TEMPLES OF SOUTH INDIA

TEMPLES OF SOUTH INDIA

V.V. SUBBA REDDY

GYAN

Temples of South India

ISBN: 978-81-212-1022-5

Published in 2009 in India by
Gyan Publishing House
23, Main Ansari Road, Darya Ganj,
New Delhi-110002
Phones : 23282060, 23261060
Fax : 011-23285914
E-mail: books@gyanbooks.com
Website: www.gyanbooks.com

Printed at : Singhal Print Media, Delhi

Contents

Preface 7

1. **Introduction** 9
2. **Buddhist Shrines** 27
3. **Rock-cut- cave Temples** 47
4. **Badami Chalukyan Architecture** 57
5. **Vengi Chalukyan Temples** 73
6. **Glories of the Pallavas** 87
7. **Chola Temple Art** 107
8. **Kakatiyan Style** 129
9. **Vibrant Hoysala Art** 141
10. **Gems of Vijayanagar** 151
11. **Madurai Style** 183
12. **Style Kerala** 201

Glossary 225
How to Get there 233
Bibliography 243
Index 247

Preface

Temples, symbolising the religious fervour of the people, are strewn all over India. Some of the temples, especially the South Indian, have large complexes. Unknown and unvisited by Western tourists, some of the temple compounds are so huge that the Senate of United States and Parliament of England can easily be housed in a single temple complex.

Dedicated to various gods and goddesses from the Hindu mythology, the temples are architectural marvels. Built in the traditional architectural style, some temples are richly decorated while others are small with simple decor. The book explores the temple civilization, one of the greatest and least known cultural flowerings in world history.

I have surveyed and studied the important temples of South India, distributed over the present day States of Andhra, Karnataka, Tamil Nadu and Kerala and dealt with their sculptural art dynasty wise, in a comprehensive and systematic manner. An attempt has been made in this book to describe legends, connected with them, usually called *sthalapuranas*, along with their architectural and sculptural significance and paintings, found in some of them. The book also depicts the significant role played by temples in ancient South India society. Though the book is intended primarily for the lay reader and general tourist, it will be useful as an elementary reference for art students, as well.

I visited the temples several times and studied their art and architecture and paintings in detail and tried to present my own reflections and enjoyment in this work, so that it can be shared by fellow art lovers. Besides, I have tried to provide some guidance for some of them, interested to visit them and derive the same pleasure as I have drawn, by providing the details of travel to the places, 'How to reach there' at the end of this work. The Indian terms and site names are shown in italics.

Of course, I have had to consult several published works in preparing this travelogue and feel beholden to their authors, for their devoted studies and presentation of the subject. I am obliged to the Archaeological Survey of India and the state departments of archaeology of Andhra Pradesh, Karnataka, Tamil Nadu and Kerala for permitting me to take photographs of the temples and sculptures from various sites. My son Mr. V. Ashok Reddy, M.S., (Computers) and my daughter Mrs. E.Himabindu Srinivas, M.Sc., (Information Systems), have helped me in DTP work and photo scanning. My thanks are due to Gyan Publishing House, New Delhi, for bringing out the book, in a short time.

V.V. Subba Reddy

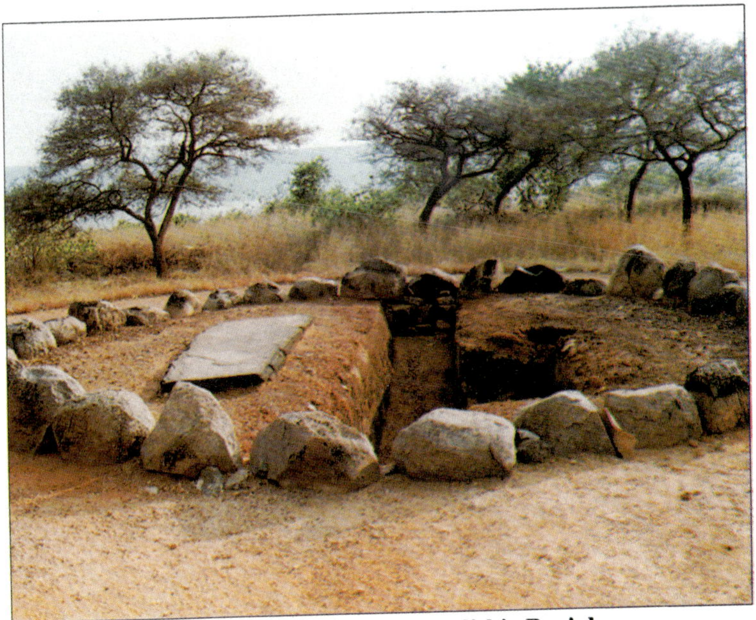

1. Nagarjuna Konda, Megalithic Burial.

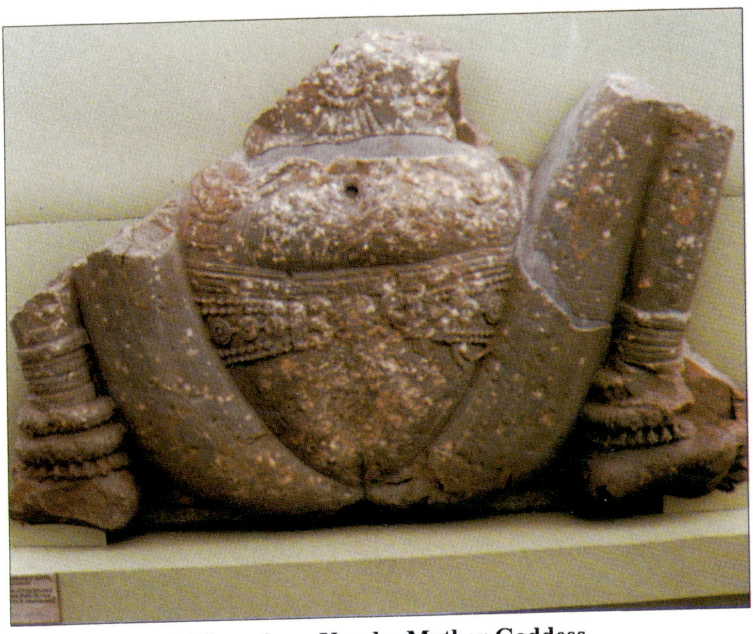

2. Nagarjuna Konda, Mother Goddess.

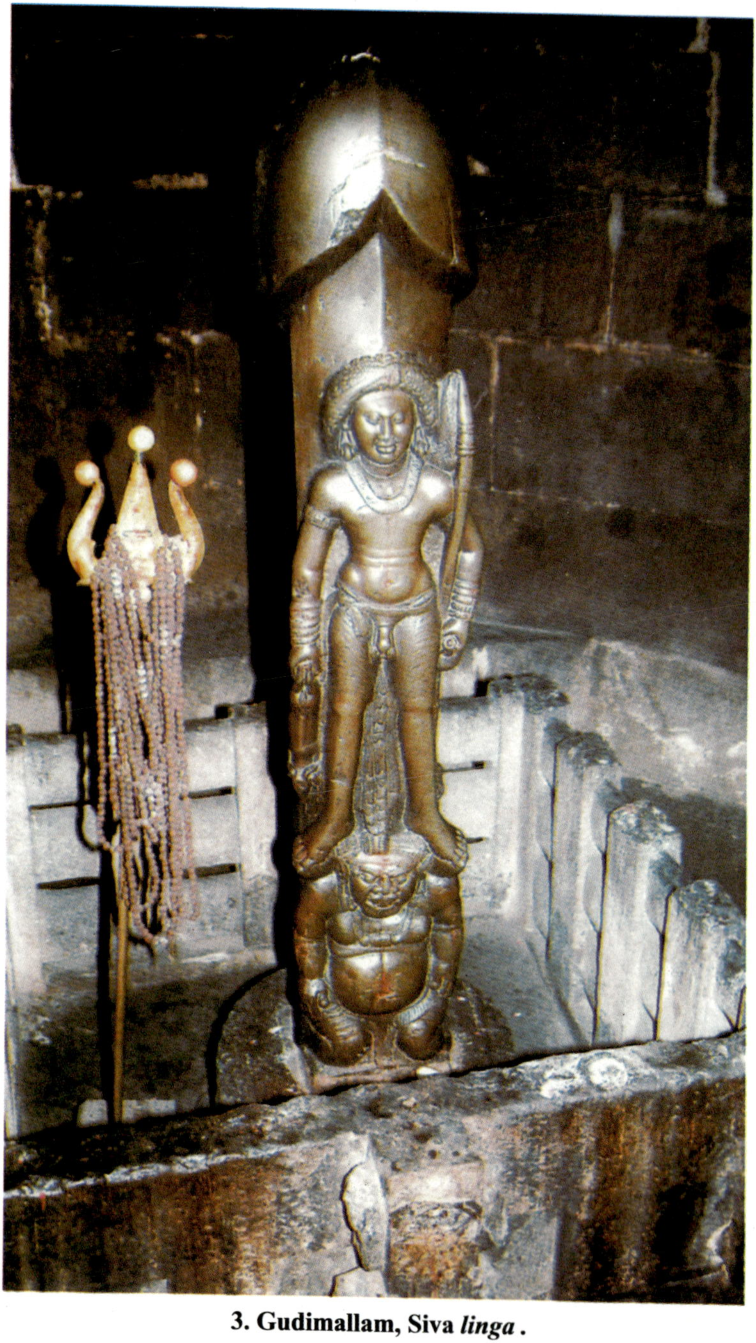

3. Gudimallam, Siva *linga* .

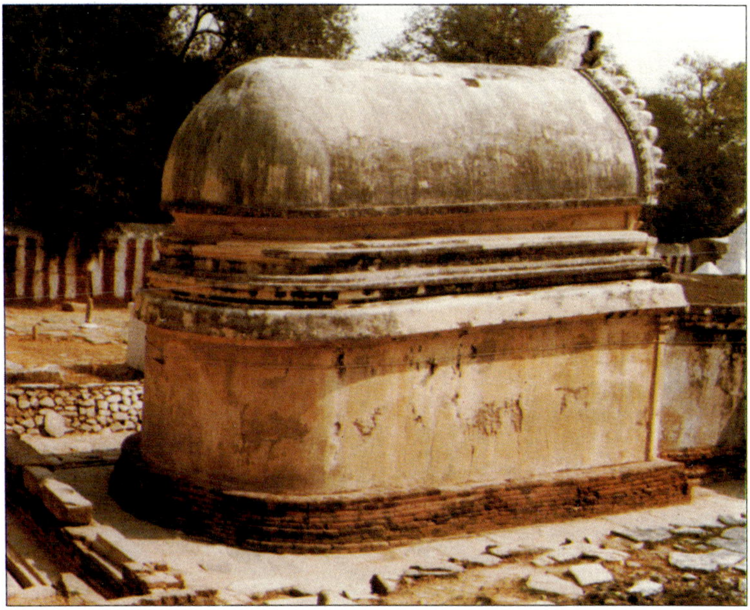

4. Chejerla, Kapotesvara temple, general view.

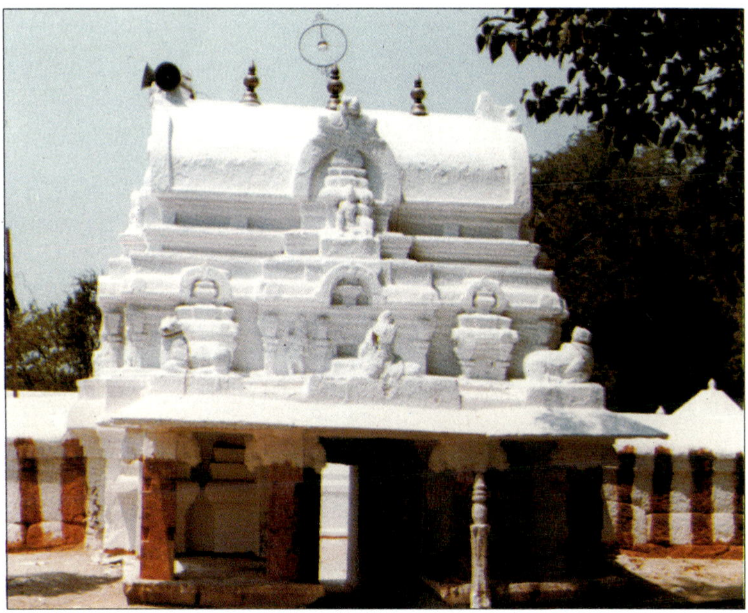

5. Chejerla, Kapotesvara temple, *gopura.*

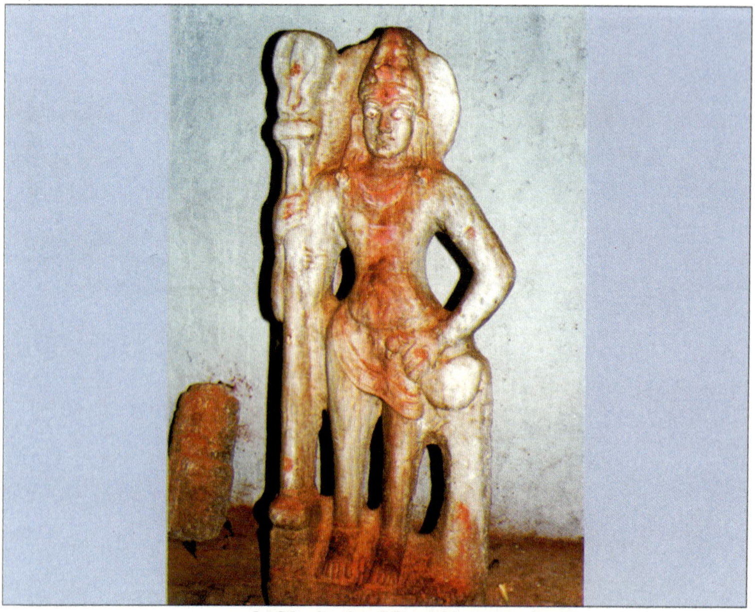

6. Chejerla, Karttikeya.

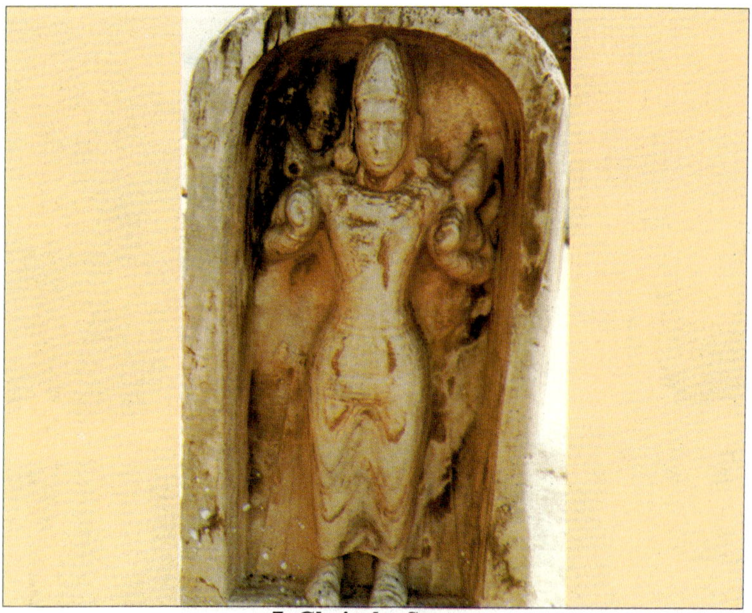

7. Chejerla, Surya.

1

Introduction

Temples, in ancient and medieval periods in South India, played a pivotal role in the life of the community. Besides promoting metaphysical inquiry into the mysterious realm of god, they served as centres of learning and imparting knowledge and also training in fine arts such as dance, drama and music. The finest marvels of architecture, which Goethe described as frozen music, are found in the temples. They were also hub of commercial and business activities. The architecture and the stone inscriptions, found in the temple precincts, help the historian discover the forgotten past and depict the picture of life of our ancestors, social, economic and cultural.

The temple, with its many pillared *mandapas,* the bathing tank and shops along outer walls, developed into a social institution, so indispensable, that it is difficult to find a village without a temple, in medieval India and it is not uncommon even today. Some of the famous temples in medieval India appear to have fostered the development of urban centres, as centres of trade and commerce. No exaggeration, when a new village was constructed, the architects used to make invariably provision for a temple. For developing a village into a flourishing town, temple was the primary instrument. Construction of temple was considered as one of the *sapta-santana*, or seven kinds of sons, that make a person immortal and thus a pious deed. Generally the construction of temples and making of images took many years and it gave employment to hundreds of artisans and Engineers.

Some of the famous temples, living to the day as immortal monuments of the accomplishments in art and architecture of our ancestors are found in Andhra Pradesh, at Chezerla, Alampur, Satyavolu, Mahanandi, the *Pancharamas* - Amaravati, Draksharama, Bhimeswaram, Palakollu and Bhimavaram,- Vijayawada, Simhachalam, Hanumakonda, Palampet, Pillalamarri, Tripurantakam, Srisailam, Ahobilam, Tadipatri, Lepakshi, Kalahasti, Tirupati, etc.

Similarly Tamilnadu has famous temples, rock-cut as well as constructional, such as those found at Mahabalipuram, Kanchipuram, Kumbakonam, Kodumbalur, Tanjore, Gangaikondacholapuram, Darasuram, Madurai, Srirangam, Ramesvaram, Chidambaram, etc.

In Karnataka great monuments of Chalukyan times,are found at Badami, Aihole, Pattadakal and the activity of art and architecture having been carried to their glory, at such subsequent monuments as at Sravanabelgola, Somanathapur, Belur, Halebid, Hampi and others. In Kerala:-Mahadeva temple at kazhakuttam, Ayyappan temple at Manjeri, Peruntirukoilappan temple at Vaikom, Vadakkunnatha temple at Thrissur, Mahadeva temple at Peruvanam, Ponmeri Siva temple at Villiapally, Padmanabha Svami temple at Thiruvanathapuram (Trivendrum) etc., are of significance.

Multifarious activities were witnessed in temples. Prof. K. A. Nilakanta Sastri rightly assessed the role of the temple of the medieval period in the following words. "As land holder, employer and consumer of goods and services, as bank, school and museum, as hospital and theatre, in short, as a nucleus which gathered round itself all that was best in the arts of civilised existence and regulated them with the humanness born of the spirit of *dharma*, the medieval Indian temple has few parallels in the annals of mankind". As it can be inferred from the inscriptions, medieval temples were governed by a council, headed by an officer called, *sthanadhipati* or *sthanapati,* helped by other dignitaries, mentioned as *sanulu* and *manulu*, consisting of the chief priest and his associates, besides others. In cases where no such committees existed, the village assembly acted as the trustee of the charities connected with the temple.

The temple was also a great land-lord and banker. Kings and the chiefs made tax-free grants of villages or lands to the temple, besides cattle for maintenance of perpetual lamps, vessels used in worship, gold and silver ornaments for decorating the deity, etc. The Mallikarjuna temple at Srisailam, according to an inscription of Prataparudra, dated 1313 A.D., owned as many as 70 villages in various *nadus* or regions under the control of Arisi-matha and Eda-matha of Srisailam alone. Some of these temples were much like *mandalika* estates with lands and villages in other kingdoms also. For example, the Srisailam temple possessed a village named Haralayapura in the Hoysala kingdom. Similarly King Prataparudra granted Salakalavidu Village in the present Prakasam district of Andhra Pradesh to Lord Sriranganatha of the Kaveri Island (Srirangam in Tamil Nadu), which was in the Pandya kingdom. Thus temples had no geographical and political barriers.

Rajaraja, the builder, donated to Tanjore temple 230 kg of gold, yet more of silver and great sackfuls of jewels. In addition, all the villages of the empire had to earmark a portion of their income to support the imperial temples and their art works. In 1118 A.D., Vikrama Chola recorded that he devoted an entire year's state revenue to glorifying his temple at Chidambaram with gold, jewels and pearls.

Officials and servants were appointed for the performance of daily rituals. The Chejarla inscription of Mahendravarman I (600 - 620 A.D.) refers that there were twelve men to supervise the services in the temple.

Some of the employees in the temple are the *sanis*, which means prostitutes in vernacular, but it was ostensibly a corrupt form of the Sanskrit term, *svamini.* Medieval inscriptions often mention respectable women of even higher social status, of Brahmins, Reddis and royal families as well, with the honorific suffix, *sani*, and thus it had not acquired the derogatory meaning at the time. As the priests in the temple, who were mostly Brahmins and well-versed with the agamic knowledge that governs the system of worship, as well as proficient in Vedic lore, were respectfully called *svamis*, and thus the *svaminis*, or the *sanis*, were respected employees.

The *sanis* of the temples were women, dedicated to temple service in the form dance and music, called *ranga-bhoga*, or service offered on the stage. *Nritya* (dance) and *gita* (music) are included in the sixteen forms of worship (*shodasopacharas)* in temples. Like any other section of temple servants, the *manis*, the *sanis* also were given *vrittis*, or lands for their livelihood, as the system of paying salaries in cash was unknown at the time. The Velpuru inscription of Mahamandalesvara Kota Ganapatideva, referring to granting lands and house site to one Bhandaramu Akkama, when she was appointed as *sani* in the temple of Lord Ramesvara at the place. They appear to have had good knowledge in literature, music and dance, well versed in *panchamaha-kavyas*, as the treatises on dance and music, were mostly in Sanskrit. As such, they were erudite in conversations and literary debates and were held in high esteem.

It appears that people used to offer a small part of their farm products, such as grain, fruits, flowers, etc., to the temple, in the harvesting season. Peasantry makes these offerings to the god in token of thanks giving. The temple serves the society by providing food to the hungry and needed. It also acts as a choultry, where people from other places could come and stay for a few days. Big temples mainted educational institutions where free board was provided to students.

Temples received donations in cash, as many an inscription refer to *gadyanas*, or *birudu-gadyas*, *madas*, *rukas*, etc. They lent the money for interest. Traders and merchants who needed capital for their commercial activities, borrowed from temples for interest. The money thus accrued in the form of interest was to be spent for the purpose of performing the stipulated services to the god. For example, an inscription at Draksharamam datable to the 12th century registers a grant of some *nishkas,* number not clear, and states that the interest on the amount is to be utilised for conducting the annual festival (*Damanotsava)* in the temple.

Mathas attached to the temples were educational institutions where *Vedas* and *Sastras* were taught, but the *agamas* and *tantras* that play important role in the maintenance of the rituals in them were given primacy. Secular subjects, literature, fine arts, various kinds of sciences, such as Astronomy, Medicine, etc., were also taught in the *mathas.* The famous Nagai temple in Karnataka was a great educational institution or *ghatikasthana* during the reign of Trailokyamalla Somesvara I. The Malkapuram inscription in Guntur District (A.P.) gives an account of the educational institutions connected to the Golakimatha, founded and maintained by the great Saivite teacher, Visvesvara-Sivacharya, who was the *dikshaguru* of the Kakatiya king Ganapatideva. It is interesting to note that the Golakimatha maintained a maternity Home and General Hospital also.

Most of the modern museums in India and abroad contain galleries with the best art pieces collected from the ancient temples and *stupas* of India. A replica of the *torana* of the Kakatiya Svayambhudeva temple is raised in the premises of the Archaeological Survey of India (ASI) in Delhi for displaying its grandeur. The temples at Mahabalipuram, Tanjore, Badami, Pattadakal, Madurai, Srirangam, Belur, Halebid, Hanumakonda, Palampet, Hampi etc. are all veritable museums of art, that belong to the times of Pallava, Chola, Chalukya, Hoysala, Kakatiya and Vijayanagara. The grand temples at Mukhalingam (Kalinganagara, the capital of early Eastern Gangas) in the

Srikakulam District (A.P.) serve as a museum of the early Kalinga art.

The temple was not merely a place of worship, for the social life of the community centred round it. As such, they were the places for religious discourses, performance of musical concerts and dances. Treatises on temple architecture provide for the construction of *ranga-mandapas* in temples, which come across often in the medieval inscriptions as well. Thus the temple was the most important public place.

All meetings of the village committees were generally held in the temples. At times their minutes were recorded on the walls of the temples. Marriages are celebrated in temples. Kings and their ministers used to interact with citizens in the temples. In short, the ancient and medieval temple was not only a place of worship but also the venue for social and cultural programmes.

Inscriptions on temple walls and pillars have helped the historian build up the story. Sri Gundan Anivaritachari, the builder of the Lokesvara (now Virupaksha) temple at Pattadakal received many favours from the contemporary Chalukya ruler of Badami. He was an expert in planning cities and constructing palaces. He won the title *Tenkanadiseya sutradhari,* the architect of the southern country.

Even today the art of temple building is known to many families in South India, bequeathed to them by generations of ancestors. Their talents are found in renovations of super structures and *gopuras* and also in several new constructions. Religion is still a living force with the people and wealthy persons make donations liberally for construction of new temples.

Religious festivals like Sivaratri attracted large number of pilgrims from distant places, singing devotional songs and dancing on their way. *Panditaradhya-charita* gives a graphic description of such processions to Srisailam for the festival of Sivaratri. The religious merit acquired by visiting Srisailam was considered to be greater than that acquired by feeding a lakh of Brahmins at Varanasi. Festivals were occasions for displaying arts and erudiation.

The festivals in Vaishnavite temples are large in number and pompous. The most important annual festival was *Brahmotsava* as at Tirupati which lasted several days. During the Vijayanagar period at Tirupati seven *Brahmotsavas* were celebrated in a year, each for thirteen days. In other temples the annual festival involving heavy expenditure was called *Tirunala*. We find a vivid description of the *Tirunala* of Lord Andhra Vishnu at Srikakulam in Vallabhamatya's *Kridabhiramam.*

Temple Architecture

Beginnings of religious thought and practices emanate from hopes and fears of the man. His hopes at the welfare and progress and his fears of uncertainities in the path of his life as well as the ultimate end of the life, in the form of death, make him pessimistic and prompts him to commit himself to the cares of invisible forces that are supposedly governing the universe. At the same time, his hopes of future prospects and his aspirations for deathlessness lead him to the concepts of life beyond life, in the form of Soul, and life through his progeny that carries on his dynasty in to future. All these ideas present at the root of religion, right from the beginning of civilisation of mankind.

The primitive animism, with belief in life after death, and thus worshipping ancestors, held ground and provided ideas and practices for the religio-philosophical developments. In fact, the upanishadic concept of rebirth was the result of the animistic influence on the Vedism. Upanishads were in the back ground to the emergence of the Jainism and Buddhism, as the two philosophical schools accepted and adopted the theory of rebirth, promulgated in that literature.

The earliest archaeological material that we come across, in the study of religious developments is the Megalithic tombs found at several places in South India. The tombs are so carefully demarcated with visible patterns of stone circle (PL. 1), etc. The care with which they were disposing their dead would lead us to surmise that the concept of soul as an immortal element in the mortal body prevailed then. Naturally, it must have brought in to existence the practice of ancestor worship and hero worship. Megalithic period registered an advance in stone cutting and planning the shape of burials. The dolmeniod-cists reveal considerable skill, not only in cutting and dressing the hard rocks to the required shape, but also the plans like *svastika* alignments of parellel rows, parallelogram, etc. Recent researches have shown that the Megalithic culture with its knowledge of iron brought a significant change in the urbanisation of South India and this period, 1000 B.C. to the early centuries of Christian era, was a momentous one in the development of religious trends.

Image worship is a natural facet of devotion. Jainism entered in South India about 4th century B.C. Probably the Jains built temples for their *Tirthankaras* at the time. Andhra and Karnataka abound in Jain sculptures and ruins. The *Bhagavatas* or *Pancaratras* popularised the image worship among the Hindus and especially among the higher sections of the orthodox people. Mention of *devakulas* or *devaghars* in north Indian inscriptions of 2nd century B.C. is worth recalling in this context. Archaeological excavations at Amaravati and Bhattiprolu suggest Buddhism was known in Deccan by 4th century B.C. itself. During the reign of Asoka, the great *stupas* at Amaravati and Bhattiprolu were built or enlarged. The *stupas* are associated with funerary as in the case of Megalithic tombs. The sculptural representations of 2nd or 1st century B.C. from Amaravati reveal shrines with *vritta-sikhara* and *sala-sikhara,* both decorated with *chaitya-vatayana* and surmounted by *kalasas.* Another important construction with South Indian Buddhists was apsidal *chaitya-griha* enshrining an image of Buddha or an *uddesika-stupa*. Some scholars hold that the Buddhists apsidal architectural traditions as a source of inspiration to Hindu constructions, since the early Hindu temples were mostly apsidal on plan. T.V. Mahalingam says that the apsidal form has travelled from the Nagarjunakonda regions to the south, the Pallava and to the west, the Chalukyan Kingdoms. The Kapotesvara temple at Chejerla (A.P.), aspidal on plan with barrel vaulted roof, is generally described by many scholars as a Buddhist *chaitya* appropriated for Brahmanical usage and is attributed to Kandara II, Anandagotrin King, who made Kandarapura as their head quarters. Longhurst first declared it as a Buddhist *chaitya* which was converted to be a Siva temple during 7th or 8th century A.D., When Buddhism was rapidly declining.

Nagarjunakonda (ancient Vijayapuri) was the peak of its glory during the time of the Ikshvaku rulers, who succeeded the Satavahanas some time in the first quarter of the 3rd century A.D. The names of four Ikshvaku rulers–Vasisthiputra Chamtamula, Madhariputra Virapurushadatta,Vasishtiputra Ehuvala Chamtamula and Vasishtiputra Rudrapurushadatta-are known from epigraphs and coins. Vasishthiputra Ehuvala Chamtamula ruled for 24 years and his regnal period marks the zenith of structural activities and artistic pursuits.

The appointment of foreigners in royal service, visits of Buddhist monks from different regions to the Ikshvaku capital and trade contacts with Rome, Ceylon and other countries seem to have resulted in a mixture of foreign element in society of that period. Society was cosmopolitan. Buddhists, Siva and Vishnu worshippers and people speaking different languages with diverge customs lived together.

The remains of several temples unearthed at Nagarjunakonda form an important chapter in the evolution of Indian temple architecture. Ruins or foundations of more than dozen temples were found around the citadel and on the bank of the river Krishna; five of them are dedicated to Siva and Karttikeya. Temple building activity was in progress from the 11th regnal year of Ehuvala Chamtamula (260-280 A.D.), the third king in the Ikshvaku dynasty and hence temple construction began around 270 A.D. in South India. In that year, Ehuvala's chief commander Elisri raised the Sarvadeva temple, is referred to as *mandapa-prasada* and the excavators call this a storeyed palatial temple.

In the 19th year of Ehuvala Chamtamula's reign, his son prince Virapurushadatta built the Pushpabhadra svami (Siva) temple, comprising of an apsidal shrine, a detached *mandapa*, a *dhvaja-stambha* (flag-staff) and a *prakara* with gate ways on all four sides. Regarding the antiquity of this temple K.V. Soundara Rajan observes "is probably the earliest Brahmanical shrine of apsidal plan known to us any where in India". The Nodagisvara svami (Siva) tempie, as the inscriptions found in the valley calls it, was raised during the rule of Ehuvala Chamtamula. It consists of an oblong cella and a *mandapa*.

The temple of Ashtabhuja-Narayana was built in 278 A.D. This temple enshrines, as the inscription records, a wooden image of eight armed Vishnu placed on an inscribed stone Pedastal. Incidentally, this appears to be the earliest reference to such a form of Vishnu so far known in India. This complex consisted of apsidal and oblong sanctuaries; each fronted by a pillared hall. At the back of the sanctuaries also an independent hall is located. A *dhvaja-stambha* surmounted by a *chakra* (wheel) was recovered from the site. The Karttikeya (son of Siva) temple consists of a square *garbha-griha* and an L-shaped pillared hall. A mutilated image of Karttikeya was recovered from this complex.

Another complex, consisting of a pillared hall, has been identified as the Burning ghat and this area yielded mother goddess images (PL. 2). The mother goddess formed a popular cult by this time as evidenced from several miniature terracotta figurines recovered.

Architecturally, the temples in the Nagarjunakonda valley did not follow any set pattern. However, to sum up the characteristics of architectural style in the valley the temples were of different shapes-oblong, apsidal, square and circular. Each temple had a *prakara* with the gateways on all sides and main entrance facing the east. All the temples were of brick, while stone played a dominant role in the construction of *mandapas* connected with temple. There were *mandapas* standing on carved lime stone pillars, had probably flat roofs.

The Hariti temple contains a *pushkarini* (stepped tank) which shows that the devotees wash their feet and hands before entering the temple. In front of the sanctum, *dhvaja-stambha* is inserted on a small Pedastal. The door jambs have at its base *purna-kumbhas* (filled jars) and not *dvara-palas*. The mutilated stone figure of Karttikeya of the time of Ehuvala Chamtamula is charming and his head dress consists of a peacock feathered bun in the centre of forehead. This recalls the Karttikeya images of Madhura. The figure of Devasena is also a note worthy example.

The uniformity in the plan of these temples discovered in the valley-*prakara, dhvaja-stambha, mandapa, antarala* and *garbha-griha*-suggests the existence of treatises on temple building which the *sthapatis* (architects) followed.

The early Pallava kings Simhavarman and Trilochana were responsible for causing damage to Buddhist establishments at Nagarjunakonda and Amaravati. As a champion of Brahmanism, Trilochana Pallava is credited with the construction of numerous Siva temples. Trilochana Pallava flourished during the last quarter of the 5th century A.D.

The Vishnukundins who put an end to the Pallava rule in Andhra region built large number of temples and also excavated the cave temples of Undavalli and Mogalrajapuram. Some scholars think that the Vishnukundins were allied with the Pallavas and Mahendravarman's rock cut architecture was inspired by Vishnukundin Indravarma.

Generally the temples contain the sculptures of Saivite or Vaishnavite themes in the niches and superstructures. The Saivite sculpture included different conceptions of Siva as

Nataraja, Somaskandamurti, Bhikshatanamurti, Lingodbhavamurti, Dakshinamurti, and Aradhanarisvara and so on. The Vaishnavite themes included the ten incarnations of Vishnu and the episodes in epics, especially of the Ramayana.

The *Silpa-sastras* broadly categorise the temples into the North Indian or *Nagara* and the South Indian or *Dravida* styles, based on the shape of the *sikhara*, but primarily based on their geographical location. The former style, which is commonly found in north India, consists of the *sikhara* like a solid tower with curvi-linear vertical ribs, bulging in the middle and ending in a very narrow necking *amalaka* (ribbed globular shaped member). Above it is the *kalasa*, the pitcher-finial. In the South, the *sikhara* has the appearance of straight lined pyramid, made up of a series of gradually receding stories divided by horizontal bands, and ending in a dome, or occasionally barrel roofed ridge. At times a combination of the two styles was attempted as in the Lingaraja temple at Bhuvanesvar. This is known as the *Vesara* style. Some scholars have tried to make the *Nagara* as hailing from the north under the aegis of Imperial Guptas and *Dravida* to have sprouted in the south.

The temples of both, the *Nagara* and *Dravida* order, are found in South India, but all of them cannot be assigned to the same period. Certainly they were the products of interaction between the styles, in the course of wars of expedition by ruling powers. The forms of art and culture of the northern origin appears to have reached Deccan via western India, which was under the rule of the Chalukyan and Rashtrakuta kingdoms, along with parts of South India as well as Gangetic plains. The periods of their rule contributed to the fusion of styles and combined art forms. It is for this reason that the earlier temples of the *Nagara* order of central India are found in Karnataka and from there they could reach Andhra. Even the Buddhist missionaries of the time of Asoka reached Andhra via the western parts of the lower Deccan.

The variation of the *Nagara* and *Dravida* styles of temple architecture is based mainly on the upper structure, to be plainly, the former consists of the curvilinear and vertical *sikhara*, while the latter, or the southern variety consisting of the sanctum in squarish plan with the *sikhara* consisting of horizontal bands, successively receding, in the form of a pyramid. It was, however, left to the innovative zeal of the early Chalukyan artisans of Karnataka to manipulate independent development of all the three styles in their region.

The subjugation of western Andhra by the western Chalukyas of Badami and later on the occupation of Vengi by Kubja Vishnuvardhana, the brother of Pulakesin II during the 7th century provided extra impetus to the growth of early temple architecture of the Andhra region. The proliferation of the Chalukyan architecture of Karnataka in the western and eastern parts of Andhra is of great significance. The Kurnool region in Andhra almost functions as a dividing line, since both southern and northern temple forms belonging to 7th century A.D., were reared at Alampur, Sangamesvara, Mahanandi and Satyavolu.

The existing structural temples of Andhra region form an interesting study. Although early examples of temples in Andhradesa are found in the excavations at Nagarjunakonda, unfortunately, they are only in the form of foundations, and nothing more. It is a pity that many valuable temples of Andhra were submerged owing to the construction of the Srisailam dam. Whatever remains is of considerable significance to exhibit the early architectural glory of Andhra Desa.

Generally, the temple complex is enclosed in an enclosure was called *prakara*, which consists of *gopuras* (towered gates), on all four sides. From 13th century A.D. onwards the temple compounds were studded with the *kalyana-mandapa*, the *utsava-mandapa*, *yagasala*, *prakara* and *matha*. Apart from the main shrine, at the corners of it, four or eight subsidiary shrines are provided; the former is known as *panchayatana* and the latter *astaparivara*. In some temples inside around the *prakara* the cloister with colonnade of pillars (*tiruchuttu mala*) became popular from 13th century A.D. onwards.

The base is the lower most element of the temple. In Andhra temples we do not find sub-base or *upapitha* till 10th century A.D. If it is used it consists of mouldings like *upana* (lowermost moulding), *kampa* (fillet), *pattika* (thick moulding), *kantha* (large recessed moulding), *kampa*, *pattika*, and *kapota* (over hanging cornice moulding) or *prati* (thick moulding). The *vastu*-texts of *Dravida* tradition classifies the bases basing on the mouldings. The base which consists of the *upana*, *jagati*, *tripattakumuda* (three faceted moulding), *kantha, pattika* and *prati*, such a one is called *padabandha*.The *vrittakumuda* (circular moulding) was invariably used in the *pratibandha* base. According to the texts the *manchabandha* type of *adhisthana* is bereft of the *kumuda* (moulding either faceted or circular).

Gudimallam, a small village is famous for its Siva temple known as Parasuramesvara. Here, enshrined the famous *Siva-linga* (PL. 3) is dated to 2nd century B.C. for its art is comparable to Bharhut and BodhaGaya. The *linga* is placed on a small circular platform, around which the railing pattern, squarish in form is carved. The *linga* is seen as standing vertically, in the same way as human phallus in the erected position probably illustrating the *sisnadeva* of the Vedic reference. In this unique sculpture Siva is carved against the *linga* and shown as standing on the shoulders of a crouching dwarf *yaksha*. The god has two hands and holds a goat in the right hand, the animal for sacrifice, an axe and a holy vessel for ghee in left hand. He wears an elaborate *ushnisa,* heavy ear rings, a wide necklace and bracelets. The *ushnisa* is arranged like a turban over the head. His undergarment is tightly tied above the thighs and held in position by a waist band. It is the earliest anthropomorphic representation of the deity which, according to Sivarama Murti, "represents, the Vedic concepts of Agni and Rudra in one figure". The anatomy of the Gudimallam figure no doubt, follows the *yaksha* model of early Indian art.

A small sculpture of *chatturmukha-linga*, made of greenish limestone, had been recovered in excavations at Amaravati. In the clearing operations around the temple of Amaresvara at the same site, a unique figure of *nandi* was recovered, datable to Satavahana period. These archaeological finds confirm the existence of Saiva sect at Amaravati, as early as the early centuries of Christian era, when it was primarily a Buddhist centre.

One of the most interesting and rare example of brick structures is the Kapotesvara temple at *Chejerla* (PL. 4). It is a place of great interest to historians and archaeologists with its apsidal ground plan and *gajaprusta-vimana*. Because of these features the temple at Chejerla is usually described as a Buddhist apsidal *chaitya* originally, but appropriated by the adherents of Brahmanical religion at a later date, so as to convert into a Siva shrine. It is undoubtedly known as a Saivite shrine as early as 5th century A.D. during the Pallava-Anandagotra time, but, the view of the earlier archaeologists, that it was originally a Buddhist-*chaitya*, but was forcibly taken away and converted into a temple of Siva is difficult to substantiate. The apsidal form appears to be a common feature to all religious structures, apsidal temples having been discovered in the excavations at Nagarjunakonda, to which time the temple at Chejerla may also be dated reasonably and thus, apsidal form being exclusively Buddhist, can no longer be maintained. Evidence brought to light in the recent clearance operations at the site exposed the *adhishthana* portion of the temple, which had been dated back 3rd or 4th century A.D. Hence, it is reasonable to treat Chejerla temple as a Brahmanical structure originally of the Ikshvaku or a slightly later period.

The Kapotesvara temple, at present, on plan features, a *mukha-mandapa* an *antarala* and an apsidal *garbha-griha*. Among these elements, the *mukha-mandapa* and *antarala* seem to be later additions, probably belonging to 5th or 6th centuries A.D. The *mukha-mandapa* and *antarala* parts have the *Padabandha-adhishthana* showing the *tripatta-kumuda* moulding, while the *garbha-griha* has the mouldings of *upana, jagati* and *Pattika.* Large sized bricks of 42.7*22.8*7.5cm were used in the construction. The interior has a flat ceiling which obstructs the inside view of the roof.

The square and cubical at the lower region and upper of the pillars of *mukha-mandapa* are decorated with half-lotus medallions, which is a feature of the Amaravati and Nagarjunakonda art, datable to about 4th or 5th century A.D. The facade of the temple, above the cornice, shows *chaitya* arch in which a miniature shrine (*kuta*) is housed and four figures of flying *vidyadharas* are carved. The *gopura* (PL. 5) at the entrance of the temple complex seems to have been constructed in the Pallava period as is indicated by the inscription of the Anandagotra king Kandara. It is rectangular in ground plan, providing the doorway at the centre, surmounted by *sala sikhara*.

Interesting legends are tagged to the history of this ancient temple. It is said that Brahma, Vishnu and Siva, the *trimurtis* wanted to test the charity of emperor Sibi. Vishnu is said to have been transformed into a *kapota,* pigeon, and Brahma in the form of vulture, chased him. Siva as a *boya* or hunter shot the pigeon with an arrow. The pigeon escaped the arrow and sought shelter with Sibi. When Siva demanded for the return of the pigeon, Sibi not only refused to surrender the bird but also offered his own flesh to satiate Siva's hunger. The three gods are said to have been so pleased with Sibi's sacrifice and charity that they granted him immortality in the form of a *linga,* called kapotesvara, to whom the temple is dedicated. Even today the *abhishekam* water is said to smell of human flesh.

A few early sculptures are preserved in the compound of the Kapotesvara temple. An excellent life size image of Karttikeya (PL. 6) has been noticed by I.K. Sarma on the hillock adjoining the Kapotesvara temple. He has rightly opined that it is in the typical Ikshvaku idiom, carved in the limestone. Another notable limestone panel at the place is of *surya*, the sun god (PL. 7) seen in the courtyard of the temple. Perhaps it is the earliest representation of the god in Andhradesa. Surya is seen as standing rigidly, two handed, holding a lotus bud by the stem in each hand upraised. The dress is typically north-Indian with a tunic and padded boots. The drapery of the undergarment is clearly marked. He wears a tall crown, ear rings and *yajnopavita*. He has a necklace and four stranded beaded ornaments on waist. The long oval face has almost straight eyebrows, long slender nose, small pouting lips, and high cheeks.

2

Buddhist Shrines

Though Buddhism originated in Gaya (Bihar), it was South India, particularly Andhradesa which nurtured it to the maximum. Ample evidence of this can be found in Buddhist inscriptions relating to 47 sites in A.P. It is claimed that Andhra Pradesh houses the largest number of Buddhist monuments. The popular belief was that Buddhism made its appearance through Emperor Asoka after the historic Kalinga war. However, evidence shows that a Brahmin teacher Bavari of Asmaka (which was part of Andhradesa in those days) who lived on the banks of Godavari sent his disciples to Rajagriha to meet the Buddha and learn his teachings. This clearly shows the impact of Buddism in the Dakshinapatha even while the Buddha was alive. However, it was during the reign of Satavahanas, Buddhism had its firm roots in the South Indian soil in 4th century B.C. and flourished up to the end of 6th century A.D. Because of its reformative nature, liberal attitude and humane approach it greatly attracted the people.

Buddhism prevailed in Andhradesa covering a vast area comprising Saripalle in the north to Nandalur in the south-west, Ghantasala and Kanuparti in the east, Kotilingala and Kondapur on the north-west and Satanikota in the Kurnool district in the south. Innumerable Buddhist settlements ranging from Pre-Asokan times (4th to 3rd century B.C.) to the reign of Vishnukundins (5th to 6th century A.D.) were unearthed in the archaeological excavations.

A welcoming feature of the Buddhism in Andhradesa was that both schools of Buddhism, namely, Hinayana and Mahayana, flourished in this land. While Hinayana which is also known as Theravada flourished more in the north coastal Andhra, Mahayana which was founded by *acharya* Nagarjuna was more prevalent in the mid coastal Andhra between Godavari and Krishna rivers. It was this Mahayana of Nagarjuna which went to Tibet and China.

Of the Buddhist shrines in South India, Nagapattinam in Thanjavur District in Tamil Nadu and Amaravati, Nagarjunakonda, Goli and Bhattiprolu in Guntur District and Jaggayyapeta and Ghantasala in Krishna District, Chandavaram and Dupadu in Prakasam District in Andhra Pradesh deserve special notice inview of their celebrity in the history of Buddhist shrines.

At Nagapattinam a Buddhist temple was built during the rule of Pallava king Narsimhavarman II (695-722 A.D.), at the instance of a Chinese king, specifically for the use of Buddhist monks coming from China. An inscription of the 11th century A.D. mentions that the Chola king Rajaraja donated a village for the maintenance of a shrine of the Buddha in the Chulamanivarma-*vihara* which the Sailendra king had erected at Nagapattinam. Also, the Kalyani inscription of 1476 A.D. refers to the Padarikarama monastery of Nagapattinam. Interestingly, nearly 350 bronze images of Buddhist deities were discovered from this place. These images belong to the early Chola to the Vijayanagar traditions.

No Buddhist monuments have survived at Nagapattinam. In 1867 the monument was demolished at the instance of a French Jesuits for use of the land for construction of a college building.

The *stupas* at Bhattiprolu, Amaravati, Nagarjunakonda, Jaggayyapeta and Ghantasala in A.P., datable from 2nd century

B.C. to 3rd century A.D. are magnificent examples of Buddhist shrines in South India. Their importance lies not only on their unique architectural features, but also on the excellent relief sculptures embellishing them. They consisted of brick-built hemispherical domes on round platforms, called *vedi,* and were characterized by rectangular projections of it, on four cardinal points. They were decorated with sculptured limestone panels richly carved in low relief, depicting scenes in the life of Buddha and scenes from *Jataka* stories, with graceful modeling of human figures as well as natural depiction of life of the people, with exquisite workmanship of the plastic art.

One of the earliest and the biggest *stupas* in A.P. is probably represented by the one at *Bhattiprolu*. Alexander Rea excavated the *stupa* site and the vicinities in 1892. The *stupa* was built in the third century B.C., probably by a local Mauryan subordinate Raja Kuberaka, assisted by the *nigama* (merchant guild) and *simha gosti* (association of Buddhist monks). The claim that it was a *maha-stupa* enshrining the mortal remains of the Buddha is attested by the discovery of a bone relic inside a crystal casket together with flowers made of gold and pearls. The importance of Bhattiprolu *stupa* lies in its wheel-shaped plan for, it heralds the beginnings of this mode in *stupa* construction.

Of the Buddhist sites in India, *Amaravati*, on the right bank of the river Krishna, occupies a pre-eminent position in the history of Indian art. The excavated *stupa* site and the Archaeological Museum are the main attractions here, the former being located close to the Archaeological Museum. The place is famous also as pilgrim's centre on account of the location of the Amaresvara temple, which gives the present name to the locality. Its neighbouring village Dharanikota was the actual site of the ancient Dhanyakataka, the capital of the later Satavahanas. It was popular in those days as a land of diamond sands or a city of lamps (*Dipala-dinne*). According to Buddhist traditions, the Buddha, sixteen years after his enlightenment turned the third wheel of law, the *kalachakrayana,* which was a branch of Vajrayana, at Dhanyakataka.

Numerous excavations done at Amaravati, Dharanikota, Chandavaram and other places have resulted in discovery of many numismatic evidences, dome slabs and other newer evidences to prove that Buddhism existed in Amaravati prior to the advent of the Mauryans. Amaravati was the nucleus of the great Buddhist culture existing at that time. Dharanikota maintained close contacts with Vaishali, Rajagriha and other cities of that time.

The *stupa* at Amravati, the bigget and finest example in South India, has invariably been mentioned in inscriptions as *maha-chaitya* (PL.8). Recent excavations at this site revealed that the *stupa* originally was of mud dating back to 4th century B.C. However, the *stupa,* during the Asokan period (in the second half of 3rd century B.C.) was well established with a pillar edict of the emperor, railing in granite having characteristic mauryan polish. The railing pillars had a height of 2.3 m. Barrett says the complete rail would have required 136 pillars and 348 cross bars. An idea of the *stupa* of this period can be gathered from its representation incised on a cross-bar fragment. It depicts a *stupa* surmounted by a *harmika* and the base of the dome carrying wavy decorations, and the *stupa* enclosed by a circular five-barred rail having 6 uprights crowned by plain copings. During the post-Asokan period whether the *stupa* was enlarged is not known, but it is fairly certain that the granite railing was replaced by a lime stone one of 1.9 m, high, mostly plain. Many of these railing cross bars bear donative inscriptions of the second century B.C. The final form of the *stupa* took shape during the 1st and 2nd centuries A.D. At present the *stupa* had a height of 1.55 m and a diameter of 49.30 m and the *ayaka*-platforms measuring 7.20*2.10m. The dome, now missing appears to have been built solidly of large sized bricks measuring 57x28*7.6cm. The *ayaka*-platforms carried originally five *ayaka*-pillars representing the five important stages of Buddha's life, Viz., Birth, great Renunciation, Enlightenment, First Sermon and Extinction. These platforms, a feature quite common in the *stupa* architecture of the Andhra country. It may be due to the fact that Mahasanghikas first settled in Andhra were largely responsible for the erection of the *stupas*. Both drum and *ayaka*-platforms were covered with lime stone sculptured slabs.

The tall dome-slabs measuring about 2.32 m and carved with *triratna* and *purna-kumbhas* covered the lower part of the dome, above which probably embellished by garland frieze in stucco.

The drum is decorated with many types of *stupa* slabs, illustrating the *Jataka* tales or the incidents in the life of the Buddha and scenes from normal social life. A broken slab (PL.9) is an example of minutely carved *stupa* with a few miniature reliefs portraying scenes from the *Jataka* tales. The dome carries in the lower registers *triratnas* and *purna-ghatas,* running animals and *Jataka* tales and in the upper portion garland-frieze probably in stucco. Undoubtedly the *stupa* was surmounted by a *harmika,* whose railing can still be seen in the mutilated part of the slab.

The imposing circular railing measuring about 54m in diameter, pierced on all the four sides by majestic gateways. Between the drum and the railing is the *pradakshina- patha* of about 4m width around. It consisted of uprights connected by cross-bars and headed by heavy coping stones fixed in tenon-socket method. The railing stood 3.57 m high on four sides, measuring 7.5 m wide. The projected railing measures 4.8 m taking turning in right angles for 1.9 m and another projection for about 2.5 m. The gateways are flanked by two pillars bearing lions in squatted position and similar figures of lions were placed on the upright slabs of the railing. The rail also splendidly carved with scenes from the *Jataka* tales and the event in the life of Buddha.

Several dynasties ruled over ancient Amaravati including the Satavahana, Ikshvaku and Vishnukundins contributing to its glory. But it was the Satavahanas and Ikshvakus who were instrumental for the popularity of Buddhism in the South. During their rule Amaravati and its great *stupa* attracted people from far and wide, including the noted Chinese traveller Hiuen Tsang who visited Amaravati sometime in 7th century A.D. The Amaravati *stupa* remained intact as late as the 14th century A.D., but by that time it had few worshippers, and the monastery too was deserted. And after that the *stupa* became a neglected monument, pillaged and desecrated by treasure hunters for several years. For almost four centuries its existence remained a mystery, buried deep under mounds of earth. A local zamindar found the *stupa* mound a convenient source of building materials and razed it to the ground. In 1797, a team of archaeologists headed by Colonel Mackenzie, rediscovered it. A series of excavations at the site by different scholars revealed a galaxy of sculptural wealth, which once adorned several panels on the drum and the railing surrounding the *stupa*. The best of the lot thus recovered however found their way to museums in London, Calcutta and Chennai during the British reign and the remaining are preserved in site museum at Amaravati.

In the courtyard of the Amaravati Archaeological Museum there is a miniature model - a replica of the Amaravati *stupa* (PL.10) which gives one an idea as to how the original would have been. Come discover the golden chapters of Buddhism, preserved for posterity at Amaravati Museum and Interpretation Centre, a repository of excavated relics from over 14 Buddhist sites in Andhra Pradesh.

The splendour of the sculptural wealth in Amaravati is superb. The earliest phase of Amaravati art emerges in 2nd century B.C. as evidenced in the lime stone stele and *yakshi*-figures, but they reflect certain advancement over Bharhut and the early phase of Sanchi. Human personalities, nature, images of Buddha, all find a suitable place here. The *Jataka* tales are exhibited in fine form in circular medallions. The subjugation of Nalagiri, a mad elephant is interesting. The figures are slightly rounder, tall, slim and in fuller and more delicate modelling. These are represented in most difficult poses and curves in action and movement, in case and relaxation, in tension and elegant languor. Ajatasatru's visit to the Lord is artistically exhibited. There are many incidents depicted from the life of Buddha- Sujata offering rice to Buddha, presentation of Rahula before Buddha, the miracle of Sravasti, *dharma-chakra-pravartana,* Buddha's visit to Kapilavastu, etc. There are four important events from Buddha's life, frequently depicted - Birth, Renunciation, Enlightenment and Salvation.

The *purna-kumbha* (a vase with over flowing foliage and flowers) on the Amaravati *stupa*, which the A.P. State Government has adopted as its emblem, was sculpted by a cobbler, Vidhika. Inscription found at the bottom of the *purna-kumbha* says that Vidhika, a leather worker, gifted the sculpture to the *Stupa*, who was a son of a teacher Nagopadhyaya. It testifies that even leather workers enjoyed high position in society like teachers (Vidhika's father) and that the gifts offered by cobblers were accepted by the monasteries with gratitude.

Architectural scenes from the sculptures are of great interest. A city gateway with *torana* is presented. The palaces have many storeys. The windows are shaped like a horse shoe. Three kinds of roofs are depicted in sculptures - barrel vault, curvilinear and circular like a hut.

Sir John Marshall rightly observes: "The Amaravati sculptures have inherited certain motifs and types which filtered in from the north-west, but these elements have become completely absorbed and assimilated with out materially influencing the indigenous character of these sculptures". The art reached its pinnacle at Amaravati in the middle of the 2nd century A.D.

The standing *nandi* (PL.11) at the ASI museum at Amaravati draws huge crowds.The fully ornamented monolithic bull, belonging to the 2nd century A.D., believed to be the first prototype in entire South India. Almost all of the *nandi* sculptures show the bull in a seating position, but the statue here is in a standing position.

The valley of *Nagarjunakonda* is noted for its rich archaeological wealth beginning from the Early Stone Age to the late medieval period. With the construction of the dam across the river Krishna and formation of the reservoir known as Nagarjunasagar, nearly 180 sq.km in area, archaeological excavations on a very large scale were done in this place by the ASI between 1954-62 and the ruins of the most important structures of this ancient place have been removed to a safer place above the submergence level on the top of the hill (Nagarjunakonda) wherein lies the newly constructed First Island Museum in India. It houses the antiquities excavated at this site. The museum can be reached by launches provided by the tourist department.

Excavations revealed a number of *stupas*, apsidal *chaityas*, monasteries, and other important remains of early Brahmanical temples; a large bathing ghat; a public assembly hall; and an imposing amphitheater.

Some of the monuments have been rebuilt in their original form and alignment, while large replicas of excavated ruins are displayed in the open air on the hill which is surrounded by the ruins of a medieval hill fort, which was built by the Reddi Kings.

The history of the place can be traced back to the Late Satavahana and Ikshvakus of the early centuries of Christian era and the place was called Vijayapuri and it was Ikshvaku's capital which stood in all its glory. Though the Ikshvaku kings were followers of the Brahmanic faith and performed Vedic sacrifices, the Princesses were Buddhists and generously supported Buddhist establishments. Nagarjunakonda became important due to its probable association with *Acharya* Nagarjuna, the celebrated Buddhist philosopher of the 1st - 2nd century A.D.

Nagarjunakonda marks a significant land mark in the history of Buddhist architecture in India. Several schools of thought converged here, giving rise to new architectural forms. All these trends confirmed to give birth to a new monastic set up. Thus, the most developed complex of Nagarjunakonda consisted of a *stupa* built on a square platform, flanked by two apsidal shrines, and a quadrangular monastery enclosing a pillared hall. But in the construction of the *stupa* all the sites followed the same style, namely, a hemispherical dome resting on a low drum, the *stupas* enshrined in the *chaitya-grihas,* however, had a high cylindrical drum. Yet we find a great change in the mode of *stupa* construction, the wheel shaped plan reached its perfection at Nagarjunakonda. In this plan we can notice not only an improvement in building tradition "but also a successful attempt at transforming an idea, a sacred Buddhist symbol (the wheel) into an architectural entity". That ideology influenced the form of *stupa* in the valley is evident also from the examples of the *svastika*-inset (a Brahmanic symbol) in the centre.

More than thirty Buddhist establishments came into existence in the Nagarjunakonda valley within hundred years. They were mainly *stupas* or places of worship, *viharas* intended for the residence of monks and nuns, and *chaitya-grihas* which served the same purpose as a Brahmanical temple with some image of deity inside. The inscriptions of Ikshvaku rulers and their queens and others provide the names of four Buddhist sects inhabiting the valley, namely, Apara-mahavinaseliya, Bahusrutiya, Mahisasaka and Mahavihara-vasin. The Apara-mahavinaseliyas were dominant sect, and together with the Bahusrutiyas, they were off-shoots of the Mahasanghikas, one of the Mahayana schools. Due to the paucity of inscriptions, the vast majority of Buddhist structures cannot be attributed to any sect or sects.

The *maha-chaitya* (PL.12), the earliest dated structure of Nagarjunakonda, with its allied units which took about a decade to reach its final form was a *sariraka* (corporeal) *stupa*, for it disclosed a reliquary containing a tooth-relic of the Buddha. The inscription alludes to it as the *dhatu* or bodily remains of Buddha (*samma - sambudhasa dhatuvara - parigahita*). It was built in the sixth regnal year of Virapurusha datta (240 - 60 A.D.). The *stupa,* wheel shaped on plan, had three concentring circles inter connected by cross and radiating walls. It had a diameter of about 27.5 m, with *ayaka* platforms surmounted by *ayaka* pillars at the four cardinal directions.

The Ceylonese monastery of Theravadin monks evidently meant for the Ceylonese monks is interesting for its two apsidal *chaitya-grihas* just opposed to each other and enshrining a callosal image of Buddha (PL.13) and an *uddesika-stupa* (PL.14) respectively, the lime stone decorated pillars of the central *mandapa* are the special feature.

The Bahustrutiyas had monastery built for them in the second regnal year of Ehuvala Chamtamula by his mother. Situated at the northern foot of the Nagarjunakonda, it comprised of a *stupa, mandapa*, two *chaitya-grihas* with *stupa,* three chambers two of which were circular and the third was oblong.

The Mahisasaka monastery, situated on the hillock adjacent to Nagarjunakonda was built by Kodabalisri, the siter of Ehuvala Chamtamula during the latter's 11th regnal year. The site consists of two *stupas*, a large four winged monastery, with out *chaitya-griha* revealing their strict adherence to orthodox principles.

The monuments (*stupas, viharas* and *chaitya-grihas*) occurring in Nagarjunakonda may be divided into four categories: (1) *stupa* with a monastery (2) *stupa,* with a monastery and *stupa-chaitya* (3) *stupa* consisting of monastery and Buddha-*chaitya* (4) Those consisting of monastery and *chaitya-griha*.

In the *stupa* construction, especially in the large sized *stupas* at Nagarjunakonda, the wheel shaped plan reached its perfection. In this plan we notice not only an improvement in building tradition, but also a successful attempt at transforming an idea, a sacred Buddhist symbol (the wheel) in to an architectural entity". The *stupas* built brick or stone, the wheel shaped ones possessed either 4, 6 or 8 spokes.

Construction of *stupas* with *svastika*–inset in the centre also came in to vogue in the valley. *Svastika* occurs in three *stupas* in sites 20, 59 and 108.

The sculptures of Nagarjunakonda, produced under the Ikshvakus, represent the last phase of the glorious Amaravati tradition, which had its beginning in the second century B.C. All the major themes depicted in the sculptures were taken from either Buddhist literature or from the life of Buddha, characteristic of Mahayana school.

The art of Nagarjunakonda may broadly be divided in to two phases; earlier phase belonging to the time of Virapurusadatta and the other to the time of Ehuvala Chamtamula. The early phase consists of drum slabs and few memorial pillars. Carvings on the drum slabs show plain *stupa*. *dharma-chakra, Buddha-pada,* column of fire, throne with *svastika* etc. These are not associated with any anthropomorphic figure of the Master. Carved in low relief and to an extent of stylization in the depiction of galaxy of *chhatras* (Umbrellas) and floral motifs. The human figures in these panels have elongated slender forms and rigid out lines.

No less than dozen *Jataka* stories the *Champeyya-Jataka, Dasaratha-Jataka, Dighitikosala-Jataka, Gata-Jataka, Maha hamsa-Jataka; Mandhatu-Jataka, Sibi-Jataka, Vessantara-Jataka,* etc. are seen, depicted in the sculptures here. Among these the *Mandhatu-Jataka* appears to be the most favourite theme of the Nagarjunakonda artists.

Some of the noted sculptures like Siddhartha in harem, the great Renunciation (PL.15), breaking of news of Siddhartha's departure (PL.16), Conversion of Nanda and adoration of the Buddha are excellent examples of Nagarjunakonda art. The artist's ability to mirror the human expression-the pathos and emotion, the joy and sorrow is the greater achievement of this period. The Poignancy and pathos are well-delineated in the panel depicting Chandaka breaking the news of Siddhartha's departure to Suddhodana (PL.16). Gautama's father Suddhodana is shocked to here the news. Yasodhara Gautama's wife almost collapses. The broken hearted Kanthaka (horse) lays its head at the feet of its stunned mistress. The situation is too deep for tears.

In the depiction of several dwarf figures in different moods infuses an element of comic and some times even sarcasim. A dancing dwarf holding a ram is note worthy (PL.17).

Not withstanding the Buddhist affiliation of the monuments and especially the sculpture on them, the art of Nagarjunakonda assigned sufficiently important place to *mithuna* figures (PL.18), numbering about 40, modelled in amorous conditions of highly delicate nature.

In one of the panels there is a remarkable scene of *sati* (self immolation of the widow) with her slim body without ornaments and reclining against a ladder, surrounded by fire. Other scenes include a woman bathing in a tub, scene of dance and revelry wrestling, etc. The last known datable piece is the toilet scene of a Saka princess. This group of sculptures displays many varieties of dress worn by people, men as well as women. The great variety of head gears, men and women, as well as the hair styles of the latter are amazingly depicted. Persons of both sexes adorned themselves with a number and variety of ornaments.

Buddha images were discovered in plenty in Krishna and Guntur districts and in small numbers in other districts. The images found at Nagarjunakonda are massive. They occupied the sanctums in the *chaityas*. Lime stone images, defaced and mutilated were found at Nagarjunakonda, Amaravati, Uppugundur, Nandayapalem, Etravaripalem, Vijayawada and Peddaganjam.

The standing figure of Buddha of 3rd century A.D. from Uppugundur (PL.19) (Prakasam District) draws our attention because of its aesthetic qualities. The hands and feet of the figure are broken, nose slightly damaged, the rest of the body retaining a delicately carved drapery exhibiting the body contours. The *urna* on the forehead, the curly hair and other features of the image recali the artistic dexterity and exuberance of the Amaravati School of art.

Another slightly mutilated panel from Kotta Nandayapalem represents Siddhartha (PL.20) wherein he is presented as a robust male, standing in *samabhanga* posture. His right hand holds a full blown lotus while his left hand is placed on his waist. His head is decorated with a turban ending in a semi circular knot. His body has been highly ornamented with heavy *vritta-kundalas* to ears, and *haras* or necklaces, armlets and wrist-lets. The drapery around the waist is tied with a *kati-mekhala*. Lengthy tassel, dangle between the legs. The physique and the ornamentation represent a royal personality. He is bear footed and flanked on either side by dwarf *yaksas* two each. The *yaksas* are represented as holding the staff of a *chhatra,* holding a basket of flowers and in *anjali-mudra.* It is interesting that the *yaksas* have curly hair decorated with *sirascakras.* It must be noted that the present image cannot be mistaken for a Bodhisattva as representation of the latter is usually in *tribhanga* posture. An image which has similarities with the present Siddhartha figure has already been reported from Goli. Thereby the figure under discussion is a true representation of Siddhartha.

The cult of Mother Goddess is of great antiquity. It is represented by a nude goddess, which is reported from Etravaripalem, now in the Vijayawada Museum, (PL.21). The lime stone plaque depicting Lajjagauri (the nude goddess) depicts an elaborated abdominal portion of a female. The *purna-ghata* like abdominal representation is flanked on either side with splayed but folded legs of a female. The legs are full of life. On art historical grounds the plaque or sculpture can be of a very early nature, in all probability representing a transition from simple *purna-ghata* motif in to a regular Lajjagauri representation. The Mother Goddess cult was prevalent from Harappan period (3500 B.C.). It was a fertility cult. The images of Mother Goddesses from Nagarjunakonda and Alampur bear striking similarity to the image from Etravaripalem. Finally this goddess is identified as Durga.

The Brahmanical temples of the Ikshvakus did not follow any set pattern as in the case of Buddhist shrines. They may be divided into two groups, namely those with a single shrine and those with more than one shrine. The single shrines are of various types of ground plan, such as oblong, apsidal and square. The palace temple of Sarvadeva seems to come under a special category, as it was designated as *prasada*, instead of the usual connotation, *devakula*. The variations in plan have no relationship with any cult, as the apsidal, oblong and square types appear to have enjoyed equal popularity; though the square plan came to be the commonly adopted in the medieval period.

Excavations at Nagarjunakonda have revealed a quadrangular construction, measuring 91.44 m x 78.9 m, with brick-built galleries on four sides, supposed to be an open-air theatre. It is a unique structure of its kind in the entire Indian archaeology, found no where else, and supposed to have been built with Roman architecture, of an amphitheatre.Ostensibly, the galleries, floored with with Kadapa slabs were arrangement for seating spectators, or some public performances, mostly sports and tournaments. The pavilion at the centre is at lower level than the stepped galleries, with the view that the sports and tournaments could be clearly visible to all, seated on them. The most interesting feature of this stadium is the fine acoustics, that has been noticed, and thus it might also have been used for public gatherings to be addressed by Buddhist monks. It has been noticed that the speeches were clearly audible to a distance of about 60 m., and the sound becomes clearer as the gallery rose up. According to Prof. R. Subrahmanyam, the excavator, the architect could achieve this "by exploiting natural environments. Its location on the lower reaches of the hill with the ledge, on which the Hariti temple stands serving as the background, facilitated a passage of air from all directions, and along with it, the sounds towards that corner".

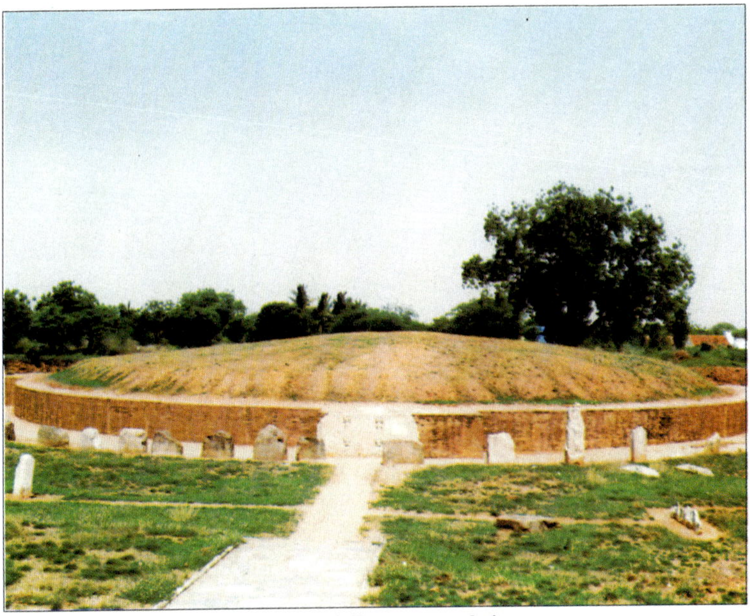

8. Amaravati, *Stupa*, general view.

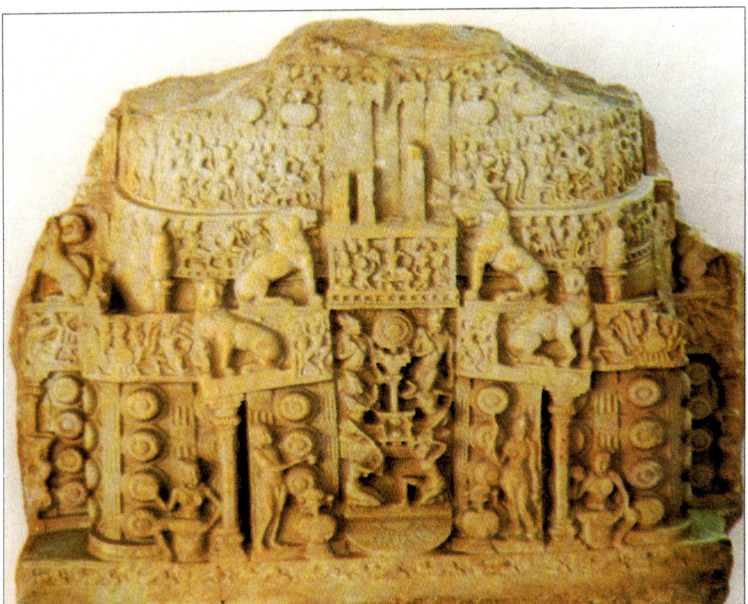

9. Amaravati, Relief of the *Stupa*.

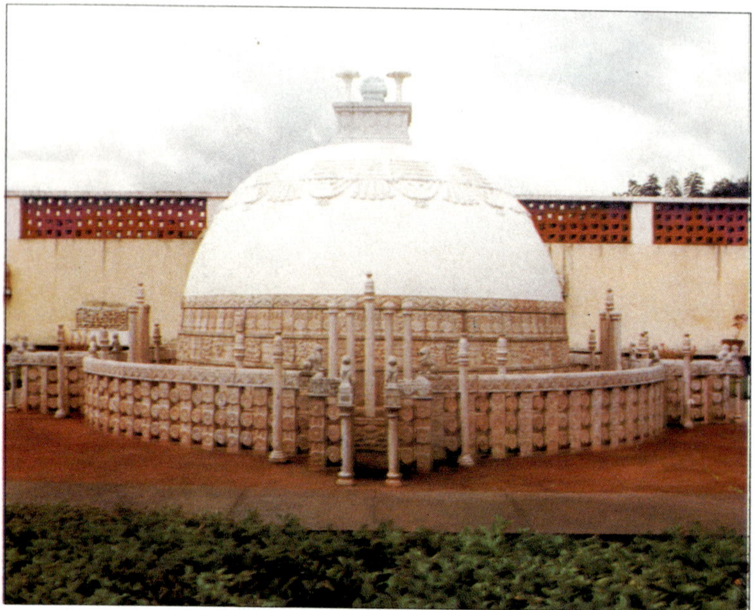

10. Amaravati, Replica of a *Stupa.*

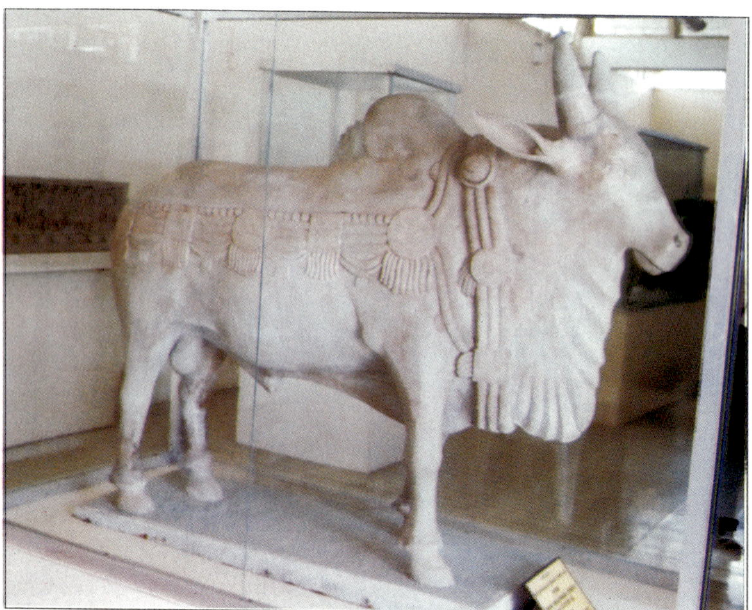

11. Amaravati, Standing Nandi.

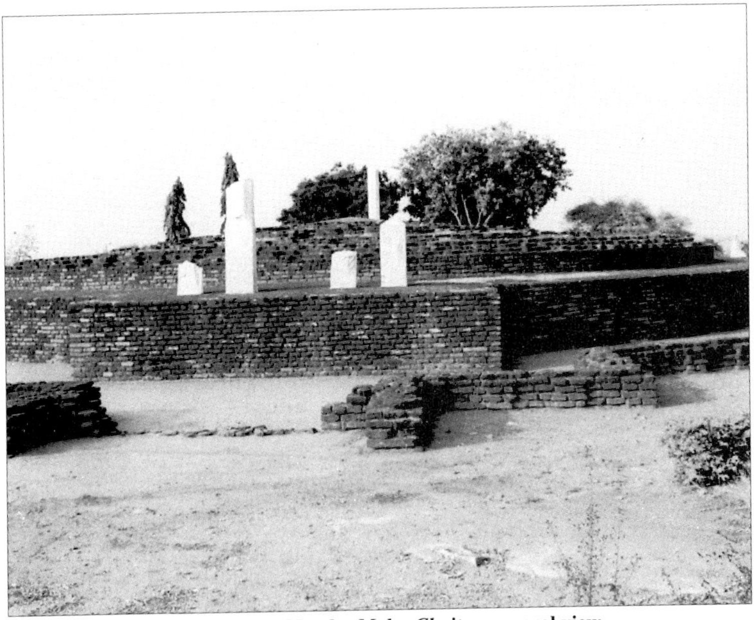

12. Nagarjuna Konda, *Maha-Chaitya*, general view.

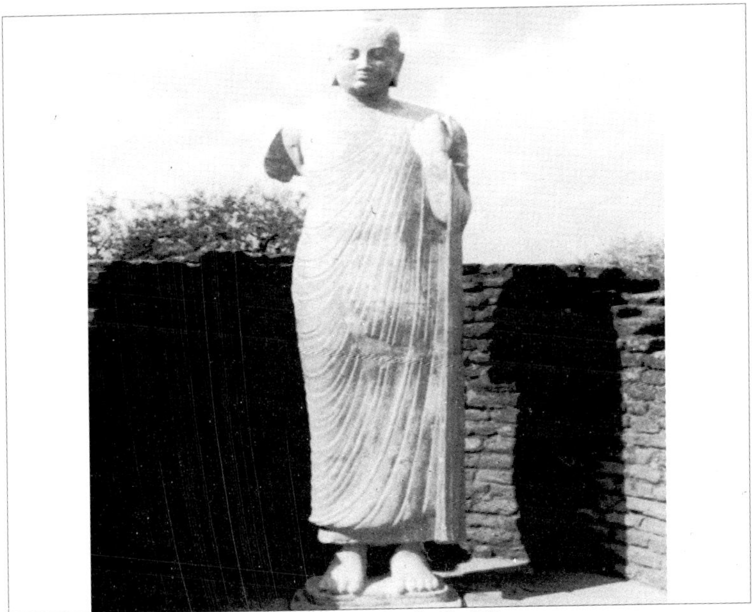

13. Nagarjuna Konda, Buddha.

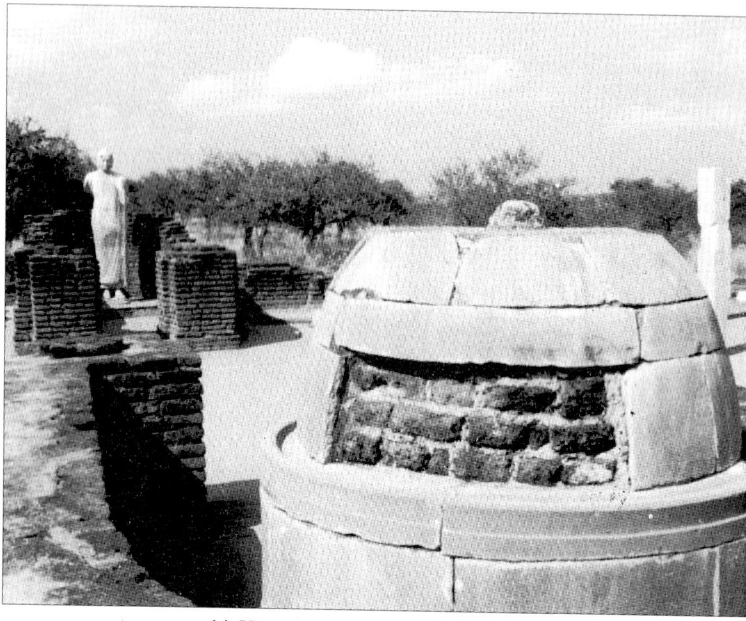

14. Nagarjuna Konda, *uddesika-stupa.*

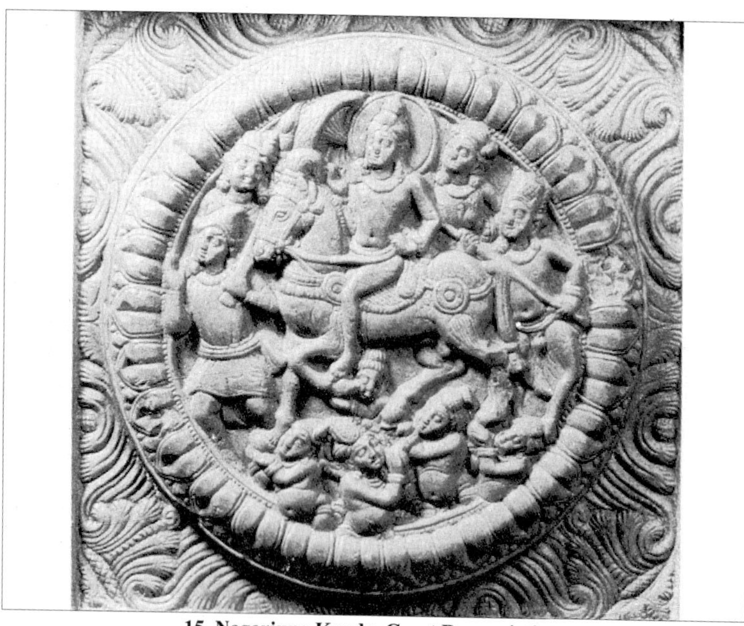

15. Nagarjuna Konda, Great Renunciation.

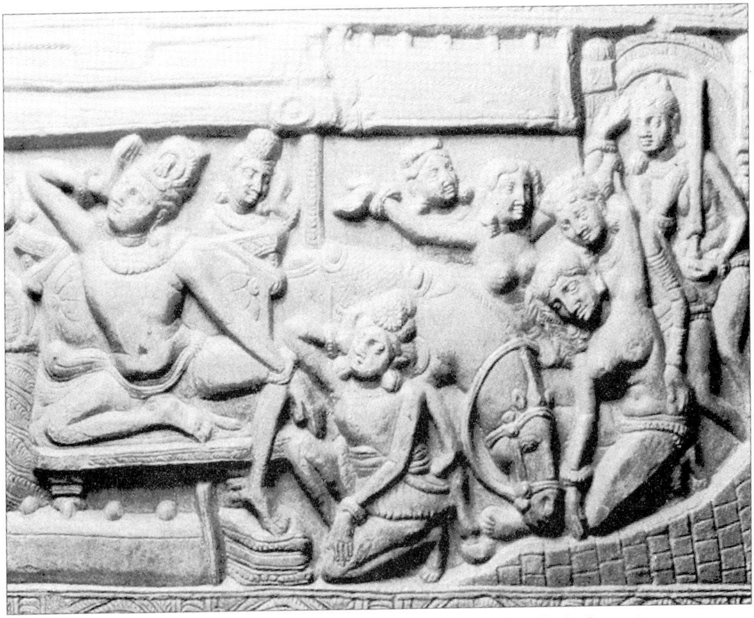

16. Nagarjuna Konda, Breaking of news of Siddhartha's departure.

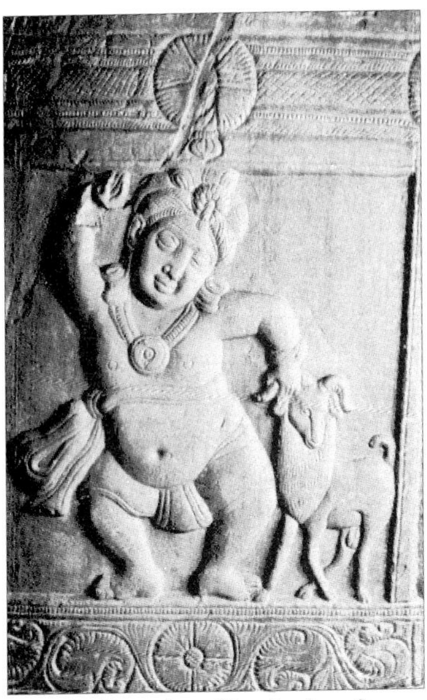

17. Nagarjuna Konda, dwarf.

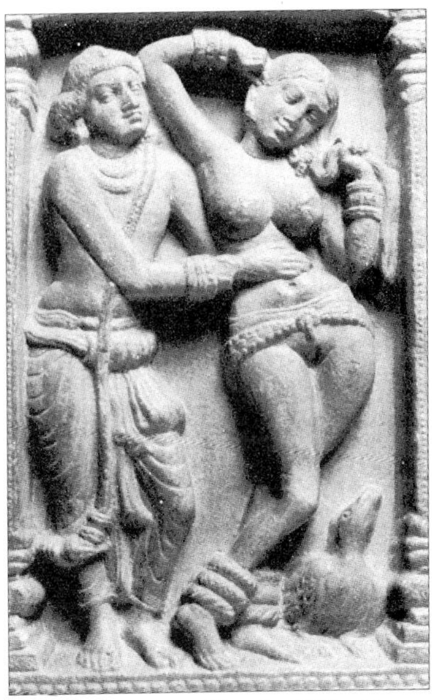

18. Nagarjuna Konda, *Mithuna*.

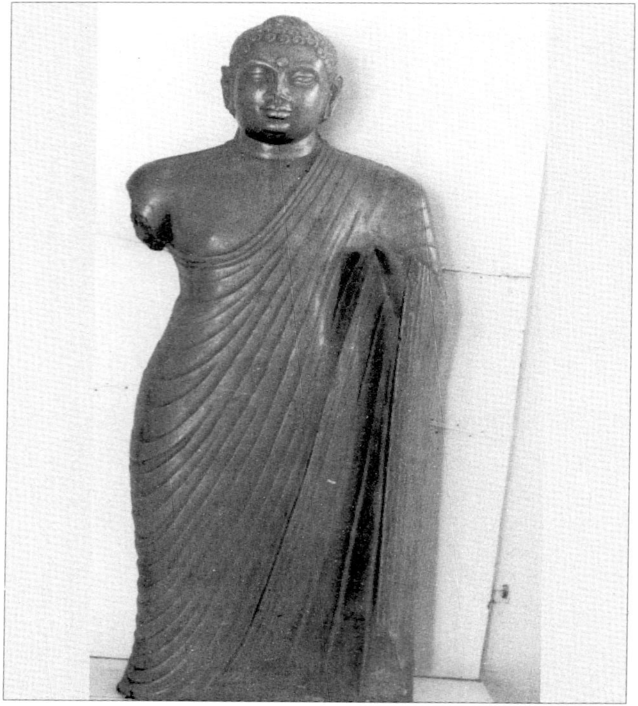

19. Uppugundur, Buddha.

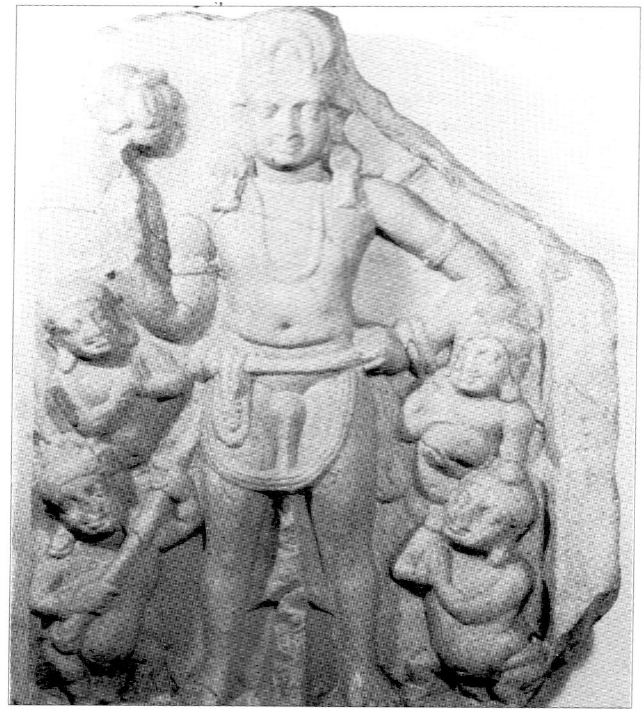

20. Kotta Nandayapalem, Siddhartha.

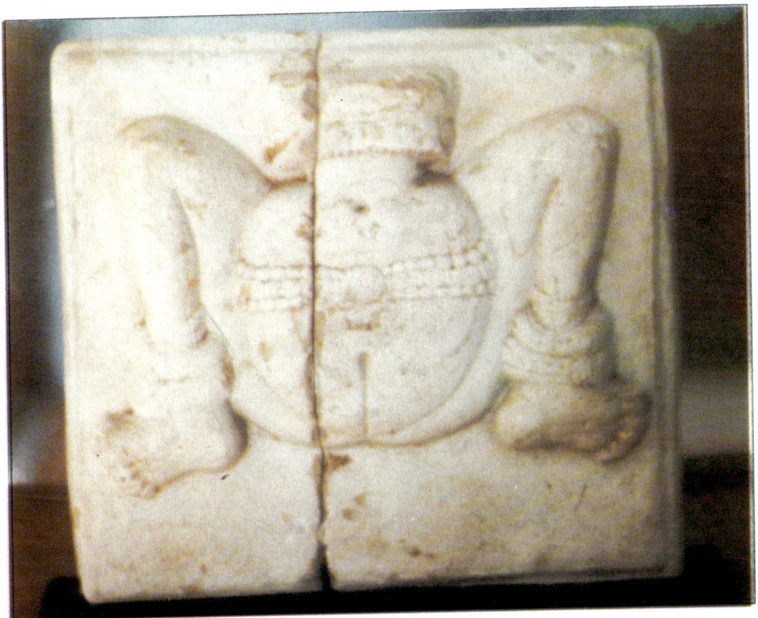

21. Etravaripalem, *Lajjagauri*.

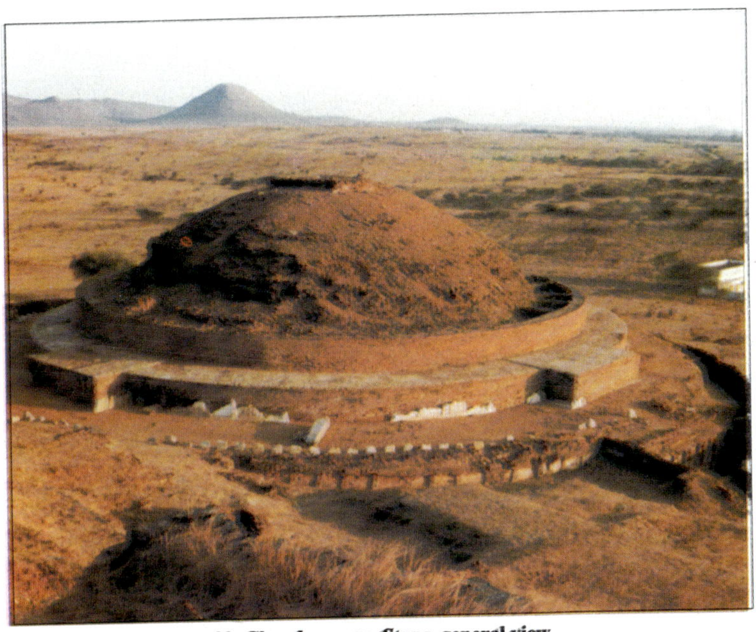

22. Chandavaram, *Stupa*, general view.

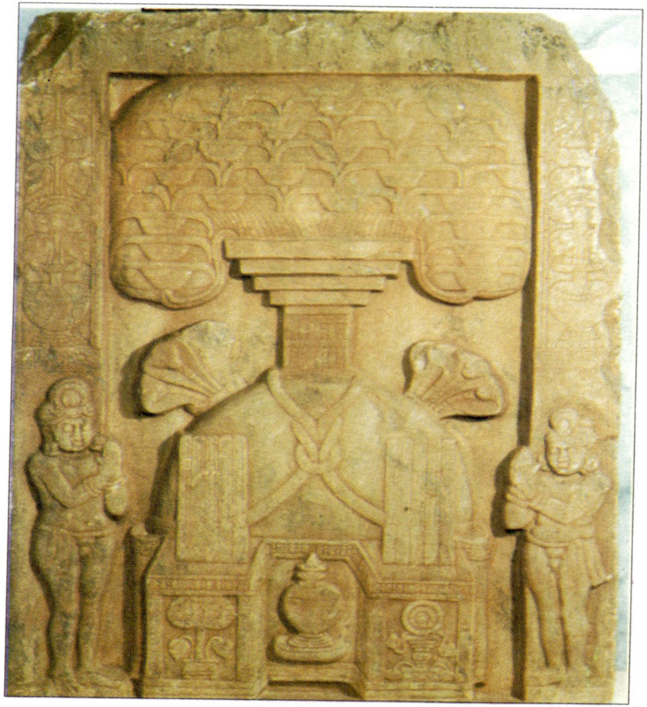

23. Dupadu, Slab No. 1.

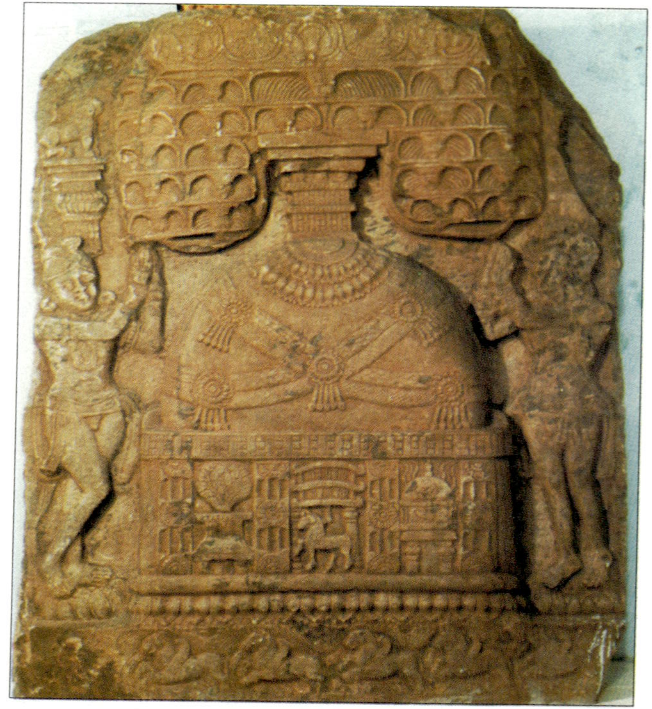

24. Dupadu, Slab No. 2.

The Buddhist remains at *Chandavaram* consist of a *maha-stupa* (PL.22), two smaller ones and *viharas* besides the remains of an apsidal *chaitya-griha* on the neighbouring hill. The remains of the *stupa* were noticed on a small hillock which is situated on the left bank of Gundlakamma River. The *maha-stupa* is a splendid structure, originally belonged to 2nd century B.C., but subsequently enlarged and decorated, as it appears, in three phases. The earliest or the original structure of the *stupa* was simple but elegant. In the second phase it was enlarged by constructing a circular brick wall around, by which the drum, or *medhi,* was enlarged, by 1.8 m in height and diameter of 40 m. The gap between the original and enlarged constructions of the *stupa* was filled in, with rubble. It has the dome, or the *anda* portion, measuring about 5.4 m in height, slightly more than hemispherical, unlike those of Amaravati and Nagarjunakonda, which were exactly hemispherical. Such shape of domes is often found in the votive *stupas* in the cave temples in Western Ghats.

In the third phase of the construction *ayaka*-platforms were seemingly provided at cardinal directions but the *ayaka*-pillars are now completely disappeared. Enclosed by brickwalls and filled by rubble packing, the *stupa* belongs to the solid brick variety. Architecturally, the distinguishing feature of the *stupa* is the terrace, made of brick infront of the railing, and fronted by stone casings. This recalls similar architectural devices adopted in the Dharmarajika *stupa* at Taxila. As the *stupa* was intended to be raised over a hill, sufficient moving space was provided by the construction of buttresses at various points, with shale stone. Most elegant flights of steps were provided from base to top in a serpentine fashion, so that worshippers, who included not only the able but also the disabled, could reach the lofty abode of the Lord without much strain.

The neighbouring hill which was connected with flight of steps supports an extensive *vihara* with a series of cells for monks. "The abode of the monks higher than that of their Lord overlooking the meandering rivulet and the purple lines of farther hills make one envious of the blissful atmosphere enjoyed by the saffron-robed inhabitants".

The exacavations at the *stupa* at Chandavaram yielded a number of sculptured panels. A few among them are now being displayed in the state museum; Hyderabad and the remaining are housed in a site museum, built recently. The panels are carved in bold relief and present very valuable pieces of plastic art belonging to 1st to 3rd centuries A.D. The sculpture on the slabs depicts multiple subjects, from the life of Buddha as well as scenes from the *Jataka* stories.

At *Dupadu*, there is a Buddhist mound locally known as Deebegutta or Rallagutta, situated half-way between a *nullah* called Tigaleru (a tributary to Gundlakamma) and the village of Dupadu. On this mound a *stupa* structure of baked bricks was exposed. The excavation also exposed the *pradakshina-patha* and *ayaka* platforms only on two sides, on the northern and western sides. The vertical face of the drum and the *ayaka* platforms were found plastered twice with lime mortar. This may indicate two phases of masonary activity. The *pradakshina-patha* measures 2.7 m wide and is bound by a 65 cm wide wall. The *ayaka* platforms which might have faced the entrances on the north and west are decorated with carved slabs. Two sculptured slabs of lime stone were recovered from two different trenches from this site. They are at present housed in the Bouddha Sri Museum, Guntur. These slabs were made from a greenish yellow lime stone available locally in the quarries along the river Krishna in Palnadu in Guntur district.

Slab No.1 (PL.23) was recovered from the *ayaka* platform facing the northern entrance to the *pradakshina-patha*. It contains the model of a *stupa*. The *medhi* portion of the *stupa* is divided into three sections. The central portion is occupied prominently by a vase. To the right side of the vase there is a throne surmounted by Bodhi -tree and to its left side a throne surmounted by *dharma-chakra*. On either side of the top of the vase there are projections which may represent *ayaka* platforms on which a group of five *ayaka*-pillars are seen. The drum is presented, as entwined by two three hooded *nagas* whose hoods come out behind the drum, on either side of the *harmika*. The *harmika* is in the form of an inverted stepped pyramid. The top portion of the *harmika* has elongated *chhatras* flowing in different directions and giving impression of Bodhi-tree. On either side of the *stupa* stands a devotee with folded hands. The central vase may be taken to stand for the relic casket and the three hooded *nagas* that entwine the *stupa* are in the posture of protecting it. Hence this sculpture may be taken to represent the Ramagrama *stupa*.

Slab No. 2 (PL.24) was unearthed from the *ayaka*-platform just facing the western entrance to the *pradakshina-patha*. It is more exquisitely carved than the other, especially in representing the *stupa*. The *medhi* portion contains three important events in the life of the *Buddha*. On the central portion a horse coming out of a gateway symbolising *Maha-bhinishkramana* or Great Departure. To its left side is a throne surmounted by the tree symbolising *sambodhi*, the enlightenment. On the right side is *stupa* on a pedastal representing the *Maha-parinirvana*. The representations of those events are seperated by four vertical *thabhos* or upright posts of railing pattern with the lotus designs and half-lotus motifs at their both ends and in the centre. The *harmika* is like an inverted stepped pyramid. Above it, there are ornamented *chhatras* flowing in different directions and giving the impression of Bodhi-tree. The top of the *anda* just below the *harmika* there are two rows of beaded garlands. The *anda* proper is decorated with garlands with pendents. The garlands are arranged as crossing each other at centre. One devotee stands on either side of the *stupa* with upraised folded hands. One of them on the right side of the *stupa* seems to be a female devotee, carrying a garland in her folded hands as if she was offering it to the *stupa* in worship. Below the *stupa*, the lower border is embellished with a frieze of winged lions in galloping posture.

It appears that this *stupa* has a *pradakshina-patha* edged by a railing around the *medhi*, which seems to have projecting *ayaka*-platforms and *ayaka*-pillars. The horse in the central part of the railing is shown as emanating from a gateway, which is three-arched, resembling the famous Sanchi gateway. But the horse is not surmounted by a *chhatra* which is generally found in Barhut and other North Indian Buddhist sculptures. The head-dress of the devotees worshipping *stupa* in both the sculptures is in typical Amaravati style.

In both the sculptures the *harmika* is elongated. In slab No.1 it is much more elongated and even the inverted stepped pyramid above the *harmika* has more steps than that in slab No. 2. This elongated *harmika* in the form of stepped pyramid might have been the result of the influence of the Buddhist art of western caves. In slab No. 2 as noted above there is a row of running winged lions. It is generally held that the winged animals are one of the peculiar features of the North-Western school or Gandhara School of sculpture.

Thus the sculptures represent a combination of several influences, i.e., the North-Western, the western, the North and that of the Krishna valley. We find such influences even in Chandavaram. This region on the basis of sculptures of Chandavaram and Dupadu appears to have been a meeting place of several influences. It is likely that the two places Chandavaram and Dupadu were at a converging point of trade routes from the North, West and East leading to Banavasi, the provincial headquarters of the Satavahanas in Karnataka.

As the Buddha is not represented in anthropomorphic form but symbolised by the Bodhi - tree, the throne, the *dharma-chakra,* the horse, the sculptures may be assigned to the early stage in the history of Buddhist art to the period before the emergence of Mahayanism.

The sculpture on the slabs is not much deeply cut, but at the same time does not show any dearth of idea or expression. It speaks eloquently of the skill and the mastery of the craftsman over his chisel and hammer, in expressing the rhythm of inner feelings. Especially the plasticity employed in the smooth flowing curves of the bodies of human figures stands incomparison with the contemporary sculptured work at Amaravati and Nagarjunakonda.

3

Rock-cut-Cave Temples

The long and prosperous rule of the mighty Satavahanas lasted more than 400 years heralding peace and prosperity in South India. The brisk trade with the Roman world not only helped raise the economy and quality of life of the people, but also contributed to the blending of the cultural and artistic norms of the East and West.

Although the rulers of the Satavahana dynasty were staunch followers of the Vedic religion and some of them performed sacrifices like *asvamedha*, yet, the noble ladies of the harem donated liberally to the cause of Buddhism resulting in the construction and embellishment of the magnificient *stupas* and the Buddhist *viharas* along the banks of the river Krishna.

The Satavahanas were succeeded by another equally powerful dynasty, the Ikshvakus. They remained sympathetic to Buddhism but they championed the cause of so-called Hinduism (the term Hindu came to be known during 12th century A.D.). It was an era of religious co-existence and mutual respect. The capital of the Ikshvakus, Vijayapuri, situated on the bank of river Krishna and close to the Nagarjunakonda, was dotted by a large number of lofty Buddhist-*stupas* and *viharas* as well as the magnificient Vaishnava and Siva temples.

After the fall of the Ikshvakus, there was no supreme authority and there seems to be a political vacuum for about 150 years. During this period a number of minor dynasties, like the Brihatphalayanas of Kudura, the Anandas of Kandarapura and Salankayanas of Vengi ruled over small parts of the region without much consequence. Later, the Pallavas of Kanchipuram controlled and ruled over the eastern parts of Andhra, probably through their governors.

The next powerful ruling house was Vishnukundins, who ruled over the entire Andhra region, during the 5th and 6th centuries A.D. Their rule witnessed an unprecedented growth and revival of the Bhakti cult, where Vishnu and Siva came to be worshipped as major gods of the Hindu pantheon. The first illustrious scion of the dynasty, MadhavaVarman, is said to have performed *asvamedha* and thousand *agnisthomas,* beside many other rituals. The other great ruler, Indravarman, was *Parama-mahesvara,* who had granted villages to learned Brahmins and Saiva temples.

The earliest phase of temple architecture in stone, commonly designated as the cave architecture, was Pan-Indian in its sweep and almost all the well known early royal dynasties patronised it. Cave temples of the Buddhist, Jain and Hindu affliations came up in different parts of India, sharing many common traits and also with many regional innovations.

The Vishnukundin supremacy heralded an era of great artistic activity and many innovations in the realm of temple architecture. The matrimonial relations of the Vishnukundins with the Vakatakas, who were responsible for the construction of some of the rock-cut caves at Ajanta, possibly inspired them to build a series of rock-cut-cave temples at Undavalli and Mogalrajapuram, near Vijayawada in Andhra Pradesh, the most important among them are the series known as the Akkanna-Madanna caves on the eastern and western slopes of the Indrakiladri hill at Vijayawada. The lower cave (PL.25) is simple in plan with three rear cells and a common corridor in front,

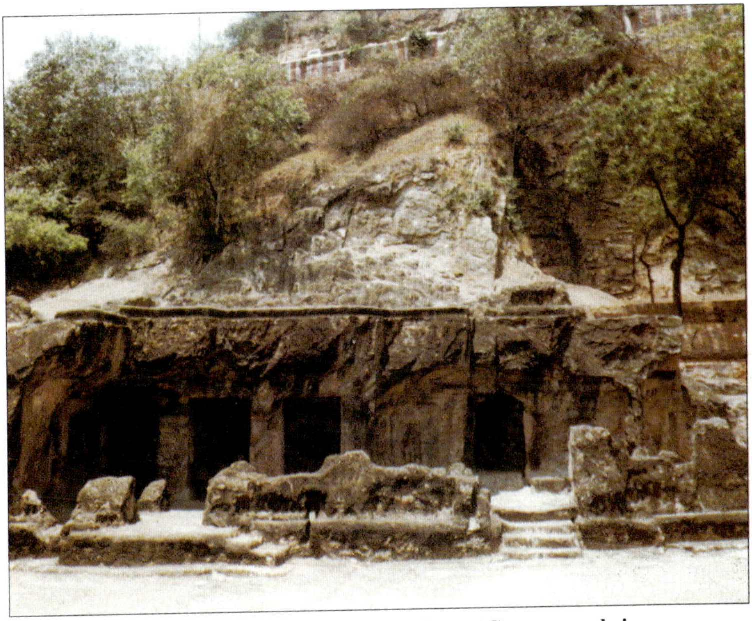

25. Vijayawada, Akkanna-Madanna Lower Cave, general view.

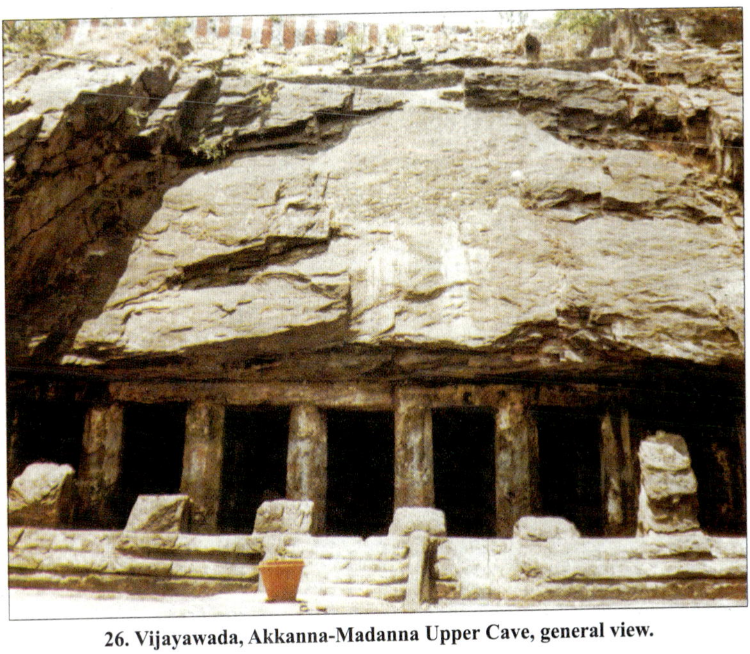

26. Vijayawada, Akkanna-Madanna Upper Cave, general view.

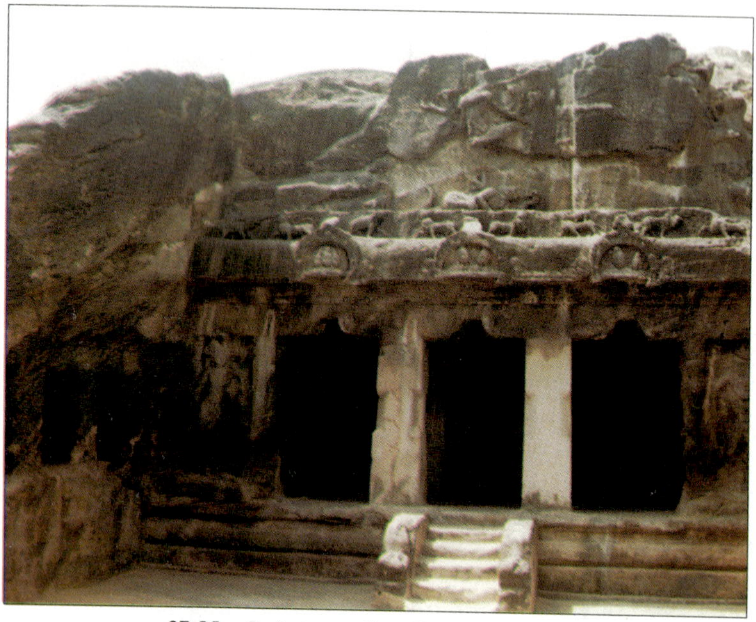

27. Mogalrajapuram, Cave No. 4, general view.

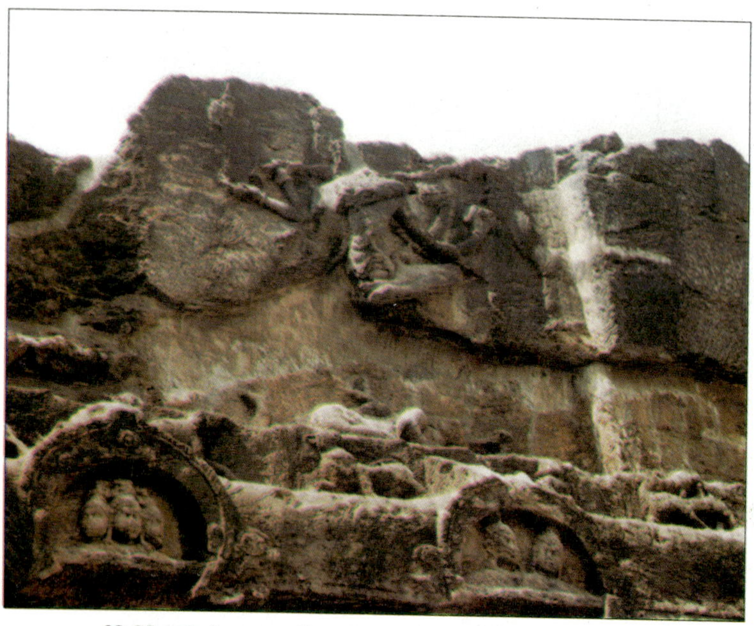

28. Mogalrajapuram, Cave No. 4 Siva-Nataraja, general view.

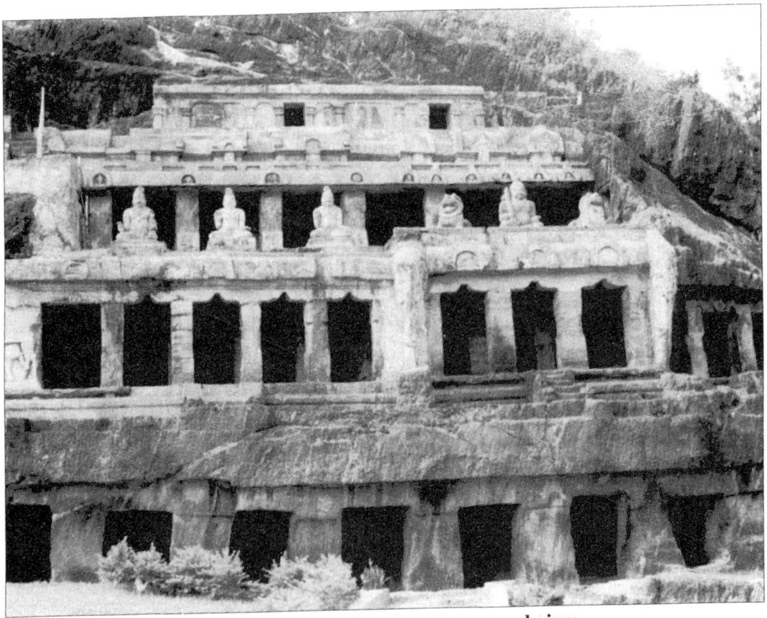

29. Undavalli, Rock-cut caves, general view.

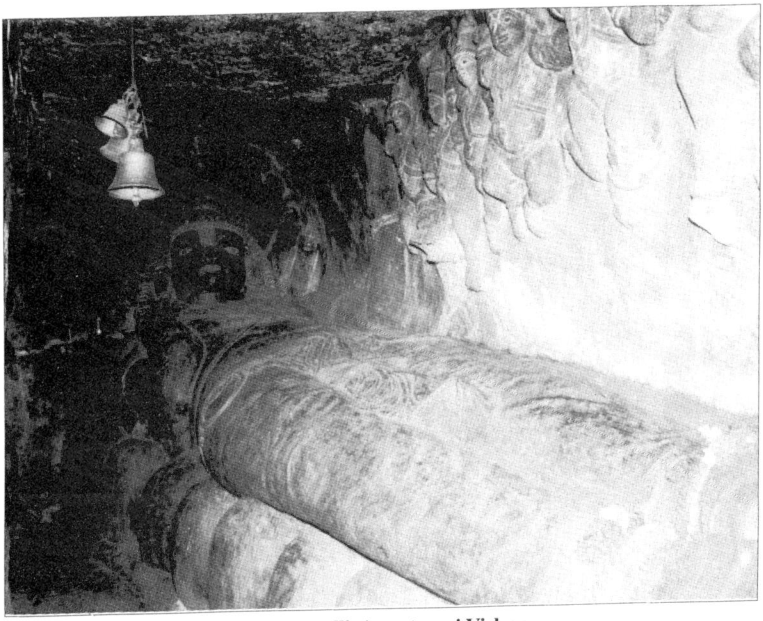

30. Undavalli, Anantasayi Vishnu.

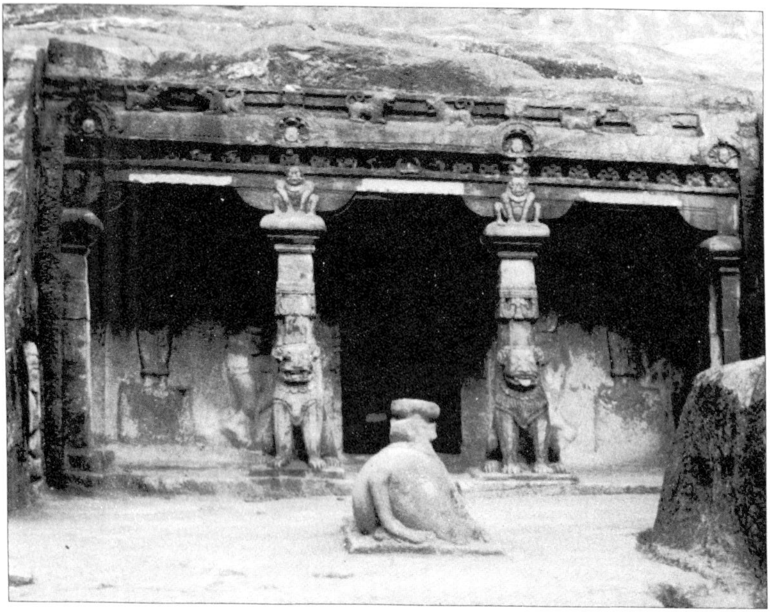

31. Bhairava Konda, Rock-cut temple No. 2.

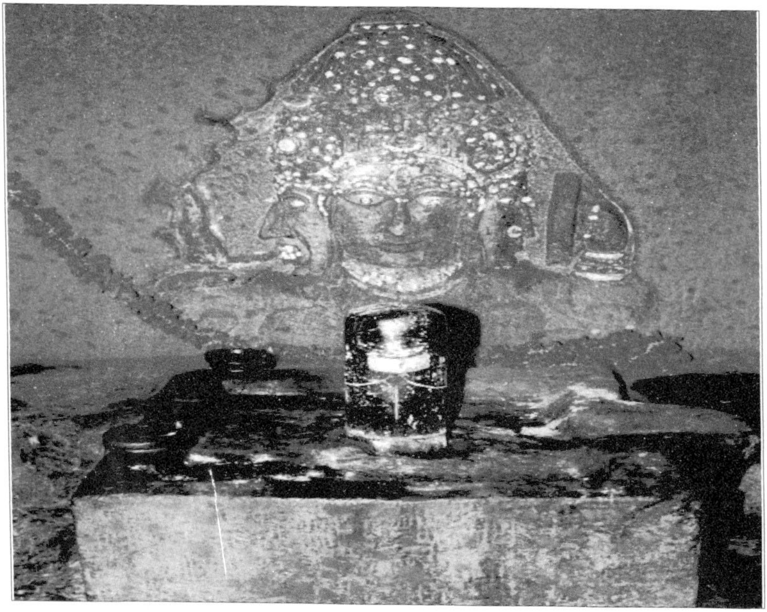

32. Bhairava Konda, Mahesa figure behind the *linga-pitha* in temple No. 5.

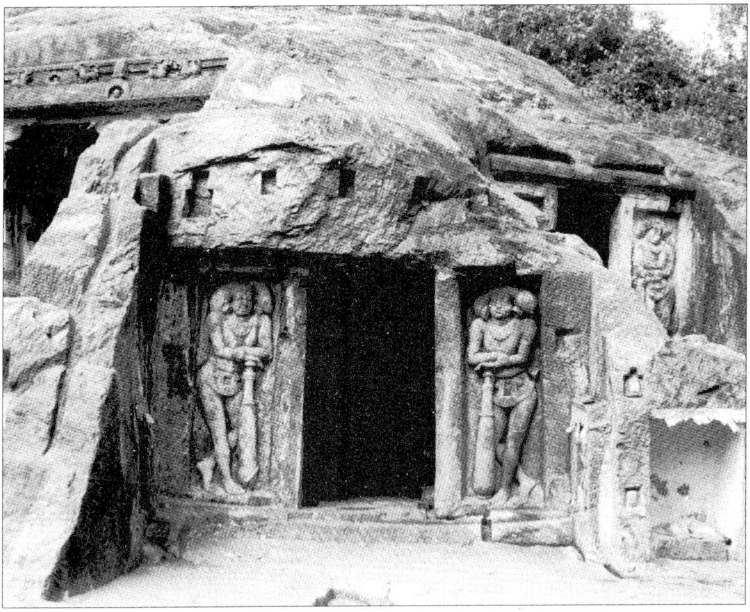

33. Bhairava Konda Cave No. 6, general view.

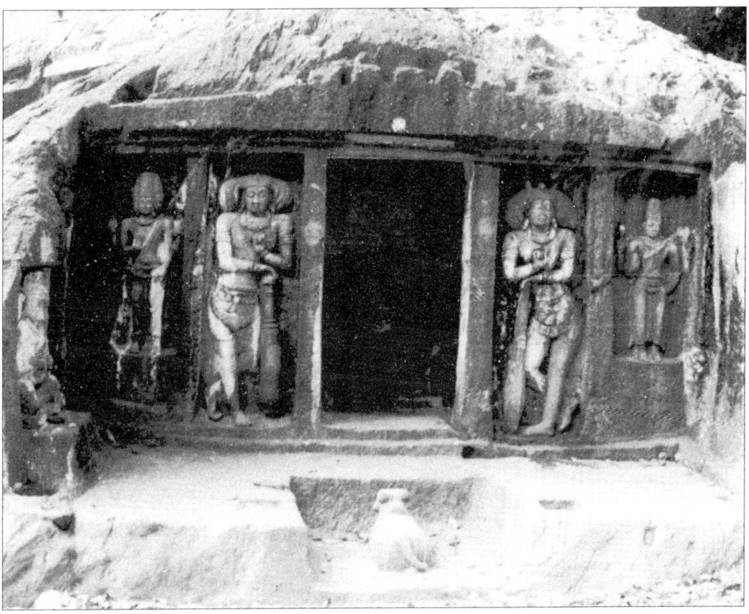

34. Bhairava Konda Cave No. 9, general view.

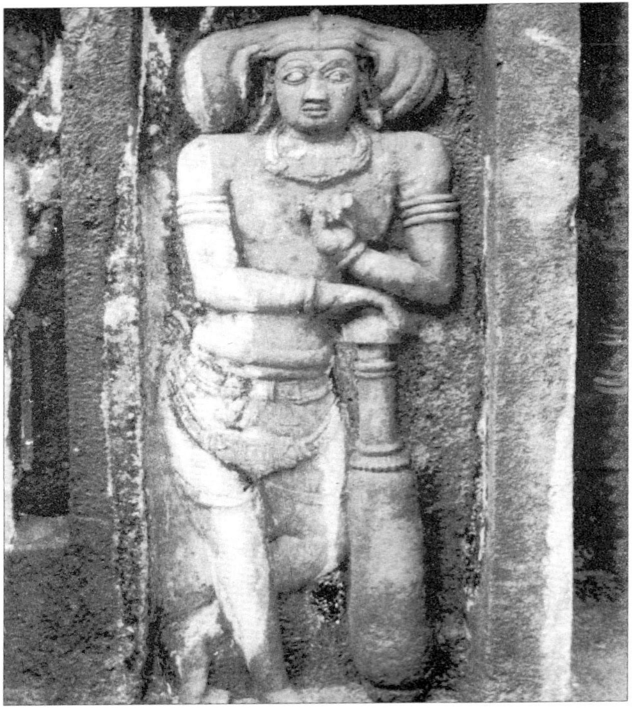

35. Bhairava Konda, *dvarapalaka*.

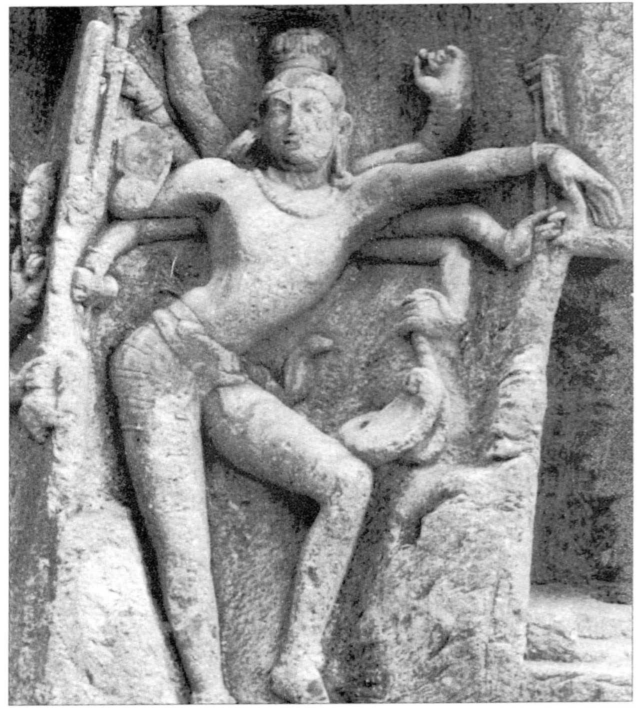

36. Bhairava Konda, Nataraja.

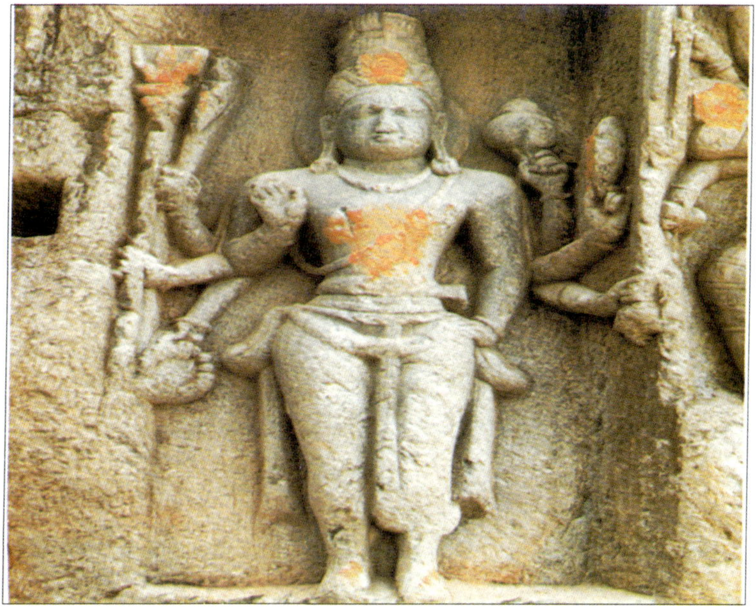

37. Bhairava Konda, Harihara.

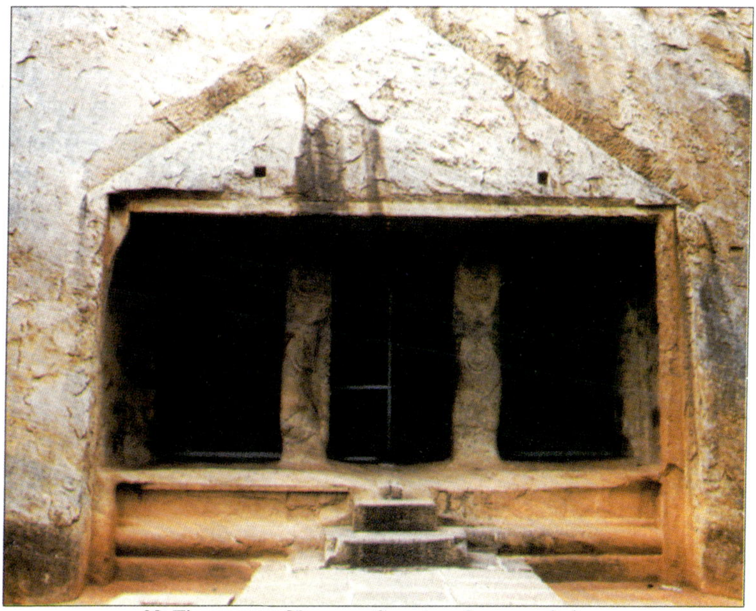

38. Tirupparam Kunram, Cave temple, general view.

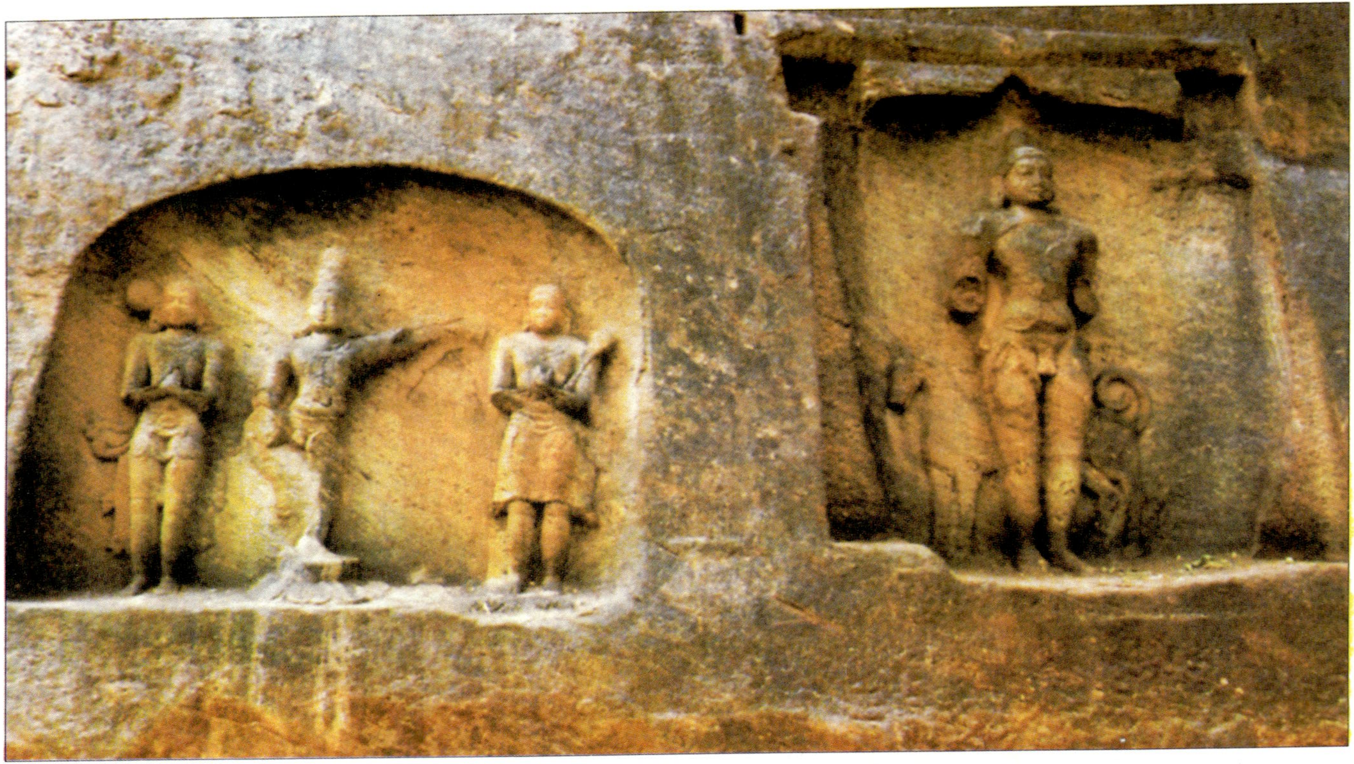

39. Tirupparam Kunram, Jnana Sambandar and Bhairava.

and is devoid of any ornamental mouldings. A series of massive and octagonal pillars divide the hall into bays. Due to the octagonal type of pillars, this cave-shrine is not assignable to the Pallavas.

On the upper slopes of the same site, there is another cave (PL.26) which is also of the same plan as the lower one. A sacred *linga* is seen in the central cell. In the other cells, on either side, no image is existing, but only the sockets are found. Especially in this cave we notice the introduction of niches to house sculpture. This cave-shrine may have been dedicated to the Trinity of Siva, Vishnu and Brahma. On the ceiling of this cave, an inscription datable to 2nd or 3rd centuries A.D. is noticed. Hence these caves appear to be of Pre-Pallava times. They are, therefore, the works of local Andhra artists. It is difficult to say in which period this was dedicated to the Trinity.

The Mogalrajapuram group of cave temples are located amidst small hills on the eastern side of Vijayawada city. In all, there are five caves, excavated on the hill on all its four sides. The cave shrines, Nos, 1, 2 and 3 are small shrines scooped out on the back wall to form a cella with a facade supported by square pillars. The cave shrine No. 3, has a carved *kapota* (cornice) relieved by *chaitya-kudus.* On the back wall of the cella has a worn out relief of Ardhanarisvara which is supposed to be the earliest Ardhanarisvara image in South India, so far known. On the eastern side of the facade is a rock cut niche with decayed figures of Brahma, Vishnu and Siva.

The cave No. 4 (PL.27) is the largest and best preserved shrine of Mogalrajapuram group. It comprises a front court flanked by vertically planned rocky sides on the right and left. The facade of the cave is decked with prominent *chaitya-kudus* having miniature figures of the trinity, namely, Vishnu, Siva and three headed Brahma along with their consorts. A beautiful frieze - of elephants and lions - is carved on the upper part of the cornice. Above them in the central zone is a decayed, almost completely destroyed, but very powerful carving of a dancing

Nataraja (PL.28), Siva, possibly the earliest of its kind in South India. The pillars in the entrance - octagonal at the middle and square in the upper and lower parts-are of early Pallava type. The inner faces of the upper square parts of these pillars are carved with themes like Gajendramoksha, Putanasamhara episode and the flying *gandharvas.* Thus, these epic themes comprising Krishnalila, etc., are the earliest Vaishnava sculptural representations in South India. This cave has two *dvarapalas* in the niches, on either side of the entrance.

The earliest depiction of the Gajendramoksha panel and the Krishnalila scenes in temple architecture are first noticed at the Dasavatara temple of Deogarh, near Jhansi in Uttar Pradesh. The same theme with similar iconographic details in Mogalrajapuram, at a slightly later date, possibly suggests the interaction of the Andhra artists with North Indian art and architecture.

A word must also be said about the interesting life-size figures of the *dvarapalas* standing in *tribhanga* position. They have horns on their heads between which the head gear is placed. The left arm of these door-keepers rests on the club *(gada)*, whereas the right hand is in *katihasta* pose. The horned head presumably signifies their relations with *nandi,* the mount of Lord Siva. Thus, the main shrine is clearly attributed to Siva with Vishnu and Brahma appropriating the lateral shrines.

On the southern bank of the river Krishna, lays the *Undavalli* village and a little higher up are the spectacular Undavalli caves (PL.28). "Oh! Ananta Padmanabha svami gudi?" exclaim the locals when asked for directions. The caves are three storeyed, excluding the ground floor. The first floor of the cave is the most elaborate of all the storeys, where the interior is fashioned into a pillared hall with an inner sanctuary to place an image or a *linga* on a pedestal. The arrangement of the excavated *mandapas* and shrine is similar to those of Buddhist caves at Ellora. The cave is named after the colossal relief of Anantasayi Vishnu carved east-west on the north end wall. The reposing Anantasayi (PL.30) measures 4.3m long under the canopy of the multihooded Adisesha along with all the other ubiquitous features of this aspect of Vishnu. Incidentally, the iconography of the relief of Anantasayi Vishnu is again similar to that of the Anantasayi Vishnu panel of Deogarh temple in Uttar Pradesh.

Another interesting architectural feature of this cave is the lions at the base of the pillars which have one paw raised. No doubt, there are lion figures carved at the base of pillars of the Pallava structural temples. However, their feet rest on the ground unlike the lions at Undavalli cave temples. Hence, the construction of the Mogalrajapuram and Undavalli cave - temples cannot be assigned to the Pallavas of Tamil Nadu. They were excavated by the Vishnukundins of Andhradesa during the 6th century A.D. The top storey of the Undavalli cave-temple remains unfinished and has three cells with a *mandapa.*

The pillars in the first floor contain sculptures depicting the *avataras* of Vishnu. These include Krishna lifting Govardhana, Varaha, Narasimha, Vamana-Trivikrama and Hanuman visiting Sita under the *Asoka* tree in Lanka, etc.

Another group of cave temples found at *Bhairavakonda* or *Bhairavakona* are the most significant of the art and architectural wealth of the modern Prakasam district in Andhra Pradesh. They are nine in number located at a picturesque spot in the Velikonda ranges, over looking the ravine at Bhairavakonda. The caves are excavated in schist rock hills. The caves are Saivite in religious affiliation, dedicated to Siva and the name of the place is obviously derived from the Bhairava image found carved on a big boulder, which came to be housed in a temple constructed at a later date.

The series of rock-cut shrines start from south. All of them have a similar plan. The temple No.1 facing east is at a higher level, than others, facing east. On plan, this temple consists of an open court-yard, an *ardha-mandapa* and a square *garbha-griha.* The facade elements consist of pillars, *kapota* and a *bhuta-mala* below. The pillars are heavy and have square *pitha* and squatted lion-bases. The shaft is short and is octagonal with a square section in the middle. The capital portion consists of the *tadi, kumbha, virakantha* and *potika*. The front faces of the *potikas* have *beki-bhairava* figures. Flanking the simple doorway of the *ardha-mandapa*, there are two figures of *dvarapalas* and Brahma on the south and Vishnu on the north. In the centre of the *garbha-griha* a square *linga-pitha* is cut. In the open court yard a monolithic *nandi* is placed, facing the temple. On the face of the southern parapet wall, a figure of Ganesa and on the northern side an image of Chandesa is carved.

Next to the rock-cut temple No.1 on the northern side, the temple No. 2 (PL.31) is excavated. It displays the similar layout and architectural and iconographic scheme. The *vyalavari* is carved over the cornice and *nasikas* as in temple No.1 are crowned by *kirttimukha* heads. An interesting feature in the *bhuta-mala* is the presence of a motif consisting of Siva-*linga* flanked by a devotee on each side. The *garbha-griha* is square on plan. The *linga-pitha* of *pada-bandha* type is found in its centre.

Temple No. 3 is excavated at lower than Nos.1 and 2. The temple can be reached by means of steps, provided on the southern side. The courtyard has high rock faces on either side and the southern one on its face has Siva-*linga* in a slit type of niche and on the northern face an image of Ganesa and the northern wall has a figure of Chandesa in a niche. Longhurst opines that these images are later additions. The style of the sculptures very well agrees with the sculptures of the temples 1 and 2 and hence there is no reason to doubt them as later additions. Although the temple follows the same layout the pillar type is of different variety. The square pillars with an octogonal section in the middle of the shaft are topped by the *beki-bhairava* motif and a bracket of semi-circular profile. Flanking the doorway the wall of *ardha-mandapa* is finished almost entirely to present life size *dvarapala* images. Only a small space on either side is devoted to carve small images of Brahma on the south and Vishnu on north. Lack of space must have influenced the architects to carve the images in smaller size.

Temple No. 4 is situated at a higher level next to temple No. 3 and is identical in all aspects to the former but for the *citra-khanda* pillars. The square shaft has a median band above the *saduram*. Over the upper region of the shaft a large sized *khumbha, virakanta* and *potika* are carved.

The other temples are small in size and lack pillared *mandapas* but have courtyard and feature Ganesa, Chandesa on rock faces and *nandi* in the courtyard and the *dvarapalas* on either side of the door way. A significant feature is the carving of Mahesa figure on the wall behind the *linga-pitha* in the sanctum of temple No. 5 (PL. 32) for the anthropomorphic representation of Siva is rather rare. The image recalls the example of the Trimurti or three faced Siva in elephanta.

Cave No. 6 (PL. 33) is situated at a slightly higher level than the cave No. 5. A small courtyard with an uneven floor and a *garbha-griha* are the features of this temple. Temple No. 9 (PL. 34) is at a higher level and has a courtyard. The wall of the *garbha-griha* has *dvarapalas* on either side of the doorway, as usual, and images of Brahma and Vishnu on either side of the *dvarapalas*. Over looking the temples a stream flowing across and on otherside of it, on the rock faces, the figures of Siva-Nataraja and Harihara are carved.

The two life size *dvarapalas* (PL. 35) on the door flanks are invariably shown as leaning on a club. The head-gear with the *sringas* (horns) is reminiscent of the Pallava tradition.

The eight armed Nataraja (PL. 36) is without *apasmara*. The god holds the fire, trident, drum, *khatvanga* or *vrishabhadhvaja* and hissing snakes as *katisutra*, with their hoods upraised, while the main hands are in *abhaya* and thrown up in glee in *ardhamattali*. He is shown dancing in a *catura* pose. The slightly smiling face reveals his serene composure. The god Harihara (PL. 37) stands in *samabhanga* pose rather rigidly and holds in his arms various attributes. True to the nature of the composit form, the god holds both saivite and vaishnavite symbols of attributes. His right portion represents Siva and the left Vishnu. The *abhayahasta* is typically Pallava in style so are the *sankha* and *chakra.* His body is powerfully rendered but the face is serene in expression.

The art of temples at Bhairavakonda points out that it is the result of the influence of both the Pallava and western Andhra traditions. Stylistically, those cave temples are nearer to the western Chalukyas, though they also bear some striking similarities with early Pallava architecture. Yet, the workmanship here is comparatively inferior to that of Pallavas.

The rock-cut temples can be dated, with the help of some inscriptions found on the rock faces. A label inscription reading *Brahmisvara-Vishnu* found between temples No.1 and 2 is in the Pallava *grantha* characters of 8th century A.D. Similarly there is another inscription on the southern end of the series near temple No. 8 recording that the shrine was caused to be made by a princes named Lokama, the daughter of a prince Rajaporeri and grand daughter of Govindaporeri. This is dated to 9th century A.D. The stylistic analysis of the temples supports the date arrived on paleographic analysis of the inscription, probably, the caves No. 1 and 2 may belong to the first half of the 8th century A.D. and the rest of the shrines may be datable to the period from 750 - 850 A.D. It is unfortunate that these caves did not get the needed publicity like those at Mahabalipuram.

Excavated in granite out crop at *Kottukal*, popularly known as Vilinjam, Kerala, and one-celled shrine enshrining a *linga* deserve mention. The east facing cave, in the centre enshrines a loose sculpture of Vinadhara-Dakshina murti datable to 10th century A.D. The cave is unique in having on either rock flank of its door opening, unfinished reliefs of Siva in *chatura- tandava* with Parvati in attendance on one side and Siva with bow as *kirata*, followed by a dwarf *gana* on the other.

Scholars have given up Pallava affliation to this monument; some hold that this cave has Pandya origin.

The rock cut creations of the Pallavas (like those at Mahabalipuram) and those of the Rashtrakutas at Ellora were well known. But Rock-cut cave temples of the Pandyas, in the southern districts of Tamil Nadu, are comparatively less known. The Pandyas were a subordinate power of the Pallavas at the time of their zenith,must have imbibed the traditions of their overlords not only in political,but also in cultural especially in art and architecture. Very close to Madurai there are cave temples at Tirupparamkunram (PL.38) and Yanaimalai which belong to the 8th century A.D. The former is noted for its beautiful sculptures of Heramba Ganapati, Skanda, dancing Jnana sambandar and Bhairava with his dog (PL.39) besides bas-reliefs of Nataraja, Gajalakshmi and Narasimha.

At *Yanaimalai* there are two cave temples-one for Narasimha and another for Muruga. The magnificent but incomplete monolithic Siva temple at Kazhugumalai, not very far from Kanyakumari, is the only one of its kind (i.e. *ratha* type) in the Pandyan country and in technique it draws comparison with that of the Kailasa temple at Ellora. Different aspects of Siva and host of other graceful beings are carved on the tiers of the *vimana*. The sculpture is similar to the contemporaneous Pallava idiom.

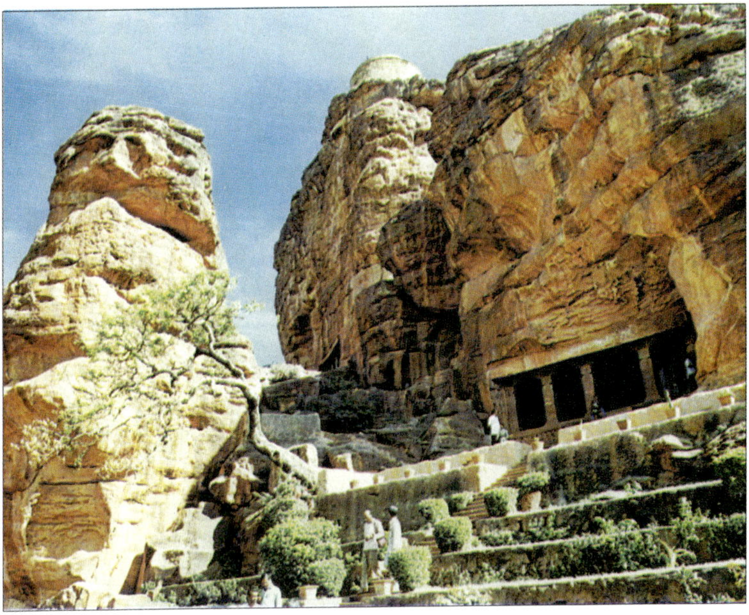

40. Badami, Cave No. 1, general view.

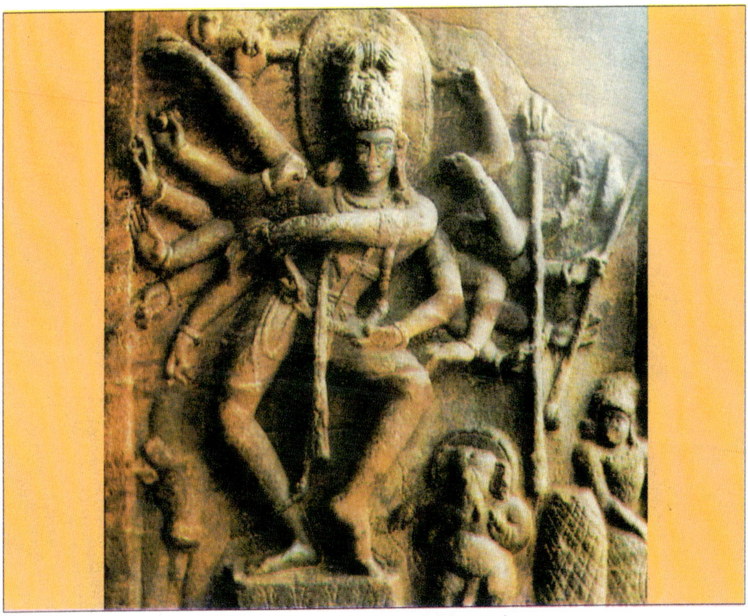

41. Badami, Cave No. 1, Nataraja.

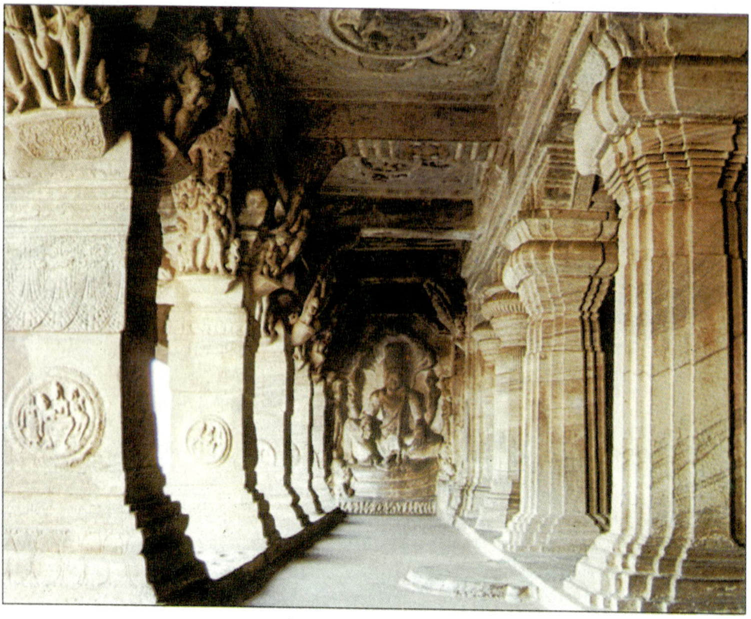

42. Badami, Cave No. 3, Vishnu seated on *Ananta-naga.*

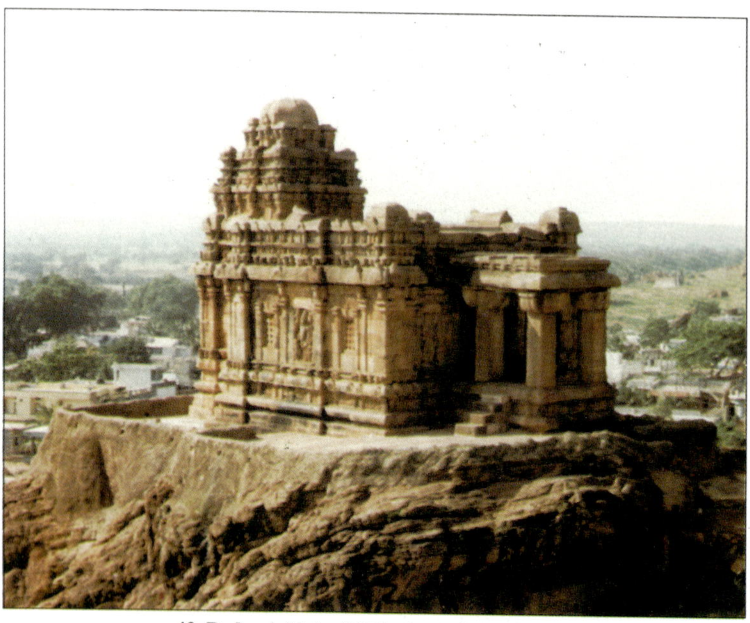

43. Badami, Malegitti Sivalaya, General view.

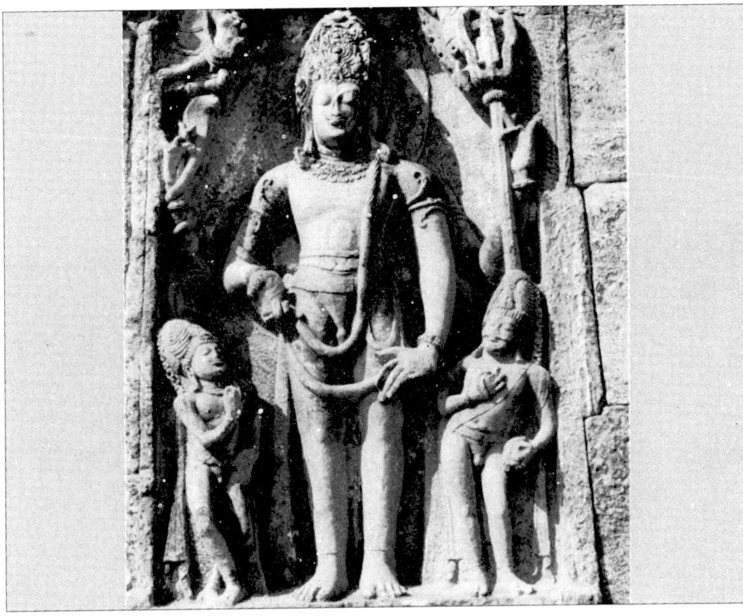

44. Badami, Malegitti Sivalaya, Siva.

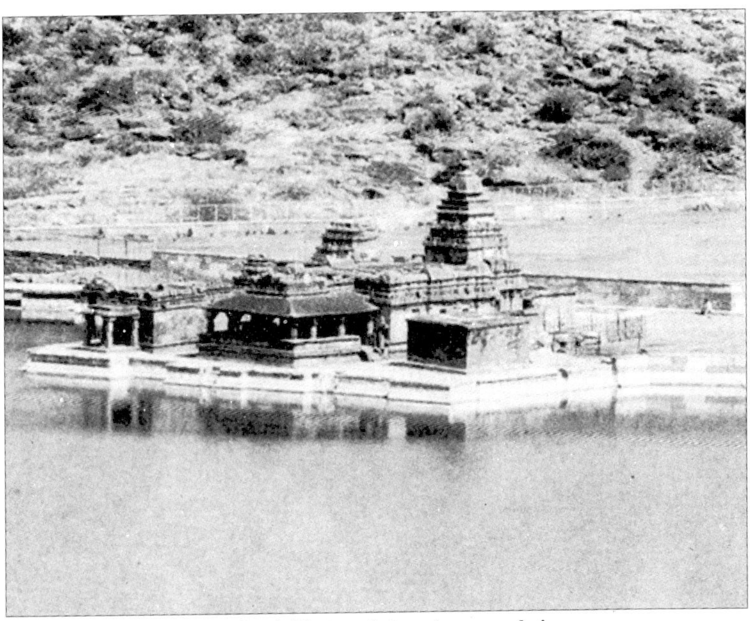

45. Badami, Bhutanath temple, general view.

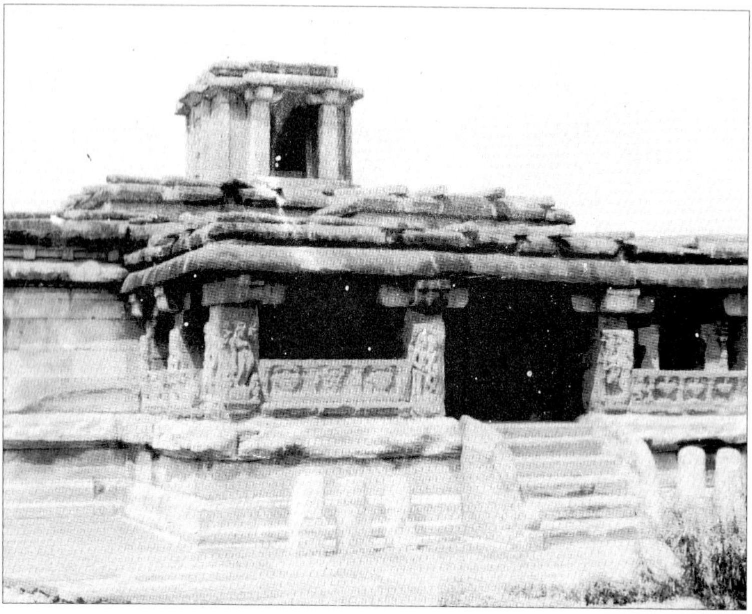

46. Aihole, Ladkhan temple, general view.

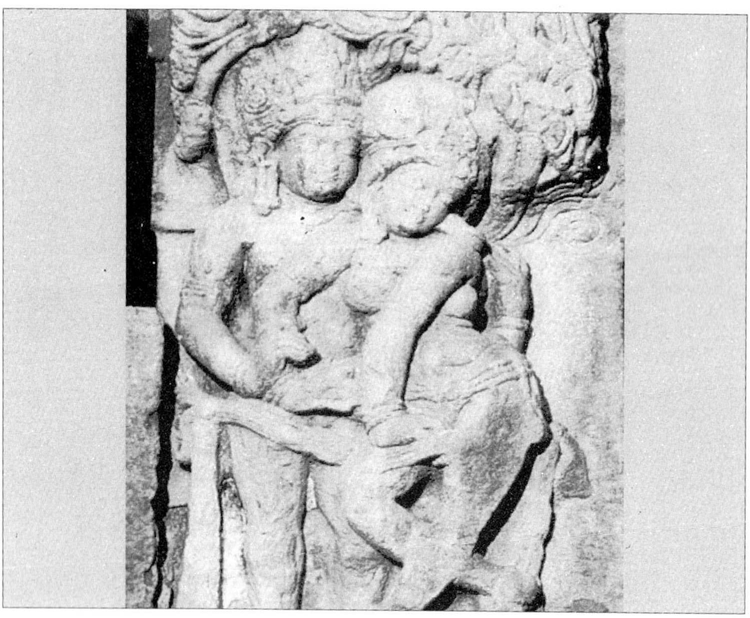

47. Aihole, Ladkhan temple, Loving couple.

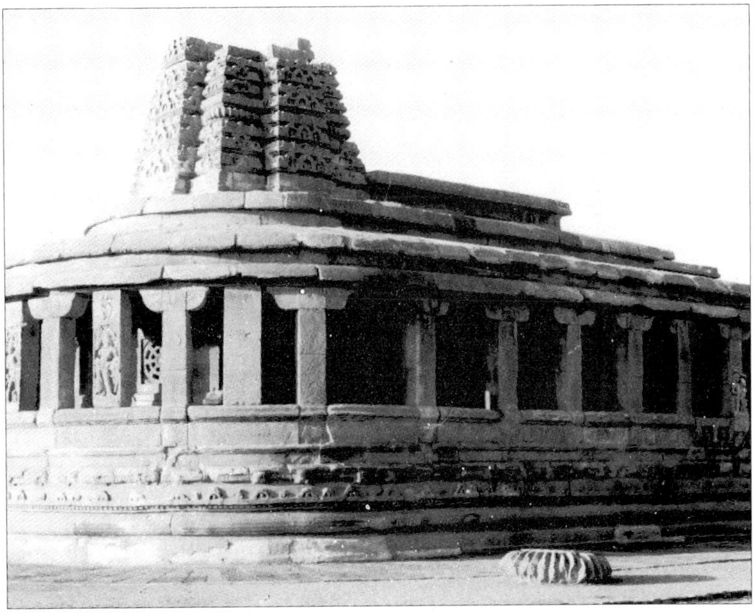

48. Aihole, Durga temple, general view.

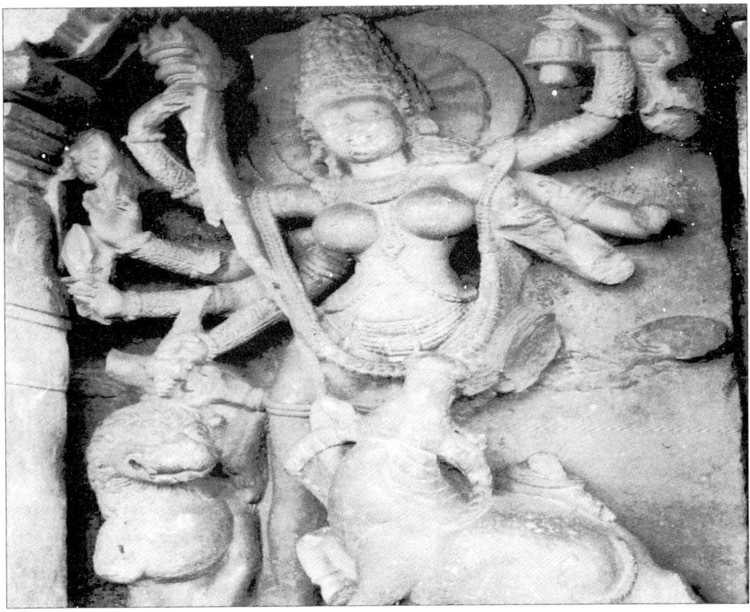

49. Aihole, Durga temple, Mahisasuramardini.

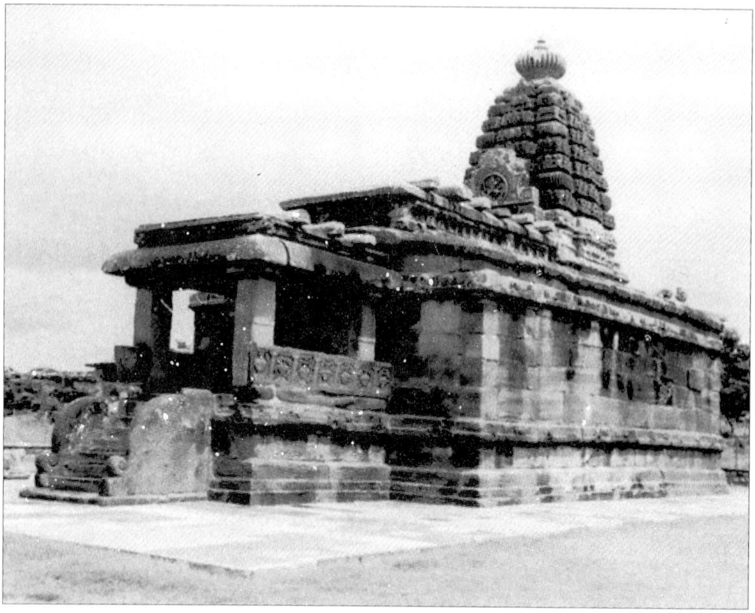

50. Aihole, Huccimalli gudi, general view.

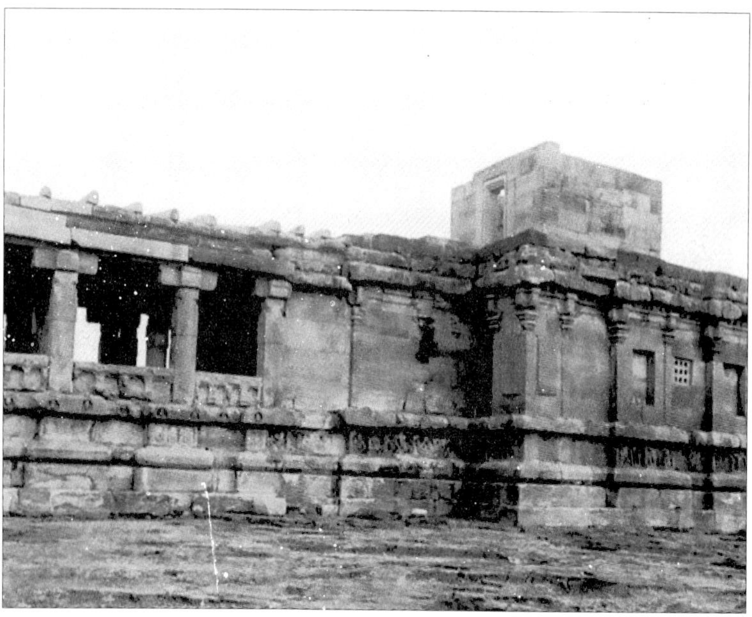

51. Aihole, Meguti temple, general view.

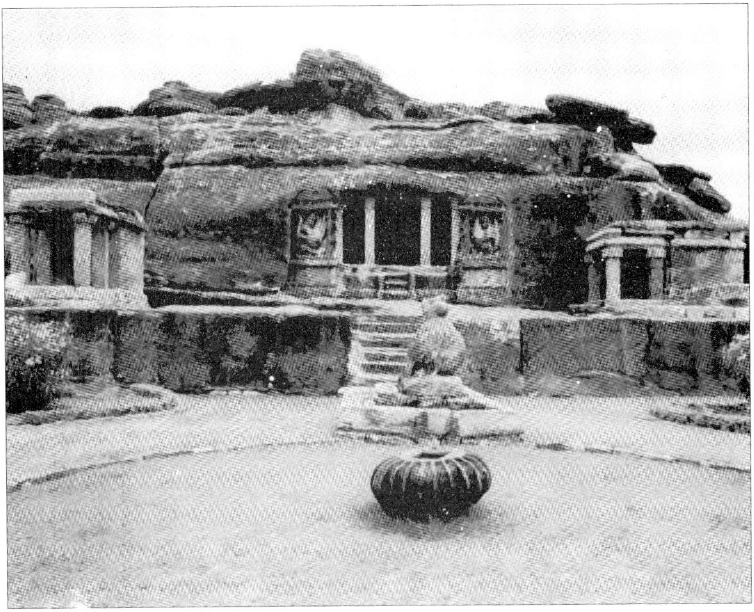

52. Aihole, Ravana pahadi Cave, general view.

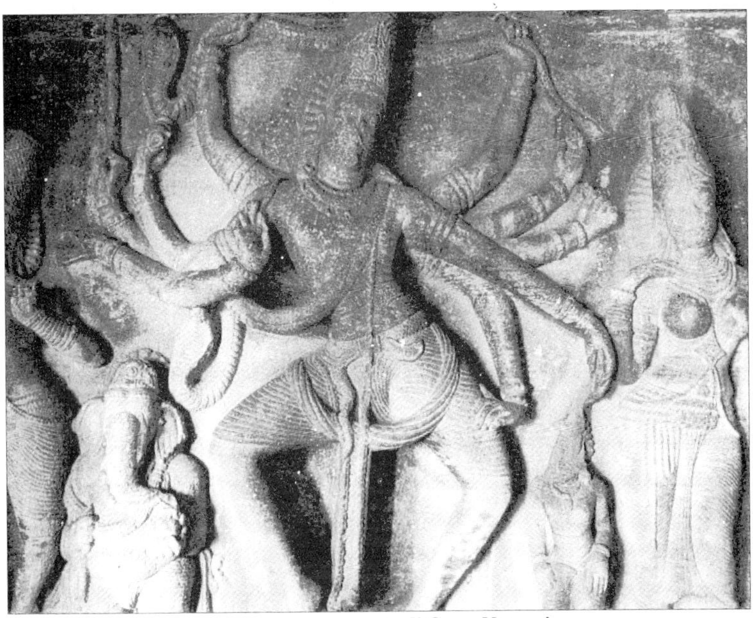

53. Aihole, Ravana pahadi Cave, Nataraja.

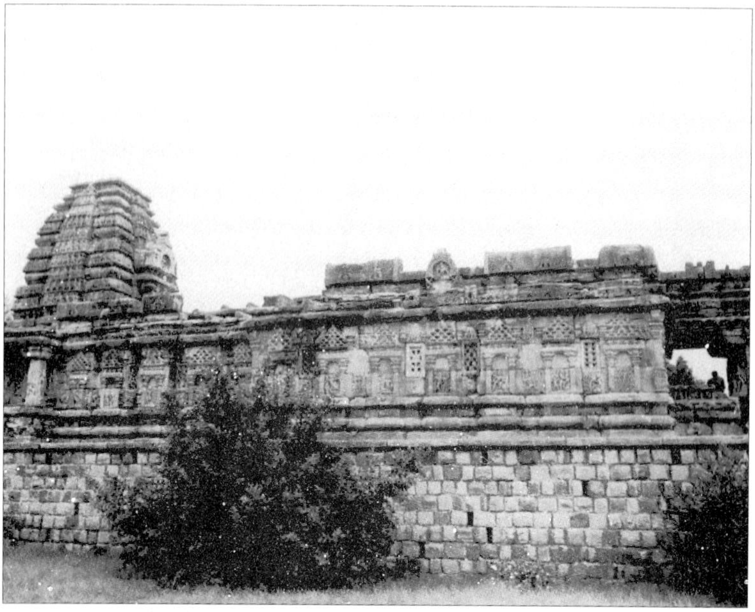

54. Pattadakal, Papanath temple, general view.

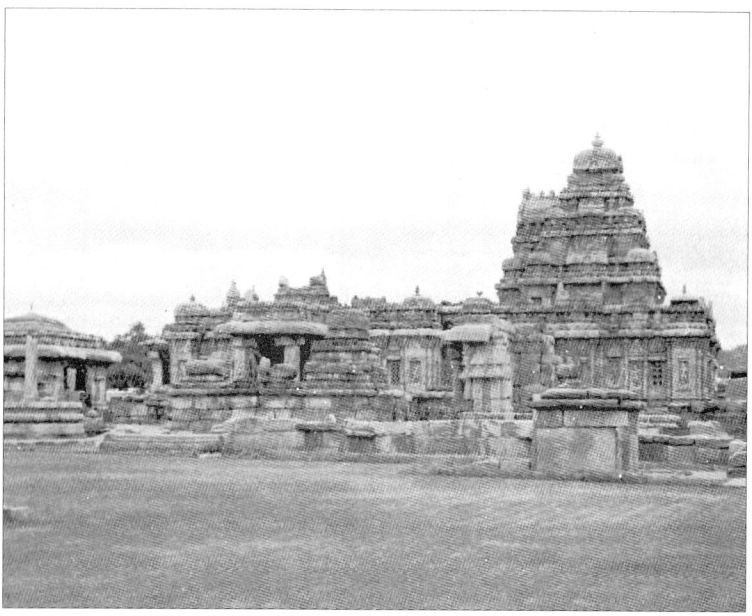

55. Pattadakal, Virupaksha temple, general view.

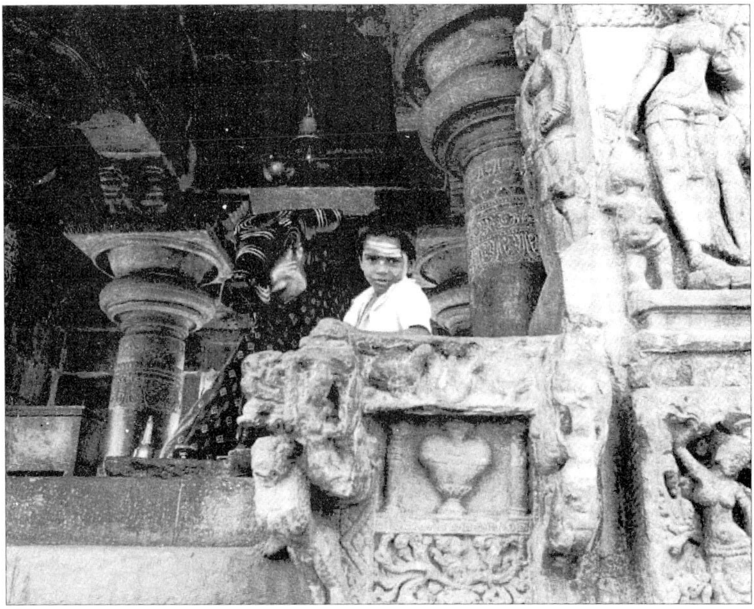

56. Pattadakal, Virupaksha temple, *nandi-mandapa.*

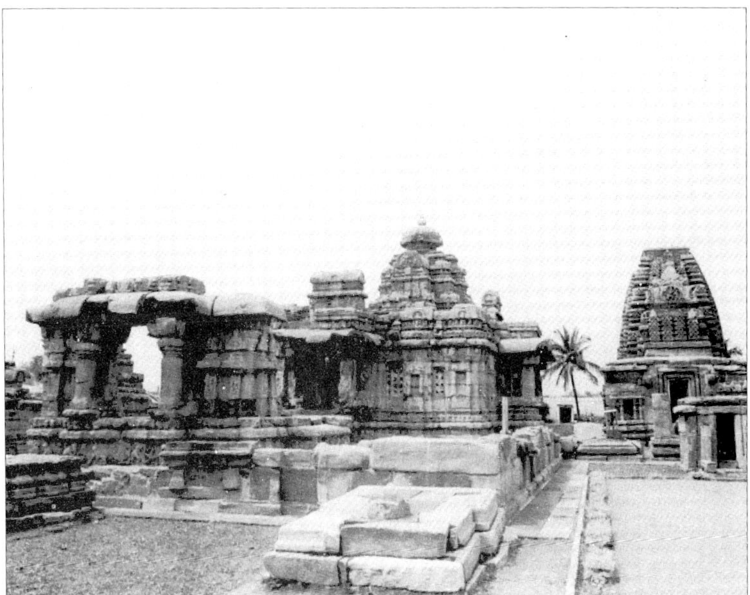

57. Pattadakal, Mallikarjuna temple, general view.

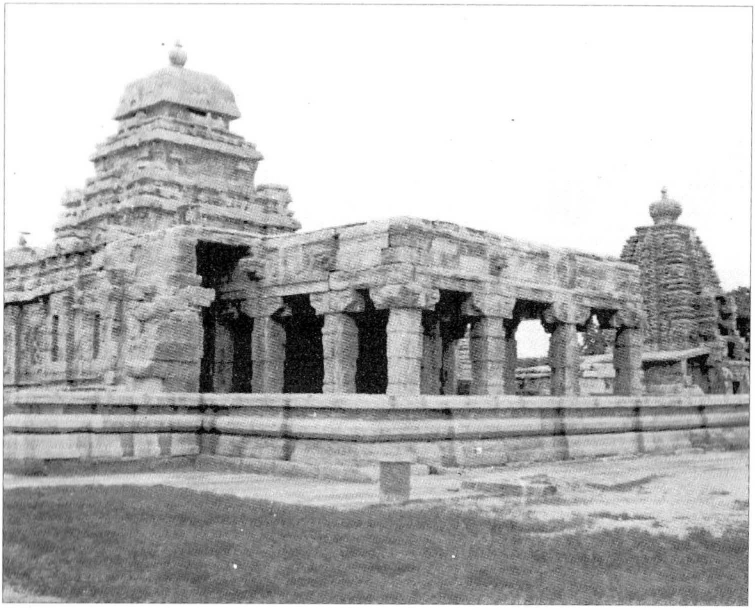

58. Pattadakal, Sangamesvara temple, general view.

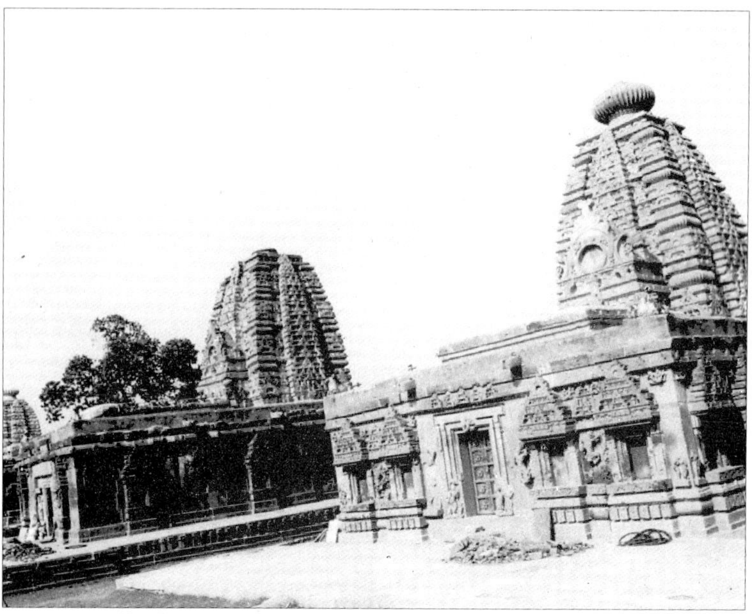

59. Alampur, Nava-brahma group of temples, general view.

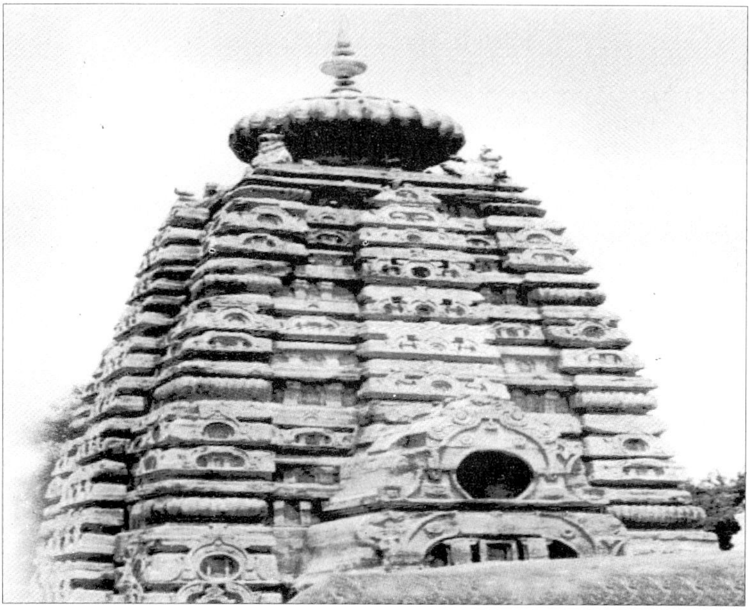

60. Alampur, Bala-brahma temple, *sikhara*.

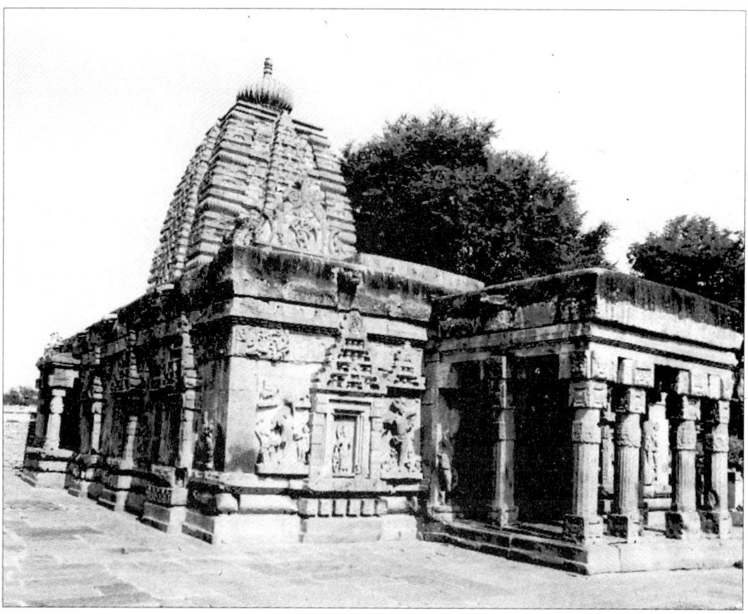

61. Alampur, Svarga-brahma temple, general view.

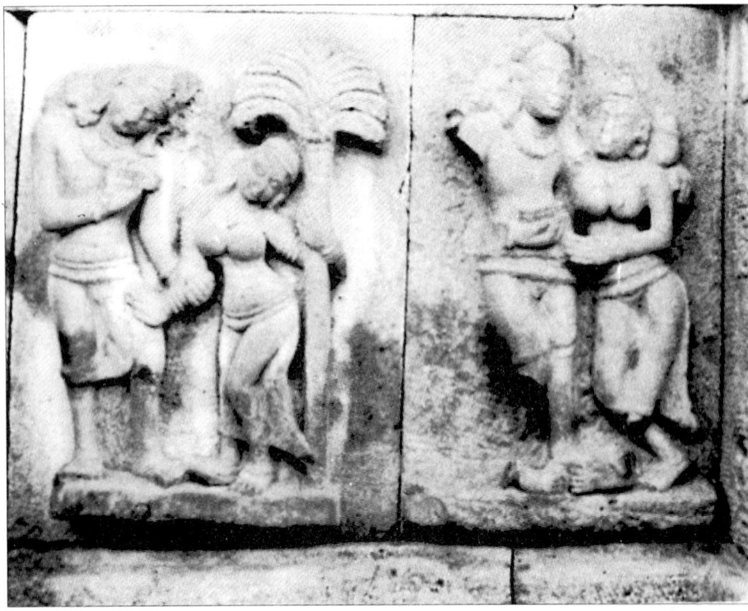

62. Alampur, Svarga-brahma temple, *mithunas*.

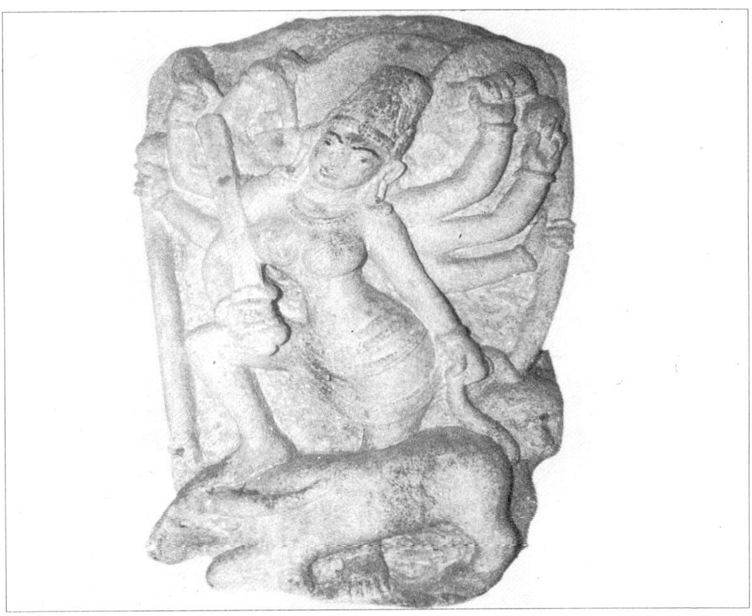

63. Alampur, Mahisasuramardini.

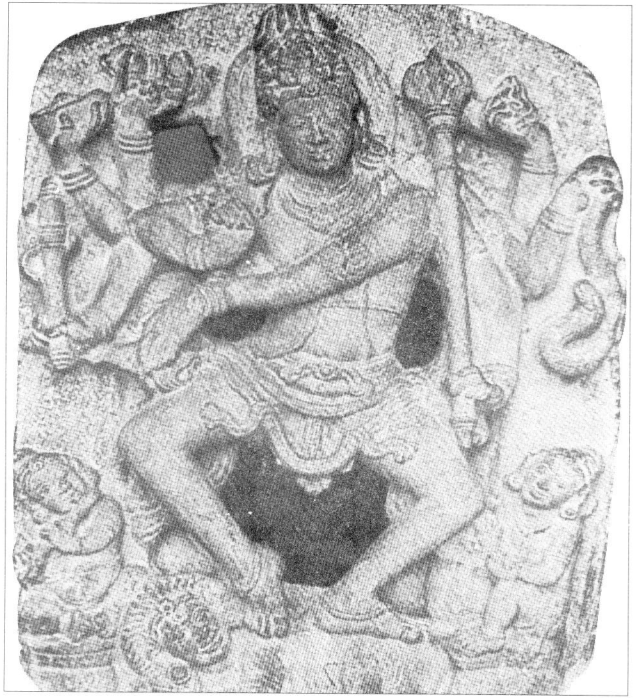

64. Alampur, Nataraja.

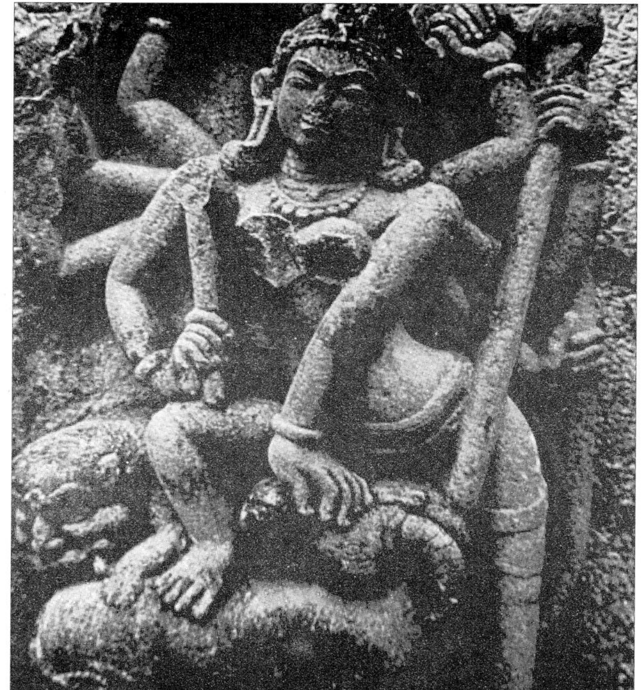

65. Alampur, Mahisasuramardini.

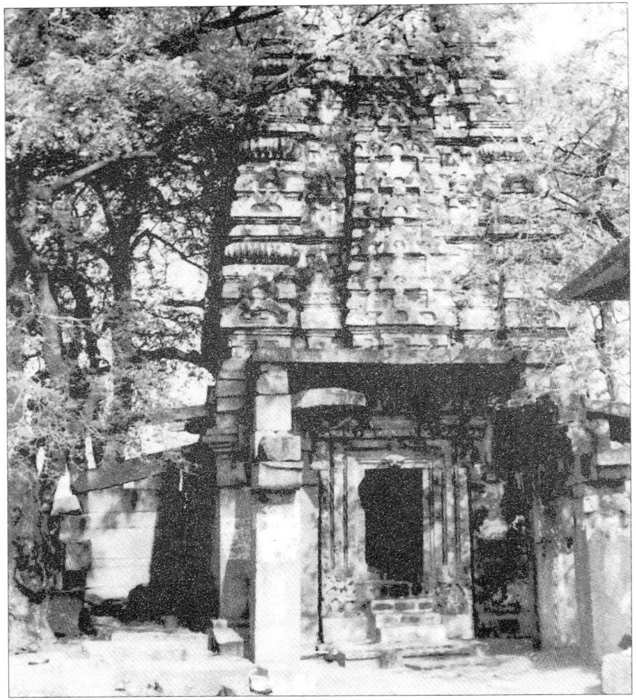

66. Panyam, Panakesvara temple, General view.

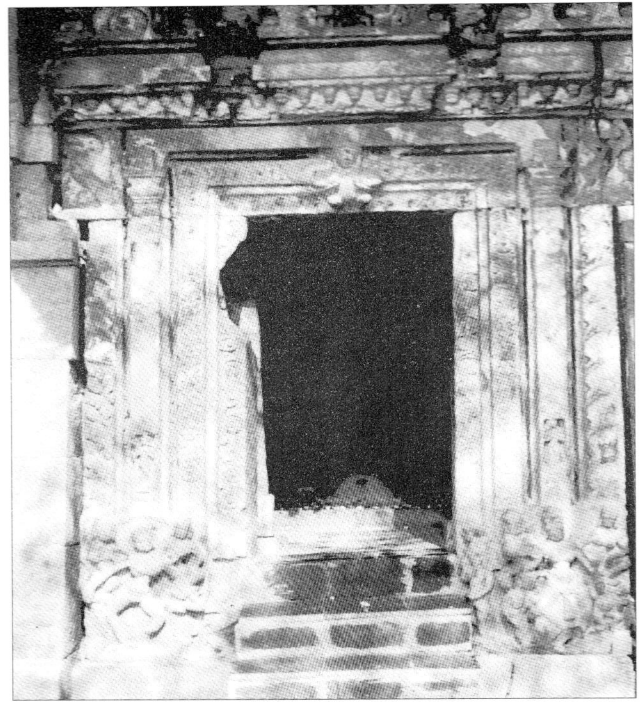

67. Panyam, Panakesvara temple, *garbha-griha* doorway.

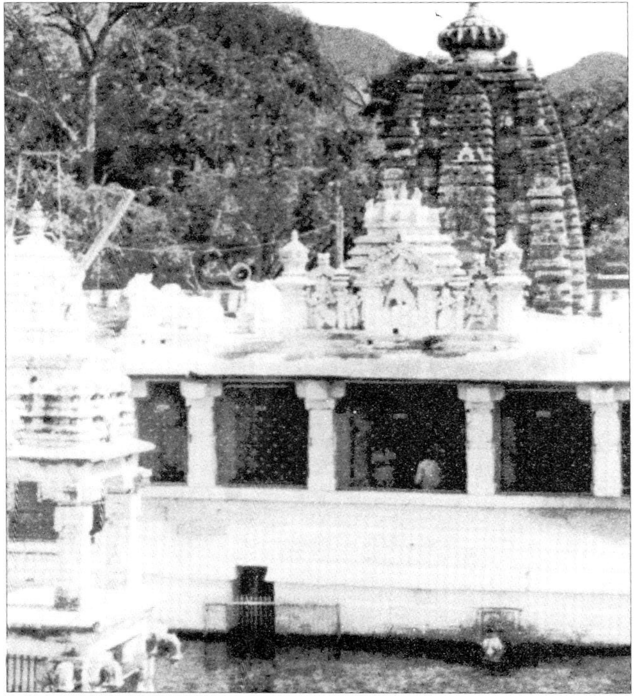
68. Mahanandi, Mahanandisvara temple, general view.

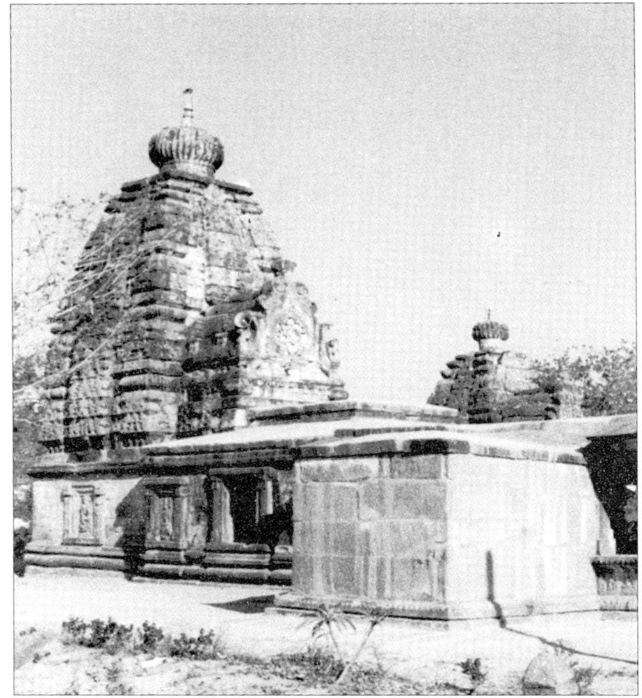
69. Satyavolu, Ramalingesvara temple, general view.

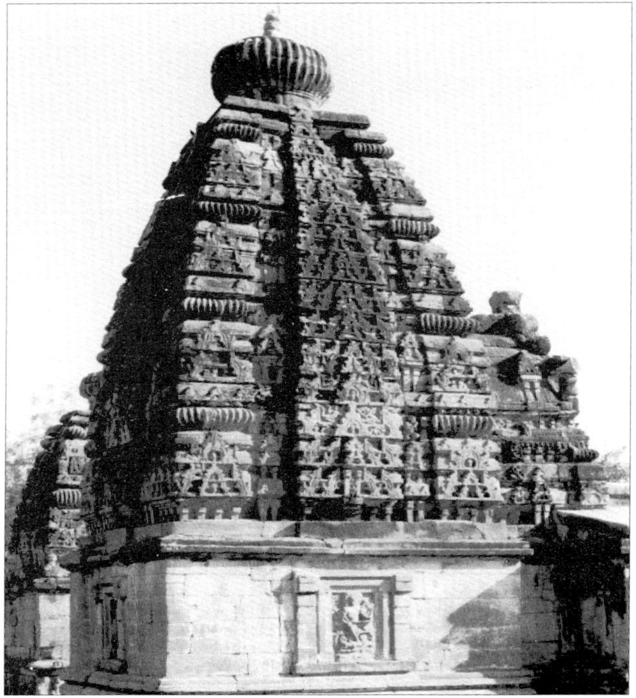

70. Satyavolu, Ramalingesvara temple, *vimana*, side view.

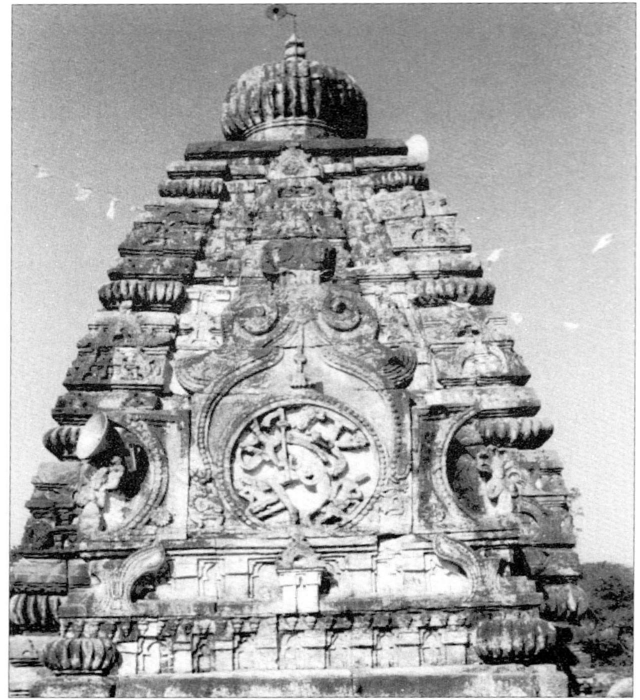

71. Satyavolu, Ramalingesvara temple, *Sukanasa*.

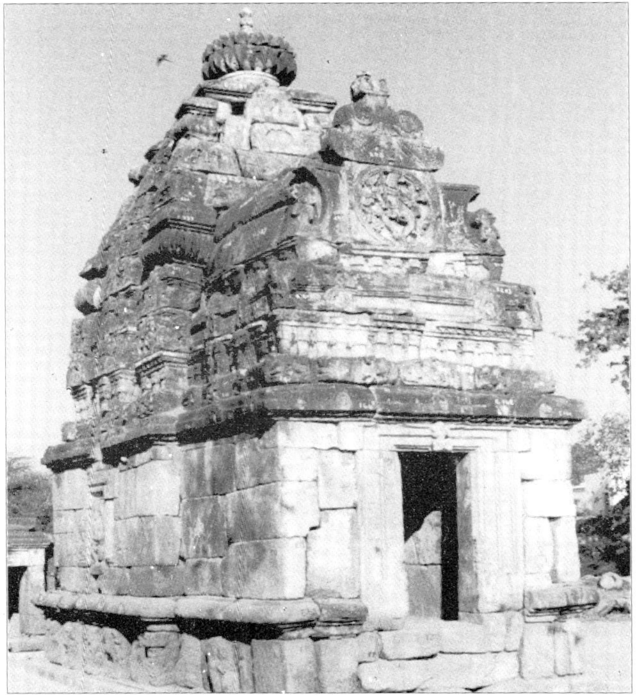

72. Satyavolu, Ramalingesvara temple, general view.

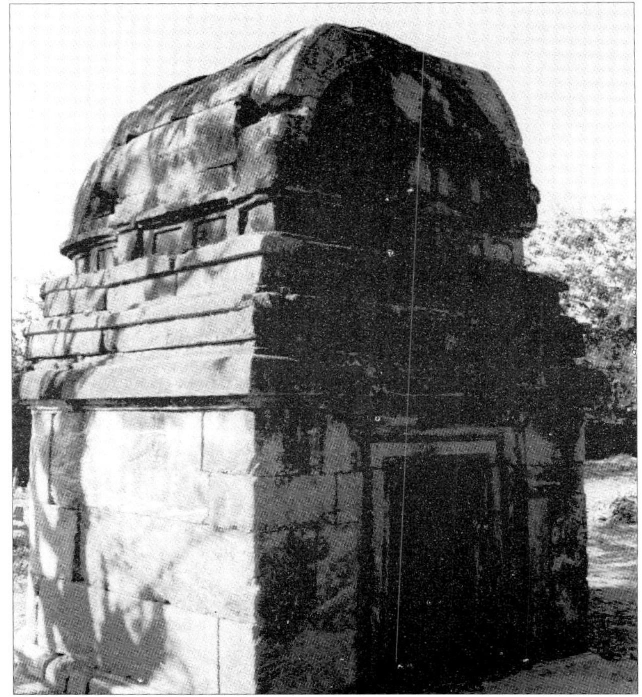

73. Satyavolu, apsidal shrine.

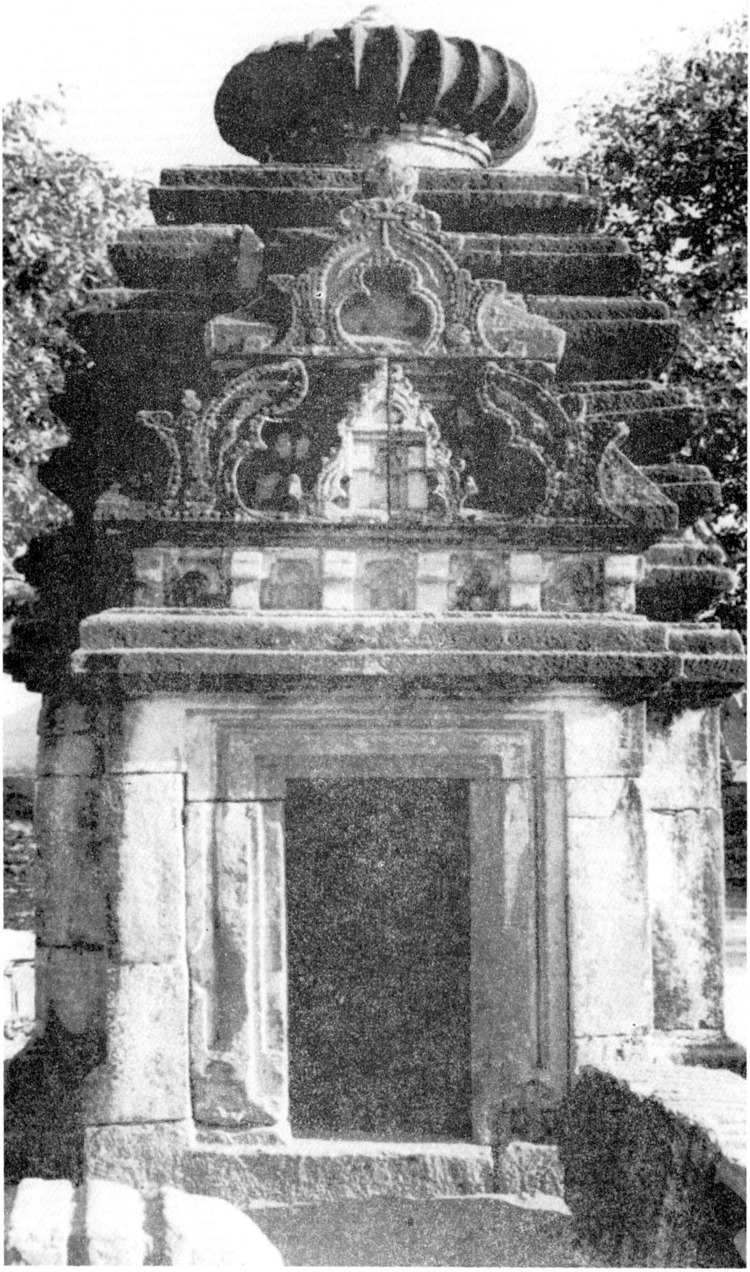

74. Satyavolu, temple with *Phamsana* super structure.

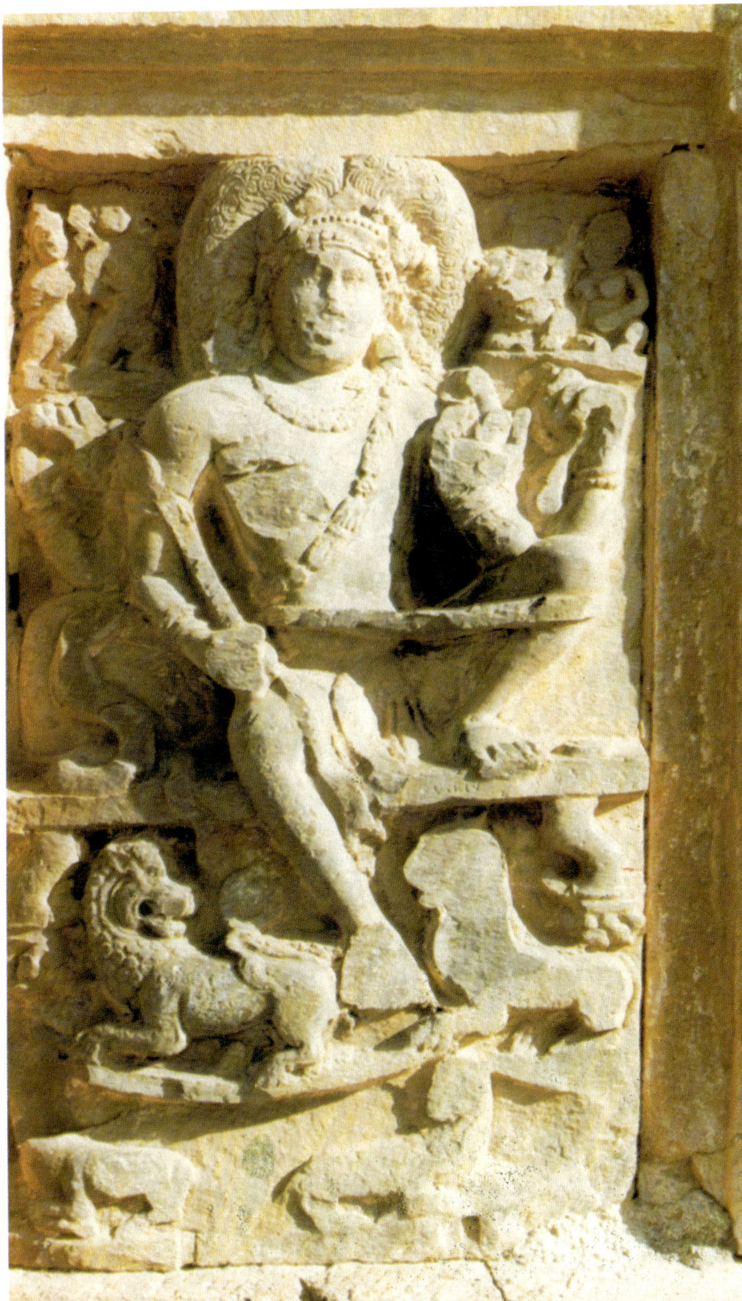

75. Satyavolu, Ramalingesvara temple, Dakshinamurti.

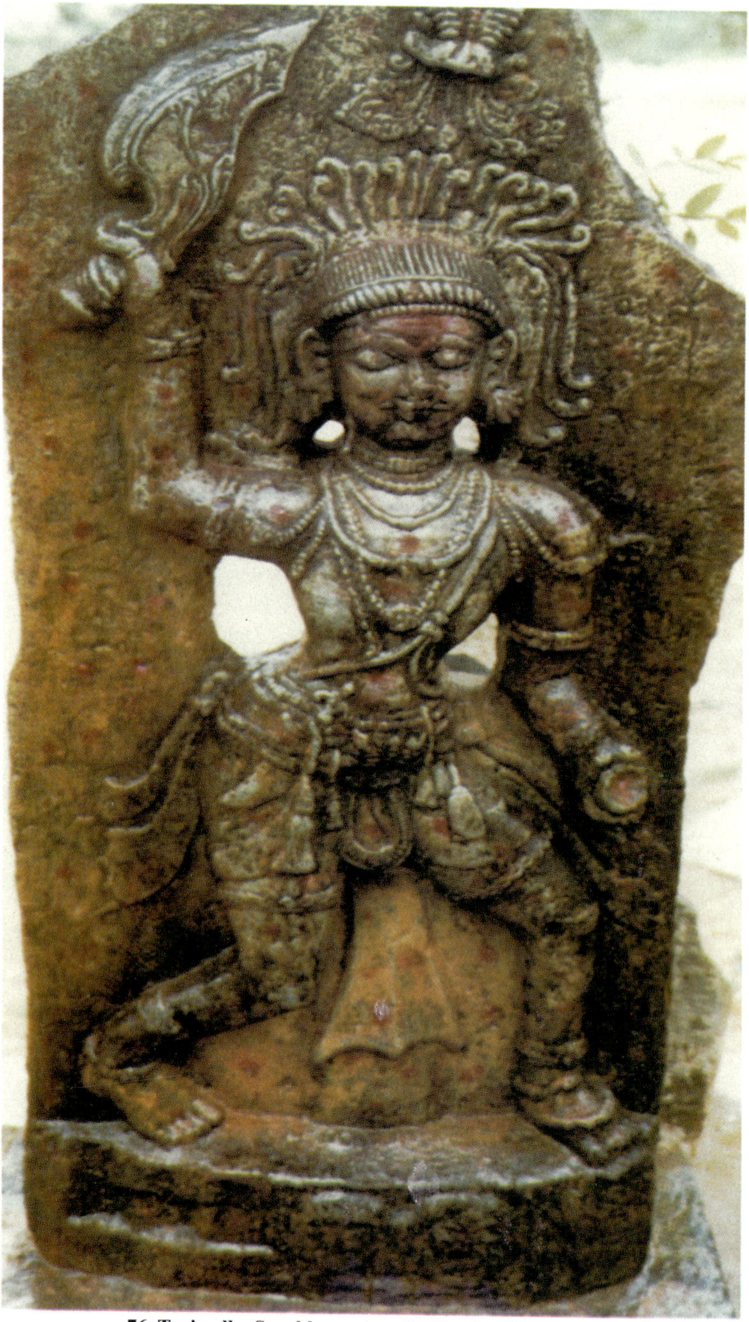

76. Turimella, Surabhesva temple complex, Virabhadra.

4

Badami Chalukyan Architecture

The early Chalukyas or Badami Chalukyas were one of the dominant powers in the Deccan from 6th to 8th century A.D. They were in general Brahmanical in their religious disposition but tolerant of other faiths, especially Jainism. In fact, the Aihole inscription of Pulakesin II has been engraved on the wall of a Jain temple, the Meguti temple, being composed by a Jain school-poet, Ravikirti. The dawn of Chalukyan kingdom began a brilliant epoch in the history of Karnataka making it till today a haven for tourists and scholars of sculpture and architecture. Perhaps the most prolific builders, they set in motion the wheel of architecture and sculpture. The triple cities of Badami, Aihole and Pattadakal, which together formed the cradle of Karnataka temple architecture, laid the foundation for the Chalukyan style of architecture.

The abundant sand stone of fine grain and quality available in the near by hills favoured the erection of famous temples and delicate sculptutre at these places. Among these the beginning was made at Aihole from about 550 to 650 A.D. and later the activity was shifted to Pattadakal, where the style of their architecture reached its culmination between the 7th century to the 8th century A.D., Badami and Mahakuta standing in between, in the chronological order. In their constructions at the above mentioned sites they made several experiments in Plan and elevation, by adopting certain existing temple styles of Guptas in the north and Pallavas in the south, the Chalukyas have introduced their own style of architecture, typically the Chalukyan.

The Chalukyas introduced many architectural traditions such as cushion capitals, bulky pillar shafts, ornate door frames, division of hall into nave and aisles, *sukanasa* over *antarala* as a projection from the *sikhara*, decoration of *kudu* arch of *sukanasa* with the figure of Natya-Siva, Ganga, Yamuna figures as *dvarapalas* on the doorframe, *garuda* on the lintel and coiled *naga* on *antarala* ceiling slab.

Architectural units like stone seats with sloping back in the portico, known as *kakshasanas*, predominantly used in the Kakatiya temples during 12th and 13th centuries in Andhradesa was, for the first time, introduced at Aihole. Even the style of roof with joints laid in overlapping fashion and covered with long narrow stone, similar to tiled roofing, was for the first time introduced by Chalukyas at Aihole. So also the case with the masonary which is composed of great archaic looking blocks dressed to level beds and placed one upon the other without using any mortar.

The first of the Chalukyan rulers of Badami, probably to emerge as an independent ruler, was Pulakesin I, whose Badami inscription of 535 A.D., gives about his construction of the fort at the place. The remains of the fort can be seen near the foot hills skirting the lake. It may be taken as the point of starting, of the greatness of the kingdom, which eventually reached its zenith under his grandson, Pulakesin II (610-642 A.D.). Pattadakal is 18 km and Aihole is 45 km, and Mahakuta is 11 km from Badami. Since these areas do not lie on the major tourist routes and are not well connected with the major cities, they have not received the prominence they deserve.

Badami, originally known as Vatapi, today, is a complex of flat roofed houses extending from one side of a huge lake, Agastya. The hills, which make Badami a natural fortress, extend on three sides of the lake. To the right of the town, facing the lake is a daunting hillock of copper-and-rust coloured sand rocks into which, at a height of 46.6 m there are four cave-temples, hewn into the rock. They date back to 6th century A.D. and are some of best examples of the early cave temples in Deccan. Of the four temples, three are Brahmanical while the fourth is Jaina. Each of the caves has a pillared veranda, a columned hall and a small square sanctuary, cut deep into the rock. Caves are ornamented with exquisitely carved animal and human figures, gods and demi-gods, floral and geometric patterns and scenes recalling the great episodes from the epics and puranas.

Although the Chalukyas were Vaishnavites, they encouraged construction of Jaina and Saiva temples also. In cave No. 1 (PL. 40) dedicated to Siva, the larger than life 18 armed Nataraja dwarfs the visitor (PL. 41). Equally superb is the figure of Vishnu in the next wherein the deity is depicted as Vamana vanquishing the egoistic Bali. The third in the series is also a Vaishnava cave, completed in the year 578 A.D., as the inscription of Mangalesa, carved in it reports. It contains fine reliefs of Vishnu seated on *Shesha naga,* under the shelter of the hood (PL. 42) and an image of Narasimha, both in the Veranda. The *mandapa* here is the most beautiful of any cave temple in this part of the country. The workmanship in these caves is marked by a high degree of technical excellence. The running frieze of *ganas* in various amusing postures carved in relief on each plinth in front of the cave deserves mention. Continuity of the iconographic tradition of the rock cut caves of the Western Deccan is observed in these images. However, the figures have become more slender. The 4th cave was dedicated to Jainism and carries relief sculptures of *Tirthankaras* like Gomatesvara and Mahavira.

The cave No. 2 and 3 have traces of the paintings. A note worthy painting here is that of betrothal of Siva and Parvati. These paintings are contemporaneous with the last phase at Ajanta. Compared to the Ajanta paintings these paintings have more soft and elastic out line and modelling is more sensitive in texture and expression.

The Chalukyas were built several structural temples along the edge of the lake and hill-top which the visitor should not miss to see. The Malegitti Sivalaya (PL.43) is, undoubtedly of a later date, of the temples of the Badami Complex perched on a hill. There are only monkeys to company here. The temple comprises an entrance porch, a square-columned hall and a sanctuary. The exterior pilastered walls of the hall carry sculptural figures, Vishnu on south and Siva on north (PL.44). Above the parapet rises the superstructure of the octagon-to-dome form, comparable to that of the nearby ruined lower Sivalaya temple. Among the temples, Bhutanatha (Siva) group of temples have a grand setting and command a good view of the lake infront (PL.45). The main temple with massive pillars and perforated windows resembles to that of Malegitti Sivalaya. The super structure here is of the square-to-dome form.

Aihole is a tiny village on the banks of the Malaprabha River, which has a great wealth of temples and temple sculptures, scattered all over. It has more than 70 temples, standing as testimonies to the creative urge and talents of giving shape to the urge of people of the time. Today, the ASI has erected barbed wire fences excluding the village enclave thrusting into the temple complexes. Three temples at Aihole, the Ladhkhan temple, the Durga temple and the Hucchimalli-gudi temple are particularly famous from the point of view of development of temple architecture at the place, exemplifying the experiments of the Chalukyan architects.

The Ladkhan temple (PL.46) was so called because a feudal Muslim chieftain once stayed there. This temple may be dated to 620 A.D. It is comparatively a low flat-roofed building, square in ground plan with a small sanctuary in its rear. In front of the square *mandapa*, a porch is set at the entrance, on the eastern front, the pillars of which bear the carved figures of the river-goddesses and loving couples (PL. 47) beneath trees. Above its roof, is a small supplementary storey, probably added at a later date, which appears rather an independent shrine of Sun-god. The remaining three sides of the temple are enclosed by walls, two of which have perforated stone grills. The interior is a pillared hall supported on square columns. At the fore-end of the hall facing the *nandi*, is the central sanctuary, not a chamber leading off the main hall, but built with in it.Because of these features, Percy Brown remarked that it was not perhaps, intended to be a temple originally, but just a moot hall, for the meeting of the village assembly, perhaps converted into a temple. The construction of the roof is also peculiar as it consists of large stone slabs grooved at the joints and held together by long narrow stones covering the entire length of the joints and fitting into groves cut in the slabs. It was originally intended as a Vishnu temple. Today it is a Siva temple.

The Durga temple (PL. 48) is an apsidal in ground plan with semi-circular rear. The temple measures 18 m x 11 m with a large portico, 7.32 m deep, on its eastern front. The temple stands on a high plinth with many mouldings, measuring about 2 m in height and has flat roof at a height of 9.1 m from the ground. A *sikhara* of north Indian type rises above the *garbha-griha* which has partly fallen and there is a veranda, roofed with sloping slabs lay on massive square columns with heavy brackets, so as to serve as *pradakshina-patha*.

As one goes around the ambulatory, the outer walls of the shrine show carved figures of Narasimha, Mahisasuramardini (PL.49), Varaha, Vishnu, Ardhanarisvara and Siva. The name Durga is misleading. The temple is not dedicated to goddess Durga but to Surya which can be dated to 6th or 7th century A.D.

The smaller and simpler with northern style super structure is the Hucchimalli gudi (PL.50), which contains a new feature, namely *antarala* between the sanctuary and the main hall. The temple contains lovely *mithuna* couples. On the ceiling of the porch is fabulously mounted karttikeya (Lord of War) riding a lovely peacock. One of the fairly early temples to be built at Aihole was the Jaina temple of Meguti (PL.51), stands on a hillock. It marks some progress in the construction of temples with better planning and execution, but it is ostensibly unfinished. Here we find the sanctum is detached from the backwall of the *mandapa,* and provided outside of it.

The other monuments worth visiting at Aihole are the sun temple whose sanctum and sanctorum has a beautiful entrance carved ornamentally. The Kontigudi is another flat roofed temple with massive square pillars, has ceiling sculpture depicting the trinity; Brahma, Vishnu and Siva. Siva seated with Devi, Brahma on a lotus and Narayana on his serpent couch. The Ravana pahadi is a small cave (PL.52) composed of a hall with two square pillars and shrines on the sides and at the rear. It carries exquisite pieces of sculpture, particularly dancing Siva trembling with motion (PL.53). Then there is the carving of the awesome Mahisasuramardini emerging fearsome, from rough rocks and shadows of a cave.

Though the early Chalukyas had their capital in Badami, they were crowned in *Pattadakal*. Now it is a small village on the banks of Malaprabha. This has been declared a world heritage site and contained in a single complex, the old stone temples, and rise out of well manicured lawns guarded by the uniformed men of the security services. Interestingly, the Chalukyas experimented with many architectural modes in this caronation city. There are ten temples here, four-Papanatha, Galaganatha, Kasi visvesvara and Jambulinga-in the Nagara style and six-Virupaksha, Sangamesvara, Mallikarjuna etc. - in the Dravida style. The Papantha temple (680A.D.) among the former, and Sangamesvara (725 A.D.) and Virupaksha (740 A.D.) among the latter, are the most notable. The Papanatha temple (PL.54) is another example for the experimentation in plan and elevation, made by the Chalukyan architects and presents the shortcomings, due to uncertainity regarding the correct relation of different parts of the temple in a structural combination. It measures 27.4 m long, too low in height, with a too small and stunted tower in northern style. It has the *antarala* too big almost like another *mandapa*, supplementing the one that is already provided for. The ceiling panels and beams of the *mandapa* are richly decorated with diverse designs. The niches in the outer walls are stereotyped with out proper spacing between one another and thus appear monotonus, showing the dearth of ideas for the sculptor. The walls illustrate incidents from Ramayana, Kiratarjuna and Gajantaka.This temple shows unsuccessful attempt to combine northern and southern features.

The Virupksha and Mallikarjuna temples were built by the two queens of Vikramaditya II, to commemorate their husband's victory over Nandivarman, the Pallava king. Originally these temples were named Lokesvara and Trailokesvara after these queens. The two temples are the finest examples of the art and architecture of Badami Chalukyas.

The Virupaksha temple (PL.55) is a memorable architectural feat-36.6 m from the front to the back of the shrine. It bears striking resemblance to the Kailasanatha temple at Kanchipuram, obviously because, Vikramaditya II brought the architects and sculptors from that city, following his victory, to his own capital and employed them in the construction of the temple. The high plinth comprising of five fully evolved mouldings. Percy Brown observes "there is a bold beauty in the appearance of the Virupaksha temple as a whole, which is best seen in the exterior". It has three porches in the east, north and south, a huge pillared *mandapa*, sanctuary, two subsidiary shrines and a *pradakshina-patha*.A detached *nandi* pavilion infront, and has a compound wall measuring 67.1 m x31.5 m.

The walls are thick and heavy. There is coherence in the construction of the *mandapa*, antechamber and sanctuary in this temple while no such harmony is observed in the papanatha temple. Even in the execution of niches we find a well thought out arrangement which is lacking in the Papanatha temple. The pillared *mandapa* has perforated stone windows and it has a coiled *naga* on its ceiling as usual. The square-based *sikhara*, typically a *dravida-vimana*, rises in four storeys each of considerable elevation. The external wall surface is divided by pilasters into well spaced ornamental niches, 35 in number, filled alternately with windows and sculptures.Thus the heaviness of stone work is relieved by increasing the amount and quality of sculpture. The sculptures include four armed Nataraja, Tripurantaka, Trivikrama, Lingodbhava, Lakulisa, Ardhanarisvara and Vrishabhantika etc. To quote Percy Brown once again: "The sculptures flow into the architecture in a continuous yet disciplined stream. So harmonious is the entire conception it conveys the impression that the deepest emotions of its creators were concentrated on its production. The amount of thought expanded, not only on the whole, but on each detail is incredible; every one of its grey weatherworn stones, inspite of the passage of the centuries, is yet warm with life and feeling. The Virupaksha temple is one of those rare buildings of the past in which the spirit still lingers of the men who conceived it and wrought it with their hands". The *nandi* in the *nandi-mandapa* (PL.56) made of black basalt is majestic.

The adjacent Mallikharjuna temple (PL.57) is almost identical in décor and detail to the Virupaksha temple. As in the Virupaksha temple the large hall beyond the porch has 18 pillars on which beautiful bas reliefs illustrates scenes from Ramayana, Mahabharata and stories from the Panchatantra and some social scenes.There is nataraja on the ceiling of the *mandapa.*

The neighbouring Sangamesvara temple (PL.58) is very much in the same style but has an open *mandapa.*Though the sculptures are massive, they look unfinished and indicate that the structure was left in complete due to for some unexepected political disaster. The temple has a massive *linga* in polished grey granite now broken. A large *nandi* faces the *mandapa*.

It is true what the guides will tell tourists that Aihole is considered a school of architecture, Badami a degree college, and Pattadakal, a university of architecture.

Though the main centres of architectural experiments carried out by the Chalukyas were mostly confined to the three principal towns in their kingdom in Karnataka, mentioned above, their architectural and sculptural styles influenced under their rule, in the modern Andhra Pradesh. The Navabrahma group of temples at Alampur, Sangamesvara temple at Kudavelli both in Mahaboobnagar district, Rupalammagudi at Terala, in Guntur district, Bhimesvara and Panakesvara Swamy temples at Panyam and Mahanandisvara temple at Mahanandi in Kurnool district, Ramalingesvara and Bhimalingesvara temples at Satyavolu in Prakasam district are a few examples of the Chalukyas of Badami. These temples were constructed exclusively of sandstone, locally available. Temple sites are generally located on trade routes or at administrative and piligrim centres. Some of these temples seem to have been centres of *Pasupata* school of Saivisim during the period.

Alampur is a small town in Mahaboobnagar District on the banks of Tungabhadra river near its confluence with the Krishna. During 7th century A.D., it flourshied as a great centre of Saivism and earned the fame as *dakshina kasi*, as well as flourished as great political centre under the Chalukyan rule, as inscriptions testify it to be the headquarters of a district, known after the Chalukyas. In view of the sanctity and importance of the place, the Early Chalukyan rulers built some of the most exquisite and magnificient temples dedicated to Lord Siva at the place.

The Navabrahma group of temples (PL.59) at Alampur represents to a major extent the developed phase of Chalukyan architecture. All the nine temples, Viz Padma-Brahma, Visva-Brahma, Vira-Brahma, Arka-Brahma, Kumara-Brahma, Svarga-Brahma and Taraka-Brahma form a single cluster with in a large enclosure.

From about the 9th century Alampur became a strong centre of *kalamukha* sect of Saivism and there are indications that *tantricism* continued here for a long time. The ancient treatise *Rasa Ratnakara* also mentions Alampur and says the presiding goddess of the place was Yogesvari, presently called Jogulamba; she was the presiding deity of gold and other forms of wealth.

All these nine temples face the east. The Bala-Brahma temple (PL.60) is the largest of the lot and is still used for worship. Here an archaeological museum exhibiting exquisite stone sculptures from 7th to 15th century A.D. is worthy of a visit.

According to the *Skandapurana,* which gives a vivid description of the place, Alampur acted as the western gateway of the famous *Srisaila kshetra.* According to Hindu mythology, Brahma made penance at Alampur to please Lord Siva and it is on this account that the nine temples are named after nine Brahmas or as the *Nava-Brahma* temples.

The Alampur temples are structurally very complete, mostly having *rekha nagara-sikhara,* except Taraka-Brahma temple which is having *Dravida-vimana*. Most of them are with *sukanasa* with an exception of Kumara-Brahma temple. In majority cases the exterior walls of the *mandapas* is relieved with niches filled with statuary and perforated stone grills. As at Papanatha temple at Pattadakal the *bhadra-gavakshas* of sanctum are provided with pillared porticos embellished with gods. The internal arrangements of the hall of each temple are in nave and aisle pattern. The door frame of the sanctum is in the *Pancha-sakha* design with Ganga, Yamuna as *dvarapalas.*

The Svarga-Brahma temple at Alampur (PL.61) reveals architectural formulation in full fledged manner. It deserves detailed consideration. Founded during the regnal period of Vinayaditya (696-733A.D.) this *sandhara* temple on plan consists of a *mukha-catuski,* a *gudha-mandapa,* an *antarala* and a *garbha-griha* and features a *bhadra-gavaksa* on the cardinal directions.

The *ghatapallava* pillars are found in the *mukha-catuski* and the *gudha-mandapa* and these are decorated with a *purna-ghata* at the base and octagonally chamfered shaft and are crowned by palmette capitals at the top. The entrance of the *garbha-griha* is guarded by *dvarapalas,* finely carved. The exterior walls exhibit new features like the flying celestials and *mithunas* (PL.62) at the top and bottom of the *kosthas* and finally the *bhadragavaksas* housing Siva–Nataraja, Trivikrama or Tripurantaka panels aside from the trellis.

The *sikhara* is four storied which is distinguished from the earlier *sikharas* at Alampur and other sites in Andhra and Karnataka as well. At the base of *madhyalata* a *panjara* is carved and succeeding layers carry small *chandrasalas* which are shown in the box-like pattern. This distinctive carving reaches to the *Pidhana phalaka* where it terminates in an elegant *simha karna.* The *suratara* is carved with *balapanjaras.* The *griva* and *amalaka* and double *kalasas* are the crowing parts. The gable of *sukanasa* contains an impressive figure of Siva–Nataraja flanked by *nagarajas.*

The sculptures of Alampur, mostly in bold relief, follow the Aihole idiom with elongate, slender forms and powerful line suggesting movement. Among the Nava-Brahma group, the Svarga-Brahma and Visva-Brahma temples are rich in sculptures. The sculptured panels of Dakshinamurti, Gangadhara, Nataraja-Siva, Lingodbhava, Tripurantaka and Bhiksatanamurti are very meticulously depicted on the exteriors of the temples. Again, in the Visva-Brahma temple, iconographic representations of Dakshinamurti in *utkutikasana;* Ardhanarisvara in Bala-Brahma temple are noteworthy. Various icons are to be found in the courtyard round the Bala-Brahma temple viz. Vinadhara-Siva, Mahisasuramardini (PL.63) and Nataraja.The *mithuna* figures (Svarga-Brahma) display the soft modelling and beauty of form that continued from the Gupta to the post-Gupta period.

A very magnificient and artistically superb idol of Nataraja (PL.64) is exhibited at the main hall of the Archaeological

Musuem, Alampur. The eight armed Siva dances in the *catura* pose on the *apasmara-purusa* in full ecstacy of eternal dance. The god holds *damaru*, *parasu* and *patra* in the upper right hands, and flame, *naga* and *trisula* in the upper left hands. His lower right hand is held in front in *pravarita* pose and the lower left in *lolahasta* across the chest. He wears a tall *jatamakuta* bejeweled with a diadem and a *mukta-haras.* He is adorned with *sarpa-kundala* on the right ear and *chakra-kundala* on the left, two *haras, graiveyaka, udarabandha, yagnopavita* and girdle. There is a corpulent figure playing the flute to the right and a drummer playing on the drums to the left. The earlier prototypes of Nataraja can still be found at Badami and Pattadakal. The multi-armed Natesa dancing beside the bull at Badami and four-armed dancing Siva on *apasmara-purusa* at Pattadakal may be considered as precursors of the Nataraja figures of Alampur.The figure of Nataraja in the Alampur museum can be dated to 10th century A.D.

A figure of Mahisasuramardini (PL.65) in red sand stone is another specimen of western Chalukyan art, exhibited in the galleries of the Alampur Museum, Alampur. The goddess is tall, supple and slender and is endowed with pleasant and relaxed expression. The forceful movement of the body, which bends the figure in an arch-like form, represents constant flow of energy and divine elegance. The eight armed goddess is killing the buffalo-demon, by piercing her lance in its neck. The qualities of suppleness, slender and divine energy are very predominant in the sculpture.

The temple of Kudali Sangamesvara, on plan, consists of a square *garbha-griha, antarala* and a closed pillared hall, similar to other Chalukyan examples elsewhere. The outer face of the *mandapa* wall is relieved with sculptured niches of Sivas various forms and perforated grills in alternate fashion. The stately presence of Sankhanidhi and Padmanidhi of the main entrance door are note worthy. The *mandapa* roof is in nave and aisles pattern. Of the *nandi-mandapa* nandi is preserved. In many respects the super structure bear a close resemblance with the Bala-Brahma but lacks *sukanasa.* The temple was dismantled and transplanted, near Alampur as it faced a threat of submergence under Srisailam dam.

The Jogulamba Devi temple at Alampur, one of the 18 *Saktipeethas* in Indian sub-continent, including Sankari Devi temple in Srilanka, was reconstructed after 615 years. The temple was razed to the ground during Muslim invasion in 1390 A.D. The local people put up a fierce resistance, killed the invaders and moved the main idol to the nearby Bala-Brahmesvara temple. The Jogulamba temple was reconstructed at the same place where it stood. The temple was designed to match the Chalukyan architecture so that the new temple would fit in to the group of temples.

The Panakesvara swamy temple at *Panyam* (PL.66) having fully developed *chatusthala* curvilinear *sikhara* is quite akin to the Svarga-Brahma in every detail but lacks the *sukanasa.* The temple as it stands now shows on plan a *gudha- mandapa* and a *garbha-griha.* The external wall and the roof of the *gudha-mandapa* are not extant. The *mandapa* is raised on bulky pillars with cushion capitals. The *garbha-griha* door (PL. 67) is of *pancha-sakha* variety and over door pattern is embellished at sides with Ganga and Yamuna figures. The wall of *garbha-griha* is decorated with flying *gandharvas* holding *puja-dravyas* in their hands. An image of *gandharva* is carved on *lalata.* The ceiling of *antarala* has a lotus medallion with coiled *naga* at the centre. The capitals and bulky pillar shafts with octogonal neck at the top are similar to those at Ladkhan temple at Aihole. On stylistic considerations, this temple may be ascribed to Vinayaditya regnal period. (681-96 A.D.).

A noted Piligrimage centre, *Mahanandi* lies in a natural gorge of ravishing beauty surrounded on all sides by greenery of thick forests of the Nallamalai range of hills and served by a sacred *Tirtha* which is famous for its curative properties. The famous Mahanandisvara temple (PL. 68) consisting of an open *mandapa*, *antarala* and a *garbha-griha* on plan with an inner ambulatory. The *sikhara* has close similarity to the Aihole *rekha* style of northen order. The *sukanasa* reaches up to the second *bhumi*. The pillars, outer walls, windows and the *sikhara* are adorned with intricate carvings. The shrines on the back of Mahanandisvara temple also belong to this period and the Ganga, Yamuna and *dvarapalas* at the base of door jambs is note worthy. The employment of *vidyadharas* and Ganga Yamuna figures reveal the impact of Nagara traditions. The *vidyadhara* figures floating in the same or opposite directions recall similar figures of the Kailasa at Ellora. There is a huge *nandi* in front of the lord's shrine, lending the name Mahanandi to the place. On stylistic grounds, this temple can be dated to the regnal period of Vinayaditya.

Underneath the *linga* of this temple, five perennial mineral springs flow into the tank in front of the temple and then to the agricultural fields. The inlets and out lets of the tank are in such a way that water level remains same and here is always 1.7 m deep. So the pilgrims can safely take a dip in the crystal clear waters.

Unlike any other *linga* the *mula-vigraha* here is very unique. It is a rough, uncut, rock with two sockets. Legend has it that one of the cows of Nanda, ruler of the domain, was feeding milk in to an ant hill in which lord Siva used to sit in the form of a child. One day, the king followed the cow and lay deep in meditation to have a glimpse of the lord. As the cow repeated its daily ritual, the surprised king disturbed the cow and it stepped on the ant hill and the divine child disappeared. Frightened at having committed *devapachara,* the king prayed for forgiveness. Pleased at his repentance, the lord ordained that the ant hill would become a *Svayambu-linga* at Mahanandi. Within a radius of 18 km of Mahanandi, nine *nandi* temples are located. The Sivarathri festival is celebrated here on a grand scale.

To the east of the village *Satyavolu* is a temple complex enclosed by a compound wall. Many features, with an interaction with Alampur idiom can be seen in these temples. The *sikharas* are in *Nagara* style and are dedicated to Lord Siva, in the form of Rama-Lingesvara and Bhima-Lingesvara. Satyavolu is the only site in Andhra Pradesh to show *Nagara* temples of *nirandhara* plan.

Rama-Lingesvara temple consists on plan a *gudha-mandapa,* an *antarala* and a *garbha-griha* (PLs. 69 and 70). The entire plan is rectangular measuring 13.7m x 5.3m. The doorway to the *antarala* is of *trisakha* variety, plain in its jambs and a *gandharva* is carved above, life-size horned *dvarapalas* flank the doorway. The *sukanasa* of the *antarala* roof is relieved with *kudu* arches further decorated with Siva-Nataraja; on either side of the *kudu*, or the facade of the *sukanasa*, two figures of Nagaraja are carved (PL. 71). The *ranga-mandapa* in front of the *gudha-mandapa* shows the finishing of pillars in the Kakatiya art, obviously, an addition in the Kakatiya period.

An identical but smaller dimensions, 6.4 m x 4.37m., is the temple of Bhima- Lingesvara (PL.72), situated to the north of the Rama-Lingesvara temple. On plan, the temple features a *garbha-griha* and *antarala* only. The *kandhara* of the *adhishthana* is decorated with figures of standing elephants, and squatted lions. The *antarala* is entered through a *trisakha* doorway. At the base of the Jambs are *purna-kumbha* motifs. An image of Vishnu on *Garuda* is carved on the *lalata.* The *kapotali* cornice is decorated with the *kudu* motifs containing images of human heads. It recalls the *kapota* moulding of the Pallava style. The *sikhara* is *dvibhumi* class. The crowning member of the spire, *Sikhara* is featured with an *amalaka* and *kalasa* surmounting it. The *sukanasa* is rather over sized and occupies the entire length of the *antarala.* A Siva-Nataraja is seen in the circular opening and on the sides of the arch, figures a Nagaraja in *anjalimudra.* The interiors of the *antarala* and *garbha-griha* are featureless.

The temple complex consists of five sub shrines, which are intended for housing the *parivara-devatas.* One of them is an apsidal shrine (PL. 73). It has *trisakha* doorway, which carries no decoration. Another shrine has *phamsana* type of *sikhara* (PL. 74). It is square on ground plan with doorway whose jambs are plain. The *phamsana* super structure has six *bhumis* and it is surmounted by a *pidhana-phalaka,* a *gala* and an *amalaka.*

The temples are dated to 7th-8th centuries A.D. to the period of rule of Vijayaditya (696 - 733 A.D.) of the western Chalukyas.

The sculptural art at Satyavolu in general is less refined. The image of Siva-Dakshinamurti (PL. 75) is found on the southern niche of the Rama-Lingesvara temple. The god is seated in the *utkutikasana* posture on a high pedastal. He holds *nilotpala* in the lower right hand, *aksamala* in the upper right; *jnanamudra* in the lower left, *sarpa* in upper left hand. He is adorned with *jatabhara, puspa-yajnopavita, keyura* and *valayas.* The fullness of the face, the flexed stoic torso and positioning of legs lend to the figure a majestic appearance and it strongly recalls the jnana Dakshinamurti from Kanchi and Kaveripakkam.

The Papavinasa temple at *Turimella* belongs to the early Chalukyan style, with its plan similar to other Chalukyan examples elsewhere. An image of Virabhadra (PL.76) is found at the entrance of the temple, looking fearful with its prominently protruding canine teeth. The image is richly decorated, holding *khadga* in his upraised right hand and *khetaka* in the left hand. His hair is finished in the form of *jatamakuta* and raging flames as emerging out of it. He wears *keyuras, kankanas, kapalamalas, yajnopavita, katibandha* of bells, anklets and short drawers. He is shown with twisted legs as if plunging in to action. His torso appears as if slightly bent forward, quite appropriately to the dynamic movement. A *kirttimukha* is seen above the head of the god and two human heads are carved on the pedestal, below his feet. The sculpture may probably belong to 10th century A.D.

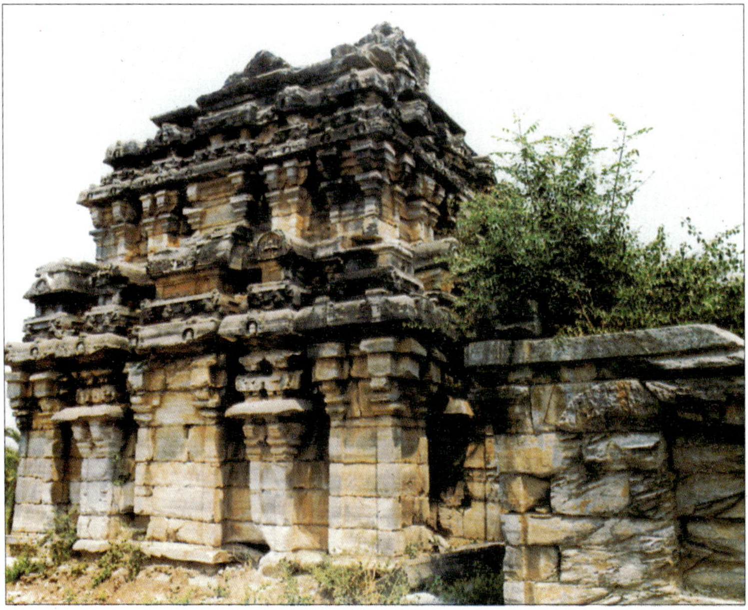

77. Pondugala, Jalpesvara temple, general view.

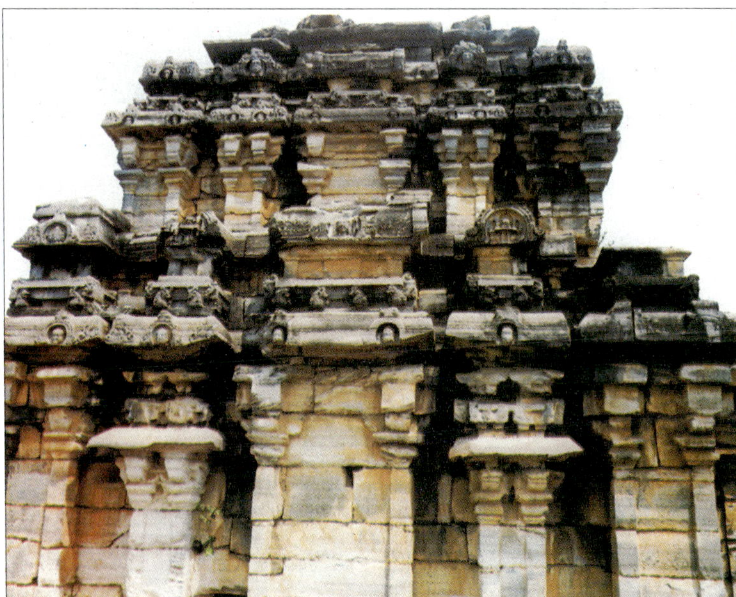

78. Pondugala, Jalpesvara temple, super structure.

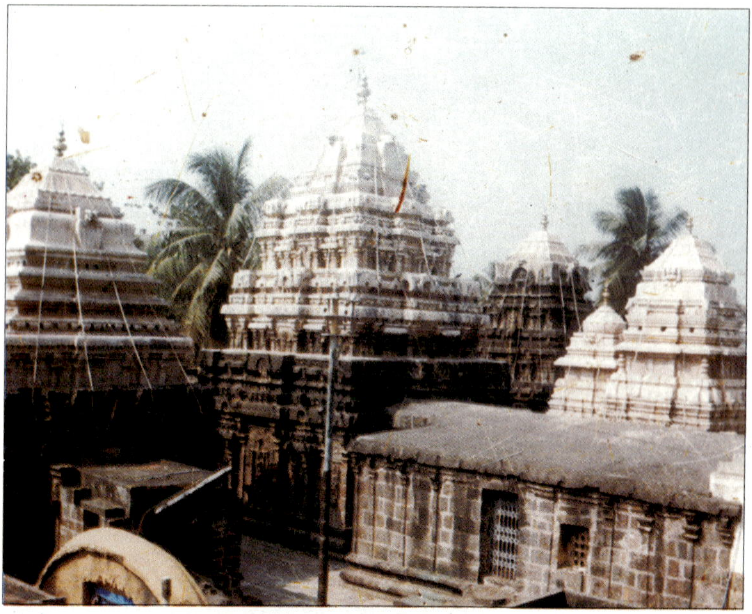

79. Biccavolu, Golingesvara temple complex.

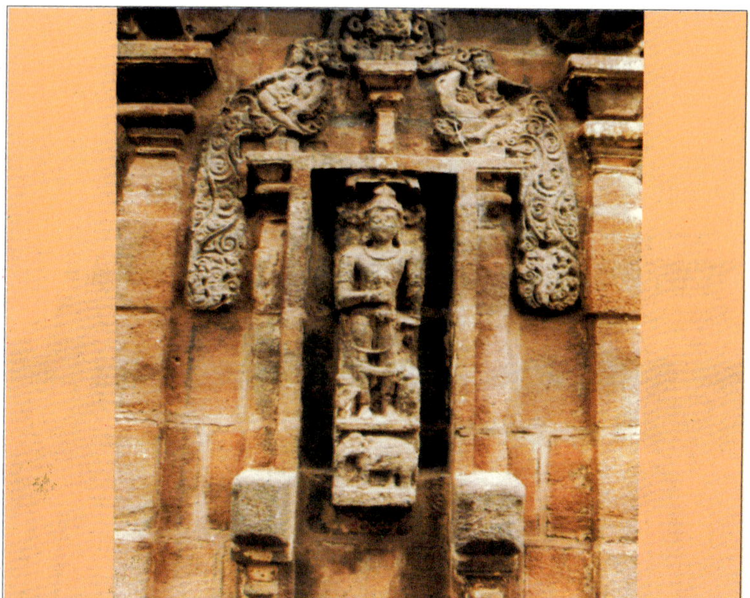

80. Biccavolu, Golingesvara temple, Indra.

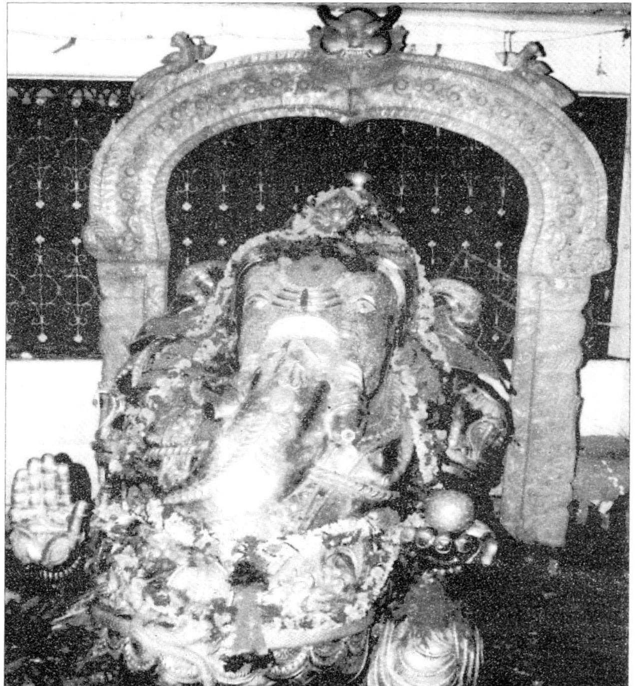

81. Biccavolu, Golingesvara temple, Ganesha.

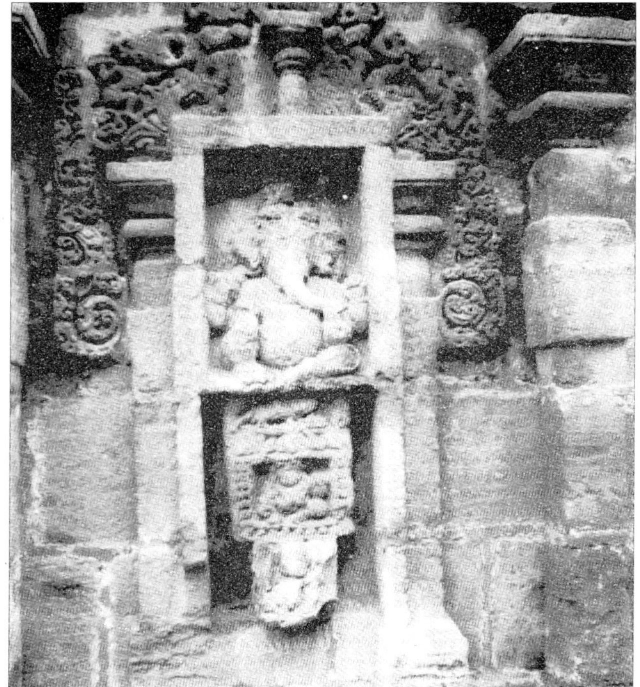

82. Biccavolu, Lakshmi Ganapati temple, Ganesha.

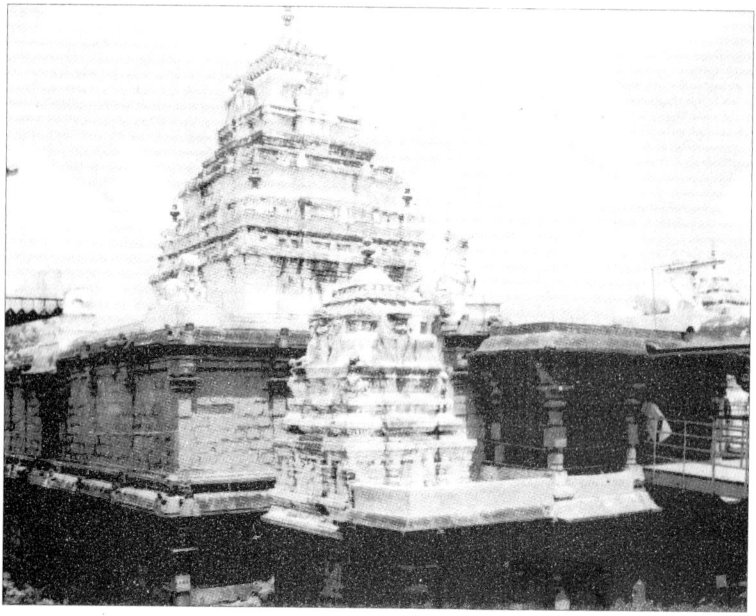

83. Draksharamam, Bhimesvara temple, general view.

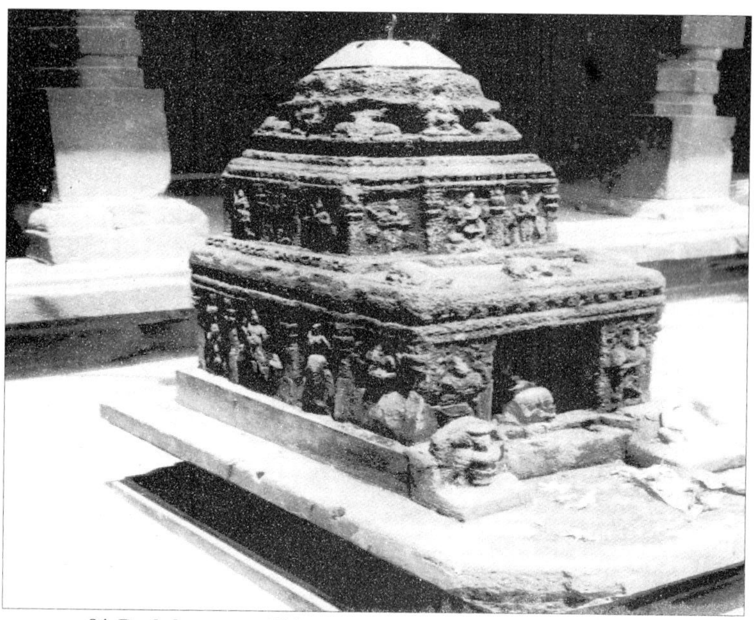

84. Draksharamam, Bhimesvara temple, miniature shrine model.

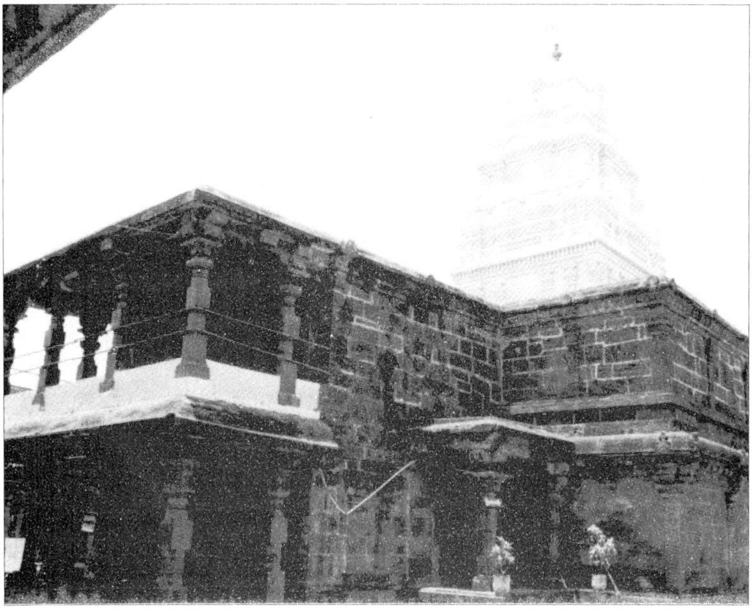

85. Samarlakota, Chalukya Bhimesvara temple, general view.

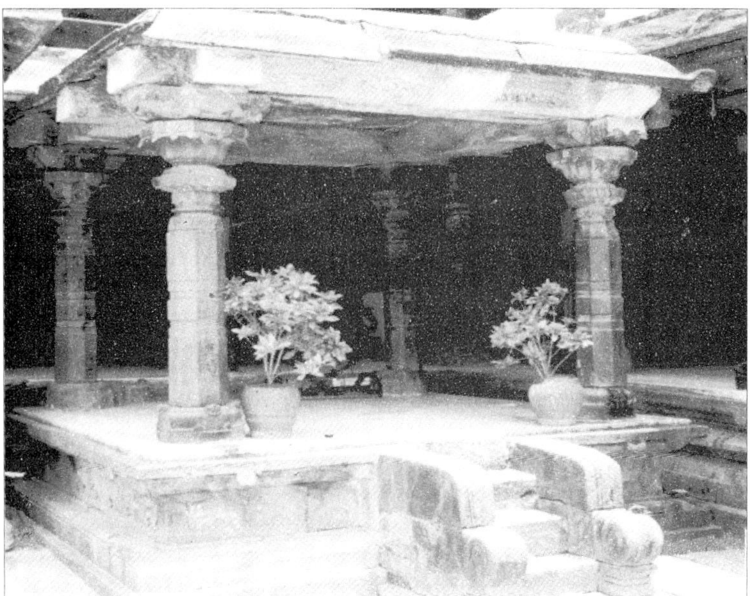

86. Samarlakota, Chalukya Bhimesvara temple, rocking *mandapa*.

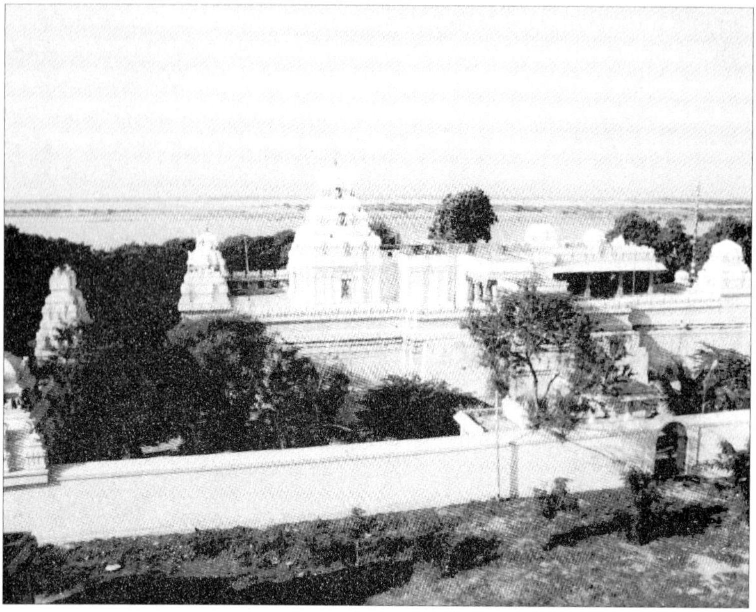

87. Amaravati, Amareswara temple, general view.

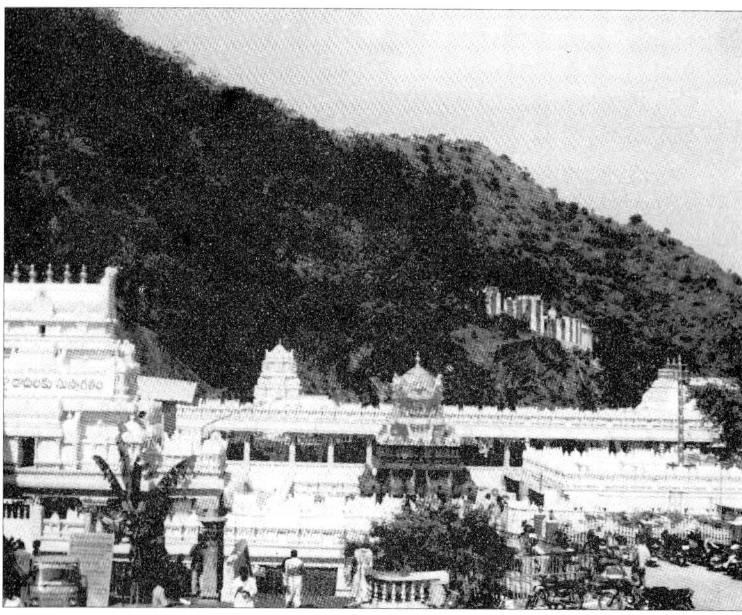

88. Vijayawada, Durga temple, general view.

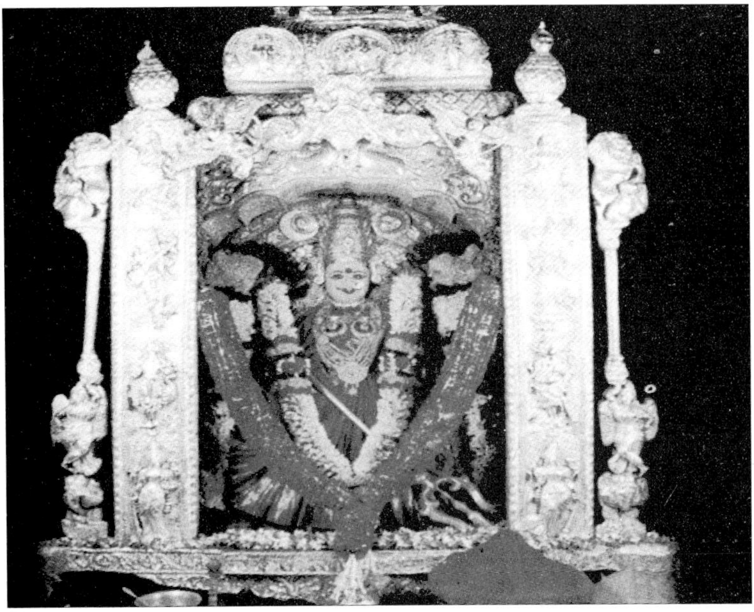

89. Vijayawada, Goddess Durga.

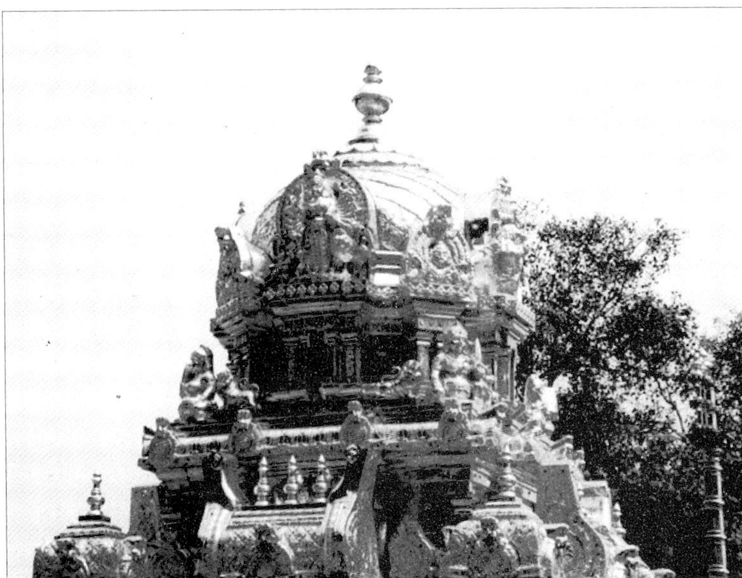

90. Vijayawada, Durga temple, *sikhara*.

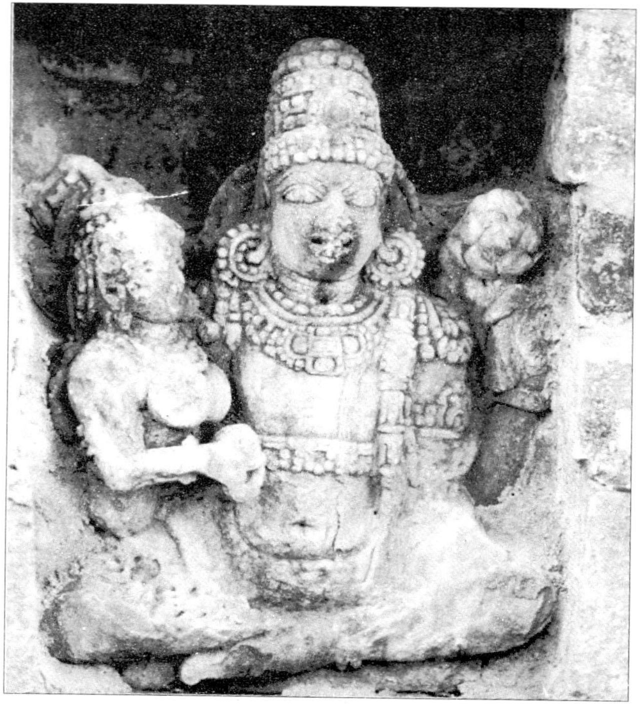

91. Samarlakota, Mandava Narayana temple, *vimana*.

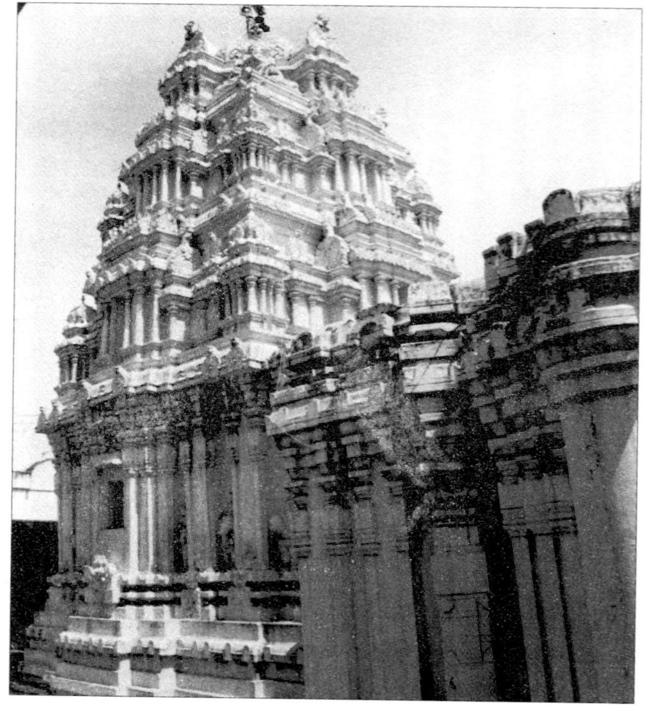

92. Samarlakota, Mandava Narayana temple, Lakshmi Narayana.

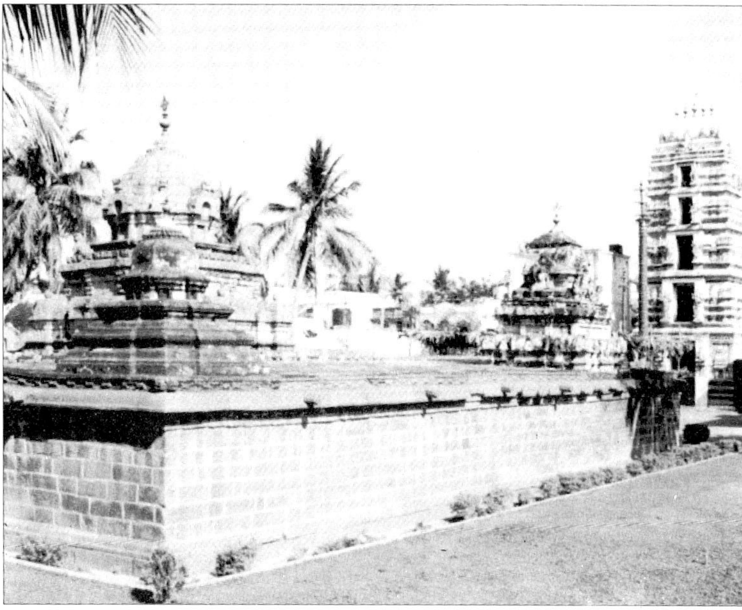

93. Bapatla, Bhava Narayana temple, general view.

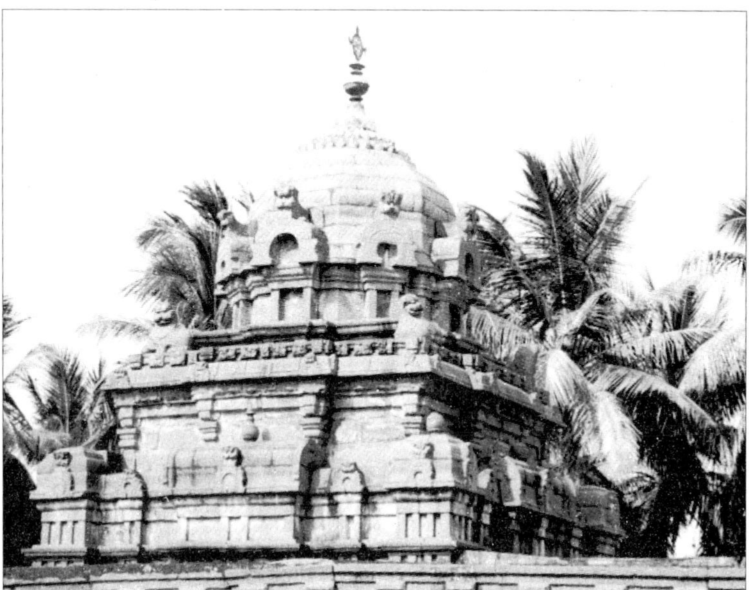

94. Bapatla, Bhava Narayana temple, *sikhara*.

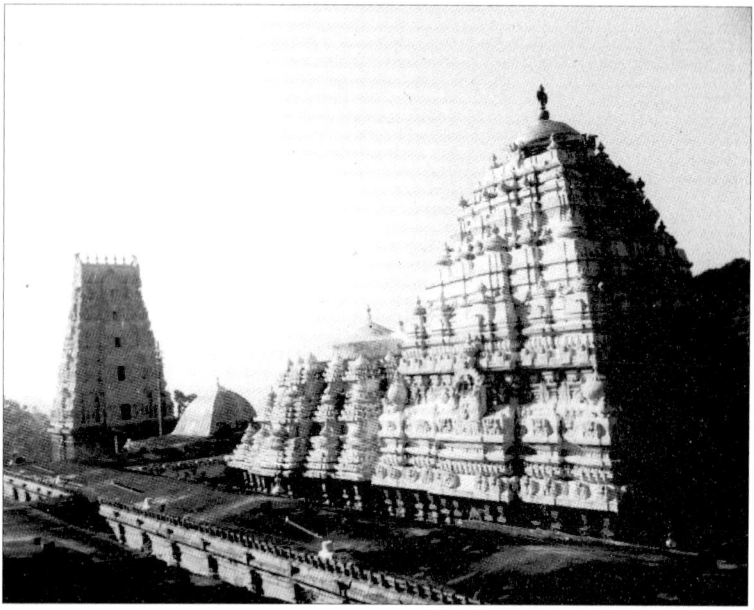

95. Simhachalam, Varaha Lakshmi Narashimha temple, general view.

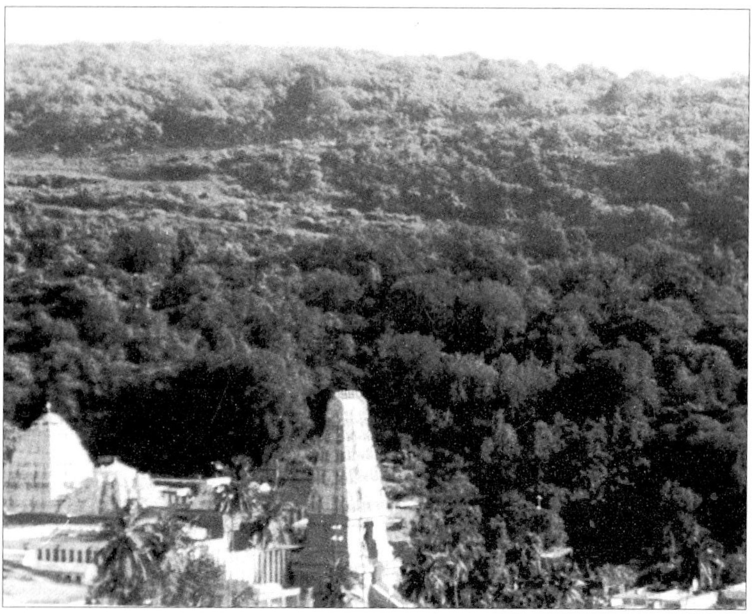

96. Simhachalam, Varaha Lakshmi Narashimha temple.

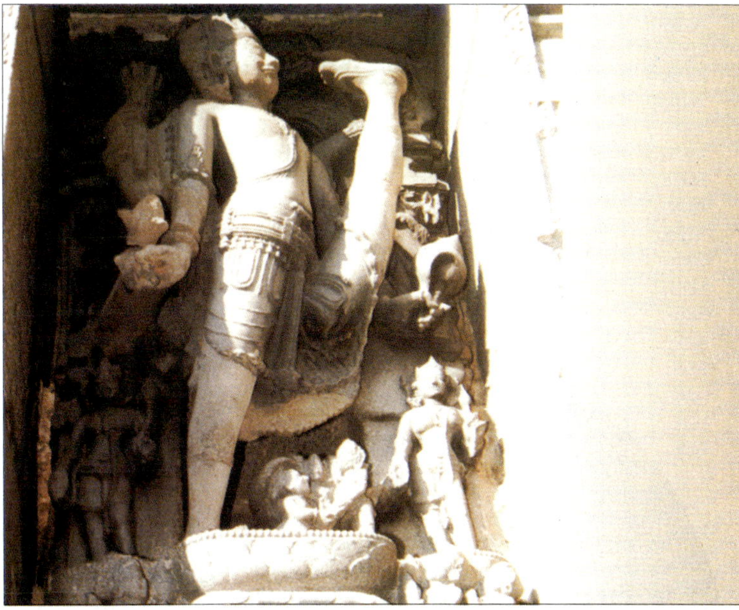

97. Simhachalam, Varaha Lakshmi Narashimha temple, Trivikrama.

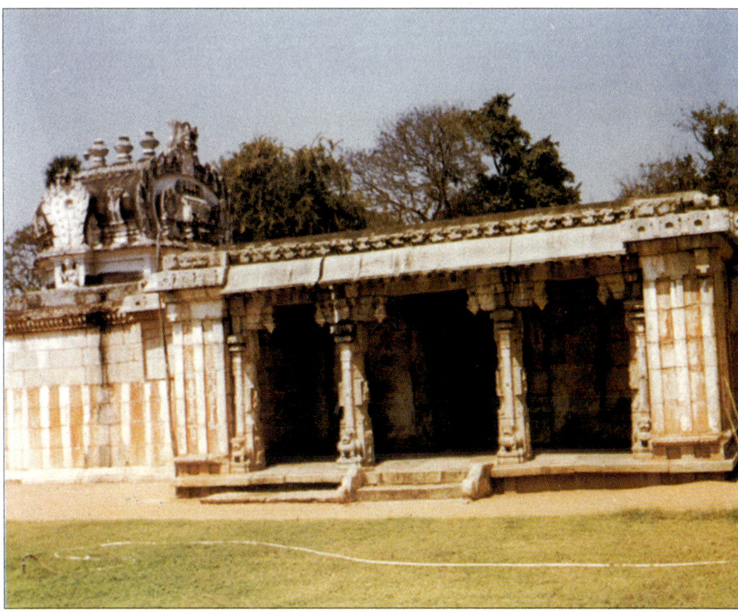

98. Gudimallam, Parasuramesvara temple, general view.

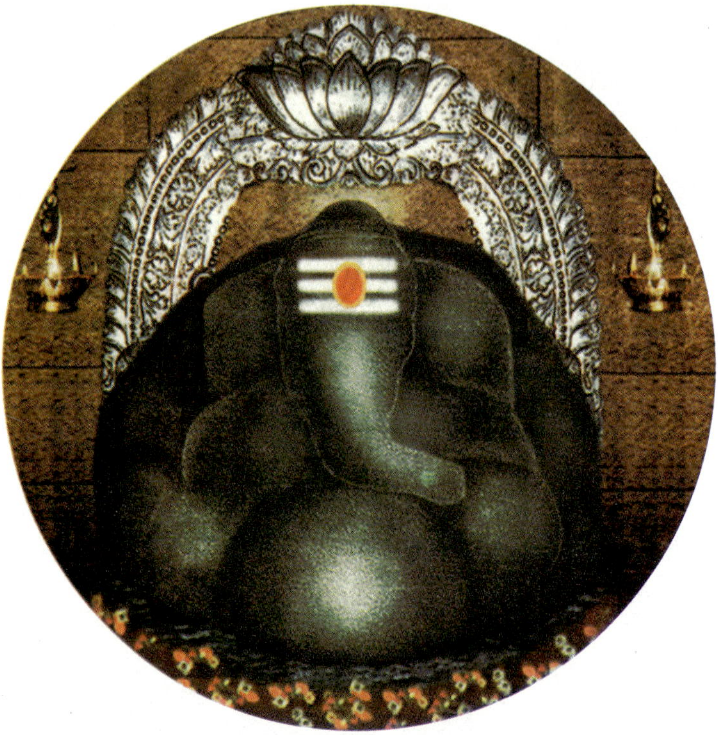

99. Kanipakam, Vinayaka.

5

Eastern Chalukyan Temples

The Vengi Chalukyas or Eastern Chalukyas ruled the coastal Andhra region from Mahendragiri Mountains in the north to the river Manneru in the south for over four centuries, from the mid 7th to the 12th century A.D. During the period of their rule, Andhradesa witnessed a brisk activity of temple building in stone, mostly dedicated to Lord Siva.

Saivite sects like the *Pasupatas* and *Kalamukhas* had evolved systematic worship of Siva in temples, receiving patronage of the Eastern Chalukyas. Some historians considered that these Saivite sects carried on militant missionary activity, which had finally culminated in the destruction of Buddhism and Jainism. The Jalapesvara temple at Pondugula, The temples of Golingesvara, Raja-Rajesvara and Chandrasekhara and the Virabhadra temple and the temples now called as Kancharagudi and Nakkalagudi at Biccavolu; the Mallesvara temple at Vijayawada, the Bhimesvara temple at Chebrolu, the Somesvara temple at Bhimavaram, the Amaresvara temple at Amaravati, all in sand stone, are notable examples of the Eastern Chalukyan temples in coastal Andhradesa. As mentioned above, the Satuluru grant of Gunaga Vijayaditya refers to the construction of 108 temples by Vijayaditya, the grand father of the donor, though it is not possible to locate all of them.

It is not easy to see the Jalpesvara temple (PL.77) near *Pondugala*. Because it is situated in remote area, far from the tourist beat. The highly ruined Jalpesvara temple and other ruined temples, locally known as *votigullu* or *nalla gullu* situated on the bank of dandivagu (8 km away from Pondugala) a rivulet finally drains in to Krishna River. The *nasikas* on the super structure show the decorative carvings like the human heads (PL.78), *Trimurti* etc; which recall similar usage in the rock cut temples at Mogalrajapuram. The temple may be dated to the late 8th century A.D.

Biccavolu is known for beautiful stone temples of Lord Siva (PL.79). These temples were built in the time of Gunaga Vijayaditya (848-891 A.D.) and his successors. The village is named after Gunaga, who had the title Birudanka-Bhima. Here, the largest temple is the Golingesvara temple which consists of a *gudha-mandapa*, an *antarala* and a *garbha-griha*. The pilasters are four sided as usual in all early temples, with full capitals. The niches are tall, narrow and rectangular in shape, with framing pilasters and the upper parts bearing *makara-toranas* the tail reaching down to the mid point of the pilaster. The niches house the images of Surya, Vishnu, Agni, Indra (PL.80), Ganesa (PL.81) Siva-Bhikshatanamurti, Brahma, Nagini, Kumara, Ekapada Siva, Chamunda, Mahisasuramardini and Siva-Ardhanarisvara. The temple has a slightly projecting cornice, on whose face, rows of *hamsas* and *bhutas* as well as the *kudu* motifs, with *kirttimukhas* are carved. The super structure is two storeyed and squattish in appearance, with miniature shrine models, the *sala*, *kuta* and *Panjara*. The sanctum adorns *Siva-linga* with its square *pitha*.

To the the west of the Golingesvara temple there is the Raja-Rajesvara temple. This temple consists of a *mukha-mandapa* and *garbha-griha* and follows the same wall pattern and design as of Golingesvara temple. The *sikhara* lacks *hara* elements over the storey. It is raised on a high *vedi* and the deeply projected *pidhana phalaka* in a prominent manner which is the characterstic feature of Eastern Chalukyan temples.

To the east of the Golingesvara temple there is Chandrasekhara temple. It is similar in size and design except for some minor variations. The figure sculpture on the storeys of the *vimana* depicts *mithunas* and divinities as in the Golingesvara temple. There are two abandoned temples known as Kanchara gudi and Nakkala gudi in the fields outside the village. These temples represent the late phase of Eastern Chalukyan style.

It you visit the Sri Lakshmi Ganapati temple at Biccavolu you would be surprised to see some one whispering urgently into Lord Ganesa's gigantic ear (PL. 82). People come from as far as Tamil Nadu and Karnataka to whisper their wishes to him, believing they will come true within a year. The two armed Ganesa idol of Eastern Chalukyan times is carved from a single monolithic stone and stands 1.5 m tall.

A new temple form was introduced during the reign of Chalukya Bhima, which consists of a storeyed building, the *madakkovil*, as the Tamilian architects call it. Essentially the temple consists of two storeys; the ground floor may be either functional or solid, consisting of flight of steps, wherein it is not solid, and the flight of steps lead the devotees to the temple proper. In those, where the ground floor is solid, the flight of steps would be provided outside. The temple proper in the upper floor consists of closed pillared hall, except for the doorways on the two sides and large sized windows are provided in the exterior wall for the required light and ventilation. Usually the sanctum sanctora of this type of temples consist of a tall *linga* emnating from the ground floor and crowned by three storied *sikhara*.

The plan and execution of this type of temples was perhaps the result of the inspiration from the Kailasa temple at Ellora, that belongs to the first quarter of the eighth century and thus the temples of the sort in Vengidesa may reasonably be assigned to a time subsequent to it. Obviously, the long-drawn warfare between the Rashtrakuts, the producers of art and architecture at Ellora and the Eastern Chalukyas of Vengidesa and the presence of Rashtrakuta princess in the Chalukya house was instrumental for the spread of the style into coastal Andhradesa. It is noteworthy that this design is adopted only at the *arama-kshetras*, the *Pancharamas*. The temples at the *Pancharamas* are plain and monotonous, with little sculptural decor and less architectural refinement, compared to the examples in the temples at Biccavolu. The emergence of *Pancharamas* was due to the Kalamukha sect of Saivism. To symbolize the supremacy of Saivism these temples were built.

Traditional accounts as to the origin of the *Pancharamas* narrate that demon-king Tarakasura, who was a celebrated devotee of Siva, used to wear the sacred *linga* in his neck; he had the boon from Siva, to remain invincible and immortal, so long as he had it in his necklace. He was tormenting the *devas* and finally the lord of *devas,* Indra had to wage war against him, armies placed under Lord Skanda, son of Lord Siva. As Skanda was aware of the boon that Tarakasura was granted by Lord Siva, had no other way except to break the sacred *linga* in the necklace of the demon-king, he broke it into five pieces, with his weapon, *Sakti.* The five pieces of the sacred *linga* are said to have fallen on earth at five places and they became highly sanctified. They are Pedda Dakaremi or Draksharamam, Skandarama or Kumararama or Chalukya Bhimavaram in the East Godavari district, Kshirarama or Palakolanu and Gudipudi Bhimavaram in the west Godavari district, and lastly Amararama or Amaravati in the Guntur District.

The Bhimesvara temple at Draksharamam, the Bhimesvara temple at Chalukya - Bhimavaram in Samarlakota in East Godavari district were built by Chalukya Bhima I (892 - 922 A.D.) and the deities named after the king Bhima.

The Bhimesvara temple (PL.83) at *Draksharamam* is one of the twelve illustrious *lingas* (*Jyotirlingas*). One of the 18 *Sakti - Peethas,* Manikyambika-*peetha* is located in the compound. The temple is a massive edifice (21.56 m x 14.2 m) enclosed by two *prakaras* and an outer enclosure featuring several *mandapas* and subsidiary shrines. The main temple and the outer enclosure with the *gopuras* were erected during Chalukya Bhima's rule and the inner enclosure, *nandi-mandapa, natya-mandapa, kalyana-mandapa, sanivara-mandapa* etc., were constructed in the reign of Anavema Reddi as referred to in an inscription of 1381 A.D.

The ground floor of the temple consists of a *mandapa* and the hall encloses the sanctum. Flanking the *mandapa*, the flight of steps is provided on either side, to reach the upper floor. The upper floor features a small *mukha-mandapa,* the *maha-mandapa,* an *antarala* and a *garbha-griha* of *sandhara* variety.

The plain walls are contoned by slender pilasters without niches. The super structure is two storeyed and slender in appearance as opposed to the earlier squattish superstructures. The *citrakhanda* type of pillars are seen in the *maha-mandapa* and they show rich carvings like Indra, Brahma, Nataraja and Uma and narrative sculptures of Kiratarjuniya, the story of Kannappa, the story of Mrgavyadha. Interesting is the placement of pillars in the circumambulatory path which was constructed by Velanati Gonkaraju II in 1148 A.D. Inside the *garbha-griha* the *linga*, as a long cylindrical pillar of about 6.1 m-7.6 m height rises from the *vedi*. Also noteworthy are the Ganesa and *nandi* images which, as in the earlier art, exhibit similar features, although the *nandi* figures become massive.

In the precints of the temples at Draksharamam and Samarlakota there aere miniature shrine models *(balalayas)* (PL. 84).

Curiously, the consort of the god Bhimanatha (Siva) is not Parvati at Draksharamam, but Manikyesvari or Manikyamba. Probably the lords of Trikalinga might have installed their goddess Manikyesvari in the shrine of Bhimesvara. It is interesting that the goddess, though recognised as one of the eighteen *saktis* or Saivite goddesses of India, is not given privilege of being called a wedded wife, but only treated as a favourite courtesan of the lord. Could this possibly be due to the contempt with which the Eastern Chalukyan kings looked upon the goddess of their vassals of Trikalinga?

Chalukya Bhima I, it is said, built the town of Chalukya Bhimavaram and in that city founded the temple of Siva, called Chalukya Bhimesvara, after his own name, Chalukya Bhimavaram is today a small village adjoining *Samarlakota*. The temple of Chalukya Bhimesvara known as Kumararama (PL.85) is identical in size and plan to that of Draksharamam. The first floor is of the same kind as at the latter place. *Simhapada* pillars are found in the porch. The temple also had grown into a big complex with double enclosures, gateways and subsidiary shrines during the Reddi times. Here the *linga* is as high as 5.5 m.

The huge rocking *mandapa* built of black granite stone (PL.86), fixed in a corner of the inner courtyard, begins to move to and fro at the gentlest touch deserves mention.

The Somesvara temple at *Bhimavaram* and the Amaresvara temple (PL.87) at *Amaravati* belong to 10th century and both have undergone reconstruction in 14th and 17th centuries. In both instances the ground floor is of solid variety. At Amaravati the *adhishthana* of the temple is *padabandha* type. Further the upper floor unlike the temples of this type is constructed in the central portion leaving the sides for circumambulation. However, the sanctum retains its old form and enshrines the tall *linga* which is about 4.6m high.

The sculptural art of 9th and 10th centuries of Vengi Chalukyan period is mainly known from Biccavolu, Draksharamam, Samarlakota, Vijayawada, Amaravati and Chebrolu.

The *makaratorana* over the niche on the wall of Golingesvara temple, which houses an image of Indra (PL.80), is carved in the form of two *makaras* facing each other, with their gaping jaws, figures of *vidyadharas* as riding on their back, holding the ends of their gaping jaws. Above the lintel, at its central point are two small pilateral motifs, with their capitals adorned with a small *makara* on both end and a *kirttimukha* atop issuing forth the pearl strands. The tails of the *makaras* are shown in bold sweeping curves of ebbing petal and flowery design. Thus the descent of tail down below the *mandi* enframing the narrow niche creates a fanciful effect.

An image of Siva now kept in the *mukha-mandapa* of the Golingesvara temple at Biccavolu is a powerful figure. The graceful flexion of the torso, broad shoulders and the not too heavy *jatamakuta* whose strands fall on to the shoulders are noteworthy. Another powerful image is the Chamunda one of the seven mother goddesses. The emaciated figure with its bizarre *jatabhara* and an open mouth is terrific in its appearance. The *nandi* from this temple shows ornaments which are forerunners of those of the Kakatiya ones.

In the temples at Draksharamam and Samarlakota the miniature shrine models contain basreliefs, depicting Mahisasuramardini, Siva-Bhiksatanamurti, Dikpalas, Durga, Ganesa, Kumara, Virabhadra, Siva-Nataraja, Gajasura-Samharamurti, *dvarapalas*, sages, etc. Although the figures are worn out, they look elegant.

Vijayawada, the political and commercial capital of Andhra Pradesh, is hallowed with several legends, thanks to the Indrakeeladri hill, the abode of goddess Kanaka Durga (the consort of the god Siva) and the Krishna River flowing by it endowing the people with both spiritual and material happiness.

In deference to the wish of Indrakeeludu to become immortal, the goddess Kanakadurga asked him to take the form of a hill so that she can live on it, Indrakeeladri hill thus became the abode of the goddess in Vijayawada making it one of the most important Durga temples (PL. 88) in the country. The temple commands a fascinating view.

There is an interesting story, as Indrakeeladri hill came in the way of Krishna River flowing to the sea, the river requested goddess Kanakadurga to provide a small passage *(bejjam)* in the hill. When the request was granted, the river gushed through the hole bringing the name Bezawada (Bejjamwada) to the city. Goddess Kanakadurga then borrowed the nose stud of Krishna River and to avoid its return, jumped up the hill and made it as her abode. The river Krishna took a vow that at the end of Kaliyuga, she should rise to the top of the hill and retrieve her nose stud.

According to legend, Lord Brahma installed Siva-*linga* atop Indrakeeladri hill and worshipped him with jasmines bringing him the name Mallesvara Svami, contrary to normal practice of the consort standing on the left side, goddess Kanakadurga stands on the right side of Mallesvara Svami on Indrakeeladri hill and her power is attributed to this position.

It was on the Indrakeeladri hill that Arjuna had under taken penance and won *Pasupathastra* after a bitter fight with Lord Siva in the guise of a hunter. As Arjuna was also known as Vijaya, the city came to be called after him. Mythology and tradition in India have been inseparable from history. It was during the rule of Madhava Varman, a Vishnukundin king that the goddess showered her blessings on the city, when a Vaisya boy was crushed to death under the chariot wheels of the Prince, his mother came to the court seeking justice, and Madhava Varman unhesitatingly sentenced his son to death. Touched by his sense of justice and impartiality, the goddess Durga rained gold on the city and brought the princes back to life. People sang in praise of her and the goddess came to be called *Kanaka* (gold) Durga since then. Though, the story is narrated in a late inscription, it cannot be said to command historical value. The only Madhava varman known to history was that name of the Vishnukundin family, who ruled in the 5th century A.D., but his association with Vijayawada is not known from any source except this late record setup by certain Pallaketa Maharaja who is again unknown other wise.

Animal sacrifice was common at the *shakti-sthalas* till Adi Sankaracharya visited the temple and appeased the goddess; He installed *sri-chakra* in the temple. Worshipping the goddess with red *kumkum* assumed significance since then (PL.89). The steps leading to the temple are smeared with vermilion and turmeric paste by devotees in fulfilment of their vows. It is the second temple in Andhra to have gilt copper *vimana* (PL.90) after Tirupati.

Vijayawada witnesses feverish activity during the nine-day celebration of Dasara festival, with great pomp and splendour. A large number of pilgrims attend the celebrations and take a holy dip in the river Krishna.

The earliest of all the inscriptions in the Mallesvara temple is that of certain Chattapa, who is stated to have installed the god Parthesvara on the Indrakeela hill with mercy of Chalukya Bhima I, son of Vikramaditya (892 - 922 A.D.). On the four sides of the inscribed pillar, we find the sculptural illustration of *kiratarjuniya* story - the penance of Arjuna to get *Pasupatastra* from Siva. From this place, a few panels representing musicians and dancers and a Narasimha, are obtained. The representation of Narisimha trampling Hiranya and fighting with other demons is noteworthy. Yuddhamalla's inscription datable to 930 A.D. records the construction of a temple for the god Kumarasvami and a *matha* for the Saiva ascetics.

Few inscriptions refer to the guild of the teliki (oil pressers) who are said to have donated the *mukha-mandapa* to the temple of the god Mallesvara.

An inscription datable to 1518 A.D. refers to Sri Krishnadeva Raya and records the construction of *antarala, ranga-mandapa* and *bhoga-mandapa* to the temple of the goddess Durga Devi of Bezawada by the subordinate Singaraju, son of Paparaju, born in the family of Madhava varman.

MEDIEVAL TEMPLES IN ANDHRA: In the ancient Vengi region the Mandavya Narayana temple at Samarlakota, the Bhavanarayana temple at Sarpavaram, exhibit the architectural styles of medieval times.

The Mandavya Narayana temple (PL.91) at *Samarlakota* belongs to 11th century A.D. and has undergone renovations and reconstructions many times. The temple consists of a *ranga-mandapa,* a *mukha-mandapa,* an *antarala* and the *garbha-griha.* Interesting is the use of *srikara* pillars in the *mukha-mandapa* and *antarala* which came into vogue during 10th century A.D. The *dvitala-vimana* has a square *griva* and *sikhara*. The *Devi* shrine is situated in the north-east corner.

The sculptural fragments of 10th century A.D. are preserved in this temple. These represent Lakshmi narayana (PL.92), Garuda narayana, Rama, Lakshmana, Hanuman, Venugopala etc. Though an early date is suggested by some scholars, these sculptures may not be earlier than 10th century A.D. The heavy beaded ornamentation of the head-gear and necklaces, ear-rings, looks like woodwork, probably, having been carried by wood carvers turned stone sculptors. The lack of simplicity in the ornamentation is also a characteristic of medieval sculpture. Even the pysiognomy and modelling of these figures is heavy and recall to our mind, the sculptures of 9th and 10th centuries, in the temples at Biccavolu, Draksharamam and Samarlakota.

The Bhavanarayana temple at *Sarpavaram* comprises of *mukha-mandapa, antarala* and *garbha-griha* to which *ranga-mandapa* was added later. This is enclosed by *tiruchuttumala*. Noteworthy features are the *pratibandha adhishthna,* the images of Vishnu's forms and Durga in the niches and *dvitala-vimana* with a square *sikhara* .The temple is notable for the shrines for the eight *parivara-devatas.*

Bapatla is said to have been named after Bhavanarayana svamy, the presiding deity, as Bhavapatla or Bhavapuri, and came to be called Bapatla gradually. There are 5 temples in the town, of which Bhavanarayana svamy temple (PL.93) is ancient and famous. The temple is assignable to the late 10th or early 11th century A.D. From early 11th century onwards, the southern parts the Eastern Chalukyan kingdom evidenced strong influence of the Chola architectural style. This is best seen at this temple. This temple proper consists of a *mukha-mandapa,* an *antarala* and a *garbha-griha* and nine shrines for minor deities dedicated to Goda Devi, Kesava, Narasimha, Kodanda Rama, Alvars, Garuda, Anjaneya, and Rajya lakshmi etc. In the exterior the *padabandha-adhishthana* with the *vedi* moulding is noticed. The walls possesses pilasters and *devakosthas.* The niches are empty. In the *prastara* region the *hamsa-mala* and the *kapota* decorated with *kirttimukha* heads are featured. The *ekatala-vimana* has an octagonal *griva* and *sikhara* (PL. 94). The doorways are carved with *latapatra* and *stambha* motifs, the lotus medallion in the *lalata* and *dvarapalas* at the base of the jambs. Inside the *garbha-griha* on a square pedestal the image of kesava is enshrined.

Sri Varaha Lakshmi Narasimha Svamy temple at *Simhachalam* (PL.95) has been hailed as most famous, richest and best sculptured shrine in this part of the country. The temple is picturesquely situated atop hill, 243.8 m above sea level, in a tiny hill - range of the Eastern Ghats (PL. 96).

Simhachalam means hill of the lion. The hills and dens are generally conceived to be the abodes of lions and temples dedicated to Lord Narasimha are generally located on hill tops. The presiding deity in the temple, Varaha Narasimha, is the combination of man, Lion and Boar.

According to *Sthala Purana* Lord Vishnu assumed the form of Man-Lion, to kill the demon-king Hiranyakasipu, father of his ardent devotee, Prahlada. It is stated that by divine ordinance, the image of the lord is ever covered with a thick coating of sandal paste. Therefore, usually the deity resembles a sandal wood *linga.* The original shape of Varaha Narasimha (*nija rupa*) is shown to devotees only once in a year on the third day of the month of Visakha (April - May) by removing sandal wood paste. According to legend, the foundation of the temple is attributed to Hiranyakasipu, who was furious at his son Prahlada's devotion to Vishnu, threw him in to the sea and placed this hill on his head. The Lord went to the child's rescue, stood by the side of the hill and tilted it up so that the boy might escape from the weight of the hill. Later, pious Prahlada is stated to have founded the shrine. The real glory of the temple began when it was completely reconstructed by a commander of Narasimha Deva-I of the Ganga dynasty in 1268 A.D. The *tiruchuttumala* and the *kalyana-mandapa* in the temple compound also were constructed in 1268 A.D. The temple reveals symbiosis of Orissan and Eastern Chalukyan architectural styles.

This Varaha Narasimha temple consists of *mukha-mandapa, antarala* and *garbha-griha.* The doorway to the *mukha-mandapa* however is of *panchasakha* variety. A *tiruchuttumala* surrounds the temple with a porch on the east. The pilasters, square in section have *gajakranta* motif at the base. The niches are of typical kalinga style. At the apex the *udgama*, in the form of a multiple arch is carved extensively with beaded and vegetal patterns. The window composed of five pillars topped by an *udgama* is noteworthy. The walls and the niches inset with images of Vishnu's forms (PL.97) and mythical figures. The four storeyed *sikhara* over the sanctum has undergone reconstruction. The *pidha* roof in three tiers over the *mukha-mandapa* recalls the conventions of the Kalinga style (PL.95). The art of Kalinga region is best represented in the bas-reliefs and sculpture in and around the temple. The art impulses from Bhuvaneswar are quite evident here.

The Parasuramesvara temple (PL. 98) at *Gudimallam* appears to have had consistent development in the form of additions and alterations in various periods, the late Pallava, Bana and early Chola times that its original form has disappeared. But the apsidal portion has undoubtedly survived from the Pallava times as it closely recalls late Pallava shrines at Vadamallisvara at Oragadam near Chingleput. The inscriptions of Vikrama Chola refer to a complete rebuilding of the temple in stone in 1126 A.D. along with *gopura*. The apsidal shrine is in low level with *ardha-mandapa* and *maha-mandapa* infront, all facing east and each higher than the previous one. In the wall, the *devakosthas* around house the images of

Dakshinamurti, Vishnu, Brahma, Durga and Ganesa. The main entrance to the shrine is, however, from the south side of *maha-mandapa,* when the walled enclosure is added by an ornamental pillared porch. The main shrine is closed allround externally by a peristylar cloister. A Devi shrine is added at north- west corner.

Svayambhu Sri Varasiddhi Vinayaka temple at *Kanipakam* was built in 11th century A.D. by Kulothunga Chola1 and expanded by Vijayanagar rulers in 15th century basing on epigraphical evidence. *Kani* means quarter acre of wet land and *Parakam* indicates flow of water into wet land, i.e., irrigation. River Bahuda nurtures the land. As the legend goes, there were three handicappcd brothers, mute, deaf and blind. They were digging a well to fetch water for their fields. The device they were using to lift the water fell in to the well dashing against a hard object. When they further dug the well they were startled to see blood gushing out and even as they were looking at the spectacle in astonishment, all the three got rid of their disabilities. People in the surrounding villages rushed to the spot and found an idol of Vinayaka. Further digging, however, failed to reveal the base. Lots of coconuts were offered and the water is said to have flowed into the channel filling a quarter of the field (*Kani*). The place acquired the name Kaniparakam and Kanipakam with a Tamil intonation.

The well in which the idol sits, is always full of water. Vinayaka is visible only up to his belly (PL. 99). During monsoon water flows over the idol. The water of the well is distributed as *Pavithra-theertham* (holy water). The lord is referred to as *nitya pravraddar,* reflecting the belief that he always grows forever. It is said a *kavacham* (breast plate) made for the idol half a century ago has become too small for it now. There arc quite a few temples around Kanipakam. In recent times the temple has undergone thorough renovation and many new buildings are coming up around the temple as a part of the master plan. The temple of Varadarajasvamy makes Kanipakam a Harihara kshetram. There are separate shrines for Sri Anjaneya (*kshetra- palaka*) and *nava-grahas.*

6

Glories of the Pallavas

The Pallava architecture and sculpture constitute a brilliant chapter in the history of South Indian art. According to Percy Brown, "Of all great powers that together made the history of Southern India, none had a more marked effect on the architecture of their reign than the earliest of all, that of the Pallavas, whose productions provided the foundations of the Dravidian style". Chronologically the structural temples of the Pallavas come next to their rock-cut caves. Massive boulders were transformed in to a world of divine and earthly beings.Caves with exquisite sculpted panels was hewn out of the hills. They are found at places like Mamallapuram, Mahendravadi, Dalavanur, Pallavaram and several others, between the riverine planes of Palar and Kaveri.

I must give you a brief idea of the history of the period.The Greater Pallavas ruled over a greater part of Tamil country together with the southern parts of Andhradesa, from the beginnings of the 6th century to the end of the 9th century from their capital Kanchipuram or Kanchi. The territory, along the coast line consists of fertile plains formed by a number of rivers and small streams that join the sea became famous for agricultural as well as industrial productions from times immemorial that enabled the people of the regions to carry on overseas trade and commerce. As such, the Pallavas had good economic resources at their command that enabled them to extend patronage to fine arts, among which art and architecture were more important. Mahabalipuram or Mamallapuram was the chief outlet to overseas trade during their time and the economic importance of the port-town is visible today in the form of wonders on rock, created by the artists and architects of the Pallava kingdom.

Simhavishnu *Avanisimha* (lion of the earth) ascended the Greater Pallava throne at Kanchi, in about 575 A.D. and conquered the whole country, south of Vishnukundin kingdom up to Kaveri. In fact, the brisk activity of art and architecture in the Pallava kingdom can be seen, to have commenced with Mahendravarman I, the son and successor of Simhavishnu, who probably ruled from 600 to 630 A.D. Southern parts of Andhradesa, which were included in his kingdom, had a record of its own, for the beginning and progress of rock-cut technique of architecture on either side of the river Krishna, at its mouth. The rock-cut cave-temples in the Krishna valley at Undavalli and Mogalrajapuram must have served examples to the Pallavas to create similar and more eloquently grand monuments in their own realms.

Mahendravarman gloried himself in the construction of temples without the use of bricks, timber, metal or mortar, as his Mandagapattu inscription states. This inscriptional statement clearly upholds not only his innovative scheme of architecture, without using bricks, mortar, timber, iron, etc., but also that he introduced a new technique (rock-cut) that was hitherto unknown in that part of the country. Ostensibly, he borrowed the technique from Krishna valley, by virtue of his political suzerainty over the area, which fact is substantiated by the Chezerla stone inscription.

Mahendravarman I was succeeded by his son Narasimhavarman I, surnamed Mahamalla, or Mamalla (great

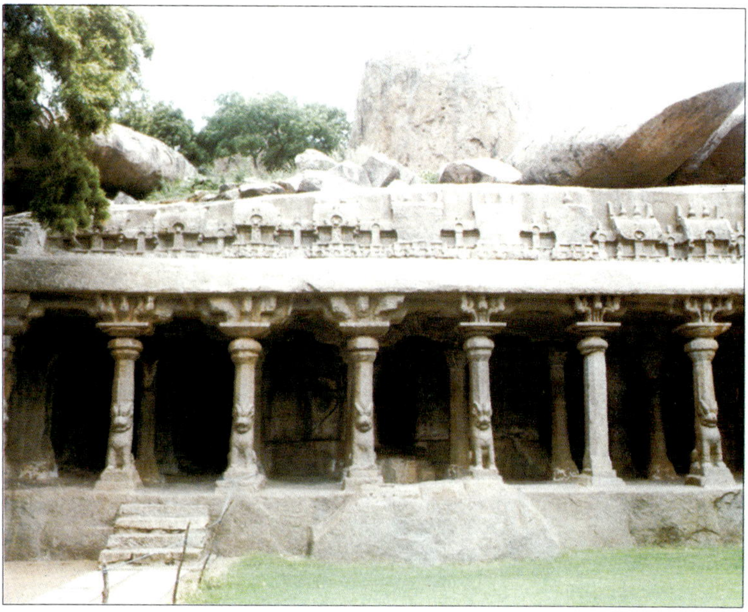

100. Mahabalipuram, Pancha *pandava-mandapa*, general view.

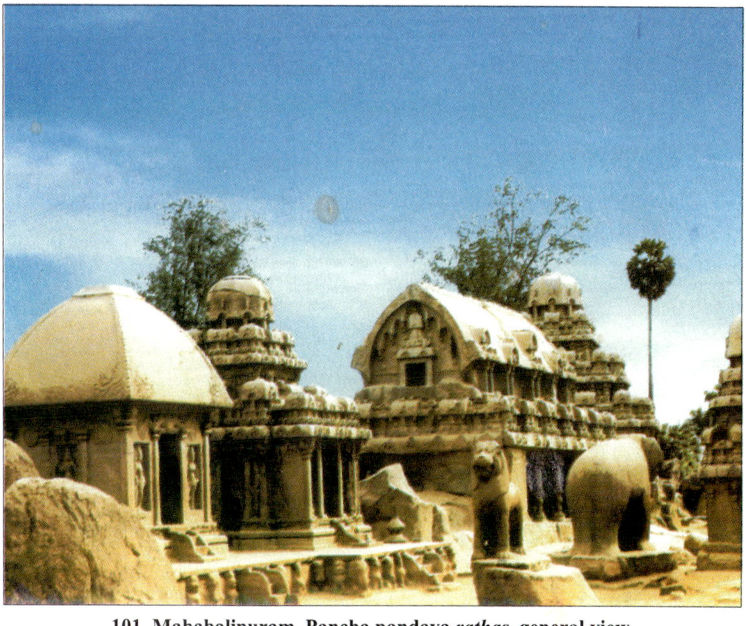

101. Mahabalipuram, Pancha pandava *rathas*, general view.

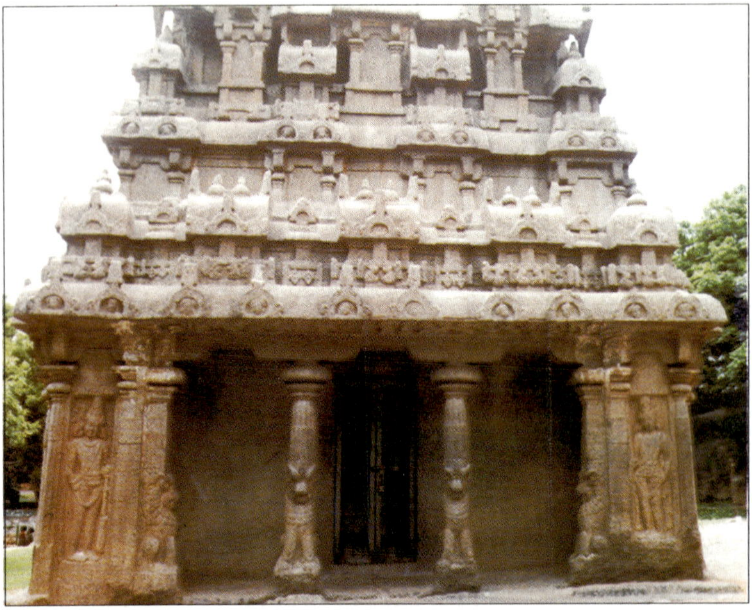

102. Mahabalipuram, Ganesa *ratha*.

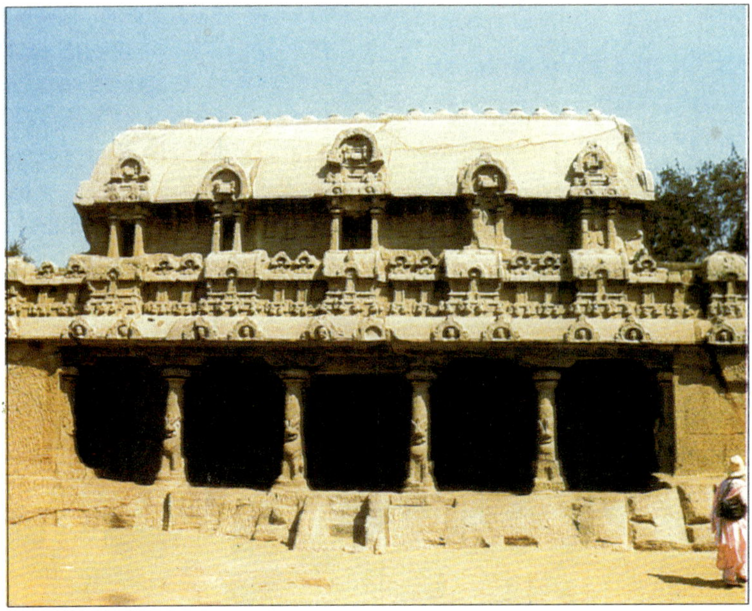

103. Mahabalipuram, Bhima *ratha*.

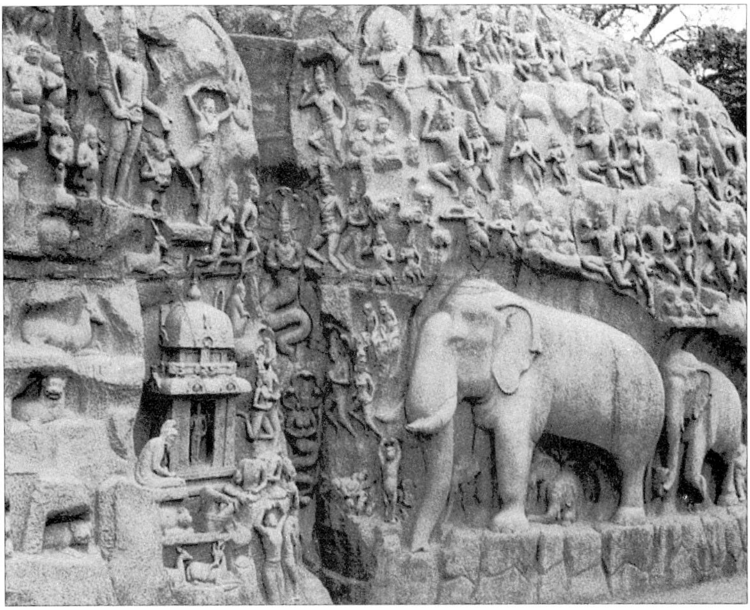

104. Mahabalipuram, Bhagiratha's penance.

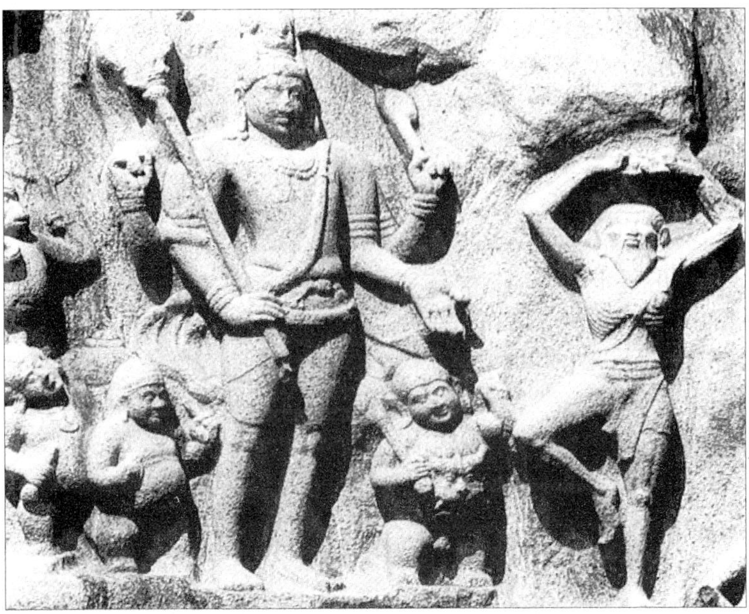

105. Mahabalipuram, *Ekapadothama tapasvi*.

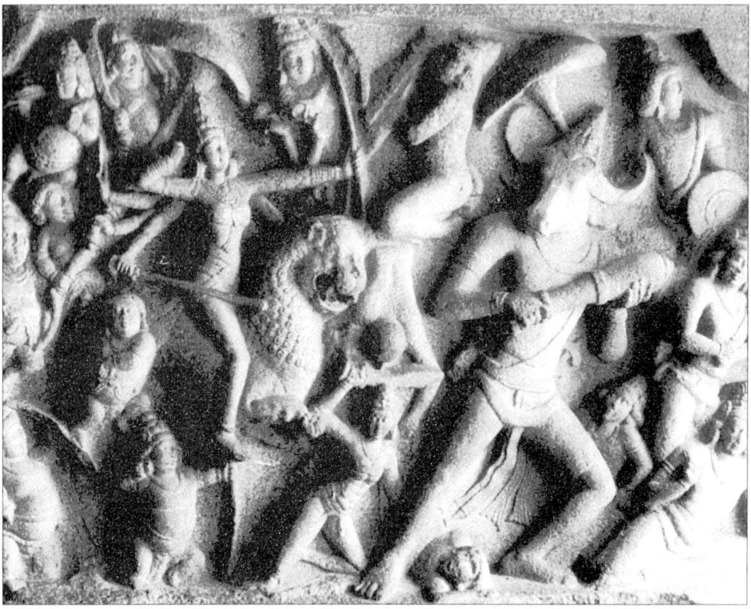

106. Mahabalipuram, Mahisasuramardini cave, the battle of Durga with Mahisasura.

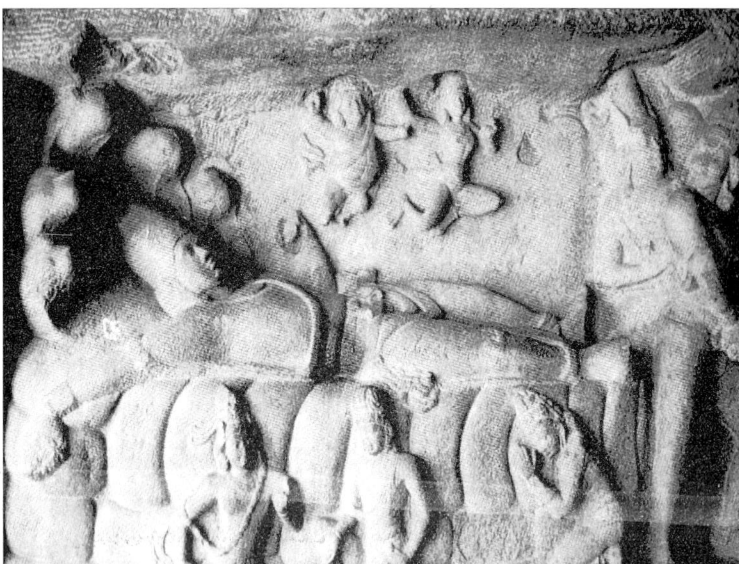

107. Mahabalipuram, Mahisasuramardini cave, Vishnu reclining on the serpent, Ananta.

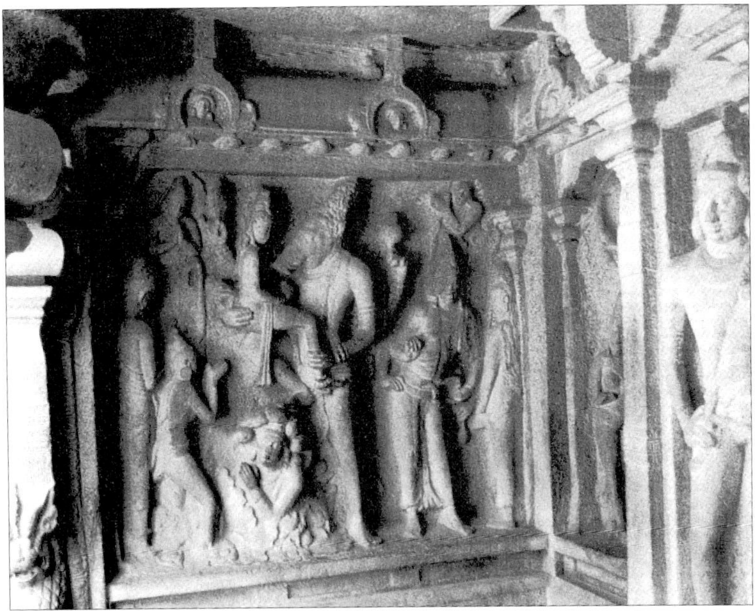

108. Mahabalipuram, Varaha mandapa, Varaha raising the earth.

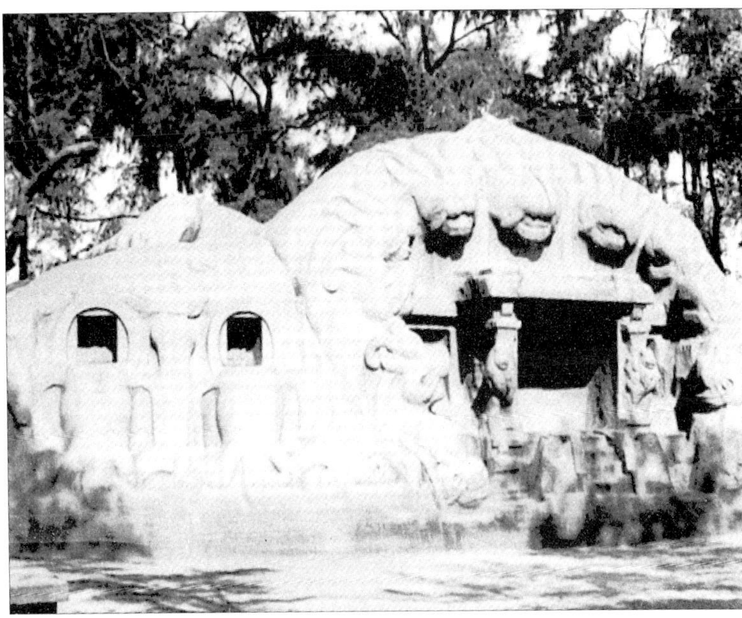

109. Saluvankuppam, Tiger cave, general view.

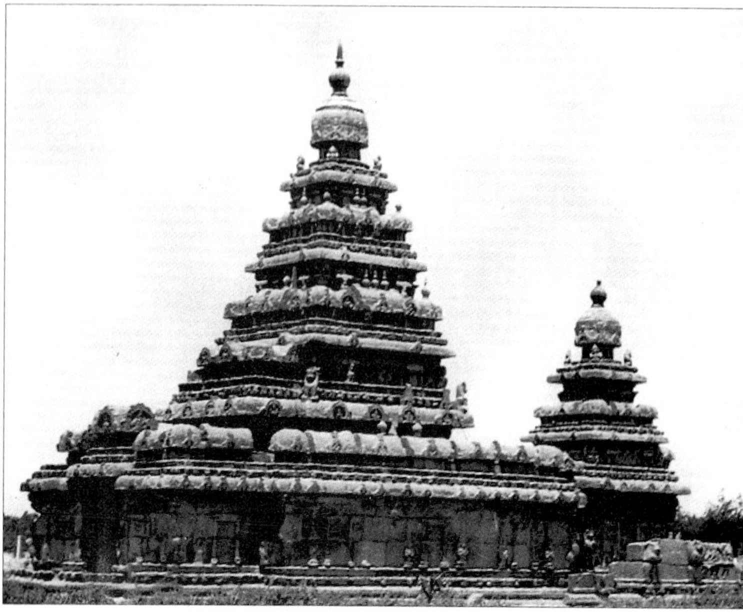

110. Mahabalipuram, Shore temple, general view.

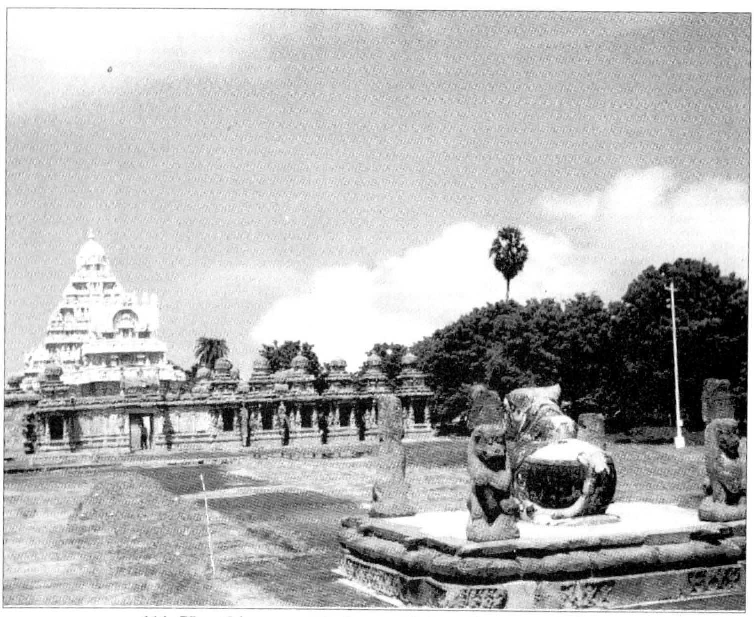

111. Kanchipuram, Kailasanath temple, general view.

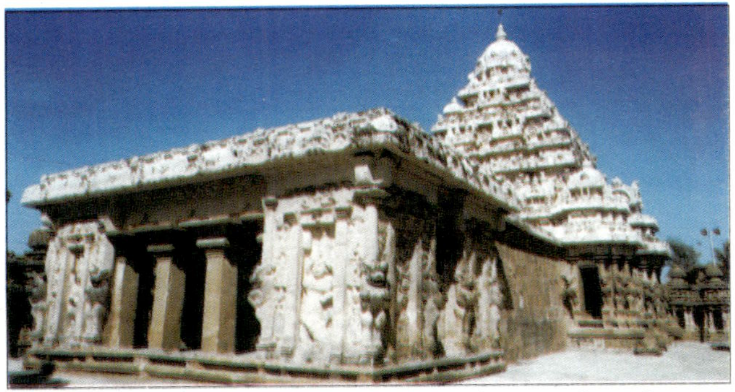

112. Kanchipuram, Kailasanath temple, *vimana* and *mandapa*.

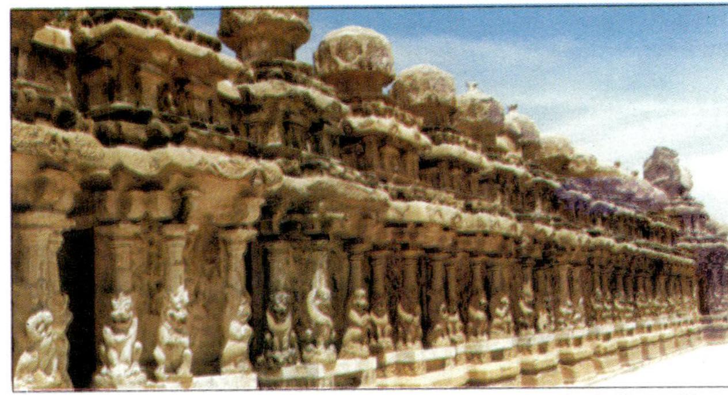

113. Kanchipuram, Kailasanath temple, courtyard, shrine cells.

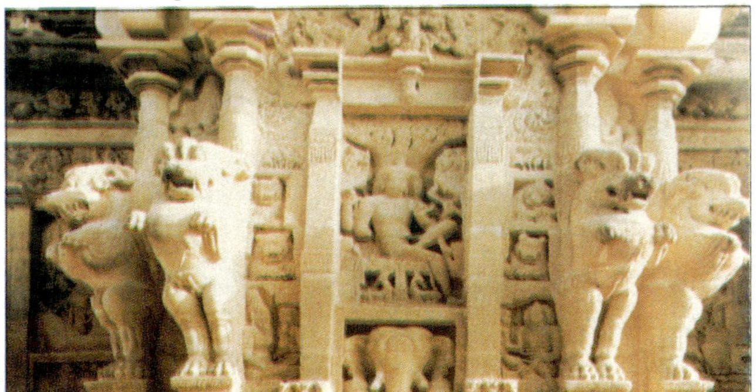

114. Kanchipuram, Kailasanath temple, Siva-Dakshinamurti.

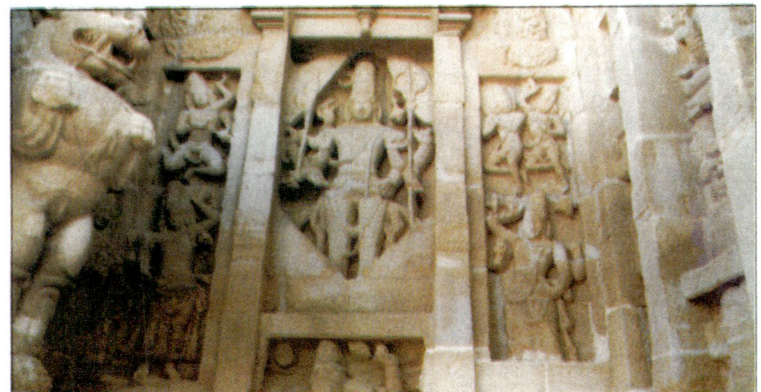

115. Kanchipuram, Kailasanath temple, Siva-Lingodbhava murti.

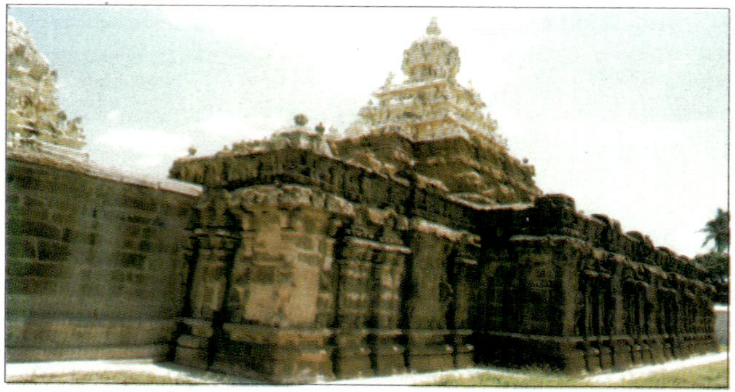

116. Kanchipuram, Vaikuntha perumal temple, general view.

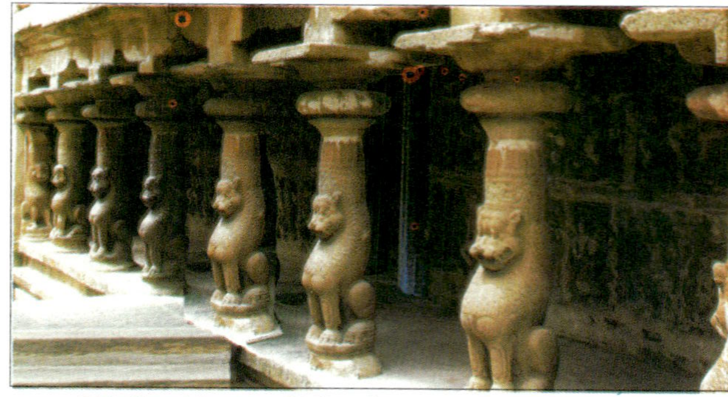

117. Kanchipuram, Vaikuntha perumal temple, corridor.

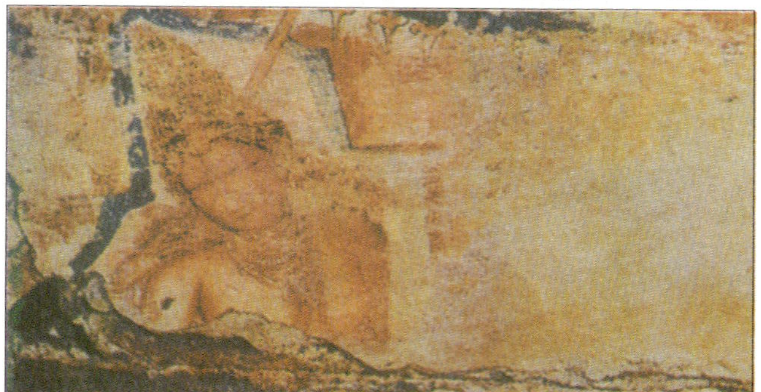

118. Palnamalai, Talagirishvara temple, standing figure of a lady.

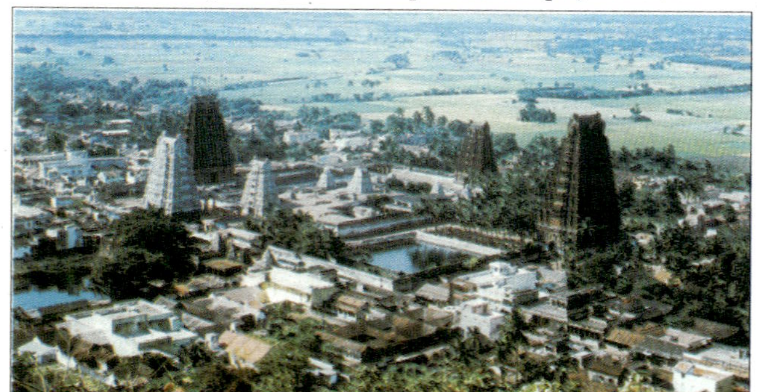

119. Tirukkalukkunram, Bhaktavatsala temple, general view.

warrior) who ruled from 630 to 668 A.D., during which period had fought several wars with the Chalukya rulers of Badami and in one of the invasions; he had even captured and occupied the Chalukyan capital of Badami. One of the most elegant records of art on stone, Mamallapuram; originally Mahamallapuram, was obviously initiated by Narasimhavarman I, and surnamed Mahamalla, after his own proud epithet, *Mahamalla.*

Among the successors of Narasimhavarman I, following his son and successor, Paramesvaravarman I who ruled from about 670 to 700 A.D., Narasimhavarman II Rajasimha 700 to 728 A.D., is very important from the point of view of the history of Pallava art. His period of rule was comparatively peaceful and thus he had more time and resources to spend on the building of temples and executing rock-cut monuments. In fact, the largest number of temples and rock-cut temples that are usually assigned to the period of rule of Narasimhavarman I, Mahamalla, are now considered to have been the works of the time of Rajasimha, Narasimhavarman II, the most notable among them being the Kailasanath temple at Kanchi and the Shore temple at Mamallapuram. The rhetorician Dandin spent many years at Rajasimha's court.

Following the brief rule of about four years, of Paramesvara varman II, son of Narasimhavarman II, a dynastic revolution seems to have taken place at Kanchi, in which Nandivarman II, surnamed Pallavamalla, who belonged to a collateral line probably ruling over the plains of Krishna valley, ascended throne at Kanchi. He had a long reign of more than sixty years, from A.D. 731 A.D. to 795. The long regnal period of the king was full of political turmoils and vicissitudes, yet, it had an impressive record of architectural activity, exemplified by the Vaikuntha Perumal temple at Kanchi among others.

Towards the end of 9th century the Cholas became supreme and the Pallavas went in to the back ground.

The Pallava capital, Kanchi, became so famous a seat of Vedic learning, that it was renowned as Kasi of South. However, the Pallavas gave to Brahmanism a stamp of Saivism. Vaishnavism also made considerable progress largely due to the preachings of Alwars. Apart from *bhakti* cult, Saivism had other types of devotees.Some of their forms of worship were grue some, and repellent to modern taste. The practice of the devotee offering his own head to the goddess is evidenced by several sculptures of the Pallava and Chola periods. The walls, pillars and several other convenient members of architecture in these examples were used to depict the stories from mythology, either the Saivite or Vaishnavite. No doubt, the Jainism and Buddhism were still living, but certainly on their way of decline.

The progress of art and architecture under the Pallavas is usually considered to have fallen into two phases, generally called the phase of Mahendravarman and the second, the phase of Mamalla. But recent researches point out that there was in fact, no such phase, named after Mamalla, and those monuments that were categorized earlier, under the name belonged to the time of Narasimhavarman II, surnamed Rajasimha.

The Mahendravarman phase consisted mostly of rock-cut examples, illustrating the proud statement of the Mandagapattu inscription of the king, and they are called *mandapas*. To be clear, they were pillared halls carved out of solid rock on slopes of hills, with cells cut into the back wall. Gradually, the carving of *mandapas* led to carving of free-standing, independent rock-cut temples, known as *rathas* probably in the time of Narasimhavarman I, or still later. The second type of monuments is the structural, instead of temples being hewn out of solid rock, they came to be planned and constructed according to the plan, which might have followed the above mentioned ones. The preliminary exercise of this architecture might have started either in the time of Narasimhavarman I, or from the time of Paramesvaravarman I, as the result of techniques, learnt from the Chalukyan centres of art, Badami, Pattadakal, etc. The technique of construction flowered in the time of Narasimhavarman II, Rajasimha.

The excavated rock *mandapas* of Mahendraverman group are simple pillared halls with one or more cells cut into the back wall. The main feature of the front facade is a row of pillars, with octagonal shafts, plain and heavy brackets, some times with horizontal flutings.

The Mahendra style shows gradual progress particularly in the evolution of pillars and capitals. This may be noted by comparing the earliest examples at Mandagapattu and Tiruchirapalli with the later series, e.g. Dalavanur, where the roll cornice appears above the pillars, and a roll moulding is added still later as at Pallavaram.

The beginnings of a distinctive Pallava style can be traced, in the elaboration of the pillars and the figure of a lion is introduced and combined with the pillar in its lower portion and another in the capital. This style was further refined and developed in the monuments of Narasimhavarman I Mahamalla. The elegance of this improved style mostly found at Mamallapuram, which can be broadly categorized under the Mamalla style.

King Narasimhavarman I, Mahamalla, is credited with stimulating the developments in Pallava art and architecture and his experiments were carried on at the port town of Mamallapuram, famous by the name *Mahabalipuram*. The port was the principal outlet not only to overseas trade and commerce of the Pallava time, but also the South Indian Culture to South-East Asia. Looking out over the palm dotted beach and the hypnotically blue Bay of Bengal, one can intuitionally visualize the harbour at Mamallapuram, in the 7th century A.D., with ships anchored, laden with gold and silver, spices, fragrant sandal wood, wine, coral, turquoise and ivory circuited through it, connecting South-East Asia with European countries. We know that Mamalla, who had a successful reign, kept the Chalukyas of Vatapi under check, and sent envoys abroad and maintained a formidable naval presence in the Bay of Bengal and the Indian Ocean.

The Pallava monuments at Mahamallapuram can be classified in to four groups, as (1) Rock-cut cave temples or *mandapas*; (2) Rock-cut monolithic temples or *rathas*; (3) Structural temples; (4) Bas relief sculptures on the rocks in open air.

There are ten rock cut cave temples or *mandapas* in Mamallapuram and two in Saluvankuppam, a village about 4 km to the north of Mamallapuram on a hill, which are remarkable, not for their size but for the exceptional character of their design and execution. The important *mandapas* at Mahamallapuram are the Varaha, the Trimurti, the Mahisasura-mardini and Pancha pandava *mandapas*. The five celled Panchapandava-*mandapa* is the biggest cave temple in Mamallapuram (PL.100). These caves are modest structures of about 7.62 m wide facade, from 4.6 m to 6.1 m high, with a depth of 7.62 m, with pillars of about 2.7 m height and 30 to 60 centimetres diameter, usually; they had sanctuaries cut into their back walls, rectangular in plan, measuring each side 1.5 m to 3 m.The Pillars, the facade with *kudus* decoration, and the sculpture in side combined with architecture, are the salient features of these *mandapas*. These are more ornamental, slender and taller than those set up by Mahendravarman.

The bases of the pillars are often found shaped into sqauatting *vyalas* and lions.The flutes and bands of their shafts, the refined necking (*tadi*), the elegant curves of the *kumbha* and its lotus-form (*idal*) above, with its wide abacus (*palagai*), are all combine very well to produce a pillar, typical of Pallava style.

Notable among the sculptures of plastic art in the Varaha-*mandapa* are the magnificent representations of the Varaha and Vamana *avataras*, the portrait sculptures of Surya, Durga and Gajalakshmi and the two fine groups of royal personages representing the donor's family-Simhavishnu and Mahendravarman with their queens. The figures present an innate dynamism, life and vitality. No less of the feature can be found in the relief sculptures of the Vishnu relcining on the serpent Ananta, and the goddess Durga in her tumultuous war with the buffalo demon Mahisha, both in Mahishasuramardini-*mandapa* as well as that of Krishna, as he was raising the Mount Govardhana, in the Pancha Pandava- *mandapa*.

Walking past by a dilapidated Vijayanagara-*gopura*, where modern light house is, a structure appears, believed to be the royal enclave, where the sculpture of the lion stands as if guarding the building. The structure of the Vijayanagara age is often referred to as the old light house, infact, a temple sans its tower, which was probably the place of harbour in olden times, the merchant navy and also the war-ships of the Pallava kings that sailed on Simhala-dvipa, or the Chola ships on the island as well as the Sailendra kingdom of Malay Peninsula might have moved.

Rock-cut temples in a monolith, or the *rathas* at Mamallapuram, are eight in number, famous among them being the five temples in one group now called *Pancha Pandava rathas* (PL.101) and their common wife, Draupadi. In addition to them, there are three more monoliths at the western end of the village of Saluvankuppam; two of them standing side by side, called the *Pidari rathas*, and the third one known as *Valayan-Kuttai ratha*, found a little south to them. Near the great bas-relief, is another monolith, known as the *Ganesa ratha* (PL.102).

Approaching Mamallapuram, wending the way by the Buckingham canal to the west, near Saluvankuppam, as said above, a few examples of abandoned monolithic *rathas* (pidari) with unfinished carvings can be noticed. They present that the rock carvings were started at the top and brought down. The *rathas* have superbly finished crowns but with an unfinished rock base bearing rough chisel marks. One is tempted to view the abandonment was the result of a cataclysmic past.

The *Pancha Pandava rathas* (PL.101) are carved each out of a single massive granite stone upon the sea-shore. The Draupadi-*ratha* which shares a common *upapitha* with the near by Arjuna ratha, is a simple hut shaped structure, with its plinths supported by animal figures, of lions and elephants alternately. This temple is dedicated to Durga whose standing image is carved on the back wall of the sanctum and inside is an incident, of a young man holding a machete to his head, ready to sacrifice him, is carved. Thus this temple can be understood to have represented cult of sacrifice, in front of the fearful goddess, the killer of the demon-king Mahisha. A statue of the lion, carved independently and free-standing is found in front of the shrine, and it is well-known that lion was associated with the goddess in mythology and said to have been her vehicle. This sculpture of the goddess, Durga, is probably one of the earliest examples in Tamil Nadu.

The Arjuna-*ratha* is a two storeyed *vimana* with an octagonal *sikhara* and an *ardha-mandapa* in front.It is noted for its graceful figure-sculptures on the outer wall of the sanctum. A portrait of Siva leaning nonchalantly on the *nandi* is the iconic representation of the Vrishabha devar. This imagery is further developed by the Cholas, who cast this concept in exquisite bronze.

The Bhima-*ratha* (PL.103) has proportionately a long rectangular barrel-vaulted *vimana,* and a sanctum in the centre with a *Pradakshina-patha,* built within the *mandapa*. The long shape is appropriate for the large depiction of Vishnu in the form of Sayanamurti, which remains unfinished inside. Since the public has no access to view the *vimana* where the rock work is better finished, it would be educative, if the site museum could have an audiovisual unit to explain the architecture and show the finer details. This need becomes critical at the Dharmaraja-*ratha* for its tower carries the most exquisite carvings revealing a pantheon of gods. Working on a challenging stone such as the granite, the Pallava sculptor has hewn a wondrous *ratha* with its beauty partly concealed from us, but at the same time, it has to admit that the hard rock has to be thanked for preserving the art, mainly against the constant battering of salty winds.

The Dharmaraja-*ratha* is the highest and stateliest of all the *rathas* at Mamallapuram, which has a three storeyed *vimana* with octagonal *sikhara* at the top. The second and third tiers adorn excellent figure-sculptures. Its plinth has many strong mouldings and its porticos with lion pillars greatly improve the appearance. In the wall, the niches house the images of Ardhanarisvara, (composite image of Siva and Parvati), Harihara, (composite form of Hari (Vishnu) and Hara (Siva)) Brahma, Siva and Skanda.

One of the interesting features of the Dharmaraja-*ratha* is the hieratic portrait of Narasimhavarman, the author of the *ratha*, in his stately and dignified personality. He appears with his high cylindrical crown, triple wound knotted girdle and long and thin nose.

The Bhima, Nakula-Sahadeva and Gaṅesa *rathas* are oblong in plan and are based on the architecture of the *chaitya* hall. They have two or three storeys (*talas*) in their *sikharas*, which are surmounted by a barrel roof with the *chaitya* gable at the ends. Of the interest is the free standing image of an elephant by the side of Nakula-Sahadeva *ratha*. The Ganesa *ratha,* originally dedicated to lord Siva. But in recent times a Ganesa idol was installed in the sanctum of the *ratha* and hence the name. The two storied *vimana* with *sala-sikhara* and nine vase shaped finials in a row adds more beauty to this *ratha* (PL.102).

The *rathas* are not of great size, the largest measuring only 12.8 m long, the widest 10.6 m and the tallest 12.2 m high. They are Saiva in character.None of their interior is finished, and perhaps they were never actually used.

Among the sculptures at Mahabalipuram, one large composition on granite rock has obtained great celebrity. It is cut down from standing solid rock of 29.8 m long and 13 m wide (PL.104). The content of this magnificent panel is usually described as the story of Kiratarjuniya, Arjuna going on in penance for obtaining the powerful weapon of Pasupata, from Siva-Mahadeva, an event in Mahabharata, but now it is held by art critics and scholars that it represents the "Descent of the Ganges". There is a crevice between the two boulders representing a river where sculptors have filled with *nagas* and *naginis* as snake-beings are often associated with water. Swans, peacocks, gees and baboons and an elephant herd represent scenes associated with a river side. To the left of the cascade above there is a standing figure of Siva. Infront of him is Bhagiratha, with his hands in obeisance in the *ekapadothama tapas*, with his ribs and long beard showing, indicative of an arduous penance (PL.105). Making light of such practice below is the clever cat in a similar pose standing on its hind legs mimicking the ascetic. In the upper panels, the *devas,* the *kinnaras* and other heavenly hosts witness the proceedings with *bhakti* and reverence and in the real world called earth, cats, monkeys and elephants go about their grooming, monkey's de-licing one another.

The walls of many rock-cut cave temples have sculptures of exceptional beauty, in the modeling of the portraits of men and women, divine or human, and in the pattern of ornamentation and in their realistic positions and postures. The Mahisasura Mardini- cave, the Varaha-cave and the Trimurti-cave still possess originality in their conception and execution of their sculptures.

Among those figure-sculptures, goddess Durga mounted on a prancing lion, attacking the buffalo-headed demon Mahishasura, is the most excellent example (PL. 106) in this treasure house of art, at Mahabalipuram. It is the quintessence of female energy, power, majestic and forceful, an expression in stone of the victory of divine nature over evil, distinctly superior in the presentation to all other depiction of this scene known in earlier Hindu art. The goddess Durga is portrayed with eight arms. She is holding ferocious weapons such as bow and arrow, sword, long club etc., and is attended by *ganas.* She is fighting against demon Mahisha's army. Unable to face her war like attack, the buffalo headed Mahisha and his army is shown retreating back.

Opposite goddess Durga is Seshasayi Vishnu. Lord Vishnu resting on the five hooded Adisesha is in cosmic sleep (PL.107). It is another excellent example of Pallava sculpture. In the Varaha-cave we find four excellent panels representing Varaha-Murti, Gajalakshmi, Durga and Trivikrama. Lord Vishnu is depicted here as Varaha-*avatara* (PL.108) as saving the earth goddess (Bhudevi) from being submerged in the ocean. The carving of the boar's snout shows the Pallava skill in art. The panel of Gajalakshmi, i.e., goddess Lakshmi seated on lotus pedestal and being performed sacred bath by the elephants, the panel of Durga, the goddess with four arms and the Trivikrama panel of Lord Vishnu subduing the proud demon Bali are all excellent sculptures of the times.

The cave temple at the Village Saluvankuppam, 4 km north, popularly called Tiger Cave (PL.109), "is a fantastic creation with a row of *vyala* heads arranged as an aureole around the cave-temple." As the *vyala* figures resemble tigers, this cave temple is called so. What ever its complex significance, Mahabalipuram bears animated witness to one of the supreme achievements of Indic art; the energy and refinement of Pallava sculpture. For instance, in the Govardhanadhari bas-relief, where the eye transits from a cosmic Krishna, holding the mountain umbrella-wide above the villagers of Brindavana, to the detail of cow's tongue, as she licks her calf while being milked.

Even today, artisans continue to work on new rocks with their chisel and hammer.Stone carving at Mamallapuram is renowned far and wide and these images are much sought after at temples old and new.

Towards the end of the 7th century A.D. the art of the excavated *ratha* or *mandapa* was apparently given up in favour of the second phase of the Pallava art, the art of structural edifices, which became predominant form of art and architecture throughout the 8th century A.D., to be continued for all the time to come. The structural temples appear to have formed into two groups, from the point of view of their plan and finishing, measured by time-the temples of Raja Simha group (700 - 800 A.D.) and the temples of Nandi Varman group (800 - 900 A.D.). The temples are splendid with their lofty towers, built tier upon tier, diminishing in size towards a summit, typifing all the wealth, munificence and the grandeur of Pallavas.

There are six examples of the Rajasimha group of structural temples; three are at Mamallapuram, one at Panamalai (South Arcot District), and the temples of Kailasanatha and Vaikuntha Perumal at Kanchipuram. The three temples at Mamallapuram are the famous Shore temple, Siva temple and Mukunda temple, of which the Shore temple (PL.110) is the earliest. It is a superb example of Pallava art, standing at the apex of evolution of Pallava art. It faces the sea and located almost at the water's edge, so that the shrine may be illuminated by the first rays of the sun. It is a complex of three shrines, with two *vimanas*. The larger *vimana* facing the sea is called kshatriyasimhesvara, and the smaller *vimana* at its rear facing the west is called Rajasimhesvara. These two are dedicated to Siva and have wedged in between them rectangular *mandapa*-shrine with out superstructure-called Narapatisimha Pallava Vishnugriha. This is built over a previously existing reclining Vishnu on the Sesha carved on a low rocky outcrop.The names inscribed on the outer walls are all titles of Rajasimha,the builder of the complex. Here the *vimana* top is somewhat narrow and elongated unlike that of the Kailasanatha temple.The lion motif, particularly, in the pilasters becomes more developed. The usual Somaskanda relief panels are seen on back walls of both the *vimana* sanctums, which are a group portrayal of Siva in the company of Uma and Skanda, their young son, seated between them. This theme has found particular favour with the Pallavas and we do not find the continuation of this practice spilling in to other kingdoms or dynasties. The couchant bulls along the surrounding wall seem to greet and invite one in to the sacred space with in.

The shore temple complex bathed in ocean spray beckons you to visit and sit a while, soaking in the ambience of this unique site. King Narasimha Varman II, also known as Rajasimha, had passion of the arts and was a creative genius, who took the art of building to new heights. This is further revealed on visiting the Kailasanatha temple at Kanchipuram where the King's creative genius is evident.

In recent years, to create a pleasant ambience and to keep the shifting sands in check, the land around the complex was turfed. Many more temples of the Pallava time have been taken over by the sea. Obviously, the effect of sea erosion must have been one of the reasons for the abandonment of the port-town at Mamallapuram in subsequent times. Mamallapuram in its entirety has maintained the aesthetic beauty and refinement from the period of Mamalla and Rajasimha. UNESCO declared it a World Heritage Monument.When the ASI feared a threat to it from sea erosion; it erected a groyne wall to stop the sea.

In South Arcot District, 21 km from Villupuram, is the Village of *Panamalai*. Here, on a small hill close to a large irrigation tank, is an important Siva temple known as Talagisvara of the time of Rajasimha. Square in plan, the little *garbha-griha* has a narrow circumambulatory, a small entrance porch, and a large *mandapa*. In the wall, the *devakosthas* house the *Siva-lingas* and images of Somaskanda. As at Kanchipuram there are rampant lions against pilasters at every corner of the shrine. The super structure is of brick with plaster. The temple is contemporary of the Kailashanatha at Kanchipuram.

Kanchipuram, the capital city of the Pallavas was one of the most pompous and wealthy cities in the country by virtue of its maritime trade, which is perhaps still reminiscent in the form of it being one of the most renowned centres for silk fabrics interwoven with golden thread, *zarin-tar*. The pure silk Kanchipuram saris are much sought after as gifts. The city was proud of being a place for a *ghatika,* or a centre of higher learning something similar to the modern universities, that flourished in the times of the Pallavas.

Kanchi is indeed a town of temples. Once this city boasted of nearly 1000 temples, both big and small, and today around

100 can still be spotted. The Kailasanatha temple (PL.111), built mostly in the reign of Rajasimha (early 8th century) who named it Rajasimhesvara after his own name and completed during the reign of his son Mahendravarman III, is one of the most celebrated monuments at the city. The builders of this temple would seem to have exercised some thought in selecting material for construction as its foundations are of granite and able to carry a great weight, while sand stone was used for the sculptured super structure. It is a wonderful example of Pallava structural art. Originally, the temple consisted of a sanctuary with its pyramidal *vimana* and a detached *mandapa* infront (PL.112). The whole temple complex is enclosed by a rectangular courtyard by means of a high wall composed of sub shrines, surmounted by cupolas, 58 in number (PL.113), contain only reliefs of Somaskanda. Eight similar shrines appear on the entrance wall and has a *gopura*, which suggests the beginning of the *gopura*. After some centuries later, the *mandapa* and the sanctuary were joined together by an intermediate *ardha-mandapa* which has spoiled the total effect. The pyramidal tower rising in several well-proportioned storeys has rhythm in its mass and elegance in its outline. But the "perfect maturity" was yet to come. The pillars of the *mandpa* and the constant repetition of the rampant lion, all fit in to the scheme admirably.

The main temple has a high *padabanda-adishthana* with intricate carvings; including a beautifully sculpted *nandi* (PL. 111) on a platform at a considerable distance facing the temple. The outer walls of the temple have sculptured panels of various gods and goddesses. Lord Siva is depicted as Uma Mahesvara and Lingodbhava with Varaha flanked by Brahma, Vishnu and flying *amaras* at bottom level respectively on the southern wall of the temple. On the west wall, Siva is depicted as Sandhya-Tandavamurthi and Urdhava-Tandavamurti with dancing *ganas* flanked by Brahma, Vishnu, Nandi and Parvati. On the northern wall, Siva is depicted as Tripurantaka with three *ganas* and Durga flanked by three *ganas* and Bhairavi, Kausiki and Jyestha.

While splendid depictions of Bhikshatana, Somaskanda and Siva in Samhara - Tandava are seen on the out side of the *vimana* walls, the inner walls of the *prakara* have unique sculptures including that of Durga, Skanda, Bhavati, Tripurantaka, Garudarudha - Vishnu, Asura Samhara, Narasimha Vishnu, Trivikrama, Siva Tandava, Siva cutting off the fifth head of Brahma, destruction of Daksha's *Yagna,* Brahma with consort, Gangadhara, Urdhava-tandava, Vishnu with Sridevi and Bhudevi, Lingodhbhava, Bhikshatana and Ravana and Vali worshipping Atmalinga Chandikesvara.

The south facing niche on the *vimana* contains a representation of Siva Dakshinamurti (PL.114). Siva beautifully carved, sits in a pose, exuding peace and tranquility. The representation of Siva's Lingodbhava form (PL.115) on the west wall of the *vimana* is interesting.

The significant feature of Pallava architecture was its pillars with lions at the base. This erect lion holding the Pallava pillar has projections at different angles - examples of these can be seen at the temple. Under the Pallava emperors, the painters stood out as masters of line, form, colour and perspective. The Kailasanatha paintings are based on mythical stories and closely resemble the later phase of the Ajanta school, not only in respect of time but also in technique form and expression.We know that the Pallavas were fond of the theme of Siva's family. Siva is regal and yet a fond family man with a beautiful wife and child. The idiom, which begins to develop here, is seen to blossom later in to a grand imperial style of painting under Cholas.

The ASI took special efforts to remove the thick layer of plaster on the sculptures of Kailasanatha temple, which was applied in the early decades of 20th century as a preservation method. The temple well maintained by the ASI, now attracts hundreds of tourists and devotees every day.

The temple of Vaikuntha Perumal (PL.116) at Kanchipuram built by Nandivarman II (717-779 A.D.) is another marvellous example of Pallava art, where the style of temple-architecture appears to have attained maturity. The temple is slightly larger and more compact, wherein; the different architectural members, the cloisters, portico and sanctuary are, instead of being separate buildings, integrated into an architectural whole and presents unity of conception and considerable architectural merit. The temple's high *Padabandha-adhishthana* has a bold *tripattakumuda.* The sanctum is square with nearly 27.4 m side. Its front is carried forward 8.5 m on the eastern side to provide a portico, which is square in plan with 3.8 m side. Its *vimana* is square in plan and has a height of 18.2 m from the ground. "It is in four storeys, each with a passage round its exterior, a cella in the center, and a corridor encircling two of these for circumambulation". The whole complex is surrounded by a wall which is decorated on its exterior with simple and effective ornamental motifs, while inside of it are the open ambulatory and the cloisters with a colonnade of pillars supported by squatting lions (PL.117). In side it the wall is decorated with narrative sculptures and label inscriptions, explaining the history of Pallava dynasty, from its origins in Vishnu down through Nandivarman II Pallavamalla ascending the throne of Kanchi.In the garbha-*griha* is the huge four-armed icon of Vishnu carved of black stone, seated as transcendent king (Vaikuntha Perumal) facing west.The walls of the sanctum contains the standing, seated, and reclaining forms of Vishnu.

The second group of Pallava structural temples, of the Nandivarman group, mostly consists of small temples which were constructed in the 9th century when their power was declining and reveal no advancement in matters of architecture, or sculptural art, over the previous age. They are more the copies of the earlier examples, rather than innovative. The principal examples are the Muktesvara and Matangesvara temples at Kanchipuram, the Vadamallisvara temple at Oragadam, near Chingleput, the temple of Virattanesvara at Tiruttani near Arkonam and the Parasuramesvara at Gudimallam near Renigunta, Chittoor (Dt.). Perhaps the earliest in the group are the two temples at Kanchipuram, which both have porticos supported on two pillars at the entrance. The other four temples of this group are all apsidal in character, possibly based on the example of the Sahadeva-*ratha* at Mamallapuram. These temples are modest, but reveal of decline of Pallava power.

Credit goes to the Pallava kings for having kept up and further developed the traditions of Amaravati and transmitted them to the countries beyond the seas. Within the country, they played a considerable role in shaping medieval cave sculpture in south India, by way of exercising influence over the rock-cut art and architecture of the Chalukyas and when the later were conquered by the Rashtrakutas, of northern Deccan, the tradition of sculpture of Badami, stamped by the Pallava idiom, was carried further up for its fulfilment at Ellora and Elephanta.

It is not easy to see the paintings in Tamilnadu prior to those of Vijayanagar period. It was because, either they were situated in remote places far from the tourist beat, (like Sittannna vasal), or are locked up and kept out of sight of the visitors (as in Thanjavur).

Sittannavasal is a remote village 15 km beyond Pudukottai town, not far from the early Chola temples of Narttamalai, and Eladipattam. It is famous for a number of natural caverns on top of the hill with beds and pillows cut in the stone floor, ostensibly for the use of monks, known to have been intended for the Jain monks, as the inscriptions at the place reveal. The cave temple has simple pillars and sculptures of Jaina *Tirthankaras* and on an "elongated mass of granite", are the paintings, probably belong to the 7th century A.D. As the paintings have striking similarities with the sculptural art of the Pallavas in the modelling of the figures as well as their dress and ornaments and present the technique of later Ajanta paintings as to have been employed here, the date appears quite reasonable.

The paintings include a *dharma-chakra* on the ceiling, a lotus tank with frolicking animals, creepers and lotuses, young men collecting flowers, dancing *apsaras* and a barely-visible king and queen, bringing to life the Jaina philosophy of *ahimsa* and harmony with nature. One *apsara,* with her right hand in the *pataka mudra* and the left in the *danda hasta,* is reminiscent of the bronze figures of the dancing Balakrishna and Bala Subrahmanya, while the other is performing the *bhujangatrasita karana,* associated with the dance of Siva at Chidambaram. The base of Sittannavasal paintings is well consolidated, with a thin lime plaster, used as binding material, which the same technique adopted in the paintings in the Ajanta caves too. The painted stucco is made up of three layers: rough plaster, fine plaster and a covering layer of paint. These paintings are gradually disappearing, thanks to the pollution from the stone quarries, which is also probably weakening the hill.

The Talagirisvara temple at *Panamalai* is rarely visited, but is notable for the single remnant of a painting, of an exquisite female figure (PL.118), apparently shaded to present three-dimensional affect. It is a standing figure of the lady, resembling Parvati of the Kailasanatha temple at Kanchipuram, with her leg gently bent and resting against a wall, standing beneath a royal umbrella. She wears a tall bejewelled *kirita* and other items of jewellery typical of the Pallava period. It is one of the most beautiful paintings in India, undoubtedly, reminiscent of the figure portraits of women in the Ajanta paintings and with no exaggeration, often mistaken to be one of the examples from the latter. There are traces of painting elsewhere in the temple, but nothing identifiable. The fresco secco method was used here as at Sittannavasal.

Situated on the hill, near *Tirukkalukkunram*, the cave temple known as Orukal *mandapa* belongs to Mahendravarman period excavated in the 7th century. On plan this cave temple features a shrine and a varanda supported by four pillars. The *dvarapalas* are large and imposing. The *vimana* of the structural temple located here closely resembles the *vimana* of Kailasanatha at Kanchi. This temple may be dated to Rajasimha's period (the end of the 7th century A.D.).

The interesting thing about this hill is that a pair of kites arrives here everyday at noon from Ramesvaram on their way to Banaras. Every day they are fed at the appointed time. The Bhaktavatsala temple (PL.119) at the foot of the hill with its large *gopuras* and high enclosing wall attracts the visitors. Inscriptions of 13th century are noticed here; the one recording the construction of the temple by the Pandyan King, Jatavarma Sundara.

7

Chola Temple Art

The period of Imperial Cholas in south Indian history, from about the beginning of the 10th to the middle of the 13th centuries is regarded as the golden epoch of medieval times. Imperial Chola power had reached its zenith, its authority having spread over the entire Tamil region and Kerala, parts of south Mysore and Coastal Andhra, and even overseas to Ceylon, the Andamans, the Laccadives and the Maldives. The political stability as well as expansion over lands across the seas, with the economic prosperity in its sequel, undoubtedly contributed to the progress of art and architecture. The rich and glorious traditions left by the the Pallavas had been the foundation for the art and architectural activity of the Imperial Chola time, which had carried them to their logical culmination and consummation.

The Chola rulers were ardent devotees of Lord Siva and built a number of temples dedicated to the god, but necessarily when they planned a new city, a magnificent temple of Siva was invariably constructed at its centre.

After the Sangam Age, the Cholas sank in to obscurity due to the invasions of the Kalabhras and the rise of Pallavas at

Kanchi. Once again, the glories and greatness of the Cholas came to be revived by the dynasty founded by Vijayalaya, when the Pallavas were fast declining. He began his rule shortly before 850 A.D. when the Pallavas were still renowned as a suzerain power, inspite of their clearly visible decline. The Cholas had overtaken the Pandyas in the race and successfully accomplished their revival and resurgence. Parantaka I (907-955 A.D.), one of the able successors of Vijayalaya, was the real founder of the revived glories of the Cholas and their eventual supremacy in South Indian politics, who swept away all traces of Pallava suzerainty and even extended his power and authority up to Nellore in the north.

The most powerful ruler of the Chola kingdom was Rajaraja I, the Great, who ruled from 985 to 1014 A.D. who was also known as Rajaraja Sivapada Sekhara, or "he, who had the feet of Siva as his crown". The title amply substantiates his ardent devotion of Siva, as he described himself as to have always been bearing the feet of the lord on his head. Quite naturally, he raised a magnificent temple of Siva at Tanjore or Thanjavur which is known as the great temple or the Brihadisvara (Great Lord) in reference to Siva's greatness. Further it was called Rajarajesvara after the king, Rajaraja I, himself.

The Rajarajesvara temple at Tanjore has been rightly said to have been the largest, highest and most ambitious production of the temple architecture, true to its name, as Brihadisvara. Every inch of its exterior has been richly carved with sculptures and the interior walls were decorated with fine paintings. The Tanjore inscription of Rajaraja gives a description of his victories. He first destroyed the power of the Pandyas and subjugated Kerala, conquered Simhala, or Ceylon and annexed its northern part, expelled the king, Mahendra V, of the country and sacked the famous cities of Anuradhapura and Polonnaruva in the country, where he constructed a great temple of Siva, in stone; conquered Gangavadi in the Western Chalukyan empire and forced Satyasraya, to sue for peace. Ostensibly in commemoration of these resounding victories on all sides, the Chola emperor built the magnificent temple of Rajarajesvara at Tanjore.

Rajendra I, the equally great son of Rajaraja, the Great, succeeded him on throne of Tanjore and ruled from 1012 to 1044 A.D. who had his surname as Uttama chola and earned the sobreiquet *Gangaikonda chola*, meaning the Chola who conquered the Ganges, obviously carrying the victorious sword of the imperial Cholas to the banks of the sacred river. He followed his father's example, not only in the imperial expansion, but also in the construction of magnificent temples for Siva, as exemplified by the great temple, also called Brihadisvara Temple, at Gangaikondachola Puram that he constructed to be his new capital. More than all his victorious expeditions within the subcontinent of India, his remarkable naval expedition over the Sailendra kingdom in Kadaram or Malaya peninsula and Srivijaya kingdom of Sumatra, made his fame unique in the history of India. He sacked the new Western Chalukya capital, Kalyani, wherefrom he carried away a fine image of *dvarapalaka* as a trophy, which is one of the important exhibits in the local museum at Tanjore.

Next in importance among the emperors who ruled from Tanjore was Kulottunga Chola I (1070 - 1120 A.D.), who was not a Chola in strict sense and his rule is said to have started the period of Chalukya-Chola phase. He was by birth a Chalukyan prince of the Vengi kingdom, but being the grandson of Rajaraja, the Great, on his mother's side, he could ascend the Chola throne, when it has fallen vacant. His son and successor, Vikrama Chola, who ascended the Chola throne with the coronation title, Parantaka II, in 1118 A.D., for years before the death of his father, is important from the present context, the study of Chola art and architecture in South India. He renovated, probably remodelled also, the temple of Nataraja at Chidambaram and improved the Ranganatha temple at Srirangam. The work on the Chidambaram temple was completed by the son and successor of Vikram Chola Parantaka II, namely Kulottunga II (1135-1150 A.D.).

In religious matters, the Chola period was continuation of the Pallava period to the largest extent, both Saivism and Vaishnavism flourished, won the royal patronage as well as popularity. At the same time, Jainism was also popular and the Jain teachers made rich contribution to the Tamil language and literature.

The Chola temple architecture has been appreciated for its magnificence as well as delicate workmanship, ostensibly following the rich traditions of the past bequeathed to them by the Pallavas. Fergusson has very aptly remarked that "the Chola artists conceived like giants and finished like jewellers". A new development in Chola art that characterized the Dravidian architecture in later times was the addition of a huge gateway called *gopuram* to the enclosure of the temple, which had gradually took its form and attained maturity under the Pandyas.

The Chola rulers built a number of stone temples through out their kingdom, but not very large in size up to the end of the 10th century. Their modest size and decorative works, obviously present the situation of their limited resources and comparatively local nature of their style. The district of Pudukkottai in Tamil Nadu contains a large number of Early Chola monuments, in a good state of preservation, which give us an idea of different stages by which later Pallava architecture was adopted, so as to evolve a distinctly Chola style of temple architecture.

The earliest and prettiest of the Chola temple is the Vijayala-Cholesvara at *Narttamalai* (Pudukottai district). This temple stands on a hill and was probably erected in the time of Vijayalaya, the first Chola ruler. It has a circular *garbha-griha* with a square *prakara*; seven miniatures of the main shrine are arranged in the open yard round the temple and facing it, which was typical of the Early Chola period. The super structure is four storeyed, of which the three lower ones are square and the

the fourth is dome-shaped *sikhara* with a round *kalasa* atop. There is an enclosed *mandapa* infront. The pillars in the *mandapa* recall the Pallava example. The *adhishthana* belongs to *padabandha* variety. The walls have simple, unadorned *brahmakanta* pilasters without *lasuna*. Niches are absent in the walls and at the top below the curved cornice a frieze of *bhutas* is carved and the cornice at intervals itself being decorated with *kudus* containing human heads or animal figures, while a pleasing scroll work takes place in the decoration at the corner. At the main entrance of the temple there are *dvarapalas* of 1.5 m height facing forwards, while their bodies are half turned towards the entrance, with one leg crossed over the other. As in Pallava monuments, they have only two arms.

The Balasubrahmanya temple at *Kannanur* (Tiruchirapalli district) is dated to the regnal period of Aditya I (880 - 906 A.D). It is another example in the same style in which *nandis* are replaced by elephants at the four corners of the roof of the shrines and below the *sikhara* in the *vimana,* the elephant being the vehicle of Subrahmanya. The *adhisthana* is of *padabandha type* and the walls are punctuated by *brahmakanta* pilasters with archiac decoration. In the false *devakoshtha* to the south, an image of Dakshinamurti has been introduced.

Kumbakonam, located in the fertile cauvery delta is an ancient royal and pilgrimage town. Unlike typical historic towns of Tamil Nadu that are concentrically centred on a single temple, Kumbakonam is a town with multiple temple centres. Studies show that it was part of an approximately 15 sq.km royal complex of the Chola period. This town is connected with almost all the religions. There are a number of Siva, Vishnu and Jain temples and you will even find a rare temple to Lord Brahma here. The notable temples at the place are: Adikumbhesvara, Sarangapani, Somesvara, Rama Svamy and Chakrapani temples scattered outside the city are the nine planetary or *Navagraha* temples.

The famous Mahamaham festival is celebrated here once in 12 years in the Tamil month of *Maasi* (February-March) when Jupiter (*Guru*) passes through the sign of Leo (*Simha rasi*). It is believed that on this auspicious day the nine sacred rivers of India appear in the Mahamaham tank here.

The beautiful little temple of Nagesvara (PL.120) at *Kumbakonam* is more or less of the same period and style. The temple shows early Chola art in its best form particularly in the handling of the human figures. The *adhishthana* is of *padabandha -padmaka* type stands on a *padmopana*. The lotus leaves of the *padmopana* are carved with vitality. In its iconographic scheme the Ardhanari, Brahma and Dakshinamurti in the niches of the outer walls are featured. The other sculptures on the walls almost life-size reflect either the donors to the temple or contemporary princes and princesses. The epic scenes are in low relief on the plinth below the pilasters of the walls of the sanctum, recalling the wood-work.

The Devi shrine is an independent structure situated in the outer *prakara*, detached from the axial unit, though it faces south, a feature common to Saiva Devi shrines.

In the Nagesvara temple complex the *mandapa* of the Nataraja temple is in the form of a chariot on wheels drawn by horses (PL.121) as in the case of Airavatesvara porch *mandapa*.

The Sarangapani temple belongs to the Late Chola period. The Koranganatha temple at *Srinivasanallur* exhibits the next stage of evolution. Probably this temple was erected during the Parantaka I reign 907-955 A.D. The *adhishthana* is akin to *vaprabandha* type with *ardhapadma*, a feature not mentioned in Vastu texts. The beautiful large *vyalas* in the *pratimukha* are among the most powerfully conceived of their kind. It is of modest proportions and consists of the sanctuary and its attached *mandapa*. The two cover a total length of 15.3 m., with its *sikhara* measuring about 15.3 m. The *mandapa* is a small hall with four central pillars, and a vestibule provided to it at its back, leading to the sanctum, which is a square chamber of 3.7 m. The lion motif is absent on the pillars though it is reappeared in friezes where ever suited. The pillars in the interior are typical of Chola art. The usual deities are enshrined in the central niches outside the walls of the sanctum. Dakshinamurti is seen seated under a tree in the southern direction, surrounded by devotees, lions and *ganas,* a standing Vishnu on the west, and a standing Brahma on the north. Other niches contain standing figures which may be portraits. All the sculptures are in very high relief and of fine workmanship. The *toranas* over the south and west niches are of good workmanship, especially that on the west, which is perhaps the finest in South India.

The *Moovarkoil* (Temple of the three) (PL.122) in *Kodumbalur* (Tiruchirapalli district) is another perfect example for another Early Chola temple-complex notable for the excellence of its architecture and the charm of its sculptures. Kodumbalur is a tiny village, 5 km off Viralimalai on the Tiruchi-Dindigul highway that connected the Chola and Pandya capitals. Obviously, this tiny village of the present day was a magnificent town in those days. A large establishment of the Kalamukha sect was located here and it was the centre of a flourishing merchant guild. All that remains of the glory in this archaeological site is the temple complex.

There are three shrines, attributed to Bhuti Vikramakesari *alias* Tennavan glangovelar who ruled in the second half of 10th century A.D. a feudatory of Chola Parantaka II. He built three temples, one each in his and in the name of his two queens. Of the first shrine (northern), only the moulded basement remains, clearly showing the layout plan. The lowest mouldings of all the three basements are shaped like petals of full blown lotus (*padma puskala adhishthanas)*. The other two shrines (central and southern) are almost intact. Each central shrine is 6.4 m square at the base. All these temples face west. The walls of these shrines are very similar, divided by *brahmakanta* pilasters with rich and graceful ornamental details on the top members. Both the shrines have *dvitala vimana.* An *ardha-mandapa,* about 5.5 m square is common to the three shrines. At a distance of 2.4 m from the edge of the *ardha-mandapas* was a *maha-mandapa* (27.7 m x 12.5 m). Infront of the *maha-mandapa,* was a small square *nandi* shrine.

In the central shrine the rear *devakoshtha* is occupied by Ardhanari, but in the northern one we find Siva, the southern niche is empty. In the southern shrine the rear niche is for Gangadhara, the northern niche for standing Siva and the corresponding southern niche is for Vinadhara. The substitution of Brahma by Siva in the northern *devakoshthas* of these two shrines and that of Ardhanari by Gangadhara in the second of them is noteworthy. The temple and the sculptures are classified as belonging to the Early Chola period; but evidence of transition from Pallava style are seen but with a fresh vibrancy. More sculptures have been unearthed and displayed neatly in a site museum. ASI's expertise in renovation is evident.

Temple-architecture during the period of Rajaraja I and his son Rajendra reached its final stage of evolution. Many temples larger than the specimens so far described, but still of moderate size were built by Rajaraja and his son.

The Uttara Kailasa temple at *Tiruvadi* (Tanjore district), the Vaidyanatha temple at *Tirumalavadi* (Tiruchirapalli district), the twin temples of Siva and Vishnu at *Dadapuram* (South Arcot district) and Siva devalam No.2 at *Polonnuruva* (Ceylon) are some of the more notable among numerous small temples of Rajaraja's reign, though none of them approaches Tiruvalisvaram temple at Brahmadesam (Tirunelveli district) from the stand point of sculpture. The well known *ananda-tandavara* of Siva-Nataraja is found on its wall perhaps the earliest depiction of this characteristically stylized and sublimated concept in Tamil Nadu and its unique contribution to Indian and world art.

Rajaraja, the Great, and Rajendra Chola were responsible for the construction of two grandiloquent examples of Chola art and architecture, and in a way the exemplary creations of south Indian art and architecture in general. Rajaraja, the Great, built the temple at Tanjore known as the Brihadisvara, also known as Rajarajesvara temple after its royal builder, about 1003 A.D., which is known to have been completed in 1010 A.D.

The second one was built by Rajendra Chola, also named as Brihadisvara temple in 1025 A.D. in his capital of Gangaikonda-Chola-puram (already inscribed as 'Great Living Chola Temples' by UNESCO). In these two temples the Chola style reached its supreme expression and also one can see the mighty resources of the Chola power at its height.

The *Tanjore* temple (PL.123) which is contemporary with the temples at Khajuraho (M.P) had many architectural features which could be classified as innovations, that is, they are more than simply a continuum of artistic developments from earlier periods. Indeed at the time when it was built, it was not only one of the largest buildings in South Asia but in the world itself, whose construction approximately took seven years, a significant achievement for such a vast undertaking.

The Tanjore temple stands within a spacious walled quadrangle (152.4 m x76.2 m) with two *gopura* gateways infront widely seperated each other on the east. The main feature of the whole scheme is the great *vimana* (PL.124) consisting of 14 diminishing tiers rising to a height of 58m over the *garbha-griha* and dominating every thing in its vicinity, the tallest of its kind, and hence called *Dakshinameru.* It is crowned by a massive dome, with winged niches on four sides, consisting of a single piece of granite, 7.6 m high and weighing about 80 tons. It is traditionally held that this dome was set into its present position after having been hauled up on an inclined plane, specially arranged for the purpose, of about 6 km long, the length necessary to make the slope gradual enough for the stone to be moved. The tower is pyramidal and straight sided in profile, in contrast to the curved shape of northern style superstructures, and it is clearly based on earlier South Indian precedents, consisting of a multiplication of elements rather than creation of a new form.

The temple is composed of many component structures such as the *ardha-mandapa, maha-mandapa* and a large *nandi* pavilion. The *adhishthana* is characterised by bold, heavily-moulded parts; it rises to a height of 2.77 m. The massive temple building is covered from the base to the top with sculptures and decorative mouldings. A second *gopura* in front of the first forms the gateway of second and inner enclosures (PL.125). In the eastern face of the second *gopura* above puranic panels there are two monolithic *dvarapalas* on either side with exquisite workmanship (PLs. 126 and 127).

The sanctum is a 13.72 m square inside with a narrow circumbulatary passage 2.74 m wide around it. The paintings in the walls of the passage are the master pieces of the Chola mural tradition but these are overlaid by later tempera work of the Nayaka rulers of Tanjore. The sanctum enshrines an enormous *linga* (4 m in height) originally called Rajarajesvara and now known as Brihadisvara (PL.128). The walls of the *garbha-griha* and *ardha-mandapa* on either side contain pilasters and large niches. Flanking the shrine-door are Nandi and Mahakala (*dvarapalas*) in life size. The roof of the transept is supported by two rows of four pillars each. In front of the transept on the same plinth an *ardha-mandapa* and a two-storeyd structure are located. Then comes the *maha-mandapa* with rows of pillars, along the middle and aisles on either side, in front of which is another transept reached by flight of steps on the north and south. There is another small *mandapa* relatively, probably added to this, by means of another flight of steps infront, ostensibly a very late accretion. Some metres away is the *nandi-mandapa* containing one of the largest monolithic bulls (PL.129), considered as the second largest in India (3.7 m high and 6 m. long); the first being Lepakshi near Anantapur in Andhra Pradesh. In the outer walls of the *ardha-mandapa*, the niches house the divinities of considerable iconographic and artistic interest.The figures of Ganesa, Vishnu, Lakshmi, Vishnuanugraha Murti, Bhikshatana, Virabhadra, Dakshina Murti, Kalantaka and Natesa on the south, Harihara, Ardhanarisvara and Chandrasekhara on the west. Ardhanarisvara, Gangadhara, Virabhadra, Alingana

Chandrasekhara, Sarasvati, Mahisasuramardini and Bhairava on the north are housed in the niches. K.A. Nilakanta Sastri remarks, "The whole temple from the heavy moulded parts of its high basement to its finial is a magnificent example of solidity combined with proportion and grace of form".

The Devi, Brihannayaki (PL.130) shrine and the *nandi-mandapa* are later additions during 12th and 13th centuries. The large entrance hall belongs to Vijayanagar period.

The present fortifications and the moats around the temple were formed by the Nayaka rulers of Tanjore during 16th century.

A.K. Seshadri dismisses the poplular belief that the shadow of the tower or the *vimana* does not fall on the ground. It is a law of nature that any object under the sun has to cast its shadow and the *vimana* or the finial of the temple at Tanjore is no exception. This, he says it can be verified in the courtyard between 3 P.M. and 4 P.M., in the day when the shadow is long, it can even be seen outside the compound wall. Again it is thought that the *vimana* is made of single stone. Seshadri examined it and found that neither the cap stone nor the *sikhara* was made of single piece.

Tanjore itself is a classical profile of fusion and a mutual adaptation of different cultures and languages. In it, can be seen the synthesis of the Tamil Cholas, Telugu Vijayanagaras and Marathas. Situated on the banks of Cauvery, it has been the capital of many dynasties from 8th century A.D. onwards. It was a famous settlement even before the Cholas came and ruled for nearly four and half centuries. Today, it is best known for the role and influence of the Cholas in fields of art, architecture, religion, culture and administration. Tanjore is a repository of contemporary art, crafts and ritual. Here the Cauvery River fans out in to a number of tributaries that provide the lowlands with a more or less constant source of water, facilitating intensive wet cultivation of rice. As in the past, this deltaic area still forms the economic ricebowl of Tamilnadu.

Erratic monsoons may one day turn Tanjore into another parched Ramanathapuram. The varieties of cuisine served by restaurants in the districts of Tanjore still retain their delicious flavour. Coffee made in iron filter with a slightly bitter taste is still available in restaurants in Mayiladuthurai and Tanjore. So is the *vathakulambu* in Kaliakudi restaurant. Mouth watering *oothappam* with onions fried to a perfect golden brown colour is the most sought after delicacy in many hotels in Thiruvarur. A meal at Vasan Cafe is not to be missed. Kumbakonam is full of street side restaurants which offer hot *idlis* accompanied with at least six different types of *chutneys* in six colours.

Rajaraja's son Rajendra Chola who was made heir apparent in 1012 A.D. followed his father's example and constructed another great temple also called Brihadisvara at *Gangaikonda-Chola-puram* (PL.131) now in Perambalur district. Rajendra Chola made victorious campaigns into north India and brought back water from the holy Ganges to South India, thus 'sanctifying' the Chola lands. Because of this, he called himself conqueror of the Ganges and founded a new capital, Gangaikonda-Chola-puram (city of the Chola who conquered the Ganges) to commemorate the event.

The temple built by Rajendra Chola in his capital city is a replica of the Tanjore temple but with more grace of curved contours in its *vimana* and a greater maturity in its sculpture. Two decades after the temple of Tanjore, the temple was erected about 1030 A.D., within a quadruangular walled compound, appears that this was in the shape of a fortress enclosure. With in the court, the principal composition occupies a rectangle (103.6 m x 33.53 m), with its long axis from east to west, consisting of a *maha-mandapa*, (53.4 m x 28.96 m) and the massive *vimana* 30.5 m square metres at the base and 50.6 m high . The number of tiers making up pyramidal body is only 8 as against 14 in Tanjore. The main entrance in the middle of the eastern wall of the *maha-mandapa* is designed as an impressive portal. There are also two subsidiary entrances in the northern and southern walls of the vestibule. The *maha-mandapa* is relatively low building with a flat roof supported on rows of pillars of ordinary design, more than 150 in number, arranged in the interior of the hall. The *vimana* is only 50.6 m high as against 58 m in Tanjore. The treatment of the lower upright section is essentially the same as that of the Tanjore temple, but in the tapering body above, the introduction of curves in the place of the strong straight lines of the Tanjore *vimana*, enriches the beauty to the creation of Rajendra Chola. According to Percy Brown, "There is voluptuousness in the later structure, the beauty of ripe feminity, in contrast to the masculine strength of the earlier type. But in comparing these two architectural productions they present much more than a difference in kind. Stately and formal as an epic may epitomise the Tanjore *vimana* while the later example has all the sensuous passion of an eastern lyric, but it seems to go even deeper than that. Each is the final and absolute vision of its creator made manifest through the medium of structural form, the one symbolising conscious might the other sub-conscious grace, but both dictated by that divinity which has seized the soul".

More graceful but less imposing than the Tanjore temple of Rajaraja, the Great, is the Subrahmanya temple (PL. 132) located in north-west corner of the court yard of Tanjore temple with its highly decorated *vimana,* less severe in the outline. It is one of the best examples of temple architecture of the Nayaka period of 16th century. The Airavatesvara (PL. 133) temple at *Darasuram* and the Kampaharesvara or Tribhuvanesvara temple at *Tribhuvanam*, both situated inTanjore district belong to the Chola period. The Darasuram temple built by Raja Raja Chola II around 1160 A.D. seems originally to have a number of enclosures with the *gopura* or gateway for each. The carvings on the *gopura* (PL.134) at the entrance of the temple – the lovely *apsaras*, *Sivaganas* and other motifs-are finely depicted. The porch *mandapa* (PL.135) in the temple is quite attractive having been modelled in the form of a chariot drawn by elephants. It is a predecessor to the famous wheel at the sun temple in Konarak. Another miniature *mandapa* adjoining to *nandi-mandapa* (PL.136) has its steps producing musical notes, *swaras*, when they are tapped. Of particular interest in the porch *mandapa* are decorated columns with rich carvings (PL.137). The growing Saivite zeal of the Chola dynasty is clear from the stories that are told in sculpture here. The Kampaharesvara temple was built by Kulottunga-I.

The Brihadisvara temple at Gangaikonda-Chola-puram and the Airavatesvara temple at Darasuram are in the world heritage list of monuments and sites. The Brihadisvara temple in Tanjore town was earlier included in the list.

The Chola statues stand out in high relief, nearly in the round, and the sculptors concentrated more on the modelling and iconographical perfection. The images appear to have been visualized and executed so as to give sculptural formats to the hagiology of gods and goddesses, in the songs of Nayanaras and Alvars. In excellence they excelled even the Pallava sculptor in portraiture when they attempted it as at Srinivasanallur and Kumbakonam (Nagesvara). It is generally employed for decoration of different architectural members like niches, pillars, plinths, etc. The Chola sculptor seems to have felt that plain spaces left at proper places would also form a part of decoration and thus left plain spaces on walls without crowding them with too many figures. He also did not adopt the method of ivory carver and goldsmith, but worked generally on hard rock with bold strokes of hammer and chisel, giving formats to his bold conceptions.

Portraits, images of deities and decorative sculpture are the main classes of Chola sculptures. Images of deities are generally found in niches of the temple walls. Saivite figures (PL.138) predominant because the Cholas were followers of Siva. However, there are some Vaishnava and Jaina images also. Regarding the portraits of men and women in the Nagesvara temple at Kumbakonam, Ajit Ghosh observes: "Here for the

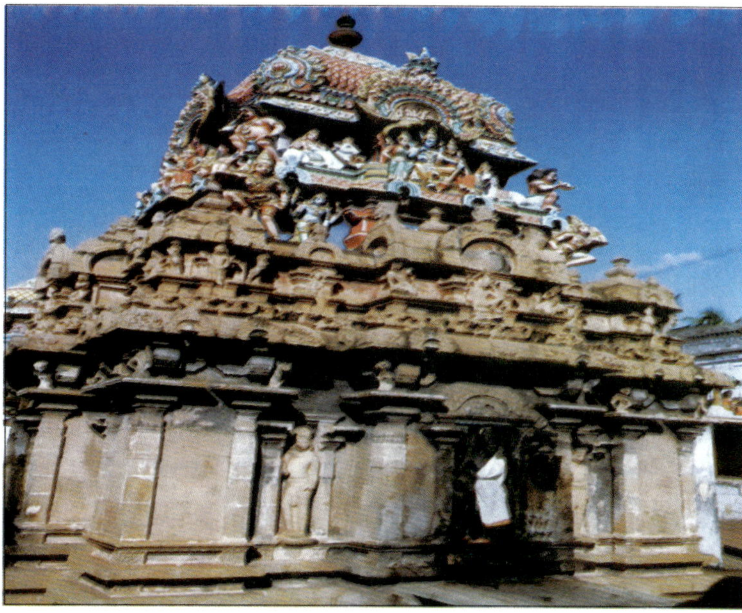

120. Kumbakonam, Nagesvara temple, vimana, general view.

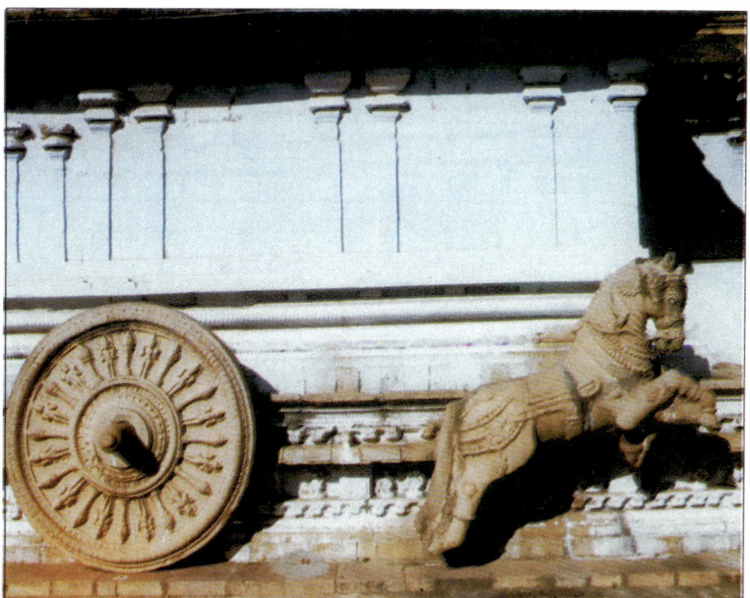

121. Kumbakonam, Nagesvara temple complex, Natraja temple mandapa.

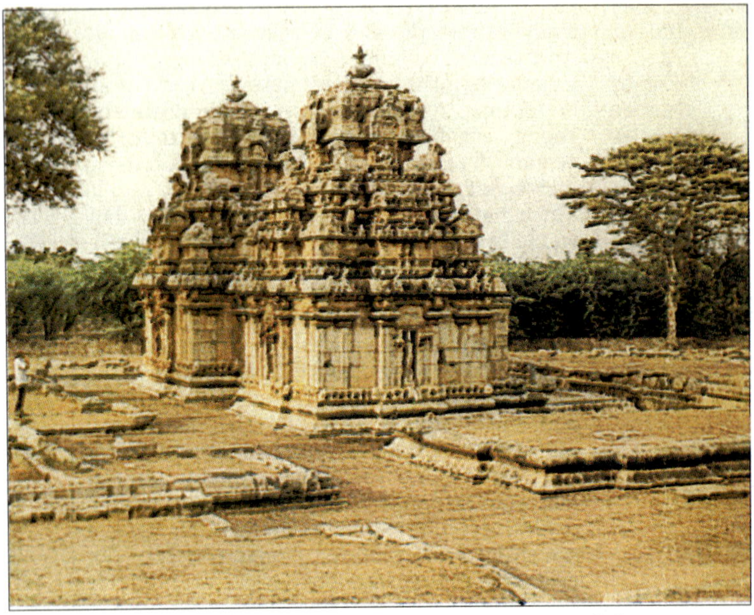

122. Kodumbalur, Moovarkoil temple complex, general view.

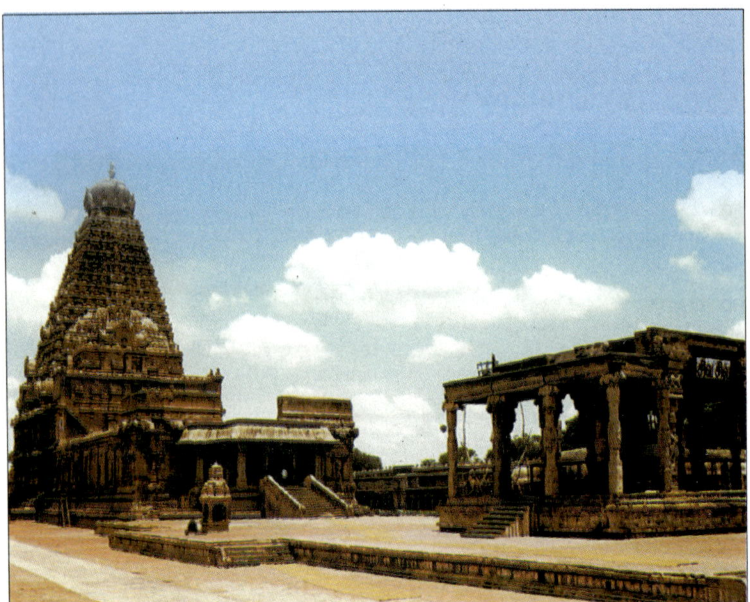

123. Tanjore, Brihadisvara temple, general view.

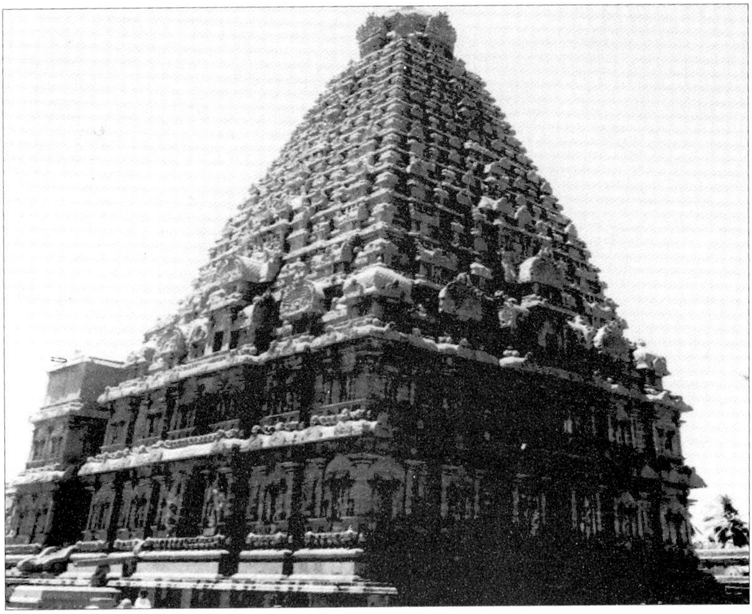

124. Tanjore, Brihadisvara temple, great sikhara.

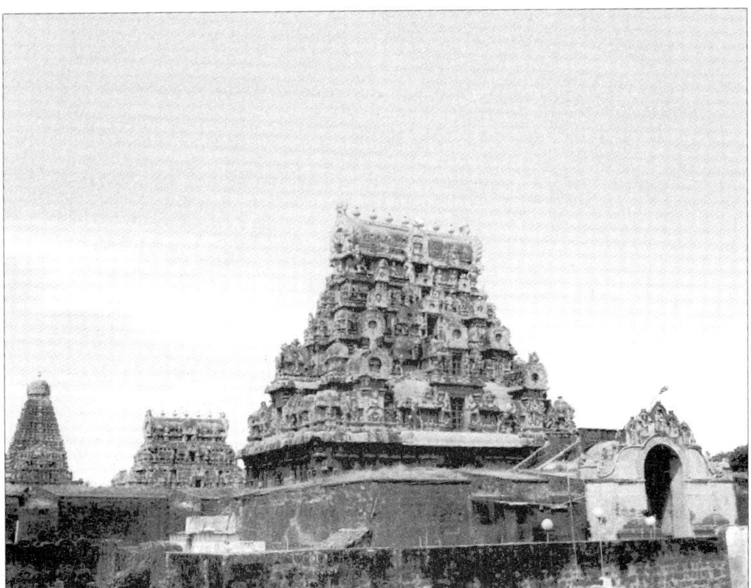

125. Tanjore, Brihadisvara temple, gopuras and sikhara, general view.

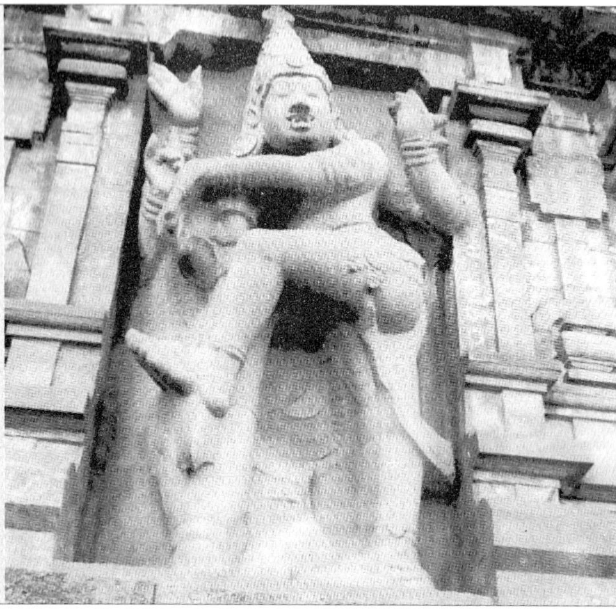

126. Tanjore, Brihadisvara temple, second gopura, dvarapala.

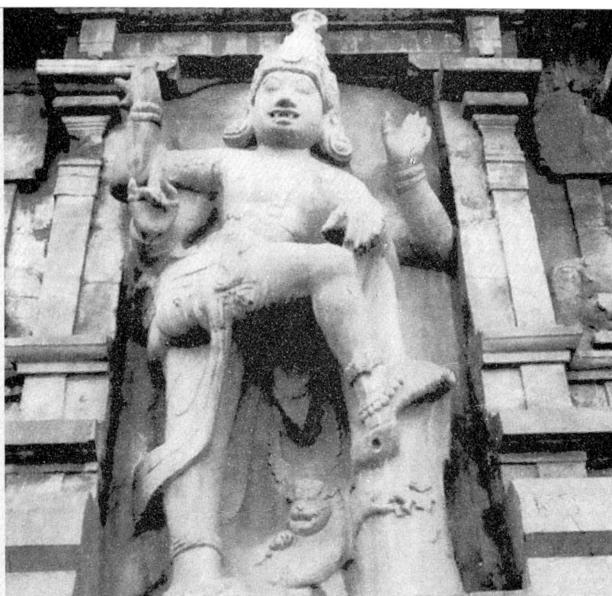

127. Tanjore, Brihadisvara temple, second gopura, dvarapala.

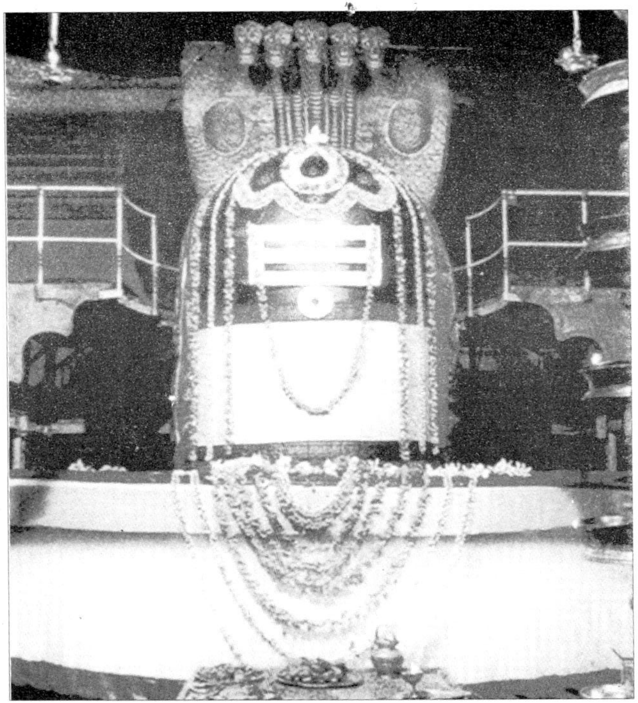

128. Tanjore, Brihadisvara temple, linga.

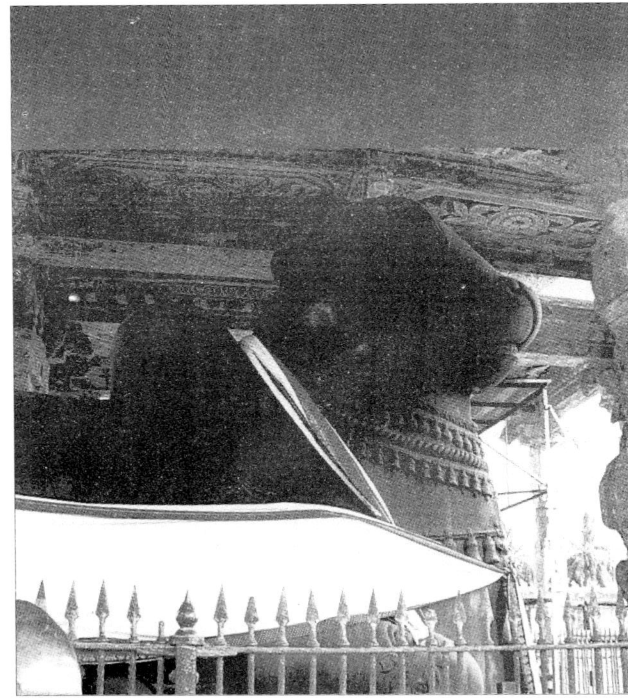

129. Tanjore, Brihadisvara temple, nandi.

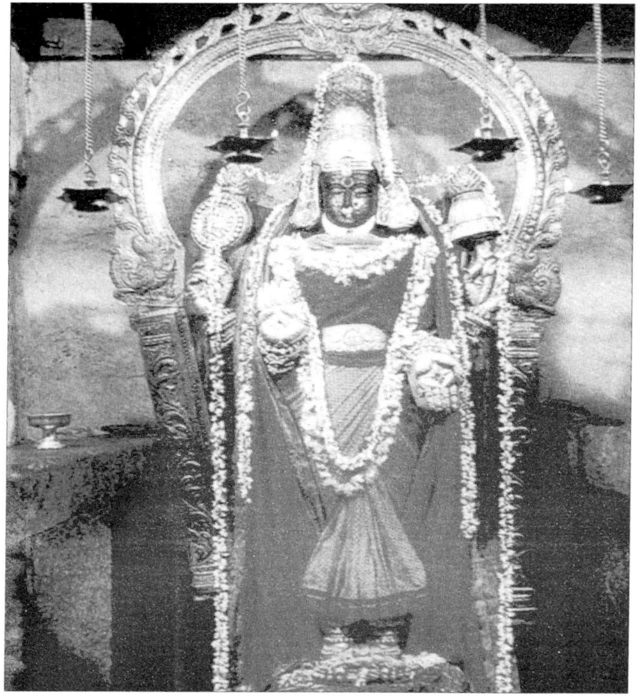

130. Tanjore, Brihadisvara temple, Brihannayaki.

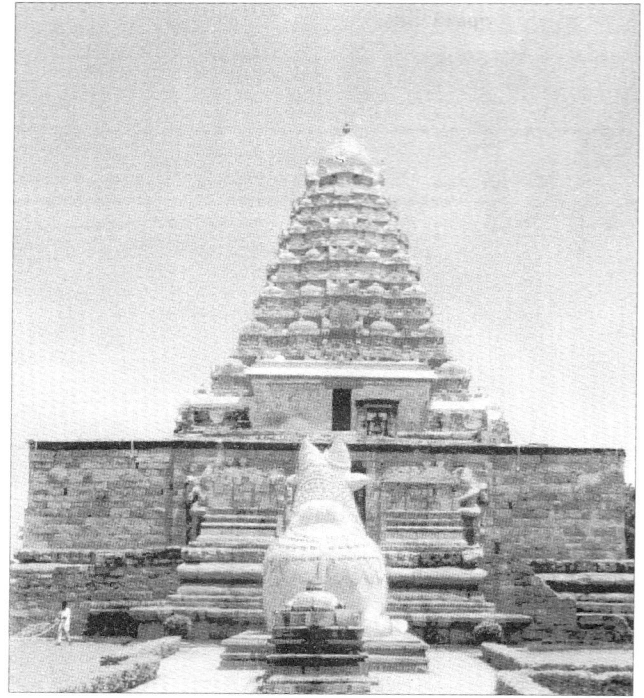

131. Gangaikonda cholapuram, Brihadisvara temple, general view.

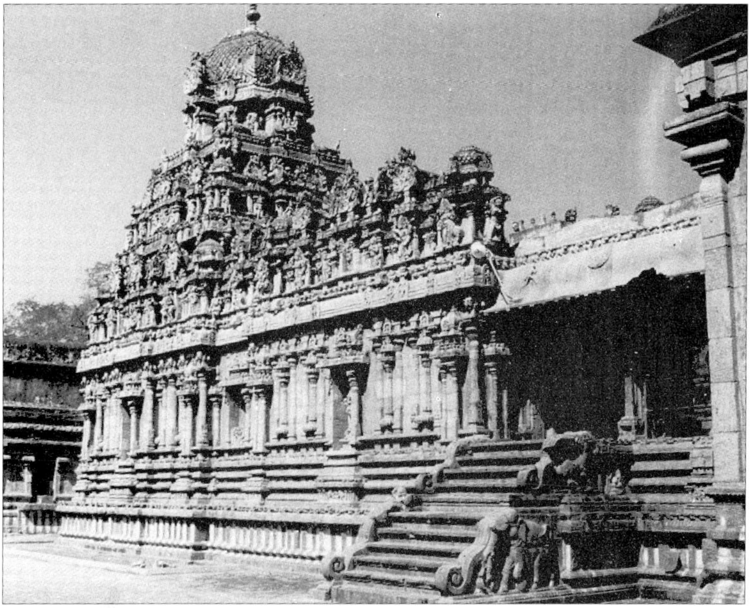

132. Tanjore, Subrahmanya temple, general view.

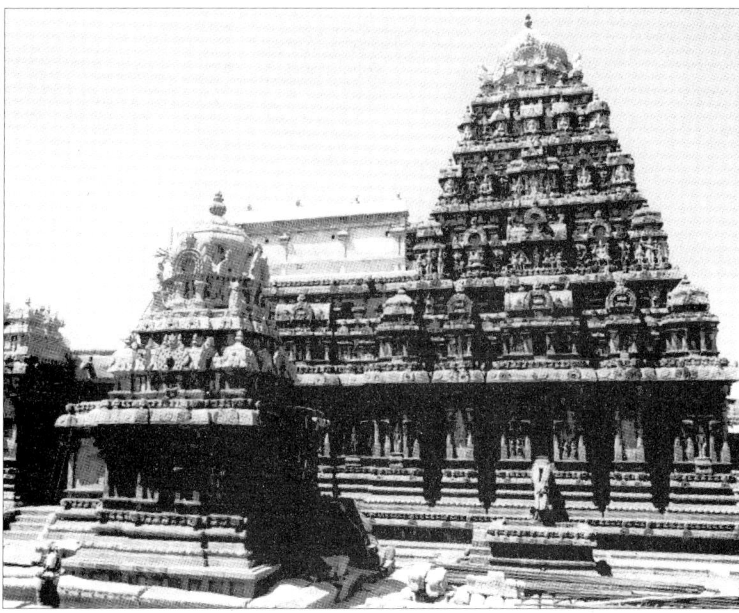

133. Darasuram, Airavatesvara temple, side view.

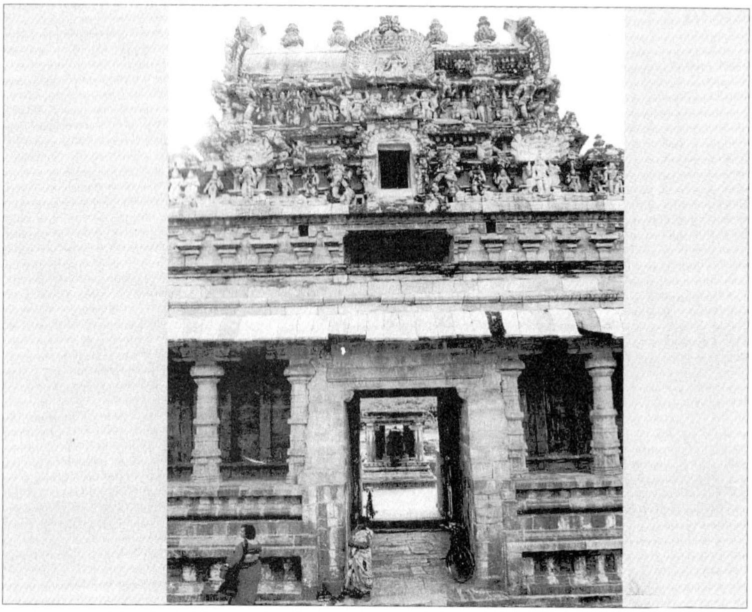

134. Darasuram, Airavatesvara temple, Interior view.

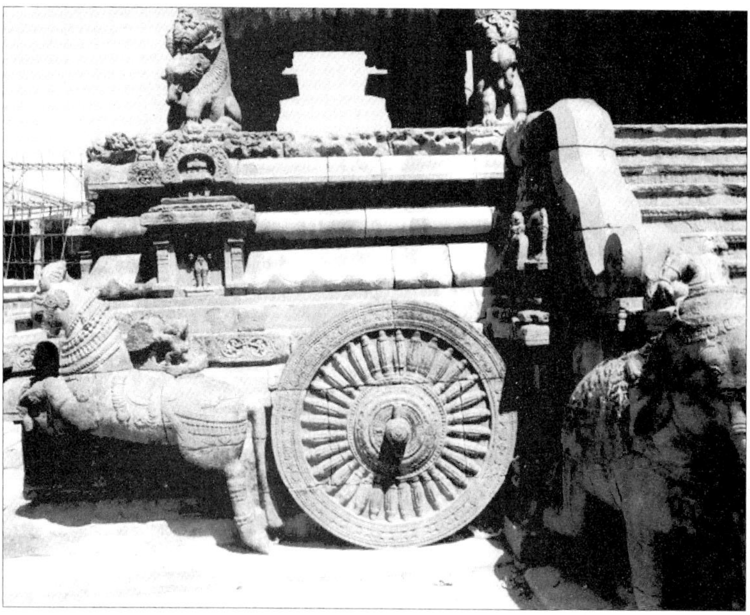

135. Darasuram, Airavatesvara temple, porch mandapa.

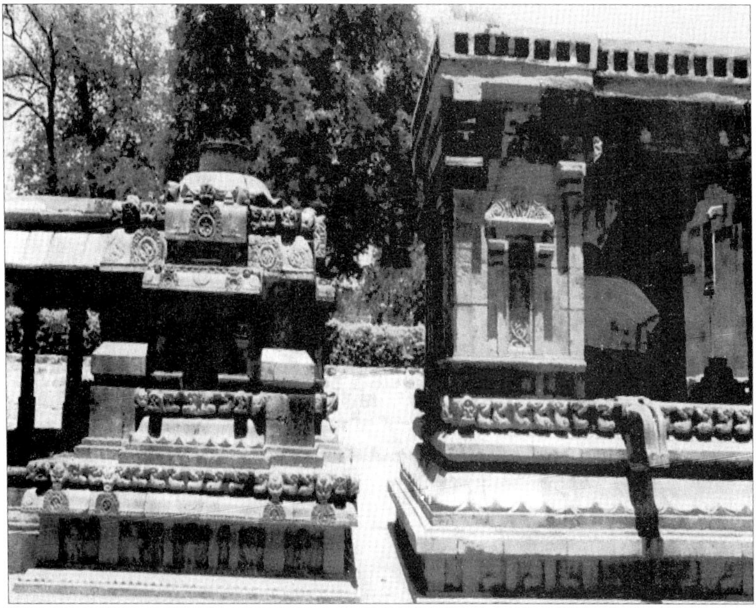

136. Darasuram, Airavatesvara temple, miniature mandapa and nandi-mandapa.

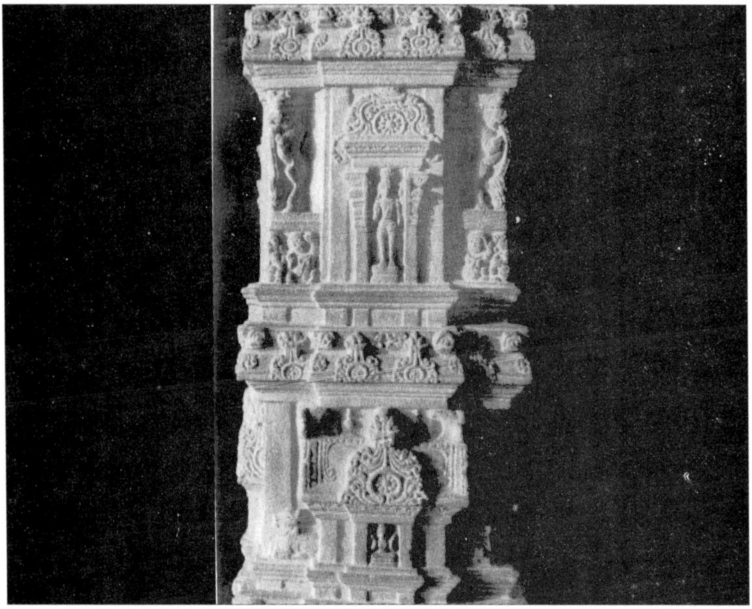

137. Darasuram, Airavatesvara temple, decorated column.

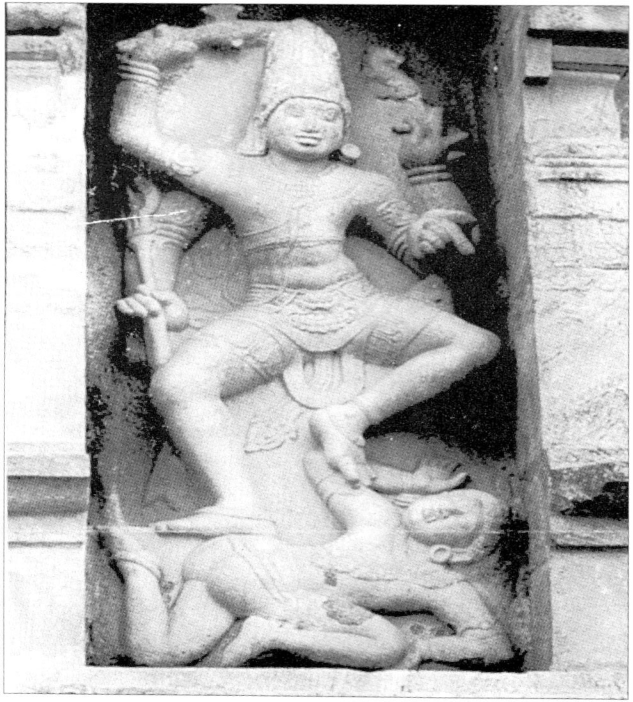

138. A sculpted image of Siva (Chola period).

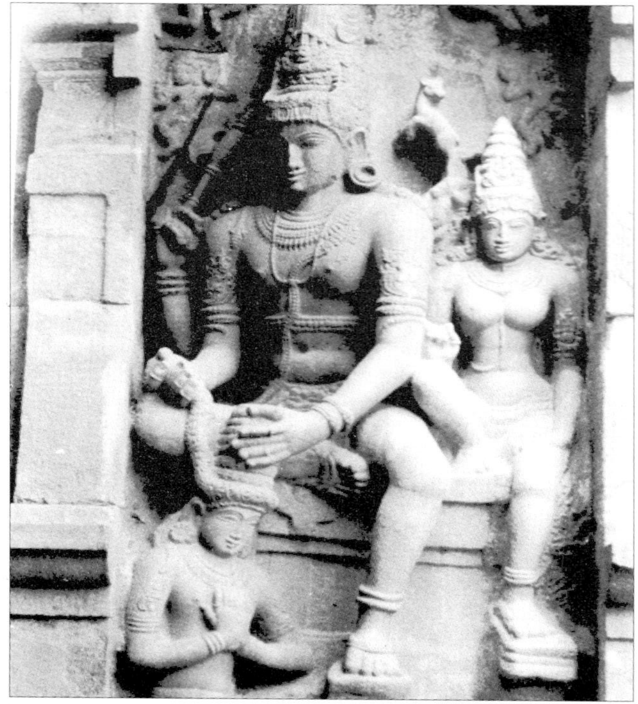

139. Gangaikonda-chola-puram, Brihadisvara temple, Siva bestowing a wreath on Chandesha.

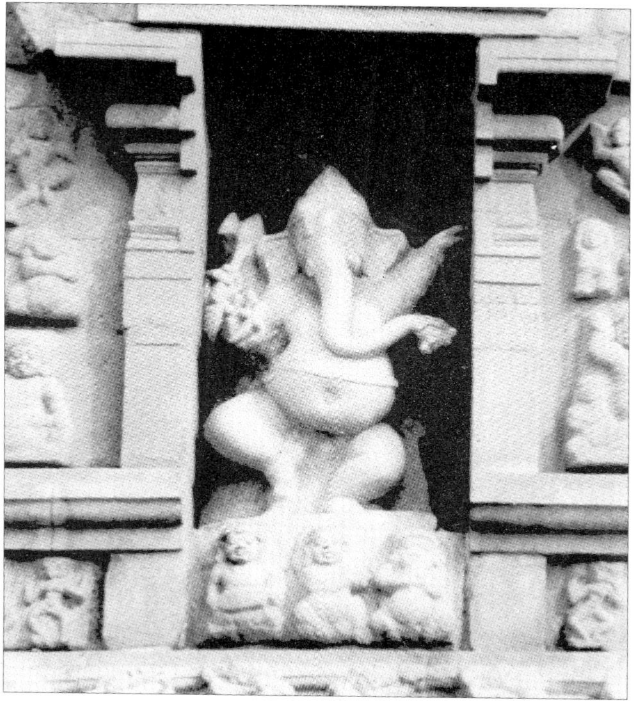

140. Gangaikonda cholapuram, Brihadisvara temple, Dancing Ganesha.

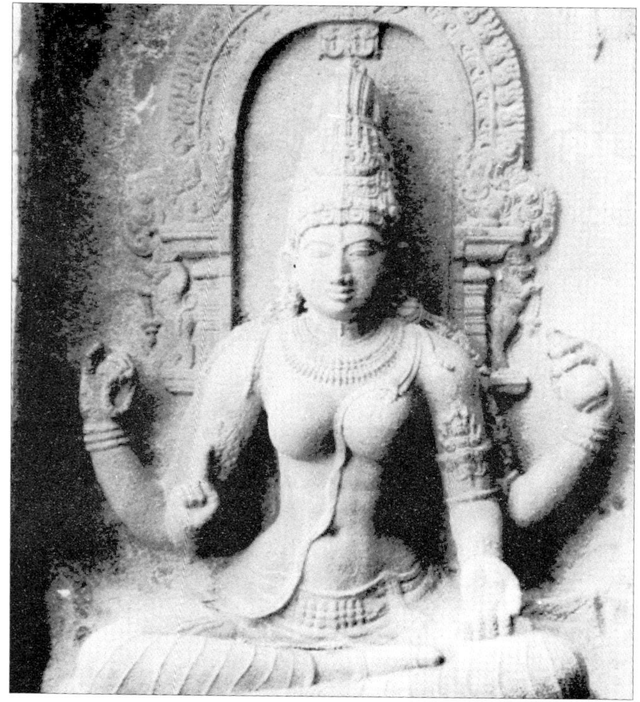

141. Gangaikonda cholapuram, Brihadisvara temple, Devi.

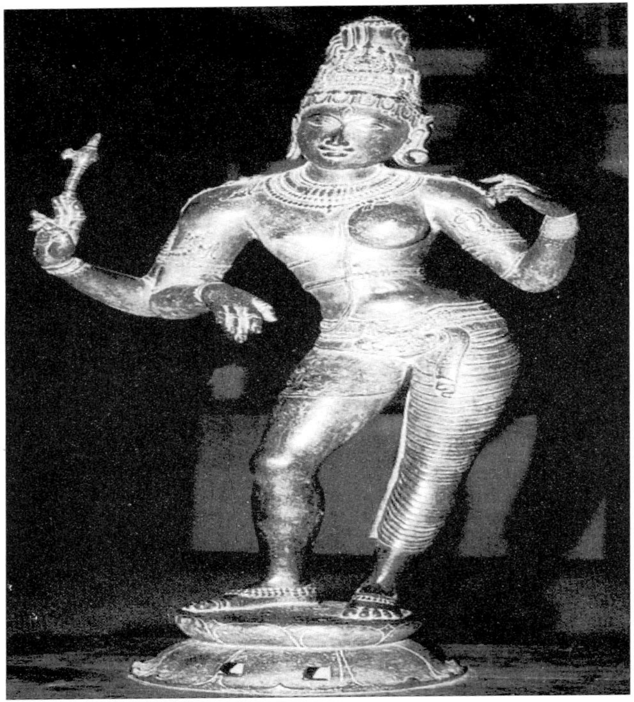

142. Ardhanarisvara, Chola bronze, Chennai Museum.

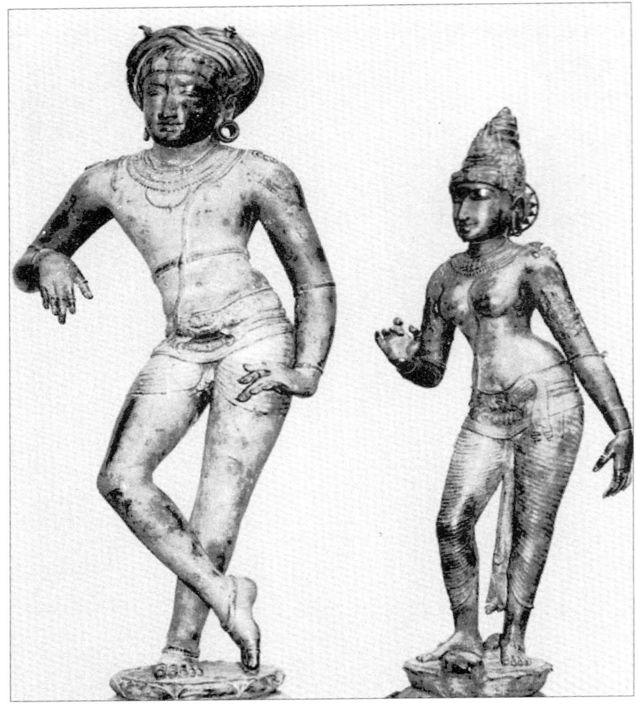

143. Rishabha vahana murti and his consort Parvati Chola bronzes, Art gallery, Thanjavur.

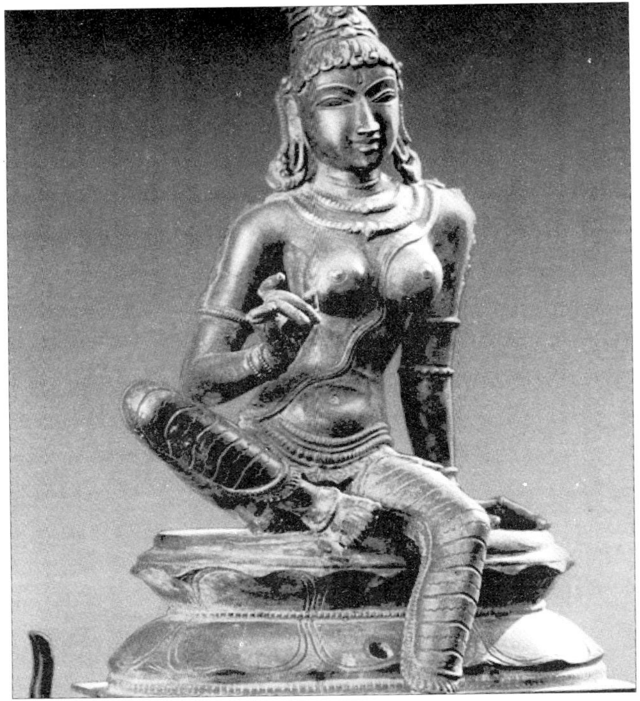

144. Parvati, Chola bronze, Chennai Museum.

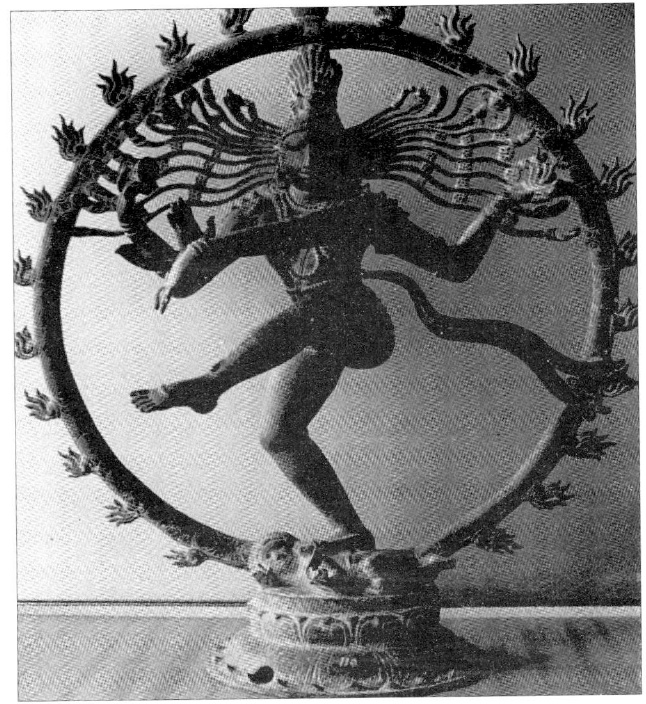

145. Nataraja, Chola bronze, Chennai Museum.

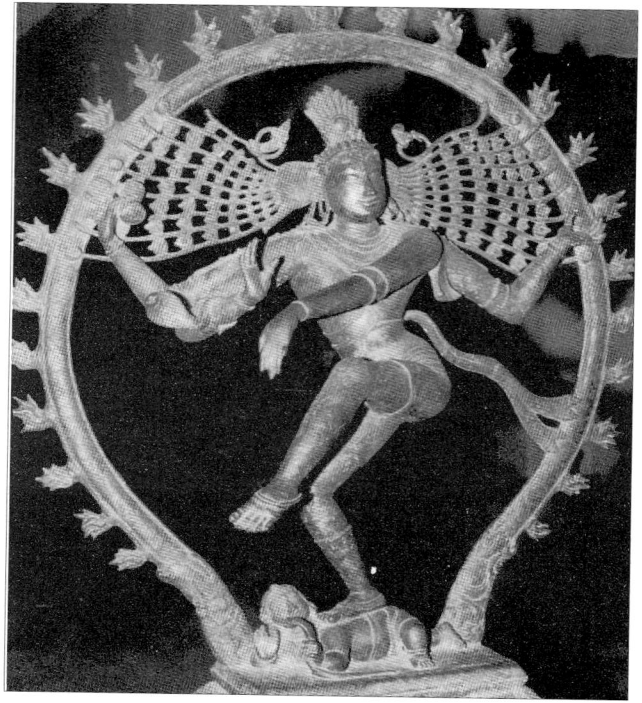

146. Nataraja, Chola bronze, Chennai Museum.

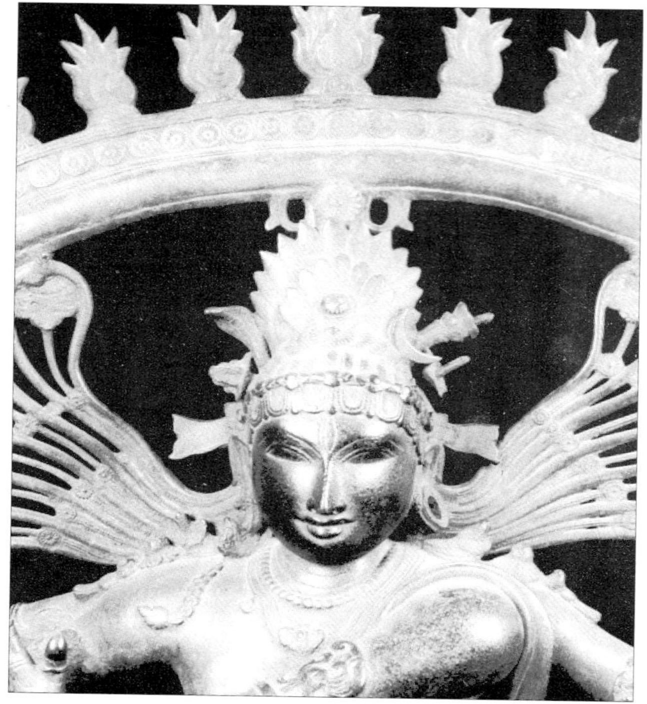

147. Nataraja, Chola bronze, Chennai Museum.

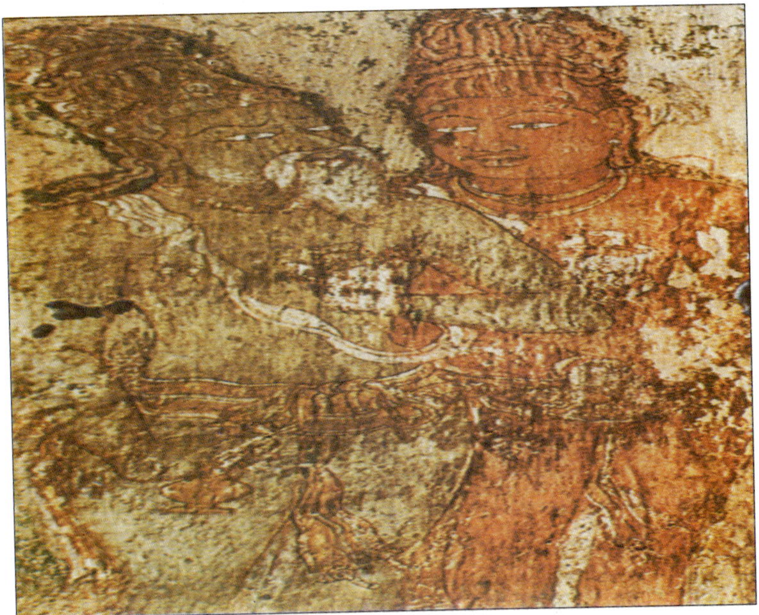

148. Tanjore, Brihadisvara temple, Rajaraja with his teacher Karuvarur, mural.

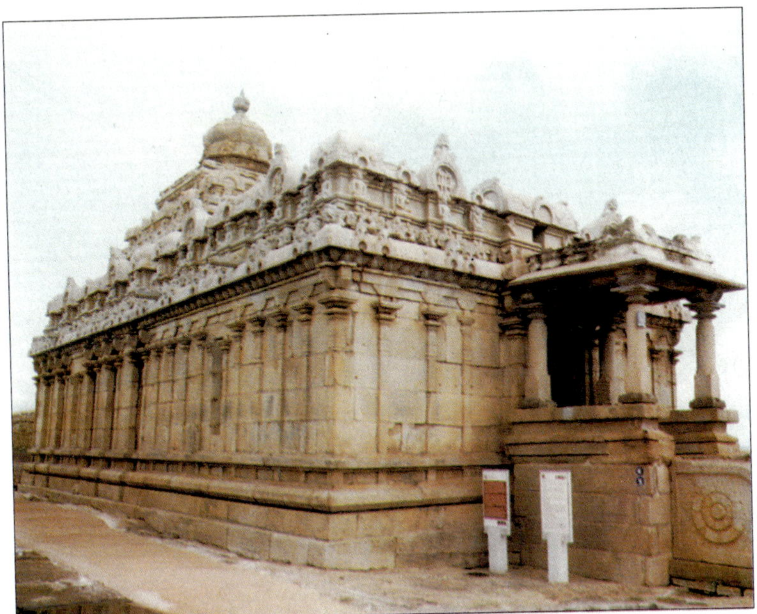

149. Sravanabelagola, Chamundaraya basadi, general view.

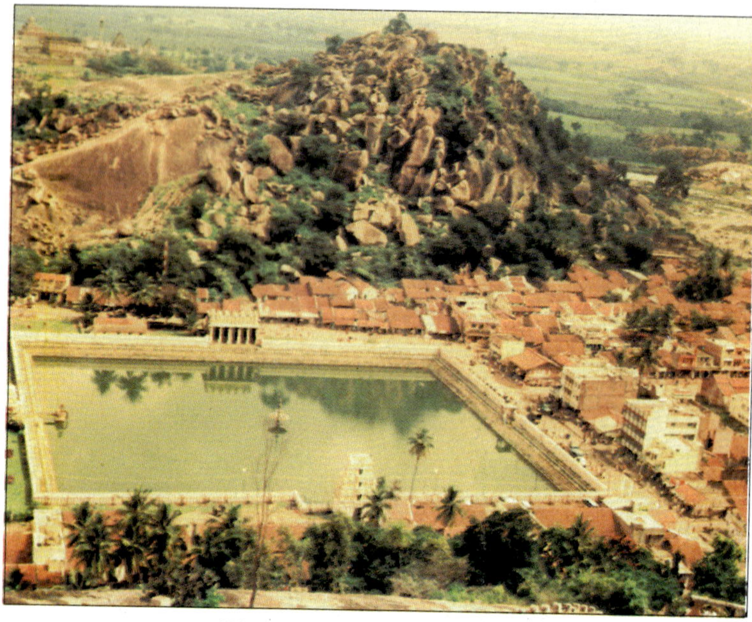

150. Sravanabelagola, Kalyani pond.

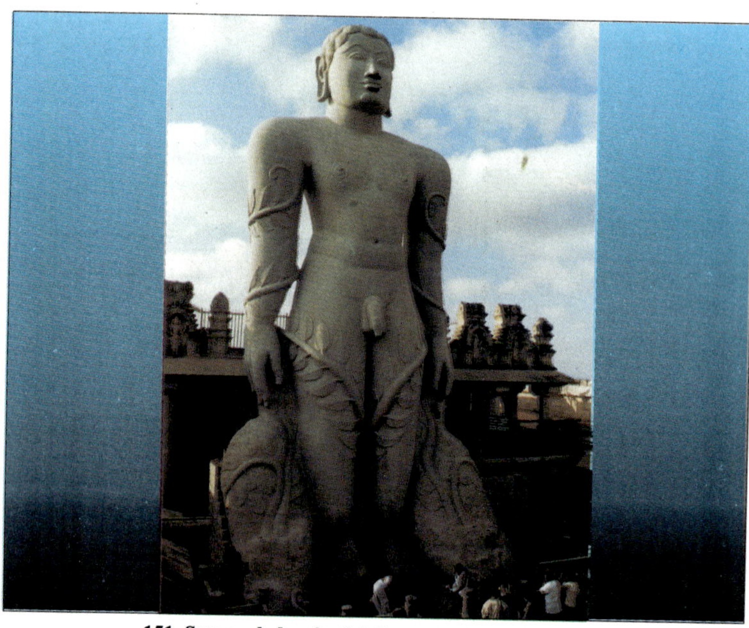

151. Sravanabelagola, Sri Gomatesvara, a Jain saint.

first time the Chola artist stands in sharp contrast with his Pallava predecessors and the latter's severely abstract, ideal, and schematic vision. There is no difference in outward bearing between a Pallava king and a god, between a goddess and a queen. But a new and attractive conception of life and beauty had dawned on this Chola sculpture. These Chola ladies are picturesque and realistic human figures, full of feminine grace and the joy of life. This intensely human quality may be said to distinguish every one of the statues in the niches of this shrine. This art, so unconventional, is thus refreshingly original in conception and spirit. This humanism is the Chola's principal contribution to South Indian Art".

The early Chola iconography belonging to Pre Raja Raja I times is best represented in the Tiruvalisvaram temple at Brahmadesam. No doubt it is a veritable museum of superb early Chola iconography. The magnificent sculptures of Siva's various forms in the niches of the *panjara* of its *vimana* and the recesses deserve notice. The iconographic scheme consists of Nataraja flanked by Vrisabharudha and Gangadhara on the left and Virabhadra and Devi on the right on the Southern side, Lingodbhava with Vishnu and Brahma on either side on the western side is noticeable. In the Vishnu temple (Partly ruined) at Olagapuram (South Arcot Dt.) the relief of eight armed Durga with two devotees kneeling on both sides and Vishnu and his consorts are noteworthy. The walls of the two Brihadisvara temples of Tanjore and Gangaikonda-Chola-puram are embellished with numerous icons of large size and forceful execution. In the Chandesanugraha murti panel (PL.139) Siva with Parvati by his side, represented as holding the head of Chandesa with his hands and tying a long flower garland round it.Siva dominates the other figures.Chandesa's happiness at this high honour conferred on him by the god radiates from his face. Among many other sculptures at Gagaikonda-Chola-puram mention should be made of Dancing Ganesa (PL.140), Vishnu and Devi (PL.141) etc.

The Chola period is perhaps unique in respect of art in the medium of Bronze, with many master pieces. Among existing specimens in various museums of the world and in the temples of South India may be seen many fine figures of Siva in his various forms, Ardhanarisvara (PL.142), Vrishabhavahanamurti and his consort Parvati (PL.143) the seven mothers, Vishnu and his consorts Lakshmi and Bhudevi, Rama and Sita with their attendants, the Saiva saints, among whom Sambandar being most frequent, the child Krishna dancing on the serpent Kaliya and many other subjects convey adequately the glory of the Chola art. The bull *nandi* is missing from Vrishabhavahanamurti but would have been placed so that Siva's arm rested on it. The Chola bronze Parvati (PL.144) is supposed to be the very epitome of feminine grace, poise and sexuality.

The Nataraja image in its various forms holds the first place among the Chola bronzes. The Nataraja of the Brihadisvara temple at Tanjore, and three others, now in Chennai museum (PLs. 145, 146 and 147), and Natraja in the Nagesvara temple are among the best masterpieces of the time. The Natraja in the Nagesvara temple is one of the largest and finest images known. About Nataraja, Grousset observes: "whether he be surrounded or not by the flaming aureole of the *tiruvocci (prabhamandala)*, the circle of the world which he both fills and oversteps, the king of the Dance is all rhythm and exaltation. The tambourine which he sounds with one of his right hands draws all creatures in to this rhythmic motion and they dance in his company. The conventionalized locks of flying hair and the blown scarf tell of the speed of this universal movement, which crystallizes matter and reduces it to powder in turn. One of the left hands holds the fire which animates and devours the worlds in this cosmic whirl. One of the God's feet is crushing a Titan, for 'this dance is danced upon the bodies of the dead', yet one of the right hands is making the gesture of reassurance *(abhayamudra)*, so true it is that seen from the cosmic point of view and sub specie aeternitatis, the very cruelty of this universal determinism is kindly, as the generative principle of the furture. And, indeed, on more than one of our bronzes, the king of the dance wears a broad smile. He smiles at death and at life, at pain and at joy alike, or rather, if we may be allowed so to express it, his smile is both death and life, both joy and pain... From this lofty point of view infact, all things fall into their place, finding their explanation and logical compulsion. Here, art is the faithful interpreter of the philosophical concept. The plastic beauty of rhythm is no more than the expression of an ideal rhythm. The very multiplicity of arms, puzzling as it may seem at first sight, is subjected in turn to an inward law, each pair remaining a model of elegance in itself so that the whole being of Nataraja thrills with a magnificent harmony in his terrible joy, and as though to stress the point that the dance of the divine actor is indeed a sport *(lila)*—the sport of life and death, the sport of creation and destruction, at once infinite and purposeless—the first of the left hands hangs limply from the arm in the careless gesture *gajahasta* (hand as the elephant's trunk). And lastly as we look at the back view of the statue, are not the steadinesses of these shoulders which uphold the world, and the majesty of this Jove-like torso, as it were a symbol of the stability and immutability of substance while the gyration of the legs, in its dizzy speed would seem to symbolize the vortex of phenomenon".

The method employed in casting these bronzes is known as 'Cire – per due' or 'the lost – wax' process. The image was first modelled in wax and then covered with a soft clay mould. When the mould was fired, the wax drains out and replaced with molten metal. Once the cast had cooled, the mould was broken and the image was filed and polished. This process allows the production of highly detailed three dimensional images, each of which is unique. The images were used as *utsavamurtis* or festival deities.

The Cholas donated to their new temple in Tanjore nearly 60 bronze images of deities, of which two-thirds were given by Rajaraja, while the rest were donated by his sisters, queen, officials and nobles. You can still see the practice of touring the bronze images of gods at any of the great southern temple festivals.

Chola painting was evolved and developed out of Pallava-Pandyan forms, but we have no good amount of specimens, survived to the day. Most important remains of paintings of the period are; of course, seen in the darkest part of the edifice-*pradakshina* passage round the sanctum of the Tanjore temple, belonging to the time of Rajaraja I and Rajendra I, depicting scenes from Saivite mythology and the story of Tamil Saivite saint Sundarar. In one of the paintings we see a magnificent Cheraman perumal on a bejewelled white horse, while an angry Sundarar Nayanar wears a white coat, Siva as an old man. Just as in some of the Pallava rock-cut caves the royal portraits appear in sculptural representations, one of the early paintings in the temple presents King Rajaraja Chola with his *guru* Karuvurar (PL.148). Unlike the formal depictions of kings to come in later centuries, this example presents the great king, standing behind his guru, portraying a sense of humility, importance given to teaching and thus to the teacher, which was lost in later times. On the top of the panel on the west wall is the Kailasa scene with Siva seated in *yogasana* on a tiger skin with the *nandi* infront and a group of *rishis* with a couple of Apsara maidens dancing at the opposite end. The scene seems to depict an anecdote in the Saivite mythology, of two devotees on their journey to Kailasa on the invitation of Siva.

There is a barely-visible Dakshinamurti, in another painted scene, beneath a banyan tree on which monkeys are playing, while *rishis* and animals live together in the forest. There is a stillness of body and reverence on the face of the sages worshipping Dakshinamurti, in contrast to the vivacious animals. Flying *apsaras* and *gandharvas* complete the scene of palatial proportions.

The Tripurantaka panel on the north wall of the Tanjore temple is one of the master pieces of the Chola mural tradition. It is a battle scene, in which Siva is standing on the deck of the chariot with his left knee bent signifying an archer, and the right leg slightly raised and moves forward, typically in attacking position in war, his eight arms holding deadly weapons like bow, arrow, *khadga*, *sula* etc., and his vibrant frame and defiant expression suggesting vigorous action. The four headed Brahma driving the chariot. Infront are the horses of Asuras, facing Siva and his *ganas* and above is seen Durga on her lion thrusting a spear in to the body of Asura while lion is holding another by neck.

In another panel, Rajaraja Chola and his wives worshipping Nataraja are seen. It was the dance of Siva, as Nataraja presented in the golden *mandapam* of Chidambaram as well, the god is presented in exquisite jewellery on his body, his head-gear bedecked with jasmine garlands, beautifully featured eyes and eyebrows like a bow and his eyes looking compassionately. The whole presentation brings an enchanting view of the massive composition in bright colours.

The Chola-age artists applied lime plaster on the wall and painted the murals on the plaster while it was still wet. This demanded that they should do the sketches and complete the painting before the lime plaster dried up. What is significant about the Chola paintings at Tanjore is great emotion in all the faces, full of life and vigour, whether it is the compassion of the *guru* counselling Rajaraja or a contemplative *rishi,* a devout queen, an animated dancer or an angry Siva. There are two layers of paintings here: of the Nayak period of the 17th century on top, and below that, of the earlier Chola period. Most of the Chola paintings were rediscovered when the upper layer was removed to be preserved separately.

The delicate nature of the paintings and the gradual erosion due to pollution has necessitated the ASI to lock them up and can be seen only on obtaining a special permission. An elaborate tableaux of domestic, public and palace scenes are an excellent source of information about the Chola period and the court of Rajaraja, who commissioned them, is a good source of information. The paintings are huge and animated, bringing alive the greatness of the lord who destroys evil and ensures peace.

Sravanabelagola is a place for Jaina monuments. There are monuments of rare excellence in and around Sravanabelagola, which means, the "Belagola", or "White tank", famous for *sramana*, which transformed into *sravana*, in popular usage. The *sramana* or Jain *sanyasi* at the place is Gomatesvara, whose colossal image had been carved in a solid rock at the top of the cliff of one of the sacred hills at the place, Indragiri and Chandragiri, between which the sacred *tirtha* was nestled picturesquely.

These monuments were executed by the illustrious Gangas and the Hoysalas who had ardent devotion to Jainism, on the two sacred hills, of which mention has to be made of Chamundaraya *basadi* (PL.149), the largest and finest, besides a number of Jaina temples on Chandragiri hill. The *basadi* (temple) measures 21.3 m in length together with the portico on its eastern front and width of 11m, probably built about 980 A.D. But it seems to have undergone improvements in the early 12th century A.D., under the Chola hegemony, as it exhibits the features of Chola architecture, a pyramidal *sikhara* crowned by a domical finial.

Traditional accounts celebrate the place, as the one whereto Bhadrabahu, known as the last Sruttakevalin and preceptor or spiritual *guru* of Emperor Chandragupta Maurya (321-296 B.C.) resorted to, leading thousands of lay followers, when the country around Pataliputra had fallen under severe and prolonged famine condition. As such, he advised Chandragupta Maurya to make suitable arrangements for mobilization of the people, and his Jain sangha, from famine-stricken region, to a safer place. After a long journey down south, he and his 1200 followers had reportedly reached Sravanabelagola, where, Chandragupta Maurya, a disciple of Sruttakevalin, abdicated his kingdom and left the world by the yogic method of *sallekhana*. There is a cave at the place, where

Chandragupta and his teacher Bhadrabahu are said to have lived and the former performed *sallekhana*. The scene of Chandragupta having left the world is carved on the stone walls of the temple, Chandragupta *basadi*.

In the heart of the town there is a beautiful pond known as the Kalyani (PL.150) surrounded by a wall with gates and towers. Opposite Chandragiri hill is Indragiri hill, about 120 m high. The Indragiri hill is one solid rock and about 500 steps have been cut in the rock. The climb is rather steep and makes it seem long and exhausting. However, on reaching the top, where the colossal monolithic Gomatesvara, son of the first *Tirthankara* stands, one can forget the stress and strain of climbing up the hill, as they stand in awe before the giant statue. The nude figure of the *Tirthankara* (PL.151) about 17 m high, stands erect, facing the north, with his face full of serenity in his enjoyment of Final Release, *Nirvana*. He appears so much involved in his state of bliss, in the austere penance that ant-hills are rising at his feet and wild foliage creeping over his limbs, of which he takes no notice. According to the Jain tradition Gomatesvara is regarded as a Jain saint and in fact is the symbolical expression of Bahubali. The monolithic image is majestic, which is said to have been installed by Chamundaraya, the prime minister of the Ganga king Rachamalla IV in 983 A.D. according to inscriptions.

The most important occasion on which people in thousands make pilgrimage to the spot is at the time of *Mahamastakabhisheka*, the grand ablution of the *Tirthankara* from head, which is said to take place once in 12 years. Just on the eve of the ceremony scaffolding will be constructed to help the priests and devotees to go up and offer worship. After sacred bath with milk and ghee, the priests arrange for the great *abhisheka* of water with 1000 pots, to the chanting hymns, in accordance with the tenets in Jain *Agama* works. The *abhisheka* with water is followed by pouring of milk, coconut water, sugarcane juice, herbal mixtures, sandalwood paste, gold and silver flowers (PL.152). The *Mahamastakabhisheka* ceremony is one of the rare religious performances in the Indian religious tradition, performed for the peace and prosperity of mankind.

A typical Jain free standing pillar opposite the main entrance of the temple of Parsvanatha at Vindhyagiri is another master piece of art. The elaborate capital and finial at the top of the pillar is the work of art peculiar to the south. The *basadi* measures 21.2m in length together with the portico on its eastern front, and its width is 10.9 m. The sacred feet of Bhadrabahu in a cave here are worshipped even now. It is said that Chandragupta Maurya worshipped these sacred feet till his last day. But it must have been built originally about 980 A.D. although in its present form it looks more like a construtction of early 12th century A.D.

In the town of Sravanabelagola there are some fine temples with beautiful architecture. A temple is dedicated to the worship of 24 *Tirthankaras*. The image of Indra in dancing pose here is beautifully carved. Two similar but smaller statues, also monolithic were made in Kanara, one over 12.2 m high at Karkala in 1432 A.D. and the other at Yenur, about 10.7 m high in 1604 A.D.

8

Kakatiya Style

The Kakatiyas of Warangal occupied a position of Paramount importance in the history of South India in general and that of the medieval Andhra in particular. They established their sway over the entire Telugu speaking area in medieval time, and the period of their rule in the beginning of 12th to the first of 14th century heralded the golden age in the field of art and architecture, though it was mostly limited to the Telingana region. Rudradeva, Ganapatideva, Rudramadevi and Prataparudradeva were noteworthy personalities in the dynasty, as empire-builders. Great generals not only fought glorious battles to extend their kings boundaries but also constructed magnificent temples. Excellent speciments of Kakatiya art and architecture are seen in the temples at Hanumakonda, Palampet, Ghanpur, Nagulapadu, Manthane, Bejjanki and Dharmapuri etc.

The Kakatiyas were the subordinates of the Later Chalukyas of Kalyani before asserting independence and quite naturally, they inherited most of the traditions of their suzerains, in matters of polity and administration, as well as art and architecture. But they were not simply faithful imitators but had many things to contribute to the life and culture of the time out of their innovative thinking, suitable to the needs of the time. The period of Kakatiya rule witnessed remarkable socio-religious reformation, with the Buddhism and Jainism having been relegated to dark corners of time by the devotional cults of militant Saivism and Vaishnavism. Society appears to have been more crystallized into castes and subcastes, undoubtedly in the wake of great progress that had been possible in fields of agriculture, arts and crafts as well as commerce. The contemporary writings of Muslim chroniclers as well as travels of Marcopolo glowing allude to the wealth of Telingana, meaning the Telugu speaking country, under the Kakatiyas. Best examples of Kakatiya temples at Hanumakonda and other places in Karimnagar and Nalgonda districts, close to their capital, were built with the locally available granite and sand stone, in the construction upto their *vimanas,* with their superstructures were built with brick and lime. A special stone of black granite or basalt was used for pillars, jambs, lintels, and other decorative motifs as well as icons.

Kakatiya temples display considerable variety of ground plans, their gradual evolution and expansion depended very much upon the alignment of the *mukha-mandapa, ranga-mandapa, antarala* and *garbha-griha.* The Kakatiya architects seems to have generally favoured *trikuta* plan, in which three shrine chambers being attached to a single *maha-mandapa* or *ranga-mandapa*, on three sides, while the fourth one, the frontal, provided entry into it. Another type of ground plan is cruciform, in which three porches are provided on three sides of the *ranga-mandapa* and thus entry into it can be obtained from all sides, except the rear, where *antarala* and a *garbha-griha* had to be provided. This form of ground plan was used in cases, where the temples were dedicated to a single god, housed in the shrine chamber. The *mandapas* or pillared halls, pavilions, *toranas* and subsidiary shrines are judiciously organised and distributed round the main temple.

The pillars in Kakatiya temples display a great variety of designs of aesthetic imagination and finish, but in general, they may be reasonably categorized as the further development of pillar-type of the Dravidian architecture. They usually have their capitals with expanding mouldings and square brackets above. In the evolution of their pattern and application of decorative designs, they exhibit strong influence of the art of the later Chalukyas of Kalyana and the Hoysalas, especially in applying a lustrous polish, quite amazing to look at. They present great amount of exuberance and variety in designs and motifs and in their bold execution, with utmost care even to the minutest detail. The door-ways are master pieces of the Kakatiya art, meticulously planned, magnificently designed and marvellously ornamented. The *ranga-mandapas, antaralas,* and *garbha-grihas* are provided with doorways.

No discussion on Kakatiya architecture would be complete without reference to the *madanikas* or the graceful female figures on the brackets above the pillars in the *ranga-mandapa* as if supporting its massive cornice, found in the temples at Palampet and Ghanapur. They are arranged in pairs, springing from the shoulders of the central square blocks of the pillars placed on the *vedibandha* of the *ranga-mandapa.* The beautiful figures of damsels, in various charming postures and poses, are the most beautiful treatment of the hair, of the drapery and of the ornaments and finally their graceful stances, the rare and uncommonly seen beauty and charm in the natural creation products, of the Kakatiya art. In the sensitiveness of the rendering of the live flesh in the creation of feminity is visible, in their long and delicate bodies and thin nails, exceptionally arresting. The smooth and resilient flesh seemingly pleasant to touch, lends·sensuous and voluptuous effect to the figure. The female beauty here, with full blooded sensuality of their firm breasts, dramatically contrasting with their slim waists is urban, sophisticated and classical in its idea and content.

The urban agglomeration of Hanumakonda, Warangal and Kazipet, is like any other city housing about ten lakh population, with narrow lanes, dingy shops. The colour and luster of oriental towns, bombarded by modernity are resplendently visible in the modern city of Warangal. The lanes, shops and the new set of people appear to have sprouted to veil the ancient monuments that are spread not only in the town, which served as the capital of the Kakatiyas in the 12th and 13th centuries, but throughout Warangal district.

The Ganapesvaram inscription of the time of Ganapatideva mentions, Hanumakonda, the first capital of Kakatiyas was "a mighty and lovely city.... the ornament of the Andhra Country, as if it was the capital of the goddess of fortune, full of delight *(rati)* like the city of cupid, raised to a great state by the rise of the excellent and full grace *(lila) of* God Siva who was there." The capital was shifted from Hanumakonda to Warangal, a nearby town, which was developed as a great city by the Later Kakatiyas, Rudramba and her grandson and successor, Prataparudra.

The excavations at the fort reveal the splendour of the city-a city that once was great as Vijayanagar. The fort consists of three rampart walls, the outer wall, built of mud, about 3.04m high, runs surrounding the villages Karparti, Kazipet and Hanumakonda. But now it is broken at several places and not easily recognizable. The second fort is another huge mud wall out side Warangal, which had four gates on four cardinal directions, surrounded by a deep moat filled with water. It was impossible for the enemy to cross the moat with water consisting of man-eater reptiles in order to get up the huge wall, of about 6.1 m high. At present there is the old town inside the fort. About one furlong inside this enclosure there is the third fort built of stone, generally called *Kanchukota*, i.e., bronze fort. A similar moat, probably deeper than the outer one is kept always full of water. This fort is provided with more bastions than the outer one. According to *Velugotivari Vamsavali*, a chronicle of Velamas in Telugu, it had 72 bastions which were placed under the charge of 72 *nayakas* or generals. One can climb over this rock fort only from inside, and from outside it is absolutely insurmountable. In side this inner fort perhaps the king's palace, the Svayambhudeva temple and the residences including officers of important dignitaries in the state service were located

At present we find only two walls, the mud wall and the stone wall along with the moats, and the four pairs of the entrance gates. After going inside we can see the four massive *torana* gate ways (PL.153) supposed to be the entrance gates of the Svayambhudeva temple, a grandiloquent temple, having been subjected vandalism in the course of warfare with Muslims. Some scholars say that these are victory gates constructed to celebrate the victory of Rani Rudrama Devi. We find nothing here but broken pieces of sculptures, pillars (PL.154) and exquisitely carved stone screens (PL.155), whisper tales of past grandeur and magnificence. There are also temples dedicated to the gods Virabhadra, Venkatesa, Sambhudeva and other deities. Ulughkhan, who laid siege to Warangal in 1321 A.D., described the city in glowing terms. Standing on the high wall of the fort he saw water fountains, on all sides, fruit gardens full of mangoes, bananas, Jack fruits etc. and flower gardens full of Champak, Jasmine and other varieties of flowers.

The earliest among the Kakatiya structures of importance is the *trikuta* or triple shrine popularly known as the thousand pillared temple (PL.156) at *Hanumakonda* (Warangal), built by Kakati Rudradeva in 1163 A.D. In the precincts of the temple, he planted a stone inscription in order to proclaim his sovereign authority.

The temple shows the transition from the architectural traditions of the Western Chalukyas to whom the Kakatiyas were subordinates in the past, imbibing the meritorious qualities of the style, before the latter evolved their own typical style of temple building. It is a *trikuta* shrine, dedicated to Siva, Vishnu and Surya has a *nandi-mandapa* infront of the temple of Siva in the centre. There is a dilapidated *ranga-mandapa,* (PL.157) in the same compound, separated from the main temple, usually called a thousand pillared *mandapa* and the name came to be eventually applied to the temple itself, but actually there are not more than 250 pillars. None of the three shrines of the *trikuta* contains a *vimana* at present and it gave scope to debates, whether the temple was left unfinished or subjected to any vandalism of the later Muslim invaders. If it were the former case, there is every possibility that the temple must have undergone some modifications probably during the reign of Ganapati deva when the present polished structures replaced the old rough ones. Of the *nandi-mandapa,* now open to sky only the *nandi* is preserved (PL.158).

The temple measures over 31 m x 25 m and is raised on a platform *(jagati) to a* height of 1 m of which a series of *kantha* and *pattika* mouldings are visible. Over the *jagati,* the base is composed of a *bhitta*, *jadya kumbha, tripattakumuda, kantha,* and *pattika.* Above this similar mouldings are repeated (PL159). The shrine models over the *kutastambhas* and on the *bhadra* niche are like the Nagara *sikhara* with a *kalasa* finial. Most of the niches do not preserve any images and the figures that survive are badly disfigured.

The triple shrine, all the three opening in to a common *ranga-mandapa* with four pillars in the central *ankana* and the dwarf pillars along the *kaksasana* is high in stature, airy and imposing. The tall *citrakhanda* pillars are cut into octagonal bands, cubical and finally *sirsa.* The pillars in the *mukha-mandapa,* the door ways, the *panavatta* of the Siva-*linga* and the *nandi* exhibit exquisite decoration and the highest degree of polishing. The ceiling in the central section has Siva - Nataraja and *astadikpalas* and the *kirttimukha* in arabesques are found on the corners. The doorways to the *garbha-griha* are of *Panchasakha* variety. The *dvarapalas* at the base, the Gajalakshmi in *lalata* are other features. Originally the entire structure might have got one thousand pillars, as the name *veyyi - stambhala gudi* indicates and obviously some parts in the main *trikuta* structure and in the *ranga-mandapa* are lost.

The 1.8 m high *nandi* is a splendid example of the art of 12th century. To quote Dhaky "The *nandi* has a cubistic head and front clarified by chains of neck ornaments that suggest gold... In general the Andhra bulls do not possess the sophistication of the Kuntala ones, like those at Balagamve; but they exhibit a considerable degree of masculine prowess".

The Ramappa temple (PL.160) at *Palampeta* forms another interesting group. In architectural and sculptural beauty it is second only to the temples of Belur and Halebid of the Hoysala Empire in Karnataka. It was constructed by Recherla Rudra, the famous general of Ganapatideva, in about 1213 A.D., states an inscription at the place. It is actually known after its architect-sculptor rather than the king who commissioned it. The temple situated by the side of the great lake called *Ramappa Cheruvu* which is about 13 sq. km. extent. An exquisite example of *vimana* form, this temple is raised over a high *Jagati* of 2m and comprises a *ranga-mandapa* and *antarala* and a *garbha-griha*. The former has porched entrances on three sides and the *pancharatha* scheme is adopted for the *garbha-griha*. The four storeyed brick super structure with its schematised and faceted *kuta, salas* and *panjara* elements has a distinctive character. The exterior of the *ranga-mandapa* has highly ornamented *kakshasanas.* The temple is remarkable for the bracket figures (PL.161) which spring from the outer pillars to appear as supporting the roof projections. Some of these figures are *nagini, nartaki, mardala,* etc., in different poses. Nude beauty *nagini* holds serpents all over her body (PL.162). She forgets herself in her ecstasy and hugs them closely. The carving of the pillars is most elegant and it represents musicians and scenes from Bhagavata, like *Gopika-vastrapaharana* and *rasakrida*. The ceilings of the *ranga-mandapa* have, lozengs, Siva-Nataraja etc. The architraves, doorjambs, lintels and friezes are all richly carved and illustrate the masterly skill of the architects.

A *nandi-mandapa,* the Kamesvara and the Katesvara shrines are situated in the compound in a ruined state. In the eastern entrance of this temple stands the beautifully symmetrical and life like image of the monolithic *nandi* with marvellous smoothness and polish, displaying extraordinary skill in carving the numerous details of its ornamental hangings.

The excavations in the fort area in Orugallu (Warangal) exposed to view some structures of the Svayamabhudeva temple supposed to have been built by Ganaptideva. The temple was built of large blocks of neatly chiselled masonry. The Kakatiya architects were adepts in using large slabs is evident from many of their temples but it is especially true in the case of present example. It is quite amazing to look at the single stone slab .6 m thick and 4.9 m square used for flooring the central apartment, which is beautifully polished to shine like a mirror. The bases of a *rangamandapa* and *parivara* shrines are extant. The more striking feature of this temple is the erection of the four gateways or *toranas* which face the four cardinal points, with freizes of fine sculpture and flanked by swans, or *hamsas* on them (PL.153). The *toranas* show the survival of this form from Sanchi until 13th -14th centuries A.D.

The *nandi* images of the Kakatiya period are regarded as master pieces of its kind. Best examples come from Palampet, Thousand pillared temple, Sambhunigudi, Ghanpur, Kolanupalli, with heavy garlands of bells in their necks (PL.158). Among the decorative sculptures scenes of folk dancers, especially in the *kolata* are frequently presented, probably suggesting that the pleasant scenes rural life were especially favourite to the sculptors. Whole panel of danseuses, with their accompanying drummers show the progress of dance and music. All the huge *ranga-mandapas* earmarked for dances are testimonies for their aesthetics.

Research on these temples and, of course, the other structures in the Warangal Fort, revealed some interesting things that the temples and *toranas* of victory, or gateways were built on foundations of sand. In modern structures it is a common practice to deposit sand at the lowest layer of the foundation on which cement and concrete are spread. The Kakatiya architects seems to have started digging the site, meant for the construction

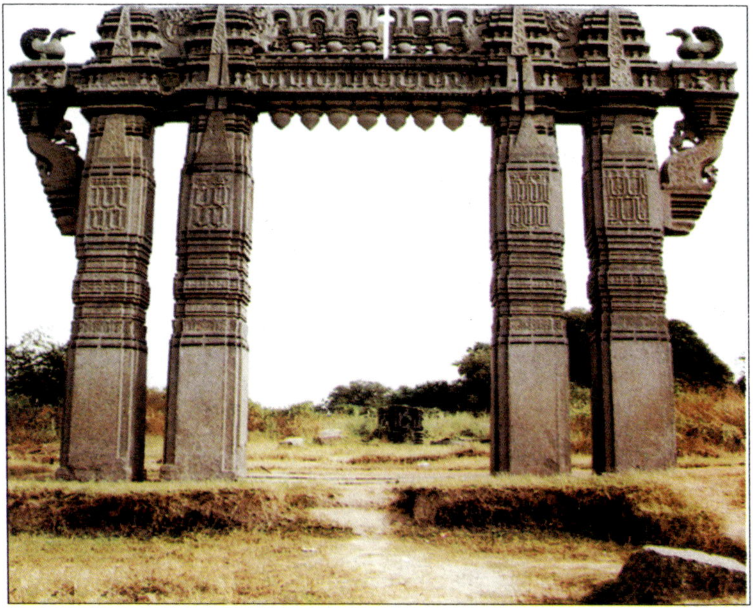

153. Warangal, Fort, *torana* (gate).

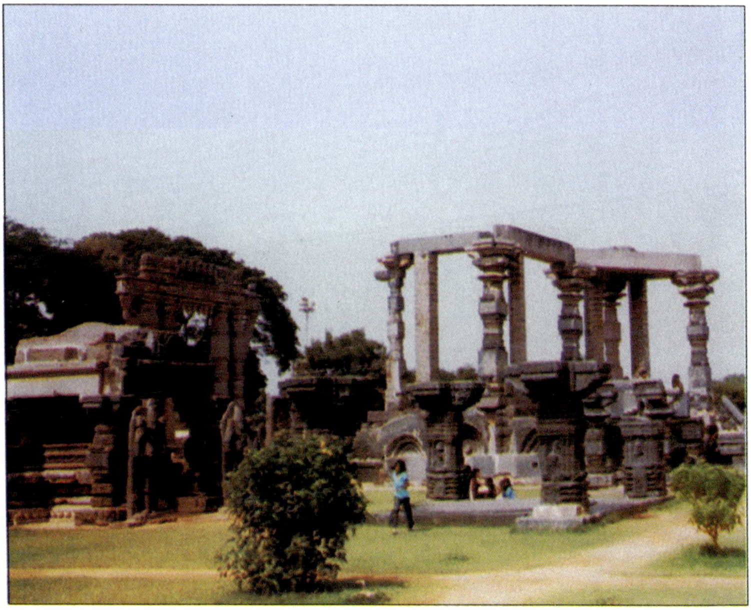

154. Warangal, Fort, broken pieces of sculptures and pillars.

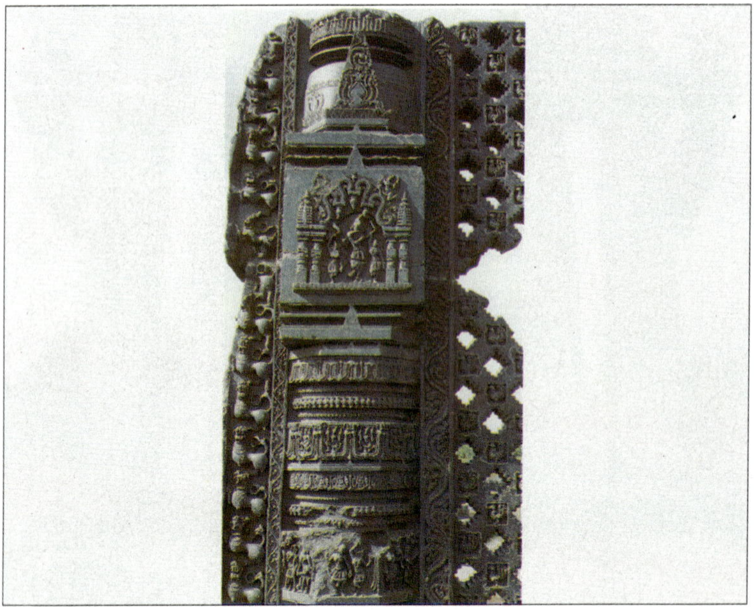

155. Warangal, Fort, stone screens.

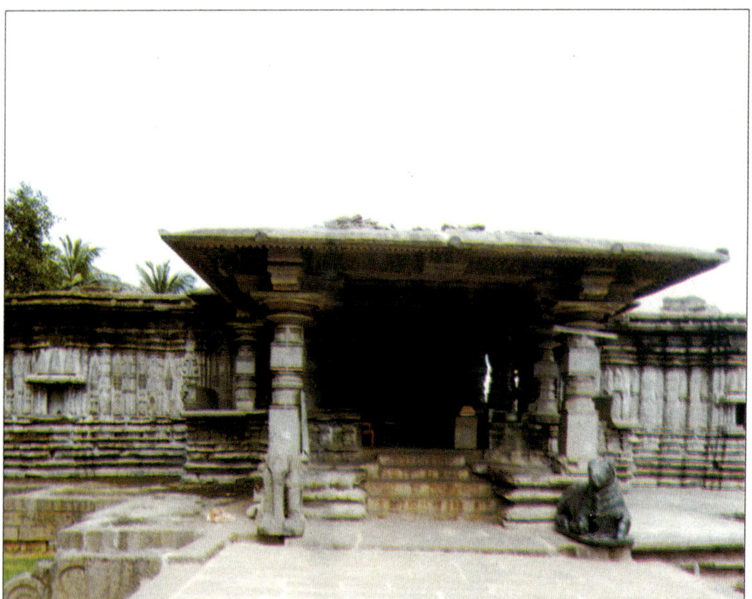

156. Hanumakonda, Thousand pillared temple, general view.

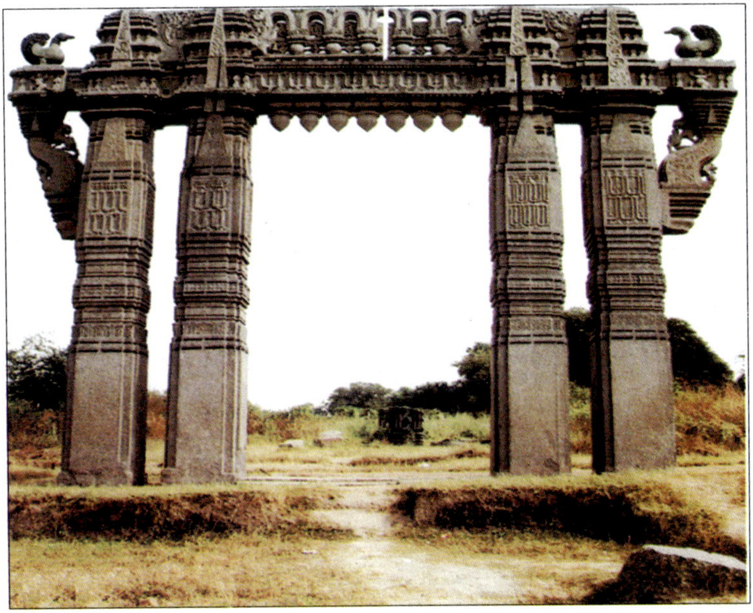

153. Warangal, Fort, *torana* (gate).

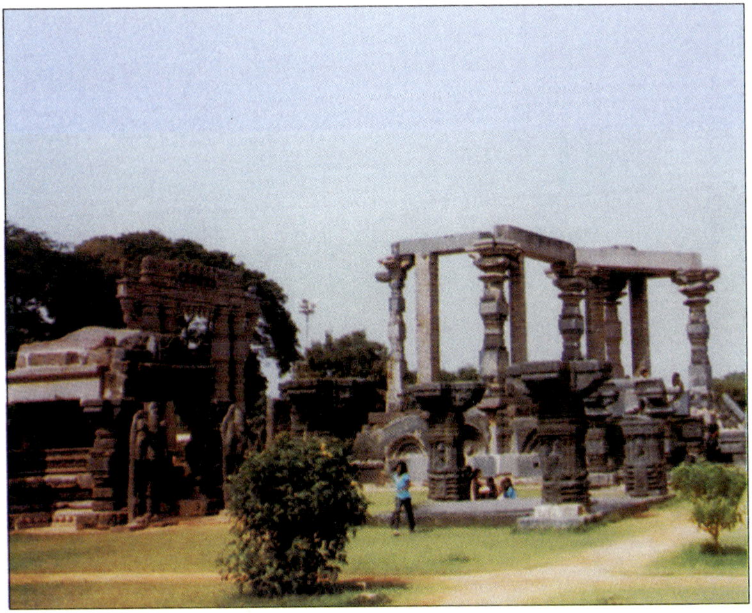

154. Warangal, Fort, broken pieces of sculptures and pillars.

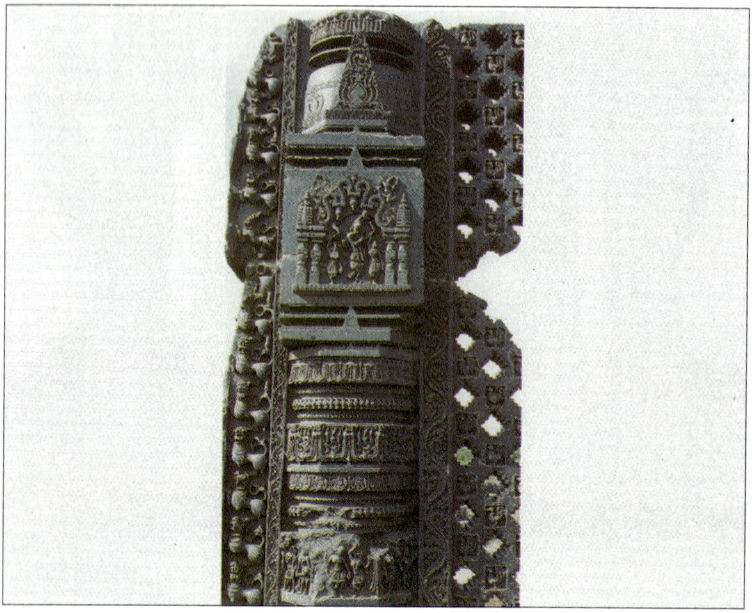

155. Warangal, Fort, stone screens.

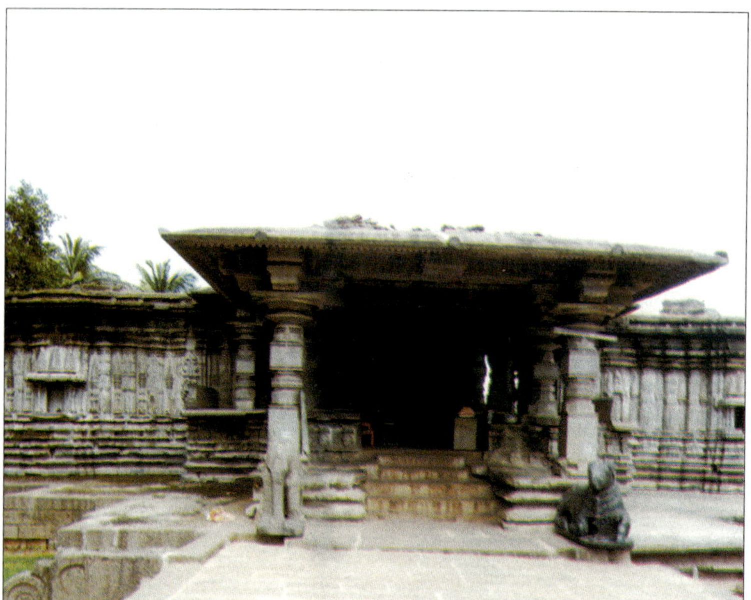

156. Hanumakonda, Thousand pillared temple, general view.

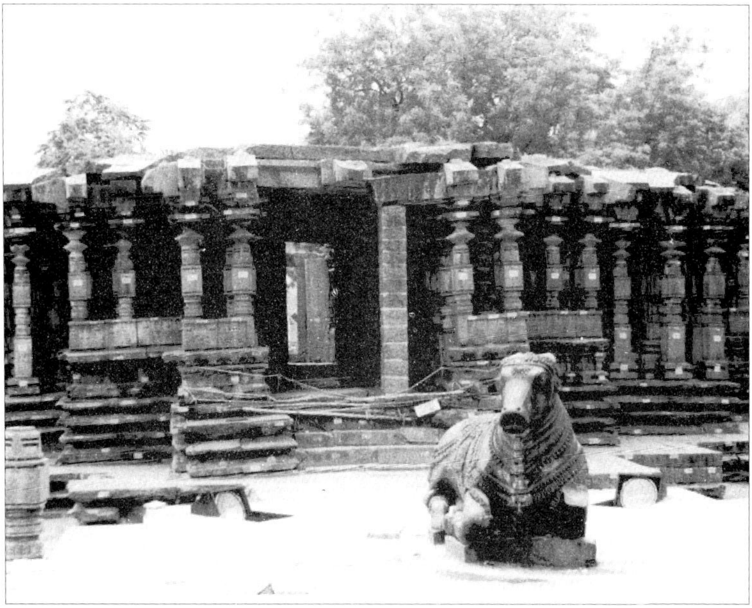

157. Hanumakonda, Thousand pillared temple, ranga-mandapa.

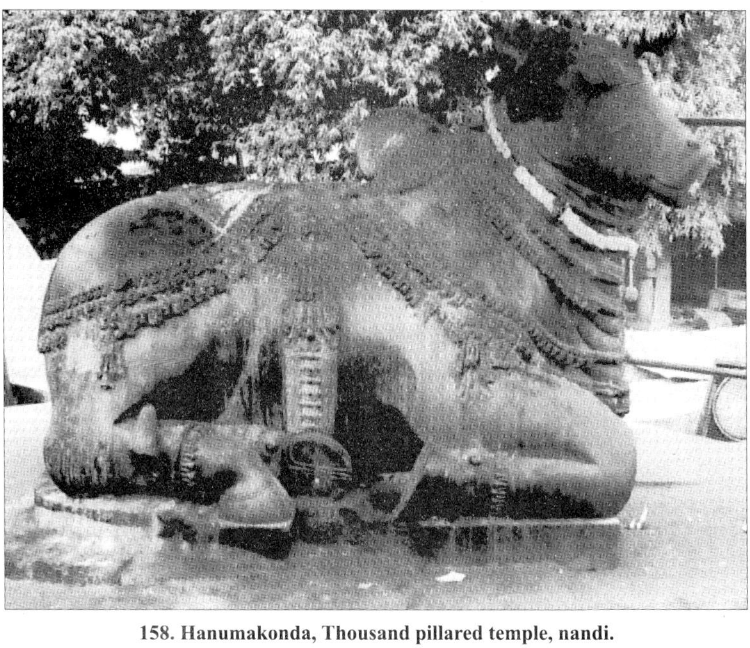

158. Hanumakonda, Thousand pillared temple, nandi.

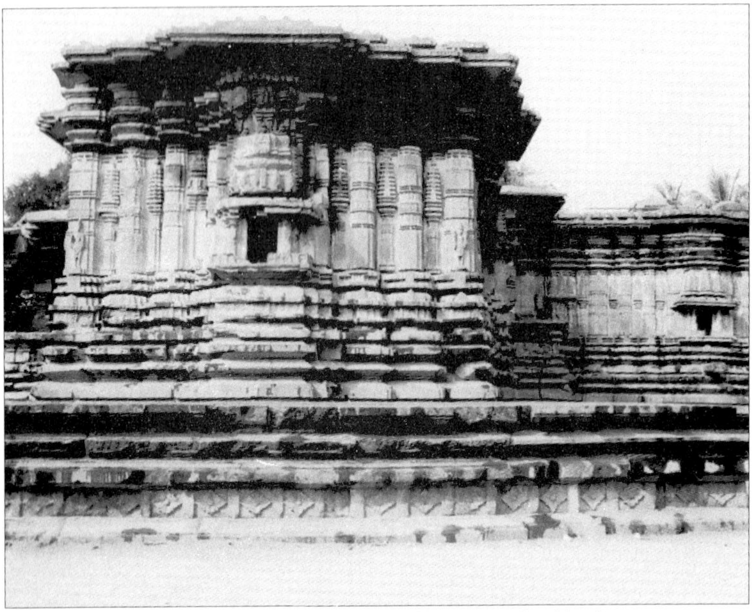

159. Hanumakonda, Thousand pillared temple, side view.

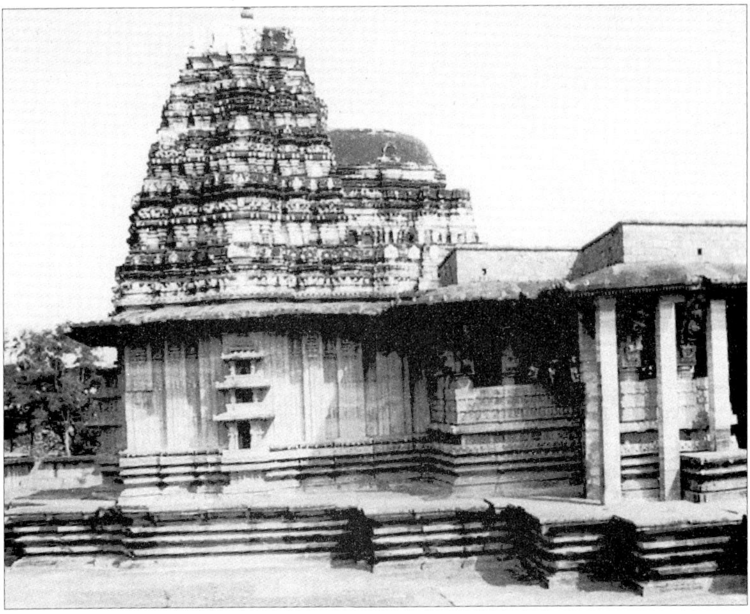

160. Palampeta, Ramappa temple, general view.

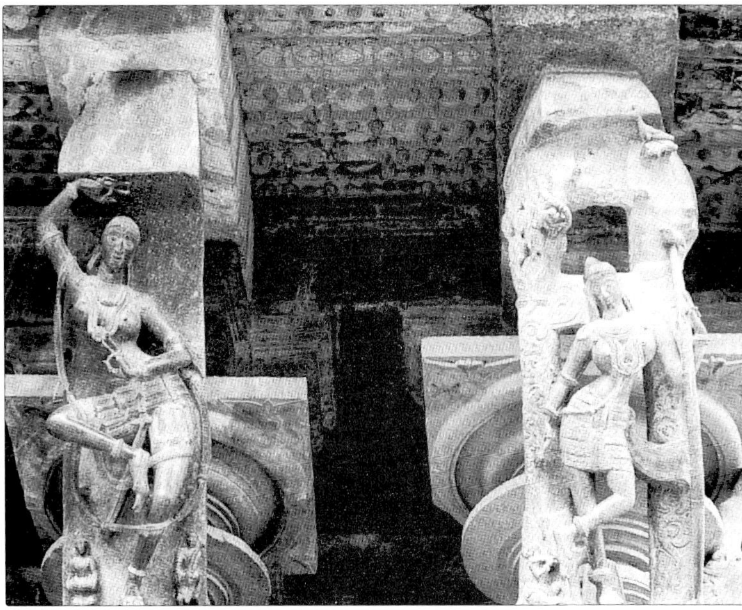

161. Palampeta, Ramappa temple, bracket figures.

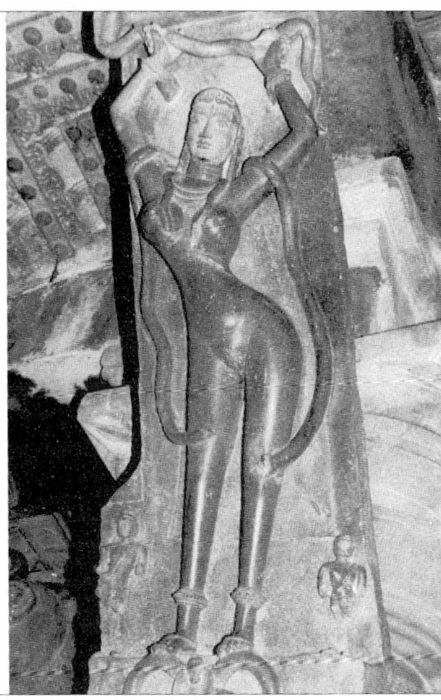

162. Palampeta, Ramappa temple, nude beauty nagini.

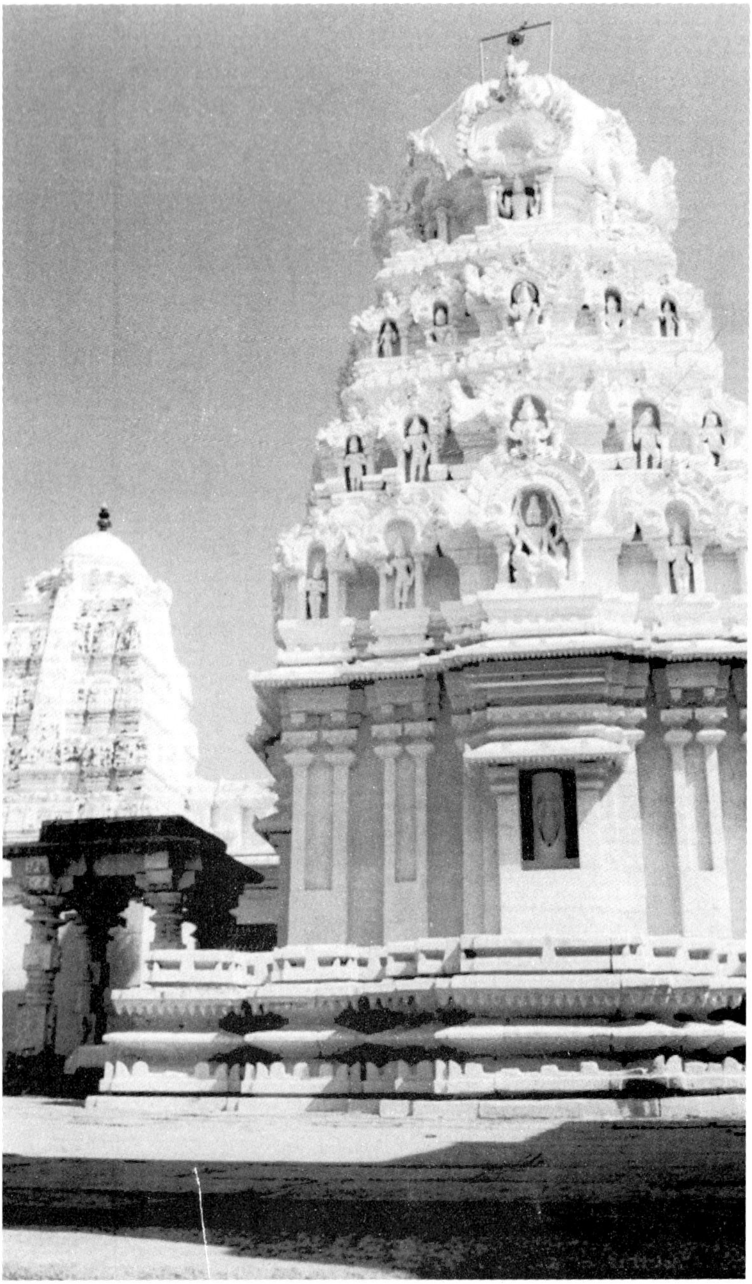

163. Tripurantakam, Tripurantakesvara temple, side view.

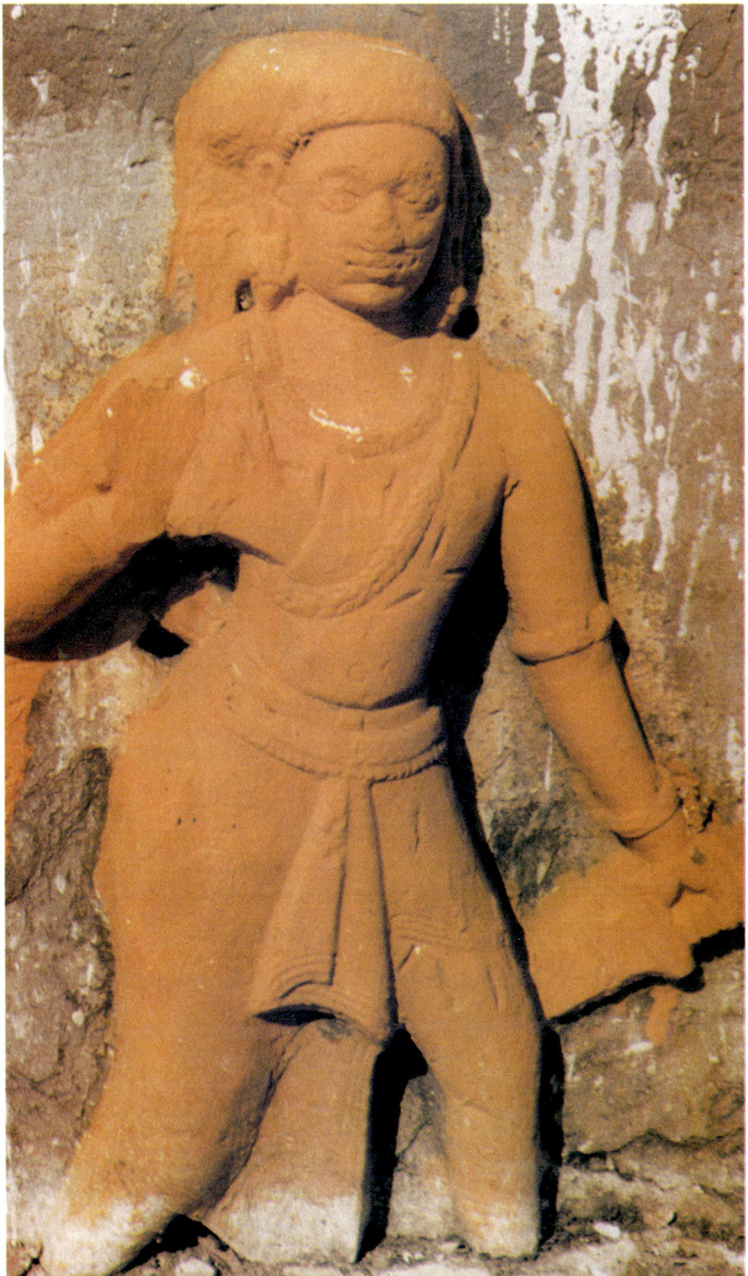

164. Tripurantakam, Devi shrine, viragal.

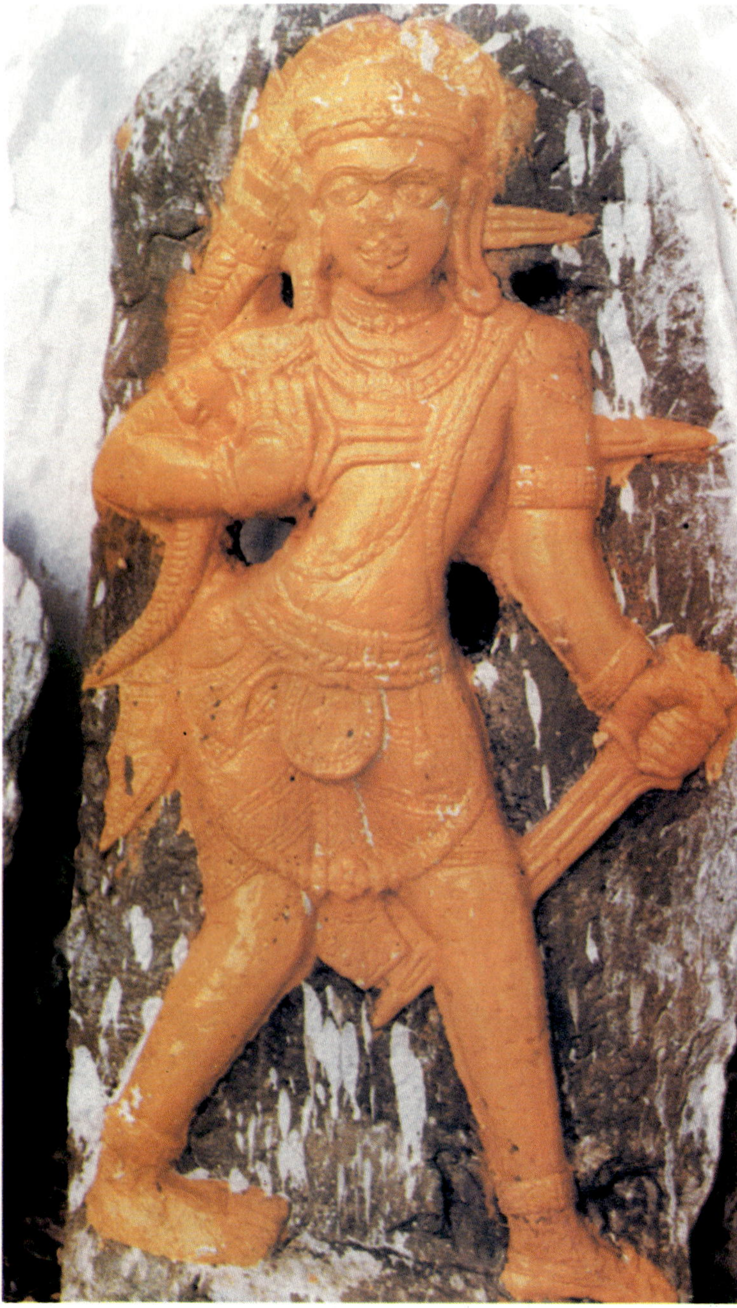

165. Tripurantakam, Devi shrine, viragal.

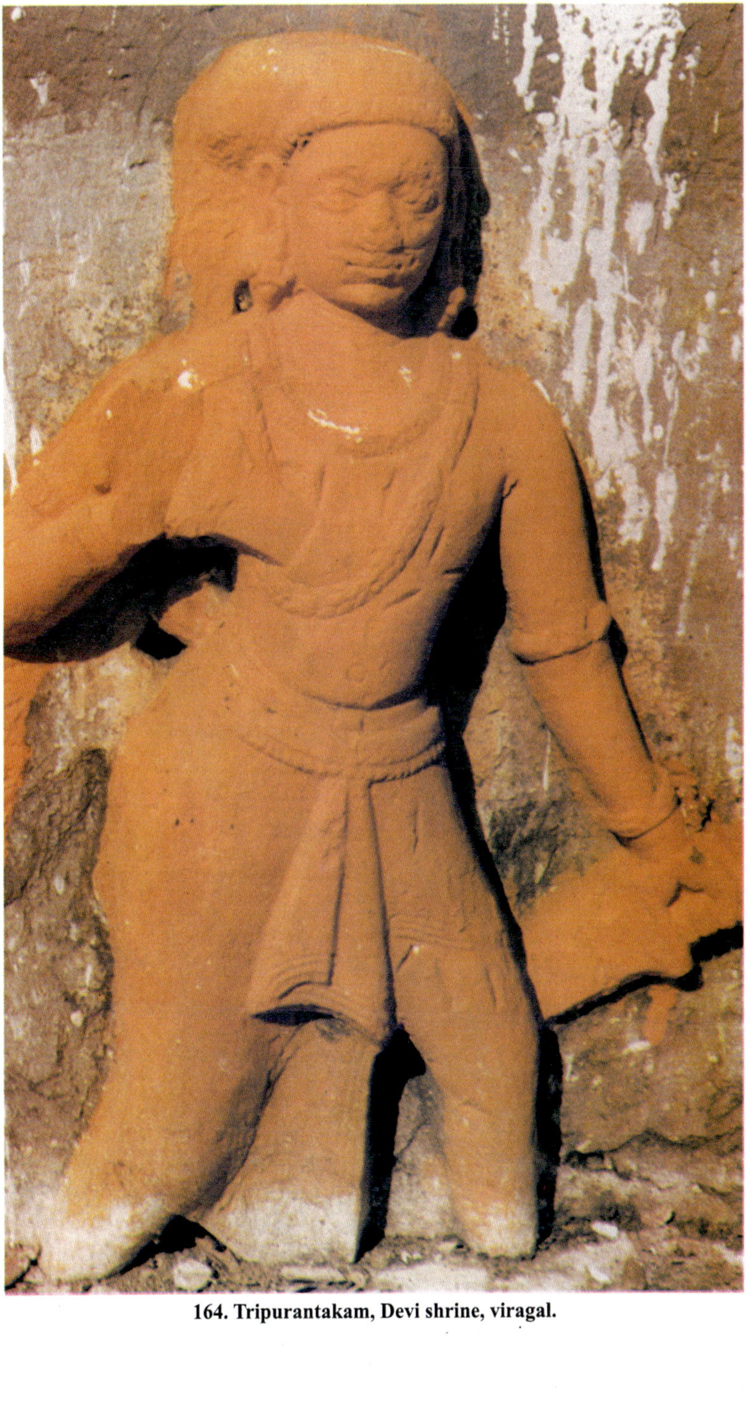

164. Tripurantakam, Devi shrine, viragal.

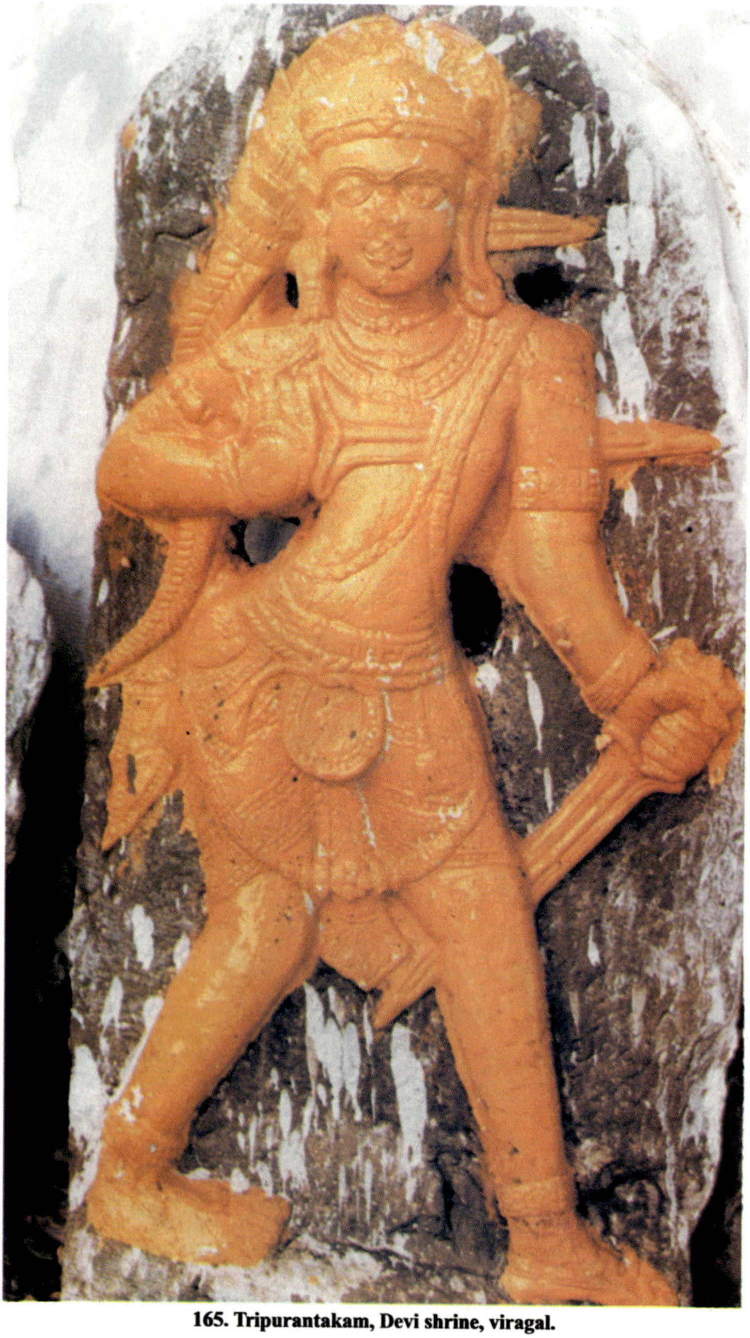

165. Tripurantakam, Devi shrine, viragal.

of a palace, or a temple, until they hit boulders, and then filled with sand, before they raise the structure. The boulders that were cut and chiseled out were piled one above the other, aesthetically one on top of the other, with out any lime or any other binding material and the structures are supported by iron girders. The walls are thick and have three layers of rock, sand and again rock-which means the hollow between the two stones, is filled with sand. If the structures have sunk due to pressure on the sand based foundation, this would have been suggested by the presence of water-logging in the foundation crevices.

It is important to note that structures in the vicinity, constructed by Chalukyas who preceded the Kakatiyas or the Vijayanagar kings who followed them have not suffered so much of destruction as the Kakatiya structures. This has been attributed to some faulty methods used by the Kakatiya architects in their construction. Chalukya and Vijayanagar kingdoms temples do not have sand-foundations as the Kakatiya structures and one can convince himself by observing the temples that they were subjected to destruction more out of natural factors than vandalism of invading armies.

The ruins inside the fort, which one has to reach through a two-layered mud-wall looks pathetic. A mere glance at the place, which is now punctuated with paddy fields and electric poles drawing wires to reach the village-settlements that have sprouted through out, reveals that there was a huge palace which has come down like a pack of cards, as suggested by the sculptural remains of trunk less elephants, the *nandi* images in hundreds, the panels- and above all the lofty *toranas*. Many beautiful faces have been chiseled out-missing are huge panelsof danseuses, *hamsa*-birds et al!

Tripurantakam is a small town in the Prakasam district, to the west of which, is a low lying hillock, known as Kumaragiri, on which a great Saivite *tirtha* and a centre of Saivite religio-philosophical culture flourished in medieval times. Under the early Kakatiyas Tripurantakam became a centre of the

Kalamukhas, probably influenced by Srisailam. Later, a branch of the Golakimatha was established in the temple.

Tripurantakam, like Srisailam, is a combination of sacred places for Siva and Sakti. The temple of Tripurasundari at the place is a *Saktipitha*, which is in the midst of a tank surrounded by *kadamba* trees; the *kadamba* trees are particularly favourite to the goddess. In spite of her name, she is a fearful goddess and local traditions say that Acharya Sankara turned the image with her face towards the back wall, so that the visiting devotees might not be frightened.

The Tripurantakesvara temple (PL.163) was constructed by Santa Sambhu, son of Visvesvaracharya under the orders of King Kakati Ganapatideva in 1255 A.D. The Devi temple was built by the sister of Ganapati in 1209 A.D. and the *chikatimidde* or *galimandapam*, the *matha* was erected by one Dharma Sivacharya in 1247 A.D. Local character is evident in the Tripurantakesvara temple, as it has a *mukha-mandapa,* instead of the usual *ranga-mandapa.* The base, the use of heavy pilasters on the walls, the *kostha panjaras,* and the massive pillars exhibit the features of Kakatiya style found in Telingana region. The *sikhara* is highly renovated recently. The western *gopura* and steps are also recently renovated. Mention should be made of the *Bhumija sikhara* of the Devi shrine.

Lithic representations of the devotee's acts of heroism attest to the prevalance of Virasaivism in certain centres. At Tripurantakam, with in the courtyard and infront of the central shrine of Tripurasundari, are arranged in a line a number of hero-stones *(virakals)* representing human figures in various postures, some with a dagger thrust into their necks or abdomen and some driving their daggers in to the left thigh with one hand and raising a weapon with the other in order to stab themselves in the chest (PL.164). One peculiar feature of some of these figures is the long braided hair which is gracefully allowed to hang right up to the knee (PL.165). An inscription on one of the *virakals* in Tripurasundari temple, which may, on paleographical grounds, be referred to the13th century, seems to explain the real situation. It runs: *svasti srimatu Somasiva gurudevaru Alladda Viramallandanu virunivariki melu gavalan=ani tana tala Tripuradevkin=ichche* (Hail! the glorious Somasivagurudeva offered to Tripuradevi his own head, so that good may befall to the hero called Alladda Viramalla). Another record, apparently a part of it lost states at its conclusion, "This is the head to the goddess". Still another refers to 'Chavundaraya Vira the brother-in-law of Telunguraya'. From these it looks as if the figures were meant to represent cases of either suicide or human sacrifice to which people in those days must have had free recourse, under the belief that the goddess would please with their sacrifice and ward off any evil. The hero-stones so full of life and animation suggest the spirit of age.

9

Vibrant Hoysala Art

The Hoysalas ruled over Mysore and the neighbouring regions for a period of two and half centuries from 1047 to 1300 A.D. Separated from each other by 14 km, the villages of Belur and Halebid, in the Hassan district of Karnataka state, are known in the medieval times as Velapura and Dvarasamudra, respectively and they served as capitals of Hoysala kings. Like the Yadavas of Devagiri, the Hoysalas claimed their origin to Yadu, the ancestor of Lord Krishna. There is an interesting legend about the origin of the name Hoysala, that an ascetic in the temple of goddess Vasanthika at Sosavur, on being threatened by a tiger, called out Hoy, sala (strike, sala), where upon Sala, the legendary founder of the kingdom, rushed forward and slew the beast. This daring event might have been commomerated by the Hoysalas by adopting the tiger as their royal emblem and it often represented in the sculptural art in most of the Hoysala temples.

From their beginnings as tribal chieftains, the Hoysalas were probably the vassals of the Western Chalukyas and following the latter's fall, they not only proclaimed independence but also involved themselves in bitter struggles with the Yadavas of Devagiri for supremacy over Karnataka and Deccan plateau.

It was under Bittideva Vishnuvardhana (1106-1141 A.D.) that major territorial expansions and more lasting contributions to art and culture were made. The Kesava temple at Belur with its lyrically beautiful bracket figures was built at this time, as also the equally inspiring Hoysalesvara temple at Halebid. The Vishnuvardhana's kingdom comprised the whole of Mysore, Salem, Coimbatore, Bellary and Dharwar districts, as well as the western parts of modern Rayalasima as well. Originally a Jain, Bittideva eventually came under the influence of the famous Srivaishnava sage, Acharya Ramanuja and became a Vaishnava; and thus some scholars suggest tha he assumed the name Vishnuvardhana, following the change of religion.

Viraballala II (1173-1220 A.D.), the grandson of Vishnuvardhana attained paramount authority over the Chola kings in Tamil country, whom he rescued from the Pandyan invasions, but it made the Hoysala kingdom to involve in continuous warfare with the latter, thereon. Undoubtedly, the kingdom became one of the most powerful in the peninsular India, by the close of 12th century, largely due to the exploits of Vishnuvardhana, but shortly after, it was subjected to Muslim invasions along with its rivals, the Yadavas of Devagiri and the Kakatiyas of Warangal. Malik Kafur and Khawaja Haji, the generals of Alauddin Khilji, in 1310 A.D., shattered the kingdom and plundered its wealth, especially in the possession of the temples at Halebid and finally, it succumbed to the invasions of Muhammad bin Tughlaq about the year 1327 A.D.

The Hoysalas built several other structures all over Karnataka, but not as large and magnificent as the temples, especially the two at Belur and Halebid.

There are more than 200 temples of this period, dedicated to various gods, but mainly to Vishnu and Siva. But the statues of both the deities together with their consorts adorn the outer walls. Thus, inspite of the Hoysalesvara temple being dedicated to Siva, a large number of figure sculptures Vaishnavite themes, depicting his *avataras*-as tortoise in the creation myth; as Rama following the golden deer; of Krishna bearing the Govardhan hill on his little finger, etc., are provided with utmost devotion and attention to their artistic treatment. More unusual are the niches in the chief cell of the Kesava temple at Somnathpur, housing the images of Ganapati and Mahisasuramardini along with main idol of Vishnu.

The Hoysala architects used soap stone (called chloride schist by geologists) which is found in abundance in the Karnataka state. It is closing textured and very tractable to the chisel. The masonary could finish the sculptures carved in more minute and exquisite detail. The main temple in general, possesses the *garbha-griha* with a vestibule infront, connecting it with the *navaranga.* In front of this there was often a *mukha-mandapa.* The single celled shrine of the earlier period was developed in to a twin-celled and some times a multi-celled temple having all essential parts duplicated.

Another notable feature of the Hoysala temples is their star-shaped ground plan, and was set on a high plat form *(jagati),* rising to a height of about 2.1 m, providing space for going around the temple, as *pradakshina-patha.* The *adhishthana* of the temple, on its exterior provides horizontal bands separated by *pattikas*, sculptured panels of processions of elephants, lions, horsemen (PL.166), *makaras* etc. A band of spiral foliage follows thereon, at the level of the eyes of spectators, a wider frieze depicting scenes from puranic stories, in a continuous way of narration, executed with great effect and a considerable wealth of detail. Above this is a border of *yalis* with spirals of foliage issuing from their mouths, and crowning all these panels, is a running frize of *hamsas.*

The lower walls of the *vimana* contained ornate niches holding images of gods under foliated canopies, and interestingly the artisans have carved their own names on pedestals of many of these.Signed works of art as at any current art Gallery. The *sikhara* seperated by the wide projecting cornice from the body of the temple below keeps the stellate formation, but its vertical lines are balanced by horizontal mouldings. Each tier of the tower adorns miniature shrines and niches.

The shape of the pillars and their capitals is another remarkable feauture of this style. The shaft is a single black of stone designed into beautiful shapes, probably by turning on a large lathe, but their bases remaining square. The lathe-turned stone pillars are made to resemble those of wooden temples of Kerala. Sloping bracket-stones were fixed to the capitals, using the technique of pegs and sockets, the brackets, also being monolithic. They are finely finished with carvings of figure sculptures as well as leafy aureoles known as *madanika* figures, with their fine finish rivaling that of the figures in the niches of the *vimana*.

These Hoysala temples were basically developments in plan and presentation of the South Indian style, in general, but distinguish themselves with the fine workmanship in stone, probably that of ivory worker or goldsmith. The jewellery, head-dresses and other details depicted on the figures give a fair idea of the social life of the times.

Belur's chief attraction is the Chennakesava temple (PL.167). *Chenna* in Kannada means "beautiful". The Belur temple is dedicated to beautiful Lord Krishna, in the name of Kesava. The temple was built by Bittideva Vishnuvardhana commemorating his victory over the Cholas at Talakad. The beautiful image of Kesava is believed to have been installed in the sanctum sanctorum in 1117 A.D. Though initially built by Vishnuvardhana, the temple underwent additions under his son and grandson.

Though its superstructure is now missing it has three entrances, on three sides of the pillared hall, "approached by a flight of steps flanked by a pagoda-like shrine, the last a useful note of architectural emphasis". The main pillars of the hall and its recessed ceiling have varied carvings. The hall measures 28 m by 23.8 m with 46 pillars of different designs. It appears that the design and production of each pillar was entrusted to a

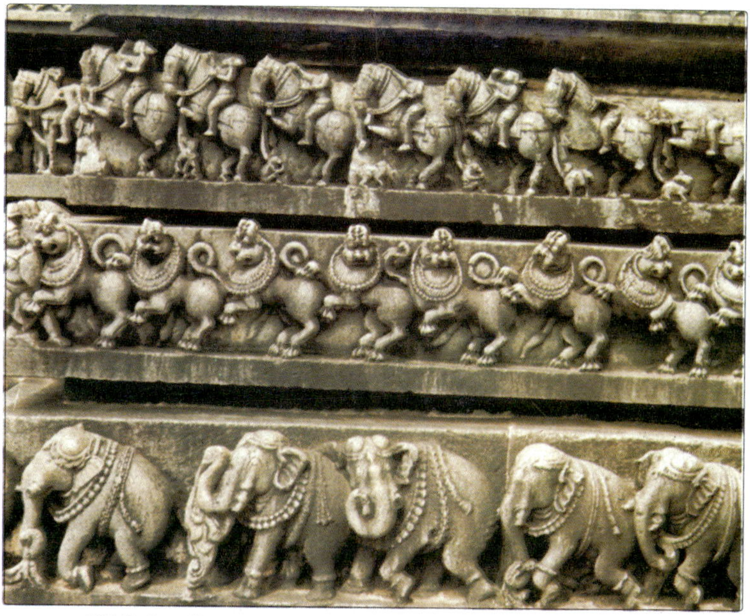

166. Belur, Chennakesava temple, adhishthna details, partial view.

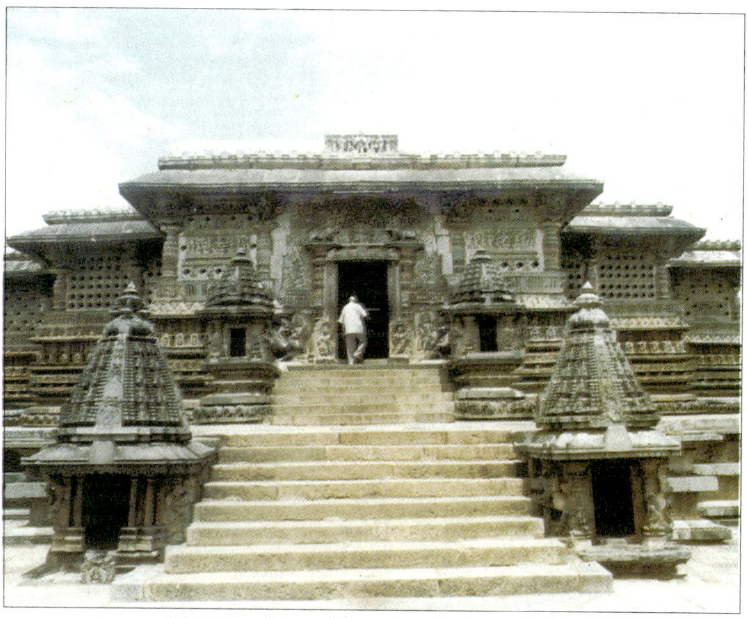

167. Belur, Chennakesava temple, general view.

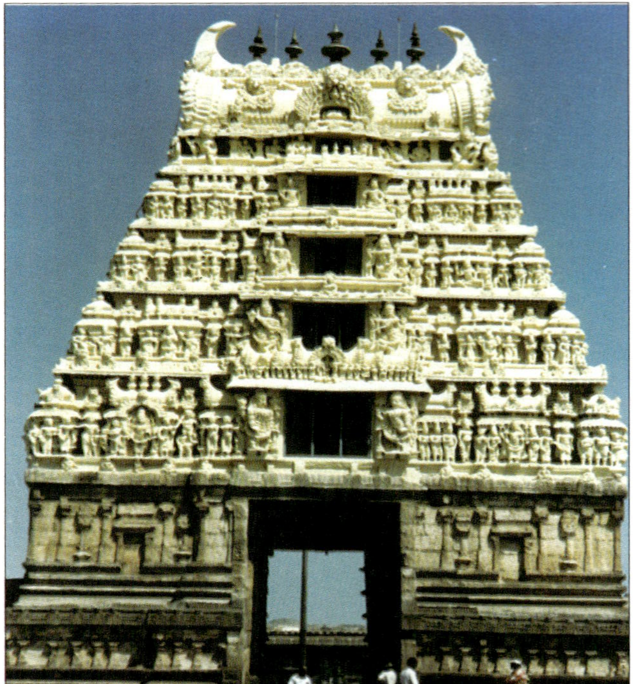

168. Belur, Chennakesava temple, gate way.

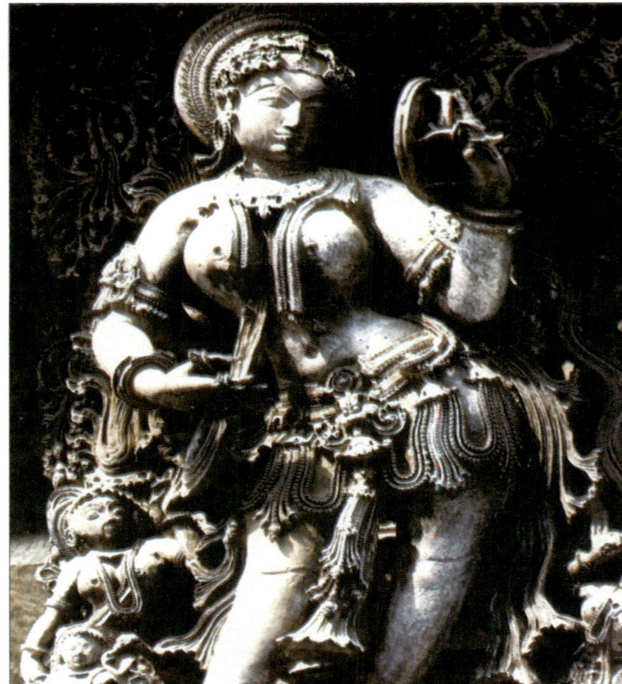

169. Belur, Chennakesava temple, Lady looking in to mirror.

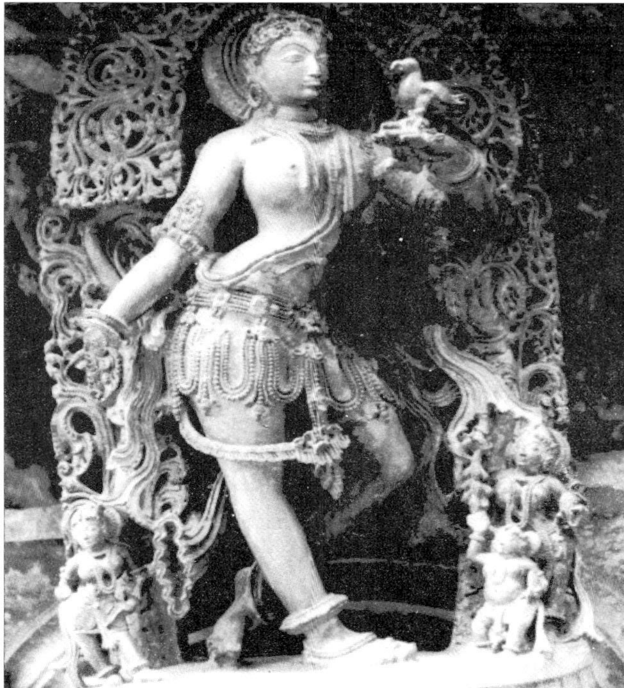
170. Belur, Chennakesava temple, Lady with the parrot.

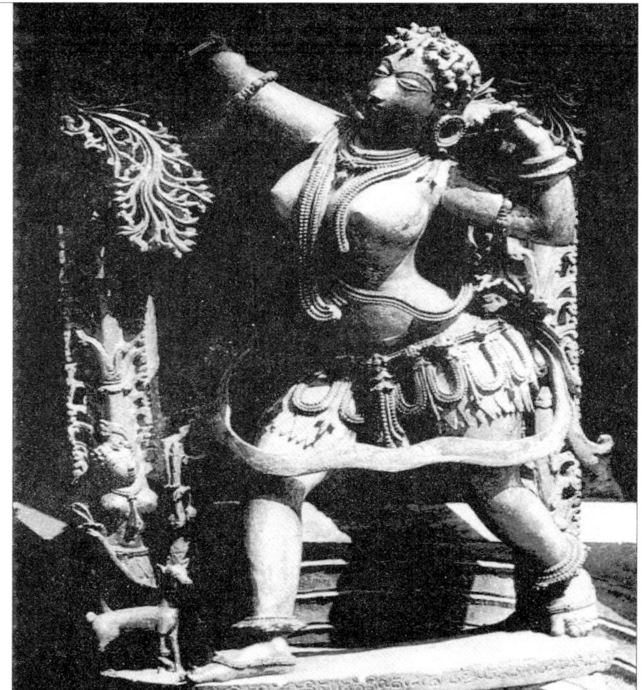
171. Belur, Chennakesava temple, Huntress.

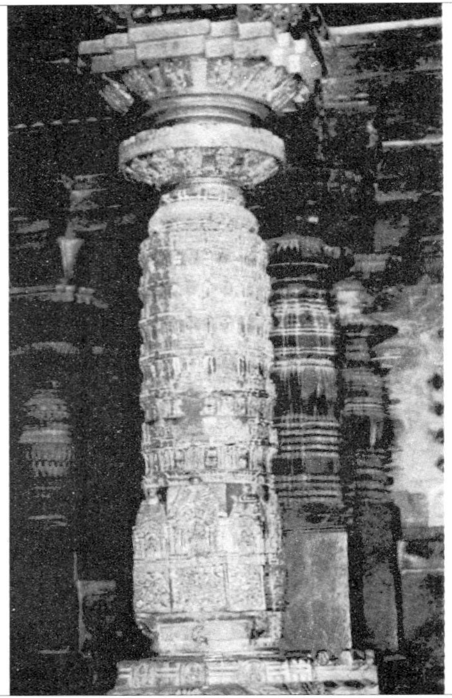

172. Belur, Chennakesava temple, Narasimha pillar.

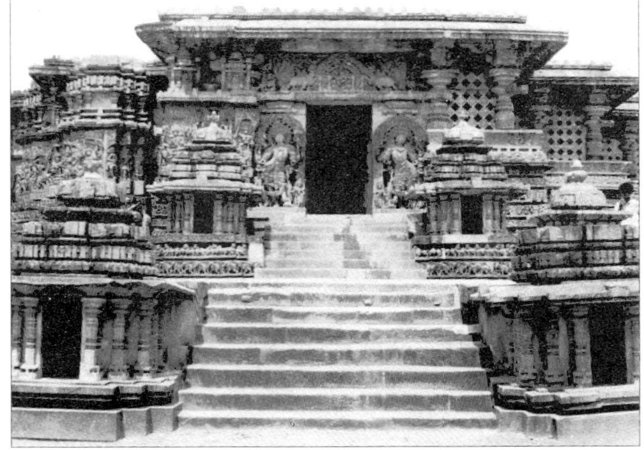

173. Halebid, Hoysalesvara temple, general view.

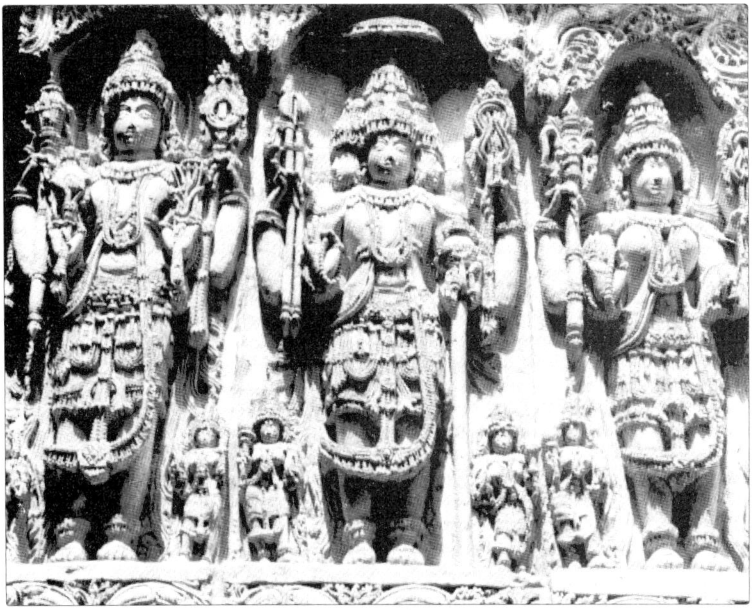

174. Halebid, Hoysalesvara temple, divinities.

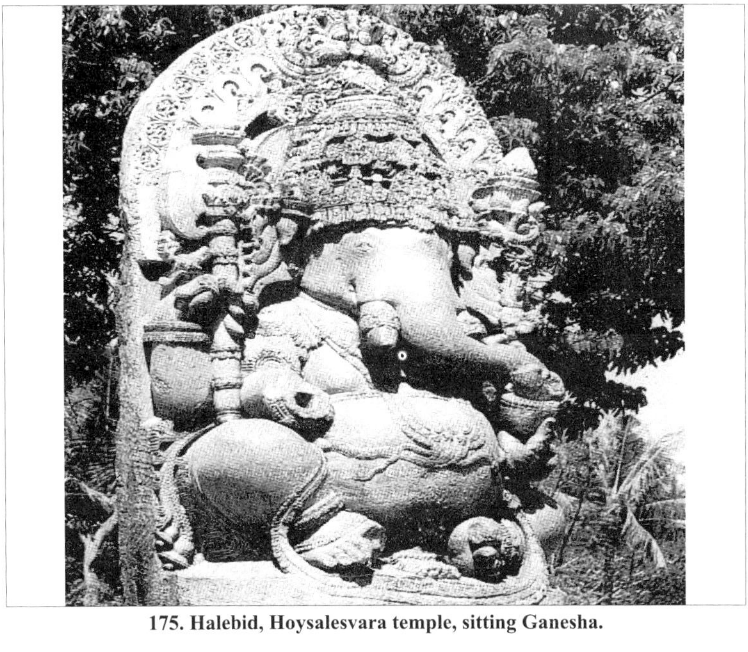

175. Halebid, Hoysalesvara temple, sitting Ganesha.

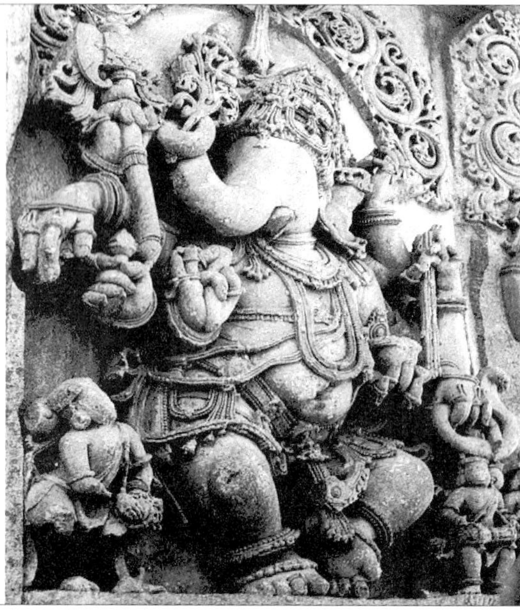

176. Halebid, Hoysalesvara temple, dancing Ganesha.

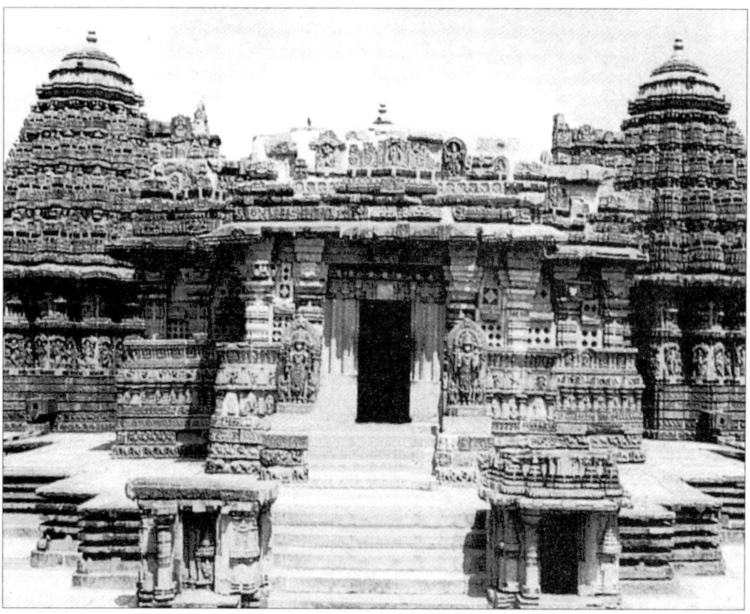

177. Somanathpur, Kesava temple, general view.

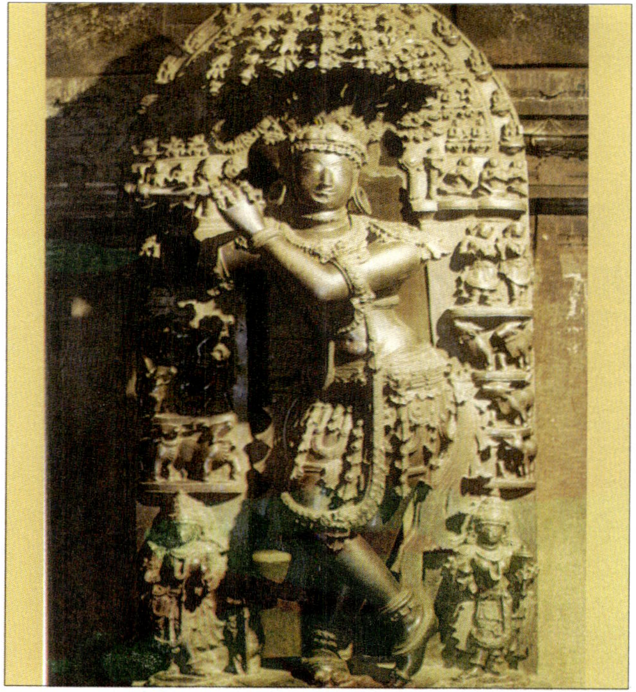

178. Somanathpur, Kesava temple, Venugopala.

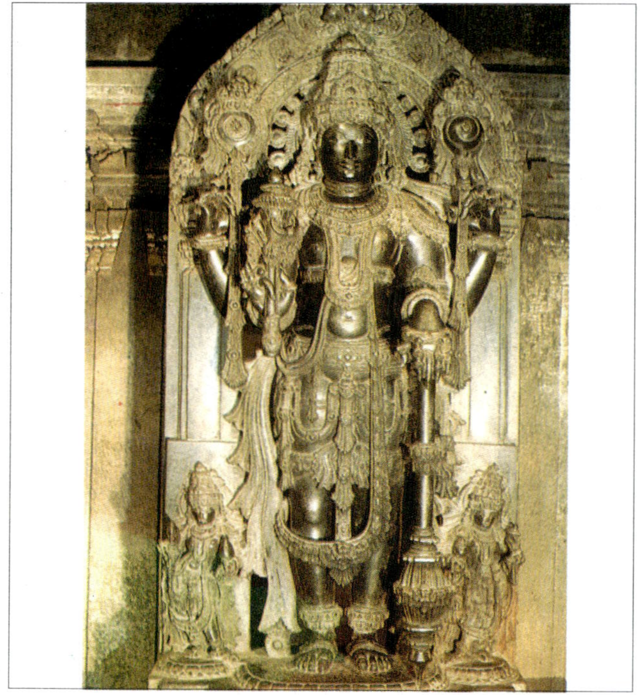

179. Somanathpur, Kesava temple, Janardhana.

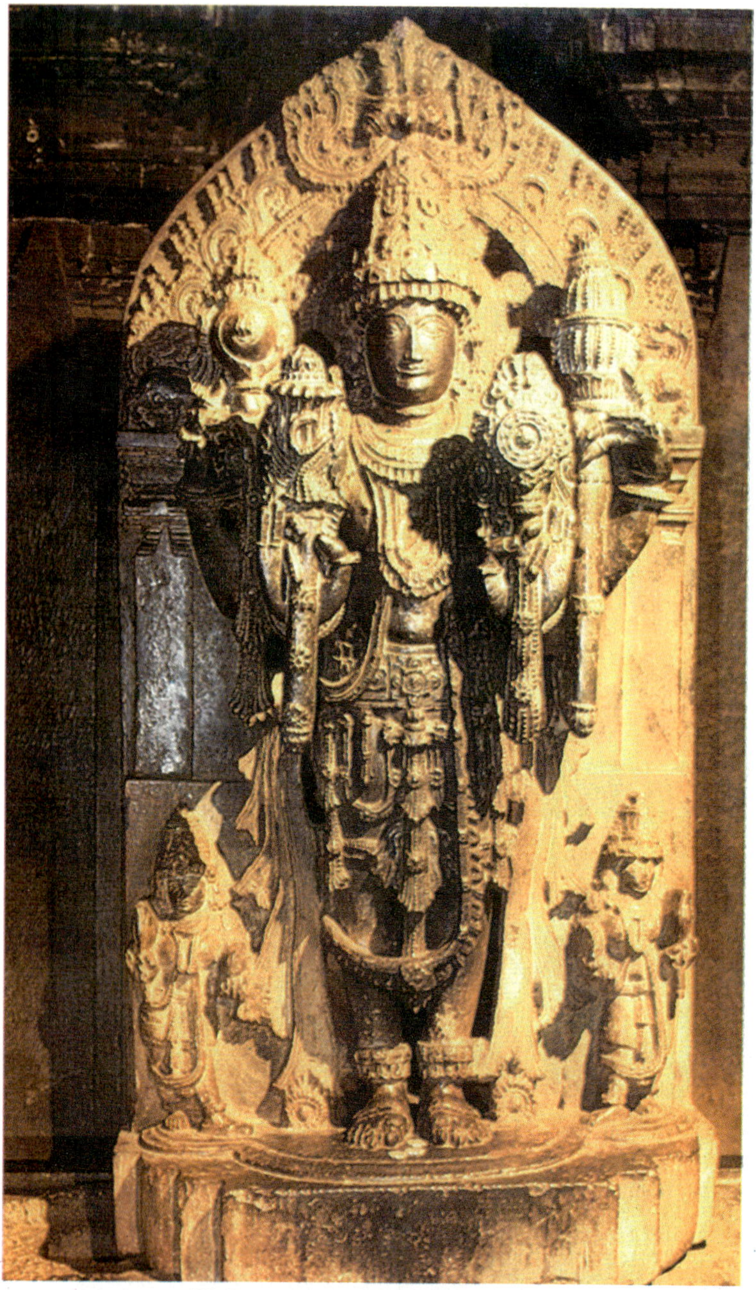

180. Somanathpur, Kesava temple, Kesava.

separate artist and his assistants, who combined as a team to produce their finest work.

The gateway (PL.168) of the temple was burnt, when the Tughlaks under the Ganga Salar laid siege to it. The seven-storeyed *gopuram,* which is seen today, was built in 1397 A.D., under the patronage of Vijayanagar rulers. Minor additions were also done by the chiefs located at Belur, under the sovereignty of the Nayaka rulers.

What specially marks out Belur temple is not its architecture, nor the exterior friezes in the typical Hoysala style, which one also sees at the Halebid temples, but the 42 bracket figures of women known as *madanika* figures, of which 38 support the eaves of the temple outside and four crown the pillars inside. Not very big in size, but exquisitely carved, with a high degree of polish and finesse, these figures - the Indian sculptor's tribute to aesthestics of womanhood: healthy, vibrant, and sensuous-virtually represent a beauty parade of ballerinas. In Fodor's words : "Most of them are voluptuous, full-breasted and full hipped women, beautifully adorned and taking any number of graceful poses beneath intricately pierced, scrolled and scalloped stone canopies".

Among the 42 figures, mention should be made of the lady looking into mirror (PL.169), the lady with the parrot (PL.170), the lady in various stages of toilet, the huntress (PL.171), the lady in various gracious dance postures, the lady playing the flute, the musician, the lady in a man's disguise, the lady with the scorpion, the lady playing the cymbals, the gypsy girl, etc.

Darpana sundari or the lady looking into the mirror (PL.169), with attendants on either side has a finely worked leafy canopy behind her. The attention that has been bestowed on the finest detail of her hair style, clothing and abundant jewellery is attractive. Each of the bracket figures is carved with similar attention to minute details. On the exterior walls we see Siva as Kamantaka, Vishnu as Narasimha, Dancing Sarasvati etc., Narasimha, or half-man, half-lion across his bent left leg holds Hiranyakasipu whom he is just killing.

Equally noteworthy are the majestic *dvarapalas,* holding the mace, the discus, the conch and the lotus. The Narasimha pillar (which was once a revolving pillar) (PL.172) and the richly carved ceiling of the central hall also arrest attention. These represent, in a way, the acme of Dravidian sculpture.

The Hoysala artist's treatment of animals in sculpture is superb, a crowning example of which is the panel of elephants on the outer walls of the Belur temple. One almost feels the movement of elephants in procession. Another outstanding piece of sculpture, not to be missed at Belur, is that of Krishna playing the flute, which depicts the Lord lost in the melody of music, while the cows and the herds listen hypnotised. By the side of the main temple are two small shrines: One, the Channagiraya temple (supposed to be built by art-loving Queen Shantala Devi, wife of Vishnuvardhana) and the other, Veeranarayana temple, the sculpture in which resembles that of the Kedareshvara temple at Halebid.

The Belur sculptor had probably the *Natyasastra* in mind while carving out the various *madanikas.* Here woman is depicted in her own pristine glory, without the interfering presence of the dominating male.

The temple of Hoysalesvara (PL.173) at Halebid is a splendid example and is dated to 1150 A.D. Like the Belur temple it also lacks the super structure. This grand temple was designed and erected by Kedaraja, under the orders of King NarasimhaI. Ketamalla, the chief officer of public works supervised the construction. It is a twin temple, the two structures being almost of identical size and joined by their adjacent trasnsepts. The god in the northern side temple is called as Shanthalesvara and that of sourthern side is called as Hoysalesvara. "The infinite wealth of sculpture over the exterior of the temple makes it one of the most remarkable monuments of the world and an unrivalled repository of religious thought expressed in plastic form". If we go around the temple we can see depicting a succession of scenes from Ramayana and Mahabharata like demon king Ravana is lifting Kailasa Parvata, shooting of *matsyta yantra* by Arjuna etc. The rows of *makara* and *hamsa* as well as swan carved on them. It will be very pleasing to see the dancing pose of Siva carved above the walls. In decorative niches or under leafy canopies, are innumerable carved figures of various gods and goddesses finely cut and ornamented in minute detail (PL.174).

In the precints of the temple, *nandi-mandapa* and an exquisite monolithic seated Ganesa (PL.175) are noticed. The seated *nandi* with rows of bells and other trappings is exquisitely carved. A fine dancing figure of multiarmed Ganesa is on the outerwall of the temple (PL.176). Mention should be made of the *dvarapalas* of *nandi-mandapa* for their elaborate decoration.

A very typical and complete example of the style is the small Kesava temple (PL.177) on the banks of the Kaveri River, in the sleepy little town of *Somnathpur*, which presents a satisfying architectural impression, since the towers above its shrines are intact.

Kesava temple is a *trikuta*, or three celled structure, opened in to common pillared *mandapa*, measuring 26.5x25.3m having entrance on the east, set with in a rectangular courtyard surrounded by 64 cells." So well balanced and finely proportioned are its parts that no element obtrudes or is out of place, and although the three stellate towers are only 9m high they are fully in accord with the rest of the building". This elaborately carved structure, built around1268 A.D., is popularly attributed to Jakanachari, who also built the temple at Belur, had left his wife and son in search of fame. Impressed by his talents, Vishnuvardhana employed him to create the structure at Belur. Many historians feel that Jakanachari was a purely imaginary character, the name a corruption of *dakshinacharya*, or 'sculptor of the southern school' and did not refer to any individual.

As usual in Hoysala temples, on the outer walls beginning from the bottom, are sculptured in succession six rows of images horizontally-caparisoned elephants, horses, scroll work, scenes from mythology. Above these rows of carvings, begin beautiful detailed friezes, depicting scenes from the *Puranas*, the Ramayana and the Mahabharata. On the walls there are 194 deities of which 114 are goddessses. Circumbulating the building, the visitor sees the dreadful Narayana's rage as he tears asunder the evil Hiranyakashipu. He is awed by the majesty of Nataraja standing frozen in the eternal dance of creation, and hears the thunder of rampaging elephants.

A line of large images each being sheltered by an elaborate, seemingly fragile canopy of leaves and flowers are noteworthy. Among these - Vishnu with his consort bless the passing multitude from beneath the shade of a blossoming tree, Ganesa dances energetically to a divine rhythm, Durga stands in savage triumph over the dying demon Mahishasura, Garuda soars over the earth effortlessly, bearing Narayana and Lakshmi on his shoulders - deserves special mention. A profusion of fine jewellery adorns each figure. The ornaments so finely wrought that one cannot believe it is all just carving on stone.

Actually this temple was built to house three versions of Krishna. In one *garbha-griha* stood VenuGopala, the cowherd (PL.178), dusky as a rain cloud. Clustered around in adoring silence were sages, cows, and cowherds. The halo-like that around the Gopala statue, had the 10 incarnations of Vishnu on it. In another cell in which stood a 1.8 m image of Janardhana (PL.179) radiating strength, obviously carved by a masterly chisel which made the stone seems like burnished bronze. The third and main statue of Kesava (PL.180), after whom the temple is named, does not bear the marks of genius that characterised the other two, possibly because it was not the original one. The *mukha-mandapa* has twelve pillars while the *navaranga* has four, all of them so marvellously rounded probably by turning on a lathe. The ASI staff might give you permission to climb the enclosure walls, from where you get a bird's-eye view of the temple.

A very important distinction between the Hoysala and Kakatiya temples is that the Hanumakonda temple is essentially three shrines connected to a common *ranga-mandapa*. The corners of the *ranga- mandapa* are not closed off. The Hoysala temple is closed, the back corners are solid walls and the front ones are enclosed by perforated screens. The Hoysala architect also adds doorways to the entrances of the pillared hall. Where the Kakatiya temple is open and light, the Hoysala temple is quite dark in its interior.

10

Gems of Vijayanagar

The foundation of Vijayanagara Empire in 1336 A.D. by Harihara I heralded the dawn of a new era in the history of South India. During the reign of the Harihara II (1377-1404 A.D.) the entire Tamil Nadu came under Vijayanagar hegemony. The Rayalaseema area in Andhra Pradesh had remained under the Vijayanagar rule since the foundation of the dynasty. The coastal region witnessed a struggle between the Gajapatis of Orissa and Vijayanagara monarchs. Krishnadeva Raya was the greatest among the Vijayanagara rulers and the credit of having brought all of South India less than one rule goes to him. His reign from 1509-1529 A.D. marked the zenith of the empire. He was a patron of Literature and is credited with the creation or enlargement of prominent temples, countless pillared *mandapas* and *gopuras* specially called *raya gopuras*.

The aim of Vijayanagara Empire being the protection of Hinduism, the Rayas extended patronage to all the sects of Hinduism, the Smartha, Saiva and Vaishnava. The threat of Islam and the influence of philosophers such as Vidyaranya reduced sectarian fanatism. Most of the kings in the Sangama dynasty were Saivites and devotees of Virupaksha. Karnataka continued as a stronghold of Virasaivism and scholars like Chamaraya made rich contributions to Saivite literature. From the time of the Saluvas, Vaishnavism became predominant and Tirupati, Ahobilam, Simhachalam, Bapatla and Srirangam were greatly developed. Tatacharya, the renowned Vaishnava teacher, had been the preceptor of a succession of Rayas. The Dvaita or the religion of Madhva also made considerable progress and Vyastirtha was honoured by Krishnadeva Raya. These different sects had their *mathas* scattered all over the country and propagated their faiths among the people. They imparted knowledge, not only in sacred scriptures, but also promoted secular arts and sciences, thereby catering to the intellectual needs of commmunity. Side by side Temple became a highly developed institution and dominated the spiritual life. The rayas displayed remarkable spirit of religious tolerance. Devaraya II allowed the Jains to build a temple at Vijayanagara in the Pansupari bazar and himself built a mosque for Muslims. In the capital, the Turukavada was greatly developed in the time of Rama Raya.

Temple architecture during the Vijayanagara period reached its final stage of evolution. The temple building activity was given due importance by the rulers as well as their subordinates. During the period, though the empire was the last stronghold of the Hindu power and cultural activity in South India, new temples were built and new adjuncts like the *gopura, kalyana-mandapa,* minor shrines, etc, were added to the existing temples. The most characterstic of such additions is the *kalyana-mandapa.* This is an ornate open pillared pavilion often with a raised platform in the centre, over which a *pitha* was placed for seating the deity and his consort during the annual *kalyana* (marriage) festival of the god. Another feature was the so-called thousand pillared *mandapa* or a huge hall with many rows of pillars. The most striking feature of the style is the varied and ornate treatment of the pillar.

Four types of pillars are discernible. In the first type, the shaft becomes merely the central core for the attachment of an involved group of statues of heroic size chiselled entirely in the round "having as its most conspicuous element a furiously rearing horse, rampant hippogryph or upraised animal of a super natural kind" - the whole of it, pillar and sculptures, being dexterously chiselled in a single solid block of stone. In the second variety, encircling the central column, a cluster of slender, miniature pillars often referred as musical pillars on account of the separate sounds they produce when they are hit by a small stone. The third type consists of the shaft composed of a series of miniature shrines. The fourth variety relates to the type where the shaft has sixteen or eighteen sides surface. Whatever the moulding of the pillar, each was provided with ornamental brackets, which formed part of the capital. These brackets had below them elaborately carved flower pendants resembling an inverted lotus bud. The *gopuras* on the east provide access to the courtyard. This is built of granite on the lower level and has a brick super structure that rises in receding storeys in typical southern style.

Buildings in the Vijayanagar style are scattered throughout the country south of the Tungabhadra. The finest and most characterstic group is to be found in the ruined capital city of Vijayanagar itself now popularly known as Hampi.

Hampi is also believed to be Pampa, the place where Rama spent a rainy season in the company of Sugriva. This ruined city on the south bank of the Tungabhadra River, amid a surreal landascpe of golden-brown granite boulders and leafy banana fields, is Karnataka's best-known heritage site.

Hampi, formerly known as Vijayanagar (the city of Victory), was established in 1336 A.D. by Harihara, the founder of the empire. When Muslims were establishing states in the north, in the south and Deccan the Hindu tradition continued although with some overlay of Islamic culture. In a few years, its fame as one of the most beautiful cities spread far and wide. The foreign visitors like Nicolo Conti and Abdur Razzak gave vivid descriptions of the city of Vijayanagar. Its circumference was sixty miles. Abdur Razzak, the Persian ambassdor (1443) describes the crowded bustling bazaars of Hampi with their pillared galleries. He says that Vijayanagar city was such that the eye had not seen nor the ear had heard of any other place resembling it upon the whole earth. It had seven fortified walls one within the other. 90,000 soldiers were always ready with arms, in defence of the city. The city was so prosperous that pearls, diamonds and other precious stones were sold openly in the long bazaar. Flowers were sold every where. According to Nicolo Conti the king (Devaraya 11) had 12000 wives, which is unbelievable.

Vijayanagar's reign as the undisputed queen of all cities came to an abrupt end in 1565 when the Deccani Muslim rulers of Bijapur, Bidar, Ahmednagar, Golconda and Gulbarga united to defeat the empire under the tutelage of Rama Raya, in the famous battle of Tallikota. He was slain in the battle and for the helpless residents of Vijayanagar, the nightmare began the next day, with unruly elements from the invading armies as well as thieves and tribes from the surrounding regions, including the Lambadis and the Kurubas began to plunder the city destroying her buildings and wealthy localities. The victorious Muslim army burnt the palaces, demolished temples, smashed idols, plundered and enslaved the people. They stayed at Vijayanagara for five months and left the city and its neighbourhood a vast heap of smouldering ruins. The kingdom was forced to shift capital for the safety of the royal family, but even in the meanwhile, the reigning king Sadasiva Raya, was killed, with whom the Tuluva line of kings came to the end. Ferishta, the late 16th century Persian traveller, describes the 1565 rout thus, "the river which ran near the field was dyed red with the blood. It is computed that 1, 00,000 infidels were slain during the pursuit." The plunder was so great that every private man in the enemies' army became rich in gold, jewels, horses, arms and slaves.

Even the city's 80 odd temples were not spared, wherein lies an interesting twist to the tale, as suggested by W.V.

Narasimham, archaeologist who has participated in the excavations at Hampi. "The emperors of Vijayanagar were Vaishnavites whereas most of the population was Saivite. So when Muslims destroyed the Vishnu temples, it is possible that some of the Saivites made most of this opportunity. At the same time they were able to save at least some of their own temples by paying money".

The city never recovered from the blow. The once proud city of victory is now a city of desolation. A handful of farmers still live here tending to the sugarcane and Paddy fields that dot the city. The few buildings which survived the holocaust, rear up from among the ruins as mute reminders of the devastation. All that is now left are the basements.

The gigantic boulders that surrounded Hampi supplied ample material for construction of the structures. Stone of two varieties; granite and the other green coloured chlorite was used for the buildings and the idols.

Truly speaking South Indian architechture owes much to the building activities of Srikrishnadeva Raya, within his ruling period of two decades. The capital city was lavishly embellished by him. The smaller east *gopura* and the *ranga-mandapa* of the Pampapati temple; the huge Lakshmi-Narasimha figure and the Krishna temple are just a few of the numerous additions made by him to the imperial city, besides making enlargements of the temples of Vitthala and Hazara Rama that were exsting before. In modern Hospet and its environs he built several new suburban cities, for example Nagulapura, in the name of his mother and Tirumala-deviyarapattana, after the name of his queen, Tirumaladevi and Tirumala Maharajapura, in the name of his son, Tirumalaraya. Many irrigation projects were also under taken and a big reservoir built near Hospet.

The early rulers adopted the name Sri Virupaksha as their signet manual and the Boar crest as royal insignia. As a mark of respect to Pampapathi or Virupakshesvara, the temple (PL.181) was raised as a massive and stately structure, standing in solitude and isolation, where Pampadevi married Virupaksha (Siva) alone remains a beehive of activity among the temples at Hampi. It is the only temple at Hampi that is still used for worship, situated in picturesque surroundings on the southeren bank of the Tungabhadra and immediately to the north of Hemakuta hill. Parts of temple predate the Vijayanagar empire and later additions, such as the *ranga-mandapa*, was built by Krishnadeva Raya to commemorate his coronation. It is a five aisled *mandapa* with various types of composite pillars carved on them with numerous sculptures of Hindu deities. Vijayanagar paintings can be seen in the ceiling of this *mandapa* in a well preserved condition. Arjuna shooting the *matsya-yantra* to win the hand of Draupadi, the *Dasavataras*, Siva as Kamandakamurti, Tripurari are some of the themes of the paintings. The three-headed *nandi*, situated near the doorway to the temple, is a unique presentation. Opposit this temple is the famous Hampi bazar, 10.7 m wide and 732 m long, a busy road even at present is lined with shops, hotels, handicraft outlets etc. At the eastern end of this bazaar, under a dilapidated *mandapa* stands a huge *nandi* carved out of natural boulder.

True to Narasimham's words, most of the Vishnu temples lie in ruins. The exquisite Vitthala temple (PL.182), on the southern bank of the Tungabhadra, which can be reached from the west by walking on from Hampi Bazaar along the river bank, or from the east through the Talarigattu Gateway. This temple, rightly called the queen of the ruins, is an artistic gem, standing as the most eloquent expression in granite illustrating the vanity of human wishes. There are 23 inscriptions around this temple ranging from 1513 A.D. to 1546 A.D. It is clear that the temple construction was begun by Devaraya II and continued into the reigns of his successors, Achyutaraya and Sadasiva. But it was still incomplete at the time of the Muslim invasion and was never consecrated. Legend has, that its deity Vitthala came to see it but thought it was far too grand for him and went back to stay in his native Pandharpur. The rectangular court yard (164 m x 94.5 m), with cloisters on the interior with a triple row of pillars surrounds the temple. There are three entrances with *gopuras,* that on the south being more ornate. The main temple is 70 m long, but height being only 7.6 m. On plan it consists of a *maha-mandapa*, an *ardha-mandapa* and a *garbha-griha*. The *adhishthana* is characterised by heavy moulded parts rising to a height of 1.5 m, with flights of steps guarded by elephants on its three sides. There are 56 pillars inside, each 3.7 m high. 40 of them are punctuated to form an aisle round the hall's outer edge, and the remaining provides an oblong passage in the centre. The huge monolithic pillars carved in to intricate compositions of sculpture and miniature pillars the *mandapa* is a marvellous testimony to the skill of carvers. The external walls are embellished with the usual arrangement of pilasters, niches and canopies. The temple entrance *gopura* is a lovely deep red, in brick and mortar, and is broken in a most striking manner. The granite base is intact, and has withstood the constant ravages of time. The remnant tower is adorned with fabulous stucco figures.

By far the best feature of this temple is its floridly elaborate pillared *mandapa* designed to produce musical notes, the *saptasvaras,* when tapped. The famous architectural gem, the stone chariot (PL.183), used by Karnataka tourism as its logo stands opposite to this temple. Its four stone wheels move up on stone axles, imparting a sense of movement to the structure. It is 7.8 m high. Ancient photographs taken in 1865 by the English man Alexander Greenlaw show a brick and mortar tower on top of the chariot, but it is now missing. This *ratha* is a real wonder with a paneling full of delicately executed figures of gods, attracting every visitor to the temple. Similar stone cars are found in other temples of the period, for example at Tadipatri and Tiruvalur.

The Hazara Rama temple (PL.184) was most probably built by Virupaksha II, intended to serve as a private shrine for the royal family, which appears less of a shrine and more an epic depicted on stone, which houses almost all the Hindu gods and goddesses. Besides the main temple a Devi shrine, a *kalyana-mandapa* and other subsidiary shrines are disposed within a massive enclosure wall. The *ardha-mandapa* features two side-porches and a pillared platform on the east. The *vimana* is rather unusual in that its lower story is of stone and the tapering tower is of brick. It is 15.2 m high.

The herds and bands of elephants, horses, infantry, dancing girls and musicians, scenes from Krishna-lila sculptured in a row come alive on the exterior of the north,east and west enclosing walls. Its walls and pillars are embellished with bas-reliefs depicting scenes from Ramayana. The four black polished pillars in the *ardha-mandapa* invite you to run your fingers over their smoothness. Their geometrical square blocks alternate with cylindrical shafts all luxuriantly carved in tangible loveliness. The name, Hazara-Rama temple is popularly taken to mean 'the temple of the thousand Ramas' on account of the numerous Ramayana bas-reliefs on its walls.

In commemoration of his victory over Gajapathis of Orissa, Krishnadeva Raya built the Krishna temple, in 1513 A.D., in which he installed the huge image of Krishna, brought from the fort of Udayagiri, which is now preserved in Chennai Museum. A large open *prakara* with high walls contains the Svami and Amman sanctams and many sub shrines. All the ten *avataras* of Vishnu including the rare form of Kalki are carved on one of the pillars in the *ardha-mandapa* is noteworthy. The large east *gopura* has only a part of its superstructure at present.

In a recent excavation, a Siva temple has been discovered and brought out, to the west of the Danaik's enclosure, which is much dilapidated and the floor of the *maha-mandapa*, the other axial *mandapas* as well as the main sanctum, are under water. It goes with the name Prasanna Virupakshalaya or Pathala Sivalayam. This temple may be assigned to 14th Century A.D. A hill near Matangaparvatham has Veerabhadra temple. The image is of beautiful workmanship, carved on one-fourth portion of a huge boulder, the southern concave part resembling the expanded hood of a cobra.

A massive stone platform known as Mahanavami-dibba or Dasara-dibba has a floor area of 1615.4 sq. m rising by a series of sculpted terraces, which was the arena of tournaments in the days of Dasara festival to which the king and queen would also attend to watch. Domingo Paes, the Portuguese traveller at the time of the hey-day of Vijayanagara Empire, noted that aristocratic women, who, "Wore collars of gold and bracelets so heavy that they had to be supported on either side", used to attend the festive tournaments, at the place. The platform sides are covered with rows of boldly-carved horizontal friezes of horses, elephants, warriors, hunters, dancers, musicians, etc., as well as foreign representatives. From here a bird's eye view of the ruins is impressive. An interesting relic near the platform is a huge monolithic stone door (3.3 m x. 9 m) faithfully imitating the wooden original in all details including even bolt- sockets.

On our way to Vitthala temple, along the river bank, we come across a huge stone structure, the King's balance (PL.185), where the benevolent king used to get weighed, against gold and gems, which were distributed to the public during auspicious occasions like coronation. A beautiful work of art, it even shows the king and his two queens in miniature at the bottom left of the Post.

In the Kodandarama temple, large figures of Rama, Lakshmana and Sita were carved on a natural boulder and the temple was later built around it. The front *kalyana-mandapa* is ornate. The entire route to this temple is full of excavated sites. From this mercifully shady spot a lovely view of the placid Tungabhadra can be had.

The Jains realising the effect of environment on their architecture, had selected a picturesque spot on the Hemakuta hill and constructed a cluster of three temples. They contain stepped pyramidal towers and have three-shrine cells, opening to a central pillared hall. These are the testimony to the religious tolerance of the Vijayanagar kings.

The elephant stables (PL.186) are a majestic row of 11 domed stalls, with arched connecting doorways. There are lofty watch towers, the queen's bath with its elaborate stucco work (PL.187) and plinths of erstwhile palaces.

The Lotus Mahal or Chitragni Mahal (PL.188), an ethereal structure, which in the moon light gives the impression of a floating palace. It is a two-storeyed open pavilion, square on plan with recessed sides. The ground floor has an ornate stone *adhishthana* and 24 square pillars carrying recessed and foliated arches. The ceiling consists of a number of vaults and domes symmetrically arranged. Here the cusped arches open to the playful breeze and the women whiled away their time. This is a fine example of Indo-Saracenic architecture.

The 6.7 m high monolithic statue of Lakshmi Narasimha, the man-lion form of Vishnu (PL.189) seated on a seven hooded serpent in a yogic pose, with the yogic band across his legs, benign yet awesome has its hands chopped off, and the original seated Lakshmi is now missing. Close by is the shrine of a 3m high stone *linga* (PL.190), beautifully polished, with its base remaining always under water. Beyond the Krishna temple there are two huge stone images of Ganesa on the slope of the Hemakuta hill. One is Sasivekulu (mustard) Ganesa (PL.191) about 2.4m high and ironically named the Sasivekalu or mustard seed. The other monolith called in the same vein, the Kadalekalu (gram) Ganesa. The huge seated god, carved in the round out of a massive boulder, is about 4.5m high and is housed in a large shrine with a fine open pillared *mandapa* in front. Narasimha and Ganesa sculptures belong to the time of Krishnadeva Raya.

Elaborate arrangements were made for providing water to the people. Aqueducts, channels, tanks and drains can be seen all over the city. The Pushkarini tank (PL.192), excavated in the mid 80s was part of the palace complex, 3 metres deep into which water was filled by a series of stone channels. Almost lyrical in its beauty, the tank has a tiered structure, made with rectangular pieces of granite. Excavations have yielded other items such as pan-supari, or the market street for betel leaves and arecanuts, dating back to the 16th century, which is now reduced to a row of pillars. Hampi was compared to ancient Rome, the mind boggles and the eye blinks at such bygone splendour, such visible artistry; which must have taken riches of an extraordinary amount, to achieve such a scale of building. The UNESCO has made Hampi a part of its preservation programmes, as it so well deserves.

Hampi is not the place to be rushed through. A stay of atleast four days is recommended. Even the most cursory visit would require two days to this "virtually a vast open air museum of Hindu monuments". Hampi ruins are mainly situated between the villages of Kamalapuram in the south and Hampi in the north. Spread over a vast area of uneven terrain of 26 sq km, with not so easily manageable path ways. The best way to see Hampi, a world heritage site and to savour the atmosphere of the place, is going round the monuments on foot and the second best option would be to hire bicycles, which are available in most local hotels. The nearest village to Hampi is Kamalapuram where there is the main archaeological museum. Thus the ruins of Hampi echo the glory of the medieval past.

Tadipatri, the bustling dusty and faction-ridden town in Anantapur district is gaining prominence in the tourist and the industrial maps of Andhra Pradesh in recent times, with the cement factories of Larsen and Toubro, a host of granite industries and the recently opened Bellum caves. For the tourist potentiality of the place, two temples symbolising the glory and the splendour of the Vijayanagara era contribute, the Bugga Ramalingesvara temple and Chintala Venkataramana temple, reflecting the grandeur and magnificence of the Vijayanagara times.

The Ramalingesvara temple (PL.193), on the right bank of the river Pennar where it takes a northward turn, such spots are considered very sacred and ideal for holy constructions. The

Rama lingesvara is located beside a perennial spring, from where it derives its name, Bugga Rama lingesvara. The *bhoga-mandapa, gopura* and *prakara* of this temple belong to late 15th century A.D.

The temple complex comprises of shrines, dedicated to Siva as Ramalingesvara, the Rama and the Parvati shrines, situated to the south of main shrine, besides other smaller shrines and *mandapas,* all enclosed within a *prakara* with gate ways. The *gopura,* the pillars in the *kalyana-mandapa* and in common *mukha-mandapa* of Devi and Rama shrines in the temple are richly carved. On plan, the Ramlingesvara temples possess a *mukha-mandapa, antarala* and *garbha-griha* exhibiting offsets and recesses and features *nandi* in front of *antarala.* The *dvitala-vimana* is of brick and plastered and has a circular *griva* and *sikhara.* The *mukha-mandapa* has entrances on all sides with the typical heavy Vijayanagara *gajakranta* based pillars, at the porches.

The north and south *gopuras* are splendid examples of sculptural art minutely carved with precision and elegance. They have *upapitha, adhishthana* and the walls in their projections and recesses incorporated the sham niches, *kostha-panjaras* with images of divinities and *kumbha-panjaras* and circular pilasters. The north *gopura* (PL.194) is preserved only upto the roof level, whereas the others are preserved to some extent. On the top central portion of the north *gopura* out side, there is a superb sculpture of Mahishasura mardini (PL.195). In the interior, on either side of the passage there is a fine sculpture of a beautiful damsel, standing under a creeper and a vertical row of circles above (PL.196). The pillars with multiple pillarates carry the figures of *vyalas* and Surasundari. The mouldings on the base are treated with intricate patterns of creepers, elephant and *hamsa* friezes. The temple is famous for the quality of sculpture found in the *kalyana-mandapa* and the *gopura.*

The Chintala Venkata Ramana Temple (PL.197), which belongs to early 16th century, has a *maha-mandapa, mukha-*

mandapa and *antarala*, before the *garbha-griha*. The wall features are identical to the Ramalingesvara but here it is more ornate. The wall is embellished with bas-reliefs depicting scenes from the Ramayana and images of divinities. The *dvitala-sikhara* has a circular *griva* and *sikhara*. The *maha-mandapa* is very high and ornate, has massive pillars with Vijayanagara capitals. The pillars are with *yali* brackets with riders, the pillar with one pillaret projecting, and the pillar with two or three pillarates projecting. Especially the pillars on the exterior are alternatively decorted with Apsara figure on the shaft. Massive architrave cut in to compartments by pilasters carry the figures of Vishnu in various forms. The main entrance to the *mukha-mandapa* is in the east with a fine doorway. There are *dvarapalas* at the base and the jambs are decorated with lotus and creeper designs and is Gaja Lakshmi on the *lalata*. Similar ornate doorways are seen on other sides and in the *antarala* and *garbha-griha* as well.

The Devi shrine has an *ekatala-vimana* and is deity figures in stucco on the *vimana*. The carving of the *kumbha-panjaras* in the recessed part originating from the base is note worthy. Thus the wall with closely spaced pilasters, the *kumbha-panjaras* spanning the entire height of the wall, niches surmounted by *kutas* and a *kapota* moulding atop, all these provide a contrast to the highly separated horizontal mouldings of the base.

A huge granite chariot (PL.198), infront of the shrine, tied to horses is preserved, which simulates the *ekatala-vimana* of the temple. It has on its body a pair of cross - shaped apertures. During the first three successive days of Maghamasam namely, Ekadasi, Dwadasi and Thrayodasi, the sun's rays shine through the apertures on the feet of the deity in the sanctum sanctorum. This phenomenon has earned the temple another name, *Bhaskara Kshetra*.

Referring to the Tadipatri temples, Smith remarked, "The best examples of the Vijayanagara style are to be found perhaps, not at the capital, but at Tadpatri (Tarpatri), Anantapur district

... in gateways erected during the sixteenth century by a prince subordinate of Vijayanagara". Fergusson, who devoted two full page illustrations of the Tadipatri sculptures, judged them to be on the whole, "perhaps, in better taste than any thing else in this style".

Lepakshi is a small village, in Anantapur district of Andhra Pradesh. The famous monument here is the Veerabhadra temple (PL.199) built in Vijayanagara style of architecture and mural paintings atop a small hill known as *Kurma-saila* (tortoise-shaped hill). There are reasons to prove that the temple at Lepakshi was already in existence in the second half of the 15th century A.D. and the additions were made by Virupanna, a treasurer of Achyutaraya of the third dynasty of Vijayanagara.

There is a popular legend about this temple which gives that Virupanna, the treasurer of Achyutaraya, conceived the idea of constructing a temple here, because the image of Virabhadra was found here. He spent the money that was collected as tribute from the vassals of the king (Achyutaraya), for this purpose and construction of the temple was about to be completed, except for the *kalyana-mandapa*. At that stage, the king found his treasury empty, came to know what had happened and ordered that Virupanna should be blinded for his crime. But, Virupanna, being a loyal servant, carried out the sentence on the spot with his own hands; and to this day, two dark stains are shown on the west wall of the southern entrance of the inner enclosure, to have been the marks that Virupanna made by his eyes which he himself threw at the wall. It is said that Virupanna did not survive long after the event and hence the *kalyana-mandapa* was left unfinished.

Achyutaraya himself made gifts to the temple and thus the story of Virupanna arises doubt as to its historicity. It may have been possible that the wars that Achyutaraya had to fight incessantly, on all sides, must have emptied his treasury and thus the construction of the temple might have stopped incomplete.

The additions to the temple that Virupanna made were probably the *maha-mandapa* and the incomplete *kalyana-mandapa*. It comprises on plan a *maha-mandapa, mukha-mandapa* an *antarala* in *sandhara* scheme. The temple exterior has a *padabandha* type of *adhishthana* and plain walls and in the interior; there are bas-reliefs on the walls, depicting the stories of Siriyala, Kiratarjuniya, etc. The *dvitala-vimana* has a circular *griva* and *sikhara*. However, this temple is renowned for its *maha-mandapa* which has 66 excellently sculptured massive pillars and painted ceiling. Life size figures of Bhikshatanamurti (PL.200), Tumburu, Dattatreya, Brahma, Narada, Rambha, Padmini, Nataraja etc., come alive on these pillars. The Rambha dances and Siva is shown dancing in the *ananda-tandava* pose are among the noteworthy sculptures adorning the pillars. The pillars are massive with single or multiple pillarets and have *pushpa-potikas*. There are also some remarkable sculptures on the pillars of *mukha-mandapa*, such as Durga, Kalarimurti and Gajasurasamhara murti etc., each measuring about four feet in height and in high relief. A pillar in the north-east corner shows fine figure of a damsel, locally known as woman of *padmini* class (PL.201), beside *Panchala-purusha* or *Vastu- purusha* (PL.202). Designed as a caryatid, the figure of the damsel stands gracefully on a *makara* holding the wine of creeper.

On the ceilings of *mukha-mandapa* and *maha-mandapa,* the paintings are masterpieces of the Vijayanagara mural tradition. Most of them portray Siva in his various forms. Scenes like Siva as a youth (PL.203), gods attending Siva's marriage (PL.204), Ravana receiving the *atma linga,* women attending on Parvati (PL.205) are noteworthy. The paintings depict scenes from Ramayana, Mahabharata and Puranas, besides a number of secular scenes too. Among the secular scenes Viranna and Virupanna with their retinue receiving sacred ashes from the priests in a panel holds prime interest (PL.206). The paintings are also a valuable visual record of life styles in one of the greatest and most cosmopolitan centres of the medieval world. The crowns and the textiles exhibit the fashion of those times.

The *kalyana-mandapa* is another magnificient structure, left unfinished (PL.207), also called *lata-mandapa* or hall of creepers having its western part made up of 42 pillars and has the *unjal-mandapa* as its eastern part (PL.208). The Vishnu shrine in the complex is a *dvitala-vimana* with a square *griva* and *sikhara.* The *naga-linga*, or the *linga* presented as coiled by a seven hooded-*naga* in protection, carved on the south, is a rare example (PL.209). On the north face of the boulder is a huge sculpture of seated Ganapati (PL.210).

The most interesting item of art at Lepakshi is the sculpture of a reclining *nandi* (PL.211) located three furlongs to the north-east of the temple, which is somewhat perplexing as to its distant location in isolation. It more than 8m in length and more than 4m in height and thus, believed to be the largest monolithic *nandi* in the country. Like the big *naga-linga* this monolith is said to have been casually carved by a party of workmen in an off hour while waiting for their meals.

Markapur, in Prakasam District (A.P.), situated on the banks of the Gundlakamma River, is a bustling town, catering to the 80% of the country's needs for slates and slate pencils.It is also a popular pilgrim destination because of the Sri Lakshmi Chennakesava svamy temple (PL.212), built by the Vijayanagar rulers during early 16th century A.D. The earliest record found in this temple belongs to 1533 A.D. This temple complex comprises of the main shrine consisting of a *ranga-mandapa,* a *mukha-mandapa,* an *antarala* and a *garbha-griha* and the temple of Lakshmi, almost similar on plan, except *ranga-mandapa.* The complex is surrounded by a *tiruchuttumala* along the *prakara*, which has massive and tall *gopura* into the temple, on the east. An *utsava-mandapa* is situated on the south east, rose around1533 A.D.

The Chennakesava temple stands on a high *upapitha*, and a *padabandha- adhishthana.* The walls are contoned with pilastrers and a niche in the central part. The super structure is single storeyed and has a square *sikhara*. The *ranga-mandapa* has beautiful typical Vijayanagara columns (PL.213) which are lofty and ornate, with rearing *gaja, simha* and *asva vyalas*, charged with vigour and movements, excellently exhibited. Inside the *mukha-mandapa* the *citrakhanda* pillars are employed, among which, there are 6 musical pillars. The *garbha-griha* houses a stone image of standing Vishnu. The Lakshmi shrine, situated to the left of the main shrine, is two storeyed with circular *griva* and *sikhara* and identical in other features to the neighbour. On the east a *dhvaja-stambha* and an ornate *bali-pitha* are situated.

According to legends the idols were installed here by Markandeya, a *rishi*, and so the place come to be called Markapuri. The unique feature of the temple is that every year, from 16th December to 14th January, the sun's rays at dawn enter the sanctum sanctorum, through specially placed windows, and fall at the feet of the deity, making it glow with golden hues which is a wonderful architectural feat that speaks volumes for the expertise of the artisans and their knowledge of planets.

Srisailam has everything that a wandering mind longs for-a liberal god who grants boons just by asking, green thickets capping the undulating hilly terrain, the Krishna cutting through the canyons, and the man-made wonder, the massive dam choking the river for human welfare and a power house built in four or five acres of artificial space created within the 'wombs' of the hills. The sacred spot (PL.214) is in the Kurnool district, famous as one of the twelve *tirthas* in India that have *Jyotirlingas* and foremost in fame and sanctity among the *Saiva-kshetras* in Andhra Pradesh. In the midst of the *nallamali* hills and forests, the plateau of Srisailam is 476 m above the sea level. The river Krishna flows touching the feet of the sacred hill through a narrow gorge of 100 m width and at a depth of 100m and is popular as *Patalaganga* (river Ganges of the nether world).

The presiding deity of Srisailam, Mallikarjuna is counted one among the twelve *jyotirlingas* ancient pilgrimage centres mentioned in *Siva Purana.* His divine consort *Bhramaramba* is considered as one of the eighteen forms of *sakti* in the country. On plan this temple comprises of a nandi-*mandapa, mukha-mandapa, antarala* and *garbha-griha.* The *mukha-mandapa* was built by Harihararaya II in 1405 A.D. The *Virasiro-mandapa* (PL.215) by the side of *nandi-mandapa* was erected by Anavema Reddi in 1378 A.D. In the central *ankana* of it four pillars are employed and *dvarapalas* at the base of the *mandapa* on the east. The door ways to the *garbha-griha* are treated with the *latapatra, purna-kalasa* and a lady holding a lotus and the Gajalakshmi in the *lalata* is seen. The nine stepped *vimana* with *simhalalata* gables is surmounted by *nagara sikhara* (PL.216). The *vimana* had undergone reconstruction and encased with gilt copper plates recently.

In side the *garbha-griha* one finds the *linga* is not fixed firmly but shaky because it is *jala-linga*, a current of water flowing underneath it. The devotees irrespective of caste are allowed to touch the *linga* probably due to the impact of the cosmopolitan traditions of *Vira-Saivism.*

Virasiro-mandapa, from the very name, can be understood to have been meant for devotees (Vira Saivites), to offer their heads severed and offered to the god, in thier frenzied devotion. If not the head, as the tradition gives, there were practices of offereing one or the other limb of the body, or tongue in order to please the god, Siva, with the hope of going up to *Sivaloka at* Srisailam. The inscriptions on the *virakals* gloriously narrating the events that no sooner did the devotees offer their heads, they had abandoned the ugly mortal bodies, received resplendent divine bodies and immediately attained *Siva-Sayujya*, speaks the esteem of the people of the time for the cruel sacrifice. The innumerable *virakals* attest to the great admiration the people had for such heroes.

The Srisailam temple stands with in a spacious and massive stone *prakara* measuring 150m x 183m x 6.7 m. This

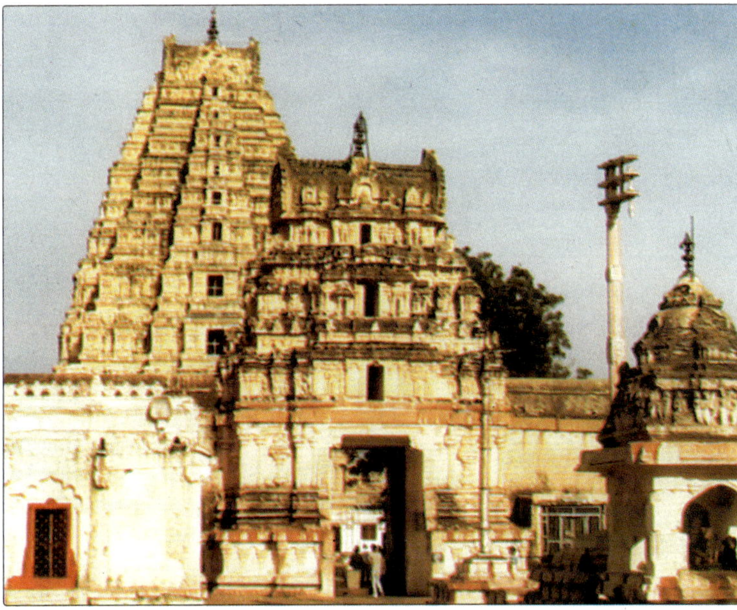

181. Hampi, Virupapaksha temple, gopuras, interior view.

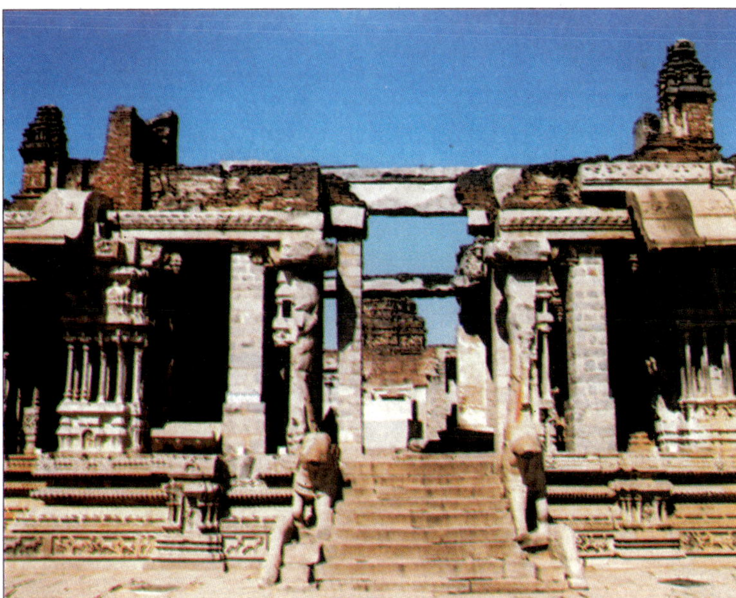

182. Hampi, Vitthala svami temple, general view.

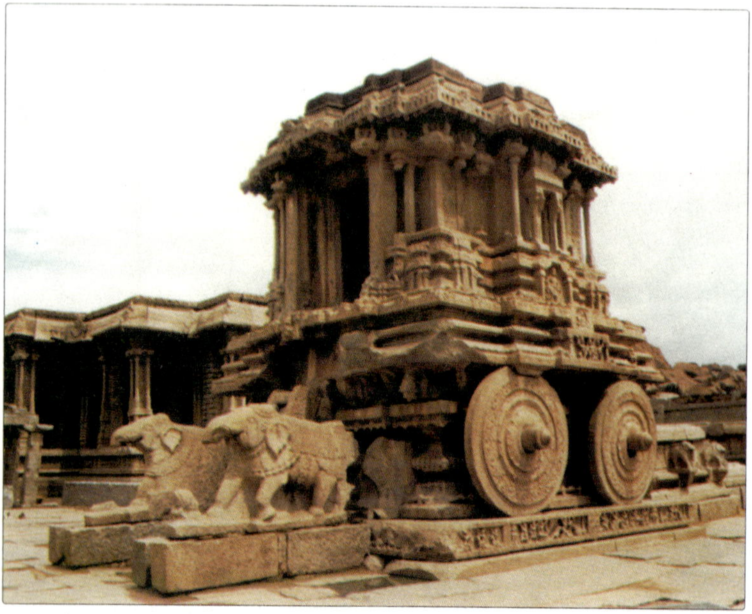

183. Hampi, Vitthala svami temple, stone chariot.

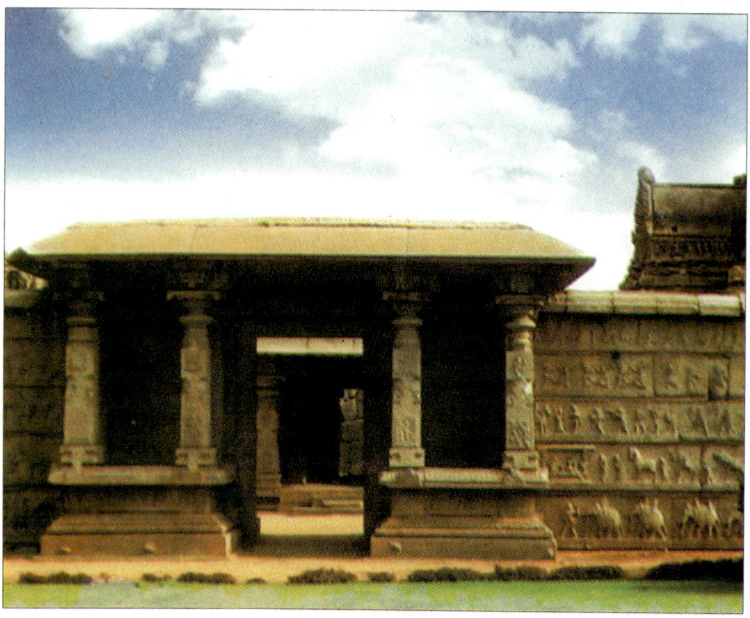

184. Hampi, Hazararama temple, general view.

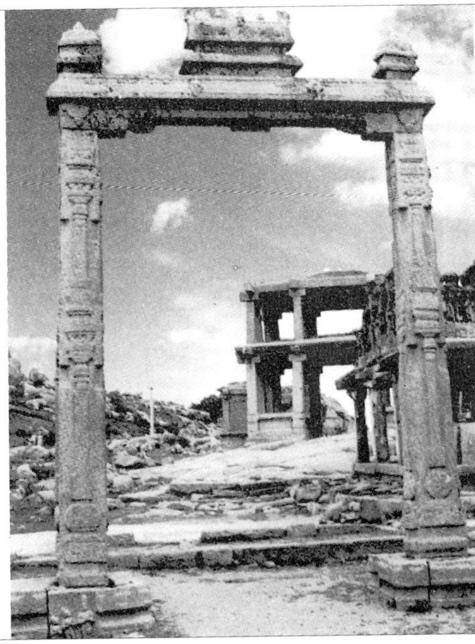

185. Hampi, King's balance.

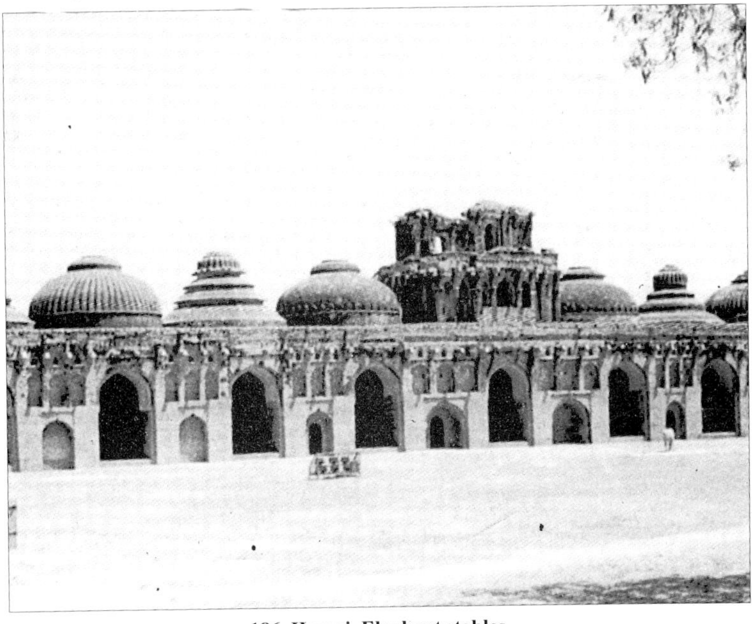

186. Hampi, Elephant stables.

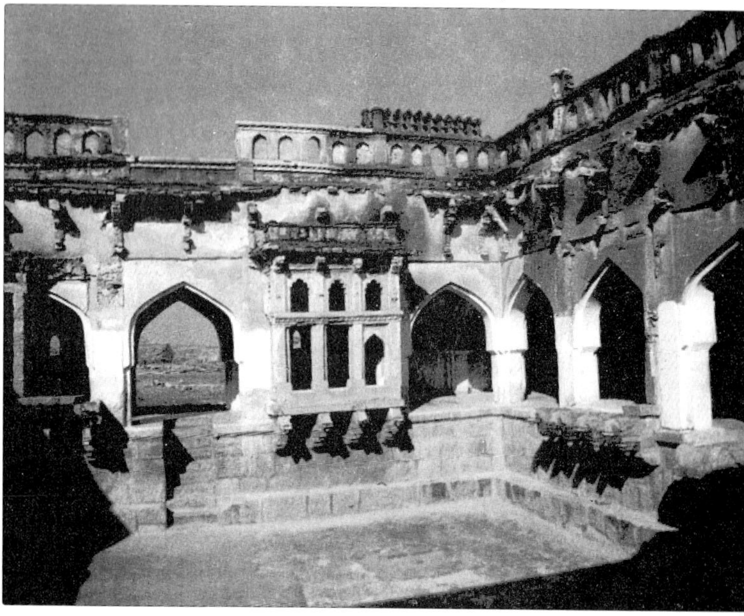

187. Hampi, Queen's bath.

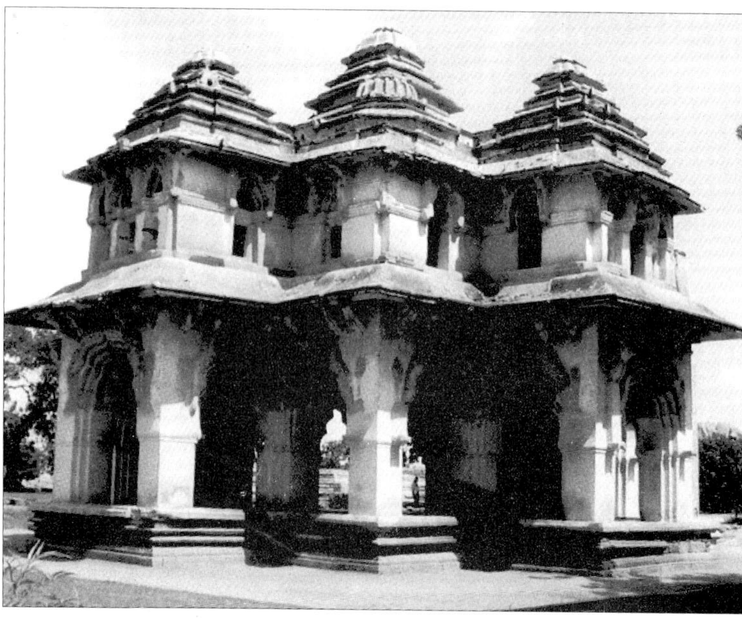

188. Hampi, Lotus mahal.

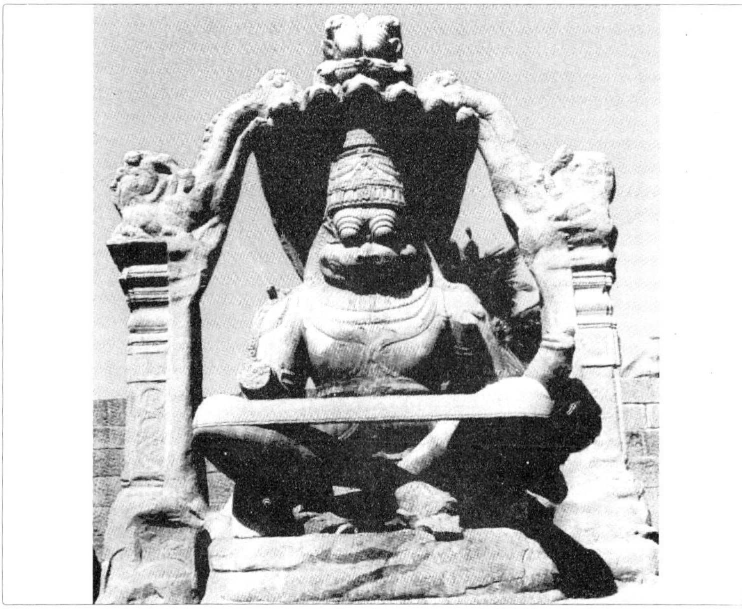

189. Hampi, Narasimha.

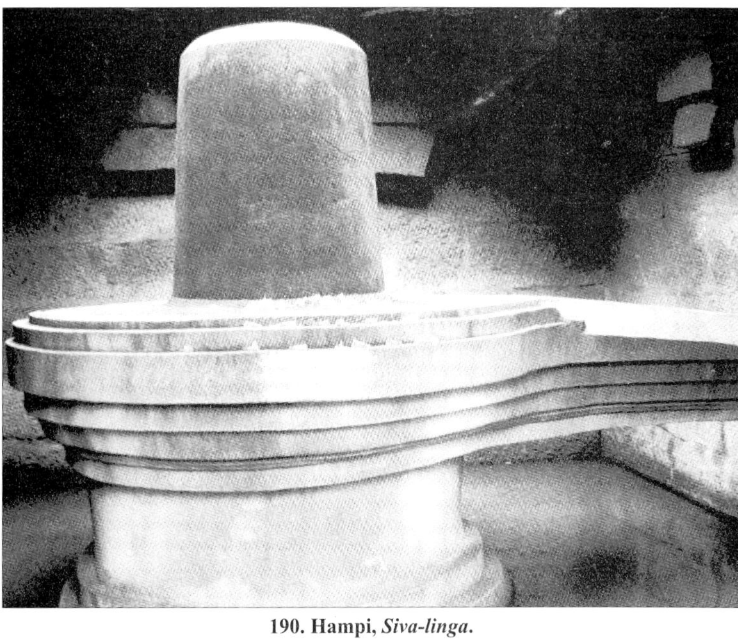

190. Hampi, *Siva-linga*.

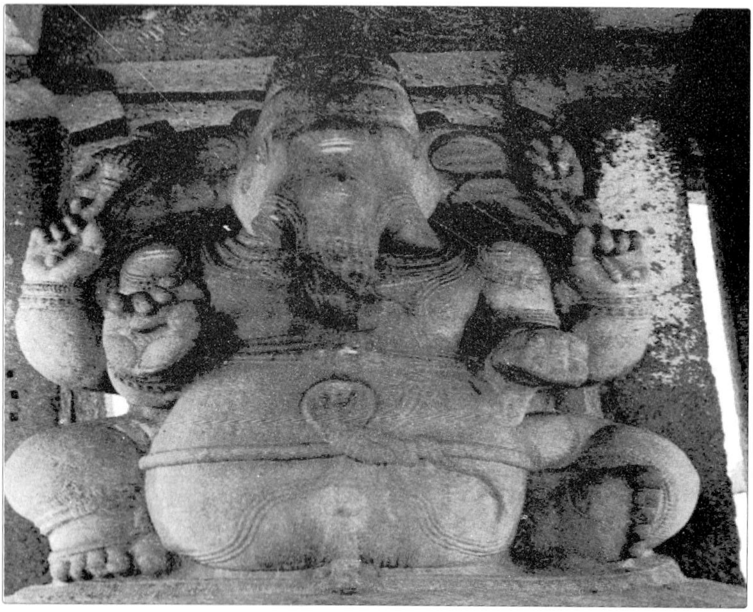

191. Hampi, Mustard Ganesha.

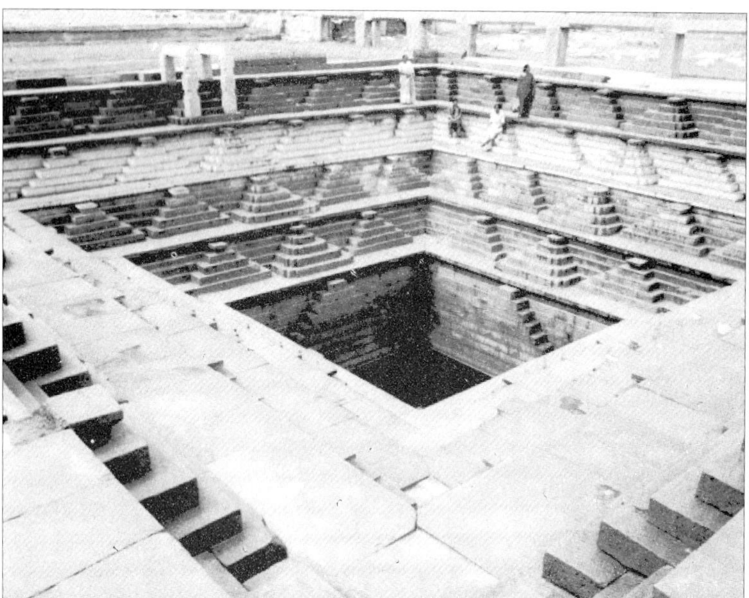

192. Hampi, Pushkarini tank.

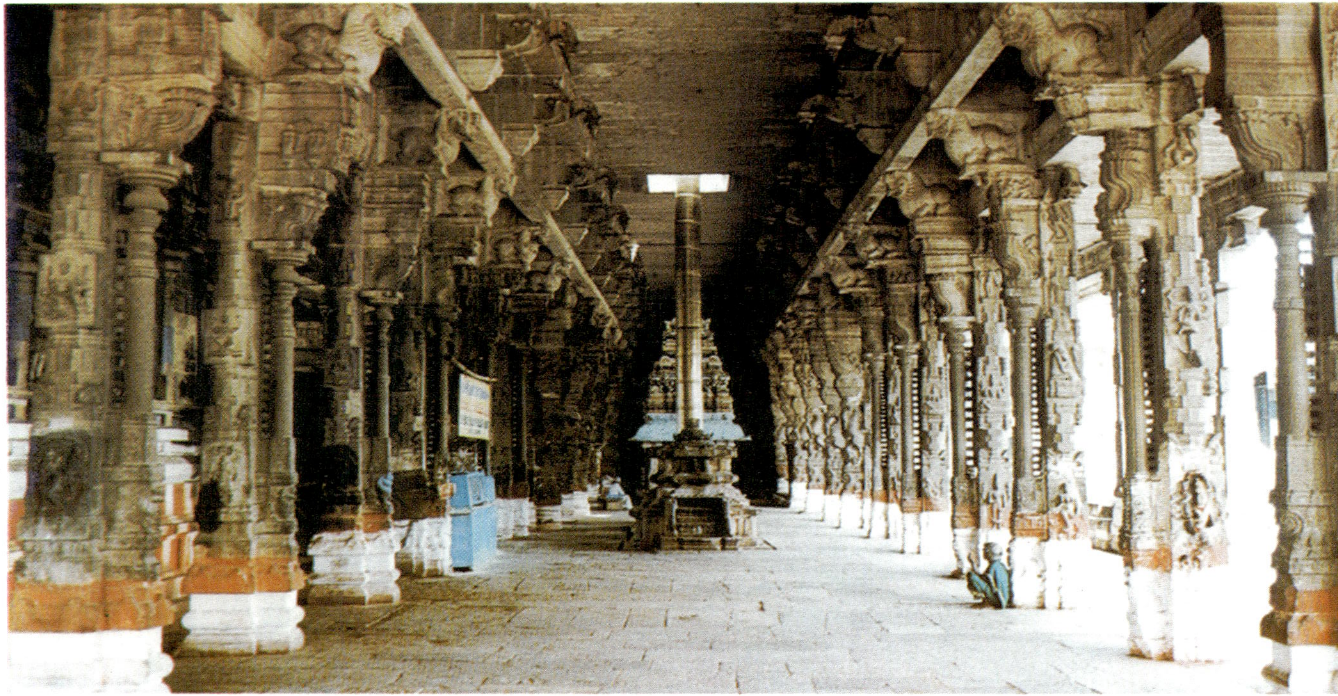

233. Kanchipuram, Ekamranatha temple, thousand pillared *mandapa*.

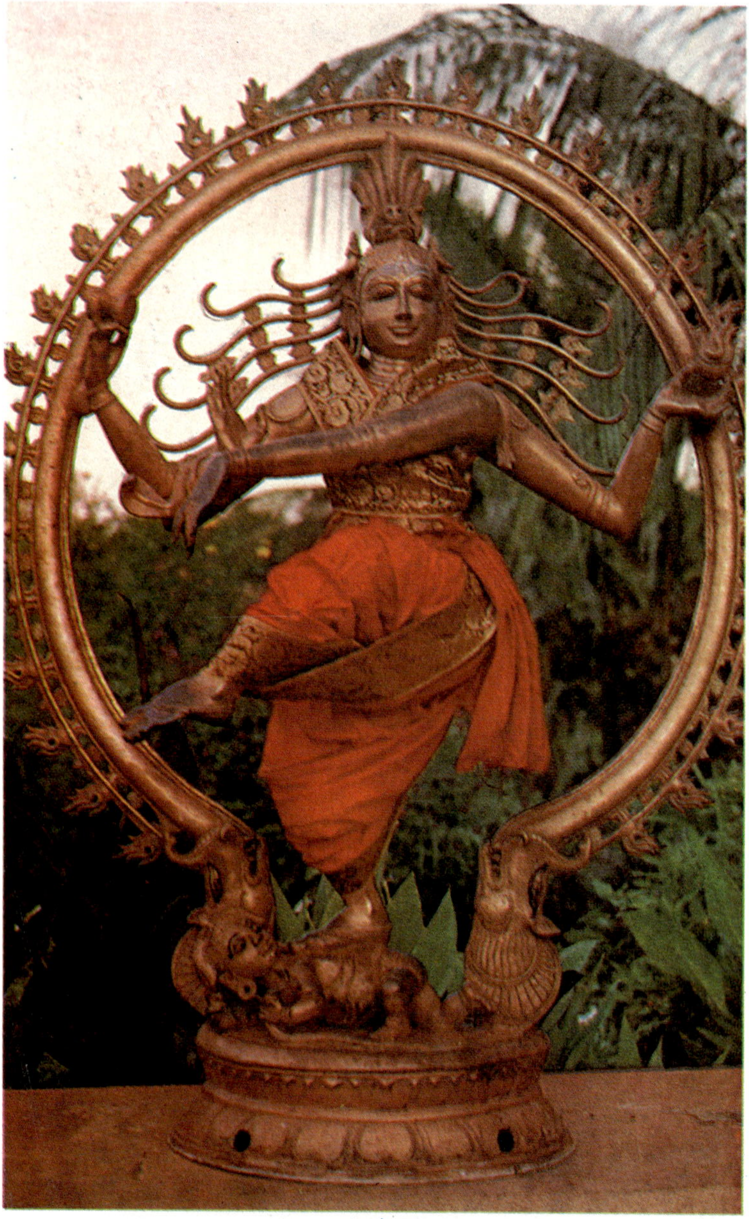

234. Srisailam, Nataraja.

sculptured *prakara* was built in 1412A.D. by one Lingayya. He was the *Dharmadhikari* of the Srisailam temple. The lofty gateways on three sides east (PL.217), north and west in the *prakara* surmounted by brick built *gopuras* are known by the names of Krishna Raya, Sivaji and Harihara respectively. The *gopuras* are datable to the 16th century A.D.

On the basis of the stepped pyramid which is the dominant characteristic of the Chalukyan style, M. Rama Rao has concluded that the temple of Mallikarjuna was built in or about the 10th century A.D. on the other hand, Parabrahma Sastry argues that even the Kakatiyas adopted the style and therefore, the temple was built about the middle of the 13th century.

The temple of Bramaramba is a small structure, with a square *garbha-griha*, enclosed by pillared porch on east, south and north. The decorative carving on the pillars consists of dancing girls, musicians and warrirors in late Vijayanagar style (PL.218). This temple on stylistic grounds may be dated to 16th century A.D.

The relief sculptures that decorate the outer *prakara* of Mallikarjuna temple complex are arranged in two or three registers. The wall is embellished with bas-reliefs depicting themes from *Siva-purana*, various forms of divinities, elephants and horse's procession, *hamsas* and *makara-toranas,* dance scenes etc. Depiction of Siva in *sandhya-tandava* accompanied by Brahma, Vishnu, Devi and Nandikesvara is interesting. Even Vaishnavite themes, particularly the ten incarnations of Vishnu find the place. The sculpture is in typical Vijayanagara style of the 15th and 16th century and closely recall the Hazara Rama example. The *Prakara* is thus a museum and library fused into one. However, the southern wall reveals that the work of the decorating the walls was left incomplete.

Prolaya Vema Reddi, the founder of the Reddi kingdom is credited with the construction of flights of steps to Patalaganga. Kataya Vema Reddi, built the stone steps leading to Sikharesvaram in 1405 A.D.

Hatakesvaram temple (PL.219) is on the way to Srisailam of about 5km away in a serene atmosphere. The temple, dedicated to Hatakesavara svamy, is stone structure datable to 12th-13th centuries A.D. and consists of *garbha-griha* and open pillared portico.

Maha Sivarathri Festival is celebrated with great fervour. The temple streets and the bathing ghats reverberated with chants of *Om Namasivaya* and *Harahara Mahadeva* by the large number of devotees. The weary pilgrims burst in to ecstasy on having a glimpse of the temple from a distance at the *sikharam* (*Sikhara darshanam*).

There were 79 temples for Narasimha in Andhra Pradesh known from epigraphic sources, of which only 27 have survived with daily worship going on, even now. Of these the most well known nine temples are at Ahobilam (Kurnool Dt.), Kadiri and Penna Ahobilam (Anantapur Dt.) Korukonda and Simhachalam (Visakhapatnam Dt.), Vedadri (Krishna Dt.), Mangalagiri (Guntur Dt.), Singarayakonda (Prakasam Dt.) and Dharmapuri (Karimnagar Dt.). Of these, Ahobilam, the abode of Nava Narasimhas situated in the picturesque Nallamali hills where nature is at once awe-inspiring and beautiful has been traditionally acknowledged to be the shrine in which Lord Narasimha accorded *darshan* to Prahlada, *Garuda* and Srivan Adi Satakopa.

Ahobilam, a famous Vaishnava Pilgrim centre and one of the celebrated centres of the cult of Narasimha is in the Kurnool District of A.P. The place can be reached by a good motorable road from Allagadda which runs up to the hill of upper Ahobilam, about 10 km from the lower Ahobilam on a plateau 853.4 m above the sea level.

Bhavanasi, a stream that cascades down the hills cradling the Narasimha Svamy temple, greets visitors immediately on reaching upper Ahobilam (PL.220), an hour's drive from Allagadda (Kurnool Dt.) through Nallamalai ranges. The piligrms can have *darshan* of *Svayambhu Murti* of Sri Ahobila Narasimha in a rock cave which can be dated to 10th-11th centuries A.D. In another cave nearby is the idol of Chenchu, bride of the Svamy. Legend has it that Lord Narasimha, after killing Hiranyakasipu, remained here forgetting his consort, Lakshmi. As she cannot remain with out Her Lord, became the daughter of a Chenchu chief. When Lord Narasimha saw her, he became enamoured and eventually married her. So, Lord's consort is called Chenchu Lakshmi.

There are eight other smaller temples (excluding the one at Lower Ahobilam) form a group known as Nava Narasimha, representing nine different forms in which Lord Vishnu appeared-Prahladavarada or Lakshmi Narasimha, Kshatravata Narasimha, Karanda Narasimha, Yogananda Narasimha, Guha Narasimha, Kroda Narasimha, Malola Narasimha, Jvala Narasimha and Pavana Narasimha. At the entrance of the shrine of Guha Narasimha is a huge Pillar which, according to popular belief is the same pillar from which Lord Vishnu emerged in the form of *Ugra* (fearful) Narasimha (man - lion) at the prayer of his devotee Prahlada, and killed the demon. Of these, the Lakshmi Narasimha or Prahlada Narasimha temple and the Ahobila Narasimha temple, both at Lower Ahobilam and the Ahobila Narasimha temple at upper Ahobilam are famous and are in a good state of preservation. Ahobilam has a pre-eminent position among all Vaishnavite temples in the country because no where else are the nine incarnations of Lord Narasimha worshipped.

The upper Ahobilam Narasimha temple consists of *mukha-mandapa* (PL 221), *maha-mandapa* and faces east, but where as the *garbha-griha* (in this case a natural cave) faces north because of the orientation and situation of the natural cave. Abutting the *mukha-mandapa* a *dhvajastamba* and an ornate *bali-pitha* are situated. This unit is located in a large open area with cloistered *mandapas* on all the sides and the eastern gate leads to Malola and Jvala Narasimha shrines.

Just opposit to the main entrance of the lower Ahobilam temple, there is the principal Sannidhi Street. This is a broad and magnificent street with an unrboken row of *mandapas* on either side and also in the middle of the street.

The lower Ahobilam temple is surrounded by the three *Prakaras*, built in Vijayanagara style. The main temple on plan features a *ranga-mandapa*, an *ardha-mandapa* and *garbha-griha* and three small shrines dedicted to Alwars, Lakshmi and Andal. There are a number of *mandapas* outside the temple. A Venkatesvara shrine is situated on the south west corner. It's *mukha-mandapa* is now used as the *kalyana-mandapa* of Lord Narasimha. However, this temple is renowned for its *ranga-mandapa* (PL.222), with 82 massive pillars arranged in ten rows; each of them has extraordinary artistic merit, most intricately and richly sculptured with subjects taken from mythological stories.

The inscriptions reveal that the temples of Ahobilam enjoyed patronage of the Reddis of Kondavidu and the Rayas of Vijayanagar. Prolaya Vema Reddi has claimed that he has constructed the *sopana-margamu* (steps) both to Srisailam and Ahobilam temples. The temple is now under the management of Jiyyars of the Ahobilamutt. A choultry also has been constructed by the Tirumala-Tirupati devasthanams recently.

Srikalahastivara temple in the form of a *vayu-linga* is situated in the town of *Srikalahasti*, at the foot of Kailasagiri on the right bank of the Suvarnamukhi river (PL.223), which originates in the Adaram hills in Chittoor District and flows in to Nellore District before draining into the Bay of Bengal. The name, Srikalahasti, is a compound of three words. '*Sri*' means a spider, '*kala*' means a snake and '*hasti*' means an elephant. Local tradition says that the three were ardent devotees of Siva, individually, and worshipped the Siva-*linga* at the place in *krita-yuga*. The spider worshipped the *linga* by way of spinning a web over it, the snake by placing gems over it and the elephant by washing the *linga* with water. Thus they all worshipped *Siva-linga* with *ananya bhakti* and were granted *moksha* by lord Siva. Hence the god Siva here is called Srikalahastisvara and the *kshetra* is called Srikalahasti.

The Siva *linga* of Srikalahasti is one of the *Panchabhuta lingas* representig the five basic elements in the Universe, i.e., earth, water, fire, air and space. Physical forms of all things in the Universe, animate as well as inanimate, visible and invisible, are made up of these five elements only. Lord Siva at five sacred places is supposed to have manifested form of each of these five elements; namely, Kanchipuram, Jumbukesvaram, Tiruvannamalai and Chidambaram represent the *prithivi* (earth), *apas* (water) *tejas* (fire) and *akasa* (space) while Srikalahasti represents the *vayu* (wind). Evidence to support this theory is that the lamps in the *garbha-griha* of Srikalahastisvara flicker continuously creating an illusion that the *vayu* (air) pervades here even though there are no loopholes for the flow of air, justifying the god's feature, *vayu-linga.*

There are many legends highlighting the greatness of Srikalahastisvara-*kshetra* in *puranas* and literary works. Tinnadu or Kannappa, an *Erukula* youth by caste was a staunch devotee of the god, Siva. In intense and innocent devotion to the lord Siva, he worshipped the Siva-*linga* with *abhisheka* by pouring a mouthful of water and offering animal flesh, he being a tribal. One day Tinnadu sacrificed one of his eyes as an offering to Lord Siva and while in the act of offering the other eye also he was prevented by Siva himself. Lord Siva was immensely pleased at the devotion of Tinnadu and restored his eyes and granted *moksha*. Thus Tinnadu is known 'Kannappa Nayanar' meaning the great one who offered his eyes to Lord Siva. There is an idol of Kannappa near the main *linga* in the temple and *pujas* are first offered to him and then only to the god. The stories of Srikalahasti and Tinnadu convey that the humble creatures and tribesmen could worship Lord Siva, implying that the worship of Siva was not monopoly of those who were learned and wealthy.

Adisankaracharya (684-716 A.D.) in his *Sivanandalahari* alluded to Bhakta Kannappa after he visited Srikalahasti and installed a pedastal of Bhuvanesvari Devi, and the crystal *linga* which shines resplendent and attracts visitors by its sparkle.

Since the temple is huge and spacious, situated at the foot of the curved hill, it is irregular in plan. The temple contains three *prakaras* of which the first is represented today by north wall with a *gopura* entrance. The second *prakara* encloses several small shrines, *mandapas* and the famous hundred pillared *mandapa*. The third *prakara* encloses the main shrine. There is a big *gopura* on the bank of the river Suvarnamukhi. This 40m-high, seven storeyed gopuram (PL.224) was erected by Srikrishnadeva Raya in 1516 A.D. At present this magnificent *gopura* presents a heraldic view of the *kshetra* to pilgrims, though it looks detached from the temple complex. The sculptures on the storeys represent Saiva mythological scenes such as the Siva-Parvati *kalyanam,* Siva as Bhikshatanamurti etc.

The entrance to the first enclosure is surmounted by another *gopura* of the Vijayanagar period. This *gopura* (PL.225) faces the north and has a narrow pillared *mandapa* in two sections, on either side of the passage in the front coverng the *adhishthana*. The brick super structure contains five *talas* decoratead with the series-*kuta*, *panjara, sala, panjara* and *kuta*. This *gopura* was erected by one of the predecessors of Krishnadeva Raya. Inside the enclosure and a few yards to the south west of this *gopura*, is the Kasivisvesvara temple (PL.226) and belongs to Chola period. This temple inside the compound wall consists of the *mukha-mandapa* in two sections; an *antarala* and a *garbha-griha*.

In the north-west corner of the second enclosure is a shrine featuring a *mandapa* at lower level, another at a higher level and a *garbha-griha* built against its back wall. The *mandapas* have typical Vijayanagara pillars. The west *gopura* belongs to the pre-Vijayanagara period. Very near to this *gopura* and touching the west *prakara* wall of the second enclosure is the hundred pillared *mandapa*. This was erected by Srikrishnadeva Raya in 1516 A.D., which stands on a high *adhishthana* and is reached by a flight of steps guarded by elephants. This high and ornate *mandapa* has 77 exquisitely carved pillars with figure sculpture of the Saiva and the Vaishnava deities and *dasavataras* (the ten incarnations) of lord Vishnu. In this enclosure there is an underground cell where Patalaganapati is worshipped.

The only entrance in the south leading in to third enclosure is surmounted by a *gopura* of Vijayanagar period. There is a narrow *mandapa* on either side of the passage infront of the *gopura*. The third *prakara* encloses the main shrine of Kalahastisvara facing the west, the *Devi* shrine facing the east. Here Parvati, the consort of lord Siva, is known as Jnana Prasunamba (flower of knowledge). There are a few minor shrines and huge pillared corridor running on the four sides in the interior. The *adhishthana* of the Kalahastisvara shrine carry Chola inscriptions. The earliest of these is dated in the 16th regnal year of Raja Raja I. The architectural style of the main shrine also reveals its affliation to the Chola period. The pillared corridor was renovated in the recent times.

The temple is famous for the *Rahu-Ketu puja* being performed here everyday.The ritual is considered to ward off the evil effects in general and those caused by unfavourable planetary movements, in particular.

The auspicious day of Mahasivaratri, every year is the occasion to largest gathering of devotees probably in lakhs to have the sight of the lord and worship him. They first take bath in the river *Suvarnamukhi,* worshippiing the *vayu-linga,* observing fast on the day completely keep themselves awake till midnight, spending time in chanting the name of Siva, performing *abhiseka* and in several other forms of service, such as *sankirtanas* and chanting *panchakshari* and listening to the stories of Siva, chanting his *stotras*, etc. Midnight worship of Siva-*linga* on Mahasivaratri day is known as *lingodbhavam.* It is a very special and sacred occasion.

The picturesque *Tirumala,* perhaps, the greatest pilgrimage centres in India, with largest income, running in hundres of croes per year is situated on the Seshachalam hills in Chittor distrct, at 860 m above the MSL. The hills spreading over more than 100 sq. km in area, are considered to have extended in the form of a coiled snake, Adisesha himself, and thus called Seshachalam, consists of seven peaks, representing the seven hoods of the divine serpant. The seven peaks are called Seshadri, Niladri, Garudadri, Anjanadri, Vrishabhadri, Narayanadri and Venkatadri, the suffix in the names, *adri* in Sanskrit meaning hill. Seshadri or Seshachalam is one of the major offshoots of the Erramalai ranges, which itself is a branch of the Eastern Ghats. This world famous shrine is next only to Vatican City in terms of the number of visitors and offerings made to the deity.

The sacred temple of Sri Venkatesvara, also known as Balaji, (PL.227) is located on the seventh peak, Venkatadri and there are several legends associated with the manifestation of the Lord in Tirumala. It was the great preceptor Sri Ramanuja who prescribed in detail the daily rituals to be performed in the Tirumala temple and created an excellent organisational set-up which continues to this day.

The abode of the lord is about 20 km north-west of *Tirupati* and there are footsteps leading to the hill as well as two separate serpentine roads to reach the shrine, by bus or a car. The glory of Tirupati dates back as early as Sangam period. Sangam literature (2nd century B.C. to 2nd century A.D.) mentions Tirupati as Thiruvengadam, which in subsequent years became Thiruvenkatadri. According to legend, god Vishnu revealed himself earlier, in the previous incarnations as Varahasvamy on the banks of the present temple tank. This manifestation of the white boar (*sveta- varaham)* is enshrined in the Adivaraha temple situated on the north-western banks of the tank.

All the great dynasties of the south have paid their homage to this shrine. The Tirumala temple on its walls carries at least 640 inscriptions. They span the period from 9th to 17th century A.D. and belong to the dynasties like the Pallavas, Rastrakutas, Cholas, Pandyas, Telugu Pallavas, Yadavarayas and the Rayas of Vijayanagara. The inscriptions reveal that the Tirumala temple enjoyed the royal patronage of the aforesaid dynasties which were greatly devoted to Sri Venkatesvara. In fact, it was during the Vijayanagara rule that the number of benefactions to the temple had increased and new adjuncts were added. Srikrishnadeva Raya had visited the temple town seven times during his reign, along with his queens and had given very great amounts of grants and endowments to this temple, in the form of jewellery and ornaments that are still adorned on the image of the deity.

The sanctum enshrines 2.4 m high image of Venkatesvara. The exiquistely-wrought idol, *Mulabera*, is believed to be self-manifested *(Svayambhu)* according to the local legends, and it is difficult to trace the history of the temple and date of the carving of the image, on grounds of tangible evidence.

The image of the lord is in the standing posture. According to the texts, he is richly adorned with flowing locks of hair some of which rest on his shoulders. On normal days the imposing idol of the main deity, is adorned with a golden *kiritam* which has a large emerald embedded on its front. On special occasions like the Brahmothsavam, he is adorned with his precious diamond crown worth over Rs. 30 crores. On his fore head, the lord has a thick double patch of upright *namam* drawn with refined camphor which screens his eyes. In between the two white patches is the *kasturi-tilakam.* His ears are bedecked with shining golden *makara-kundalas.* He has four arms, the upper two being culled to hold the *sankha* and *chakra.* The lower right hand is in the *varada-hasta* style and the left lower hand in the *katyavalambitha* pose.

His dark-complexioned body is clothed with a *pitambaram* tied with a golden string and a golden belt to which are attached tiny, jingling golden bells. He is adorned with precious ornaments. He has a *Yajnopavitam* flowing down cross-wise from his left shoulder. He bears Sri Lakshmi Devi on the right side of his chest and Sri Padmavati on the left side. His lotus feet are covered with gold frames and decked with clinging golden anklets.

The *ananda nilaya-divya vimana* (PL.228) was covered with gilt copper and surmounted with a golden vase, in the 14th century during the reign of the Vijayanagar king Bukkaraya. Neither the pilgrims nor the TTD personnel, however, top he might be in the officialdom, are allowed access into the sanctum sanctorum, only the priests and their authorised representatives can enter it, touch the deity and perform the prescribed rituals. Many of the pilgrims have a dip in the sacred pond, *pushkarini* (PL.229), tank adjacent to the temple at Tirumala, before having a *darshan* of Lord Venkatesvara. According to legend, it was originally meant for the sport of Vishnu in his celestial abode, *vaikuntha,* and was brought down to earth by *garuda* for lord Venkatesvara. During the *Brahmotsavam* season, lakhs of pilgrims visit the temple. The holy *prasadam* is in the form of *laddus.* Being a rich temple, it funds Venkatesvara university and several other institutions dedicated to the *vedas*, oriental studies, Engineering, medicine etc.

The Lord of Seven Hills, Venkatesvara, or Venkatachalapthi, or Balaji has become the first 'e-god' on the planet, with the introduction of *e-hundi, e-sevas*, *e*-accomodation and *e*-flowers. The latest addition is the on line booking of the *darshan* timings. Even though, the science and the religious beliefs never travel together, the application of the latest technology in the service departments in the TTD has received overwhelming response from the devotees spread all across the globe. Earlier every devotee was invariably to come all the way to Tirumala to make offerings (cash/kind), but the situation is different today, with the revolutionary changes in the field of science and techonology one can fulfill his vows even without his personal visit to the temple.

The Venkatesvara temple-complex stands with in the massive *prakara* built of large blocks of stones. It measures 126.2 m by 80.2 m. There is only one entrance in the east surmounted by a *gopura* known as the *maha-gopura* (PL.230). The base of the *gopura* was in existence prior to the 14th century

A.D. though the superstructure belongs to a later date. Passing through the entrance of this *gopura*, one enters the outer courtyard of the temple. Immediately adjacent to and touching the *gopura* is a small *mandapa* of Vijayanagara times with two wings, one on each side and path way in the centre. The *ranga-mandapa* with small porch is situated on the south-east corner of court yard. Towards the southern end of the *mandapa* are a pavilion and a shrine. The pavilion, now painted, is of black granite and used to house a *vahana*. The shrine is a fine structure consisting of an *antarala* and *garbha-griha*. The walls on the sides are decorated with series of pilasters, *kumbha-panjaras*. This shrine on stylistic grounds may be dated to 14th century.

To the west of the *ranga-mandapa* is another *mandapa* known as the *anna-unjal-mandapa* or Tirumalaraya *mandapa*. This comprises two parts, the front part being at a lower level and the rear part at a higher level. The rear part was erected by the Vijayanagara ruler, Saluva Narasimha, in 1473 A.D. and the front part was added by Araviti Tirumalaraya in the 16th century. The front and rear parts contain two rows of four pillars each, on each side. The pillars carry a few Vaishnava divinities.

In the centre of the *mandapa,* at the western part of the coutrtyard, a *dhvaja-stamba* and a *bali-pitha* are situated.

To the left of the entrance *gopura,* a small shrine dedicated to Varadaraja is found, and consists of a high *adhishthana,* an *antarala, a garbha-griha* and a *vimana* above, belonging to the *vesara* order. The doorway in the front is flanked by a pilaster on either side and surmounted by a *kapota* decorated with *nasikas* surmounted by *simhalalata*. In side the sanctum a stone image of Varadaraja is found.

In the sourthern part of the courtyard is the *kalyana-mandapa,* 24.4 m by 9 m, which is reached by a short flight of steps in the east. It possesses plain and *vyala* bracket pillars. This *mandapa* is datable to late 16th century A.D. Towards the western end of this *mandapa* there is a pavilion of black granite containing four pillars, each with three projecting pillarets. The sculptures on these pillars represent Narasimha, Krishna and Venugopala. Behind this pavilion is a small shrine on a finely carved *adhishthana.*

The shrine of Narasimha is in the north-east corner of the courtryard built in a pillared verandah touching the eastern wall of the *prakara.* The shrine has an *antarala* and *garbha-griha*; its outer walls are relieved with pilasters. In the sanctum theYoga-Narasimha image sitting cross legged is enshrined.

The main temple where the deity of Sri Venkatesvara enshrined is a complex of multiple structures, starting with the *tirumamani-mandapa* (open pillared hall) at the east and ending to the *garbha-griha* at the west. Its northern and southern wings of the *mukkoti-pradakshina* inside, is enclosed by a stone wall, and set on a low *adhishthana.* Two *mandapas,* the *tirumamani-mandapa* and the *snapana-mandapa*, project to the east from the front wall between the two side wings of *pradakshina.* Thus the main shrine appears to be in three sections when viewed from the north.

The *dvitala-vimana* above the *garbha-griha* carries the series of *kuta, sala, and panjara* elements in each storey and has a *gala* or neck adorned with a *salakoshtha* surmounted by *simhalalata* in the centre with a *panjara* similarly surmounted on each side. Above this is the round domical *sikhara* adorned with lotus design all over and on the top is the *kalasa.* The *vimana* with its Vaishnava divinities is enclosed by gilded plates.

To the west of the *tirumamani-mandapa* is the front wall of the *snapana-mandapa.* In its centre is the doorway, known as the *bangaru-vakili* (golden door). In its jambs have lotus petal designs and the *dvarapalas* at the base and the Gajalakshmi in the *lalata.*

Passing through the *bangaru-vakili* one enters the *snapana-mandapa* which contains four central pillars. The front part of this *mandapa* has been converted into two rooms, one on either side. Beyond this *mandapa* is a narrow compartment, about 3.7 m x 3 m with a raised pial on either side of the way. A number of metal images are found on these pials. Obviously, this was originally another *mandapa* and rooms must have been built on the sides leaving a narrow pathway in the centre. Further west is another *mandapa,* now known as the *sayana-mandapa* (bed room). This must have been originally the *antarala.* Next is the *garbha-griha* enshrining the image of Sri Venkatesvara.

The actual date of construction of the temple is not known as there is no direct evidence and any attempt must therefore be based upon inference. Inscriptions found in the temple only refer to its renovations and rebuildings and additions and alterations, but none gives the date of the construction of the original temple. One such renovation is known to have been made in the 13th century, by way of building thick stone walls, so as to strengthen the earlier ones. It is therefore not possible to examine the outer side of original walls of the sanctum and estimate the date. Basing on the available evidence it may be concluded that a shrine with *garbha-griha* and *antarala* existed in the 8th century A.D. at the latest, which are the present sanctum and the *sayana-mandapa,* which were enclosed, as mentioned above, by means of parallel walls in 13th century. The outside of the original walls of these two structures in their decor exhibit similar features noticed in the Krishna temple, adjacent to the Govindarajaswami temple at Tirupati, which can be dated to later Pallava period. In all probability, the image of Sri Venkatesvara stood in an open *mandapa* for a long time before the 8th century A.D.

In the rest of the Vijayanagara Empire some of the temples at Vellore, Virinchipuram, Kanchipuram and Srirangam all in Tamilnadu, are in Vijayanagar style. The *kalyana-mandapa* of the Jalakantesvara in the fort temple at Vellore is considered to be the most beautiful structure of its kind, with typical Vijayanagar pillars and *gopura.* The decorative carvings on pillars consist of *yalis* and rearing horses with riders in different hunting poses. The temple of Margasakhesvara at Virinchipuram

(North Arcot District) is also noteworthy for the exuberant treatment of its *kalyana-mandapa.*

At Kanchipuram there are two temples with pavilions of Vijayanagara period, that in the Varadaraja temple, a "hundred pillared-*mandapa*" being composed of a maze of closely set pillars decorating with rearing horses and hippogryphs with riders (PL.231). Monolithic stone chains cut out of single stone,adorn the corners of this *mandapa* deserve mention (PL.232). The "thousand pillared- *mandapa*" (PL.233) of the Ekamranatha temple is decorated with the same fantastic form of sculpture. The so-called horse-court or *Seshagirirayar-mandapa* at Srirangam had "a colonnade of furiously rearing steeds each rearing upto a height of nearly 2.7 m, the whole executed in a technique so emphatic as to be not like stone but hardened steel".

The bronzes of the Vijayanagara period are well distributed all over in the temples of South India. Among these the life-size portrait statues of Krishnadeva Raya and his two queens and of Venkataraya from Tirupati, standing Ganapati, Somaskanda and Nataraja from Srisailam (PL.234), Virabhadra and Bhadrakali from Lepakshi are notable. They show how bronze casting of the period retained the excellence it had attained under the Cholas.

11

Madurai Style

The Nayakas were military generals appointed by the Vijayanagar kings, at various political centres of the empire, but the Nayakas of Madurai and Tanjore, came to be pre-eminent among all others. When the Vijayanagar kings were decimated in the battle of Talikota in 1565 A.D. they became powerful, eventually independent and occupied the entire Tamil speaking country, sharing between them. They ruled, carrying on their mutual wars for supremacy, for generations together, till the end of the 18th century. Inspite of the political turmoils, due to their mutual wars on one hand and the invasions of the Sultans of Bijapur and Golconda, as well as the Marathas, on the other, the Nayakas made rich contributions to art and architecture of Tamil Nadu.

Tirumala Nayaka (1623-1659 A.D.) the greatest of the Nayakas of Madurai invaded Travancore twice and held the Setupati king under his control, made Madurai his capital about 1634 A.D. and adorned the city with many fine buildings. His palace and the temple of Meenakshi and Sundaresvara are standing testimonies to his contribution to art. It was under him the Madurai temple was altogether rebuilt on a new integral plan.

Temple building activity was given due importance by the rulers. During this period old temples were enlarged with additional high enclosure walls and towering *gopuras* at four cardinal points and adjuncts like huge halls with massive pillars, a sacred tank, etc., were added to the existing temples. The rampant animals, figure sculptures and portraits of royal persons on the shafts of the pillars are often bigger than life size are the most favoured. To some extent it was a revival and continuation of building traditions of the Pandyas. Notable representations of this style are the temples of Madurai, Srirangam, Jambukesvaram, Tiruvallur, Ramesvaram, Tinnevelly and Srivilliputtur. The temples of Chidambaram and Tiruvannamalai have some of the features of the Madurai style. In Madurai style temples, the corbels of the pillars show at their ends a plantain flower like motif. Again the corridors in the temples of this period are provided with ceilings which are invariably painted.

Madurai, with its 2500 year historical heritage, is a thrilling city in Tamil Nadu, on the banks of the river Vaigai, has always been at the crossroads of trading routes into different parts of Indian subcontinent as well as to countries abroad, since the time known to history. According to some local legend, Madurai was located in the midst of a *Kadambavana* and thus embodied its sweetness and hence obtained the name. The rule of the Nayakas and their contribution to arts, letters and culture were the last flickers of the glories of Madurai.

The Meenakshi temple is of course largely the focal point of Madurai, the magnetic force drawing every denizen and Visitor. Year-long festivals thrill the town, culminating in the celestial wedding of Meenakshi with Sundaresvar, conducted for over a week, devoutly enacting all the legends associated with it. It is about 1 km from the Madurai railway junction. The temple is a town within a town, each part of it having been built at different times, by different kings. As it is presently seen, one can never figure out where the shops end and where the

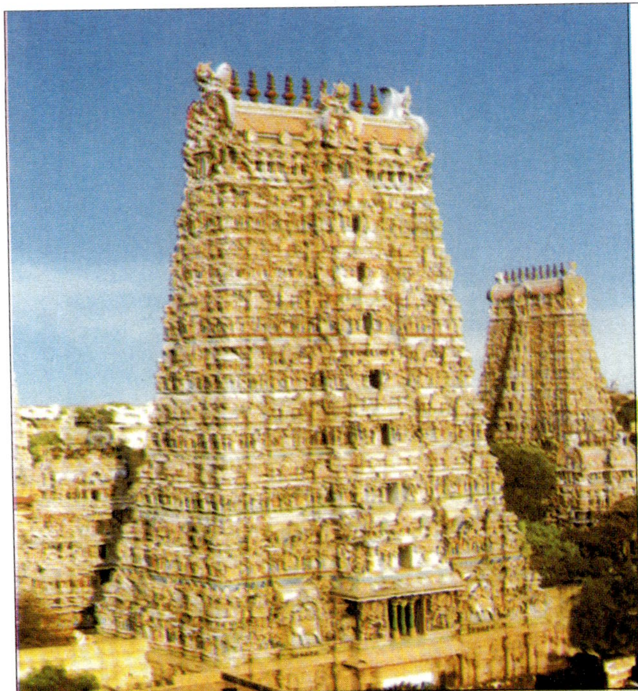

235. Madurai, Meenakshi Sundaresvara temple, *gopuras*.

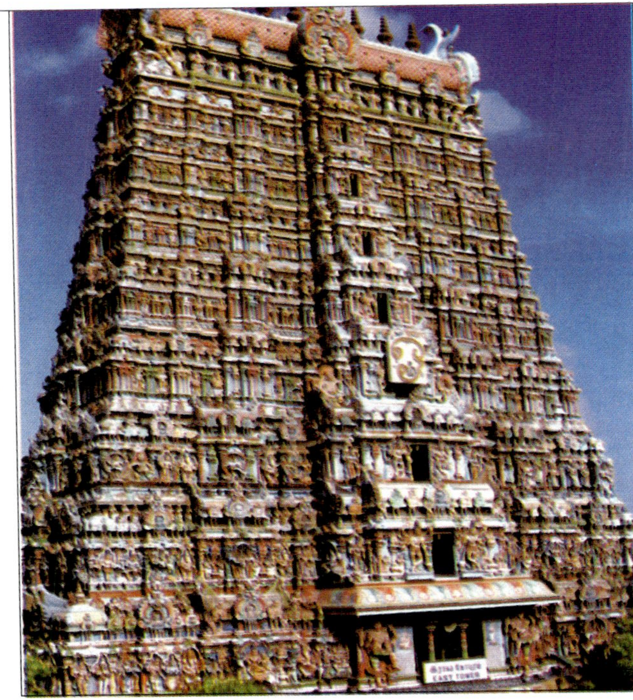

236. Madurai, Meenakshi Sundaresvara temple, East *gopuras*.

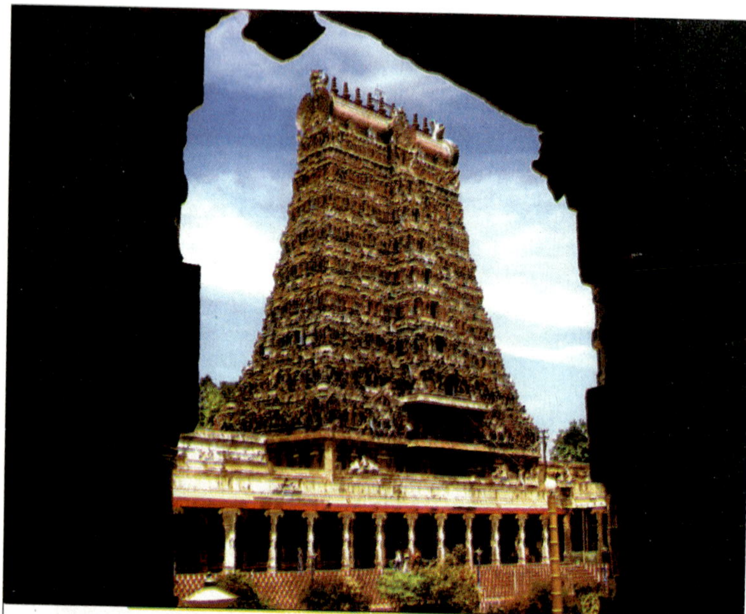

237. Madurai, Meenakshi Sundaresvara temple, pond of golden lilies and Southern *gopura*.

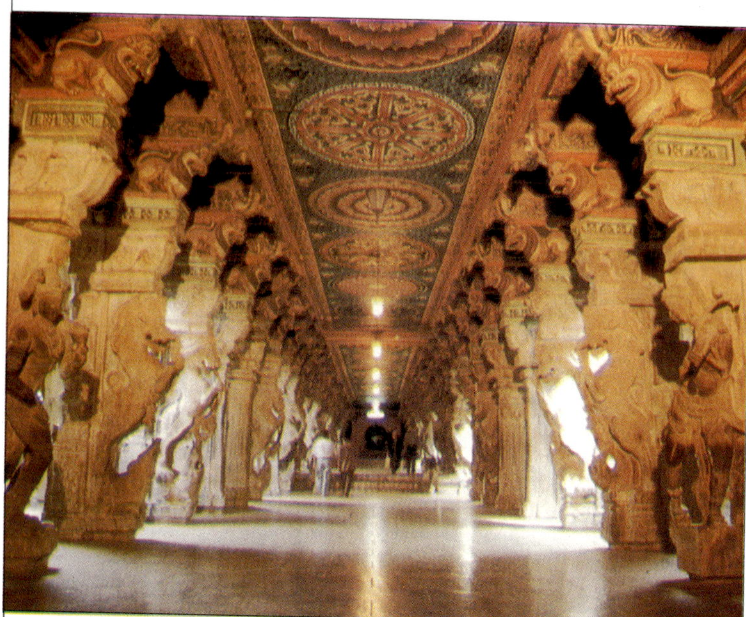

238. Madurai, Meenakshi Sundaresvara temple, Thousand pillared hall.

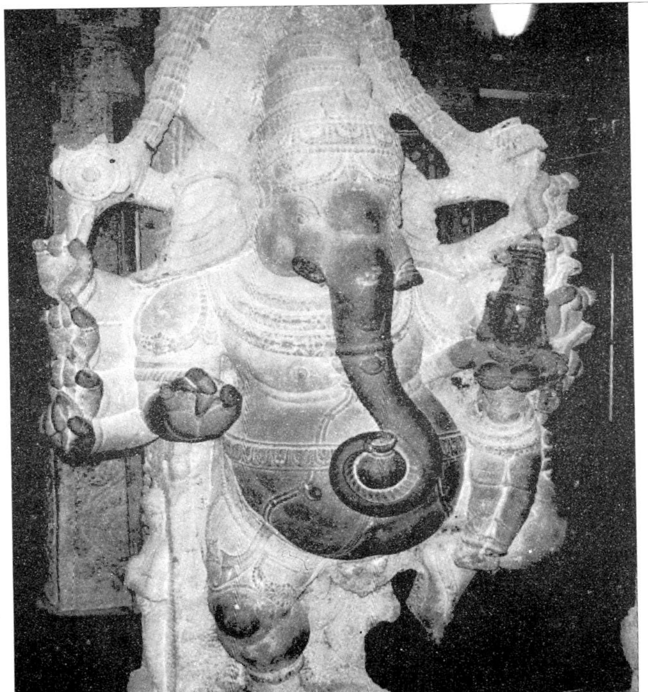

239. Madurai, Meenakshi Sundaresvara temple, Thousand pillared hall, Dancing Ganesha.

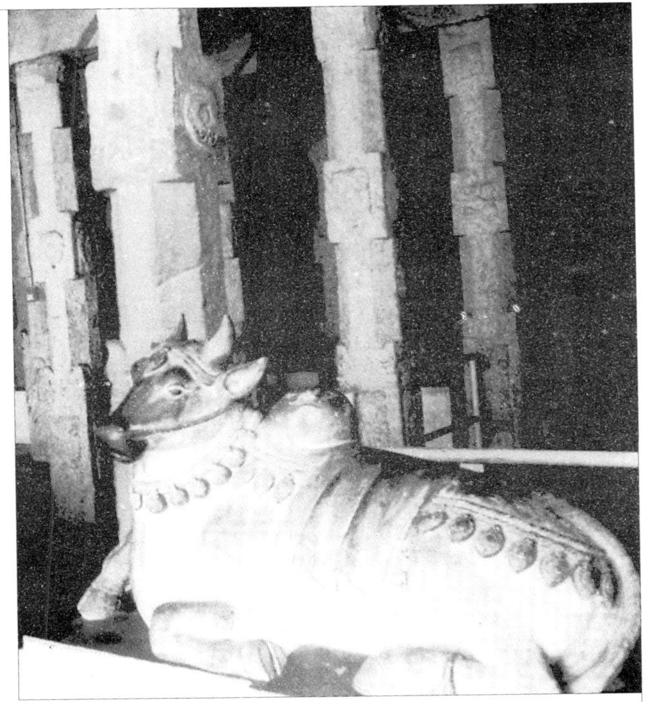

240. Madurai, Meenakshi Sundaresvara temple, Thousand pillared hall, museum.

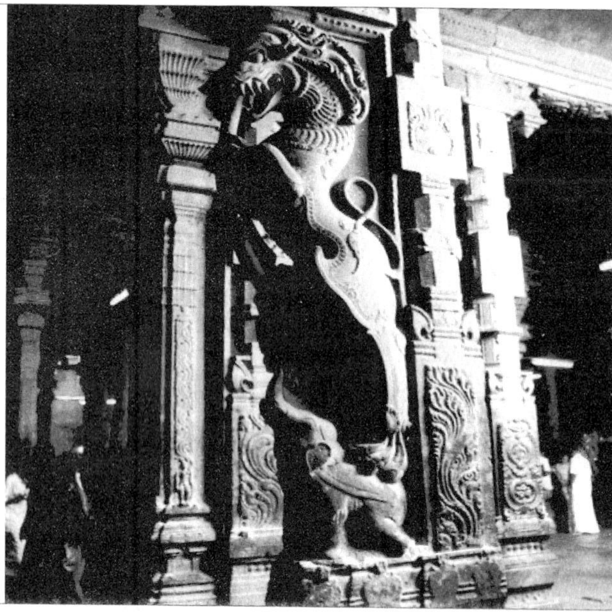

241. Madurai, Meenakshi Sundaresvara temple complex, pillar.

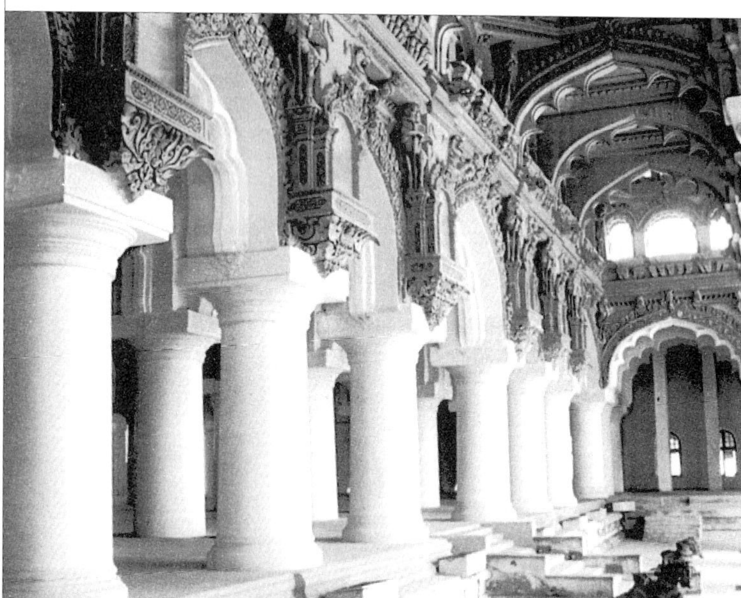

242. Madurai, Tirumala nayaka mahal, corridor.

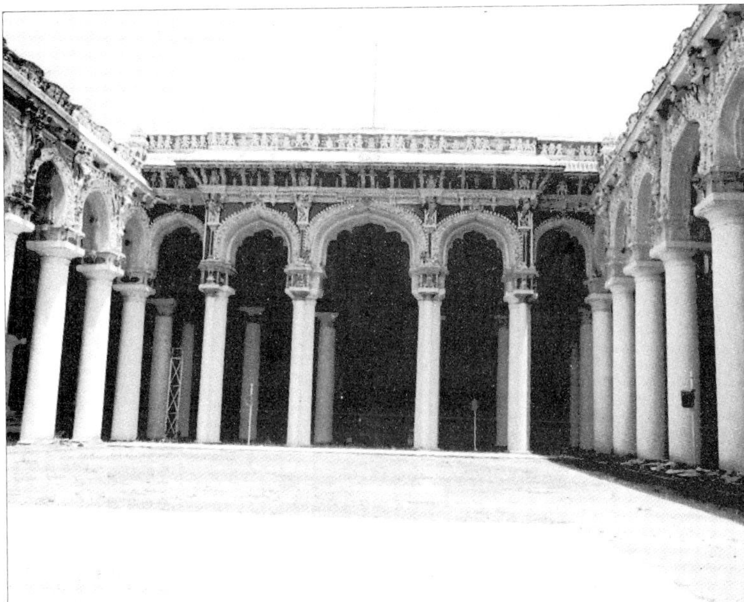

243. Madurai, Tirumala nayaka mahal, Swarga vilasa.

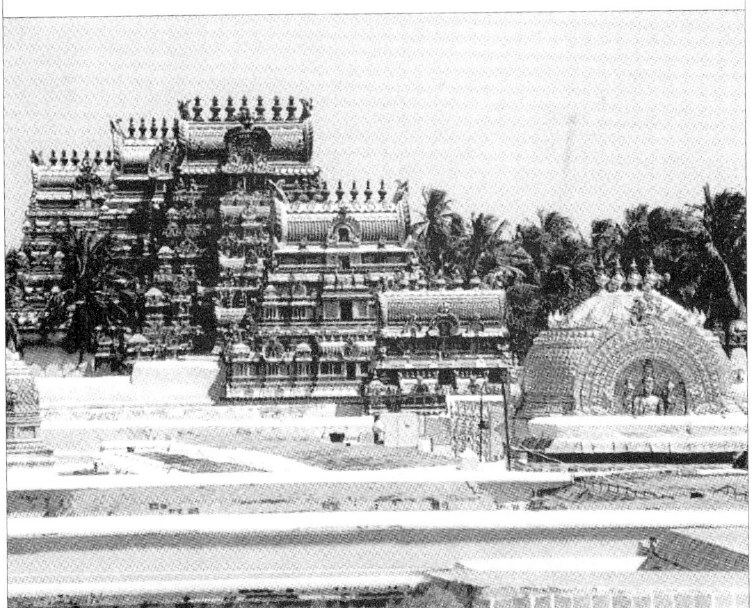

244. Srirangam, Ranganatha temple, *gopuras*.

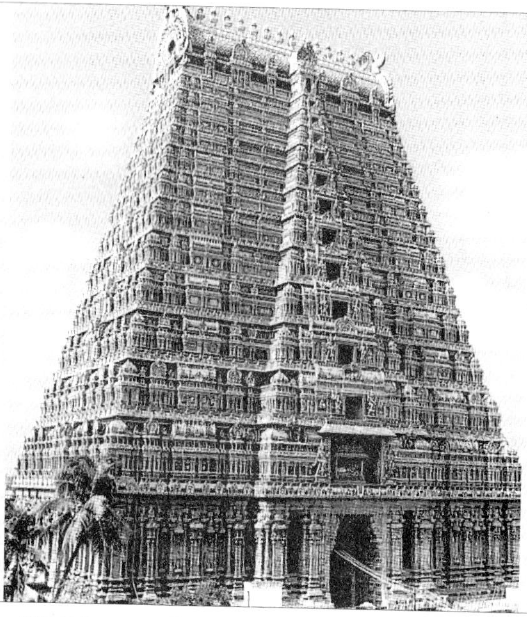

245. Srirangam, Ranganatha temple, *Raja gopuras*.

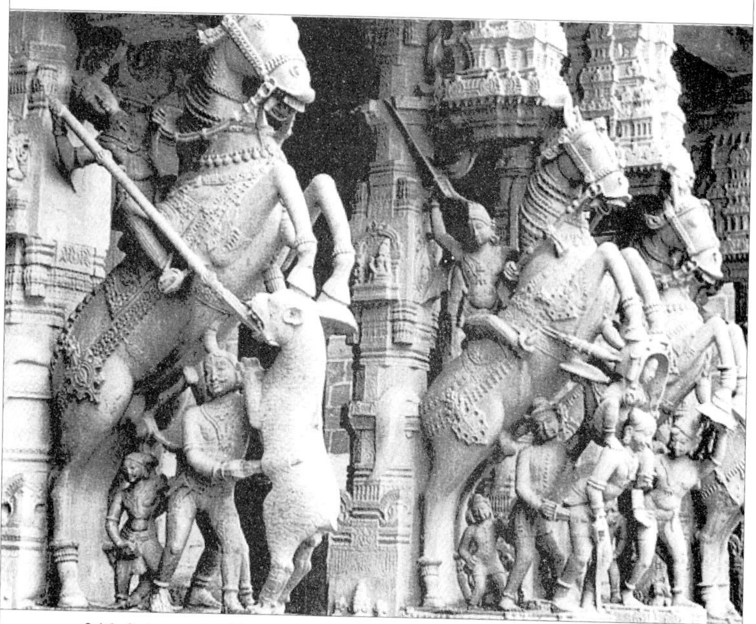

246. Srirangam, Ranganatha temple, horse court, details of pillar.

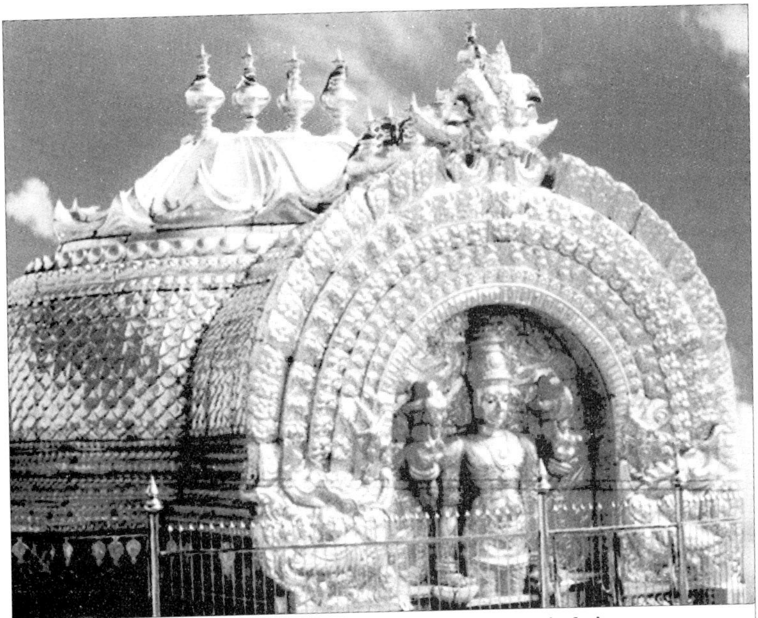

247. Srirangam, Ranganatha temple, golden domical *vimana*.

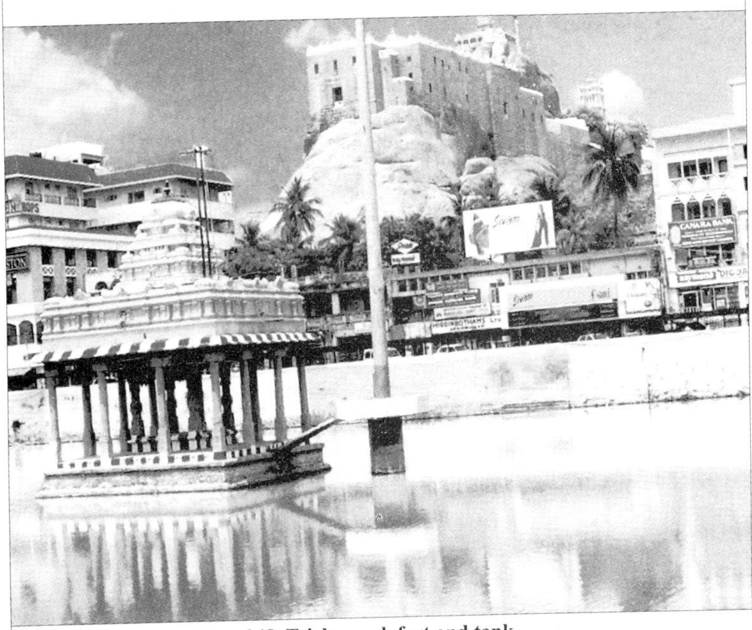

248. Trichy, rock fort and tank.

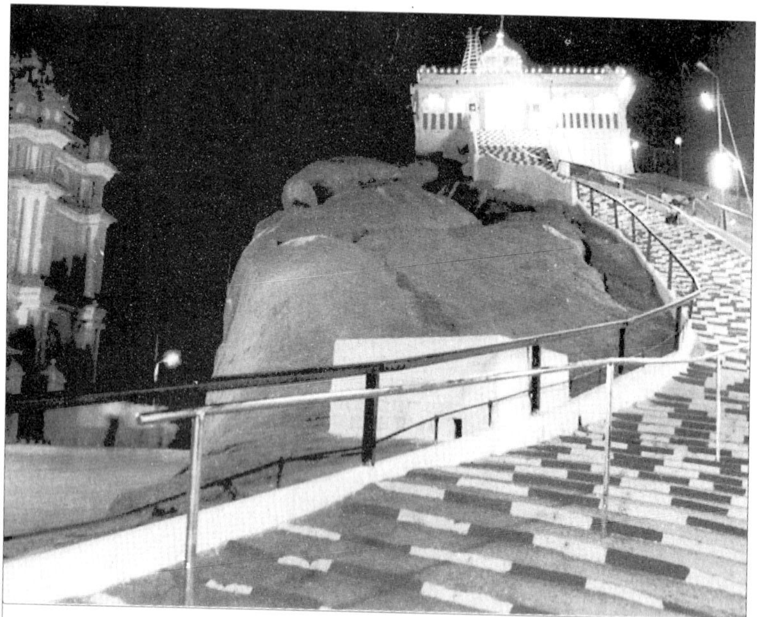

249. Trichy, Uchipillayar temple.

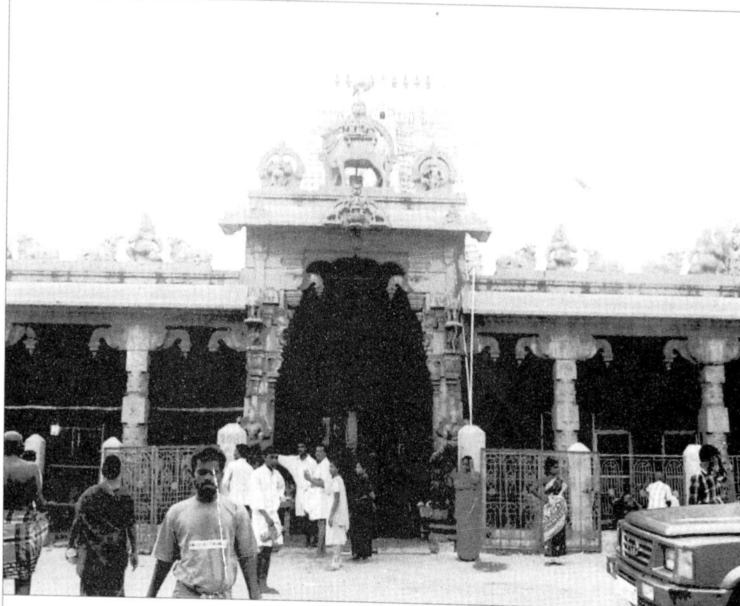

250. Ramesvaram temple, entrance gateway.

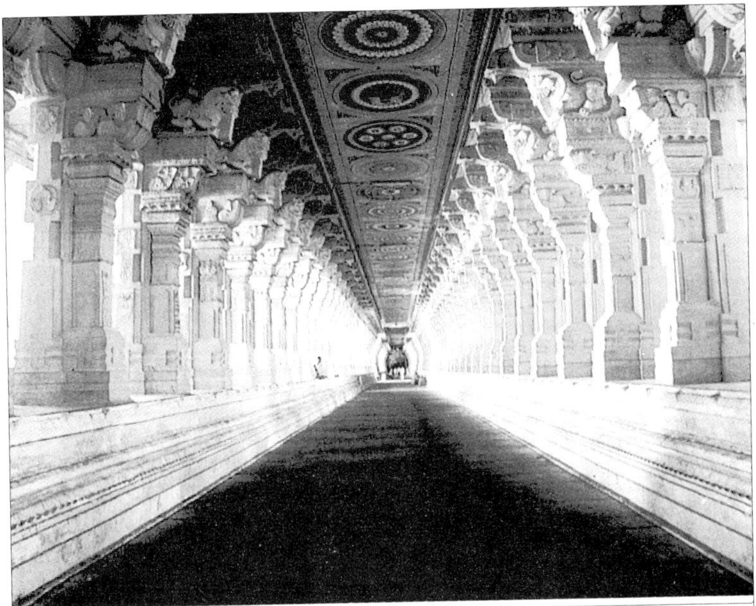

251. Ramesvaram temple, third corridor.

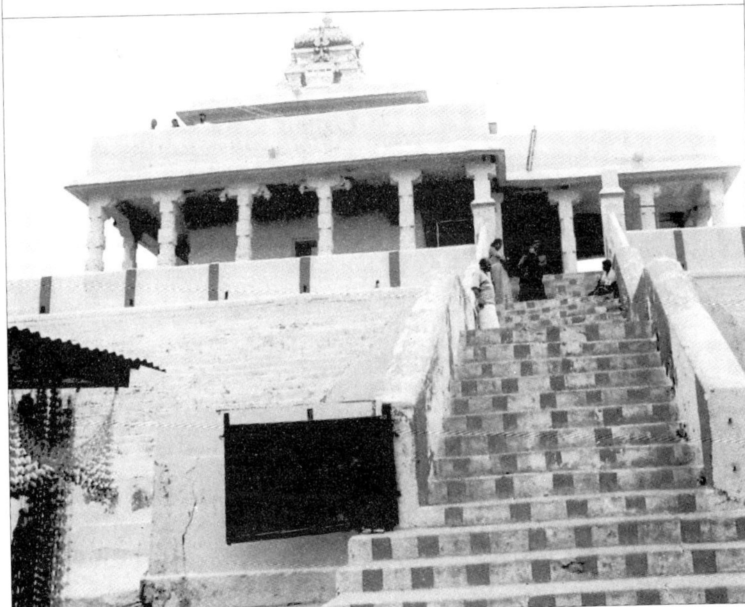

252. Ramesvaram, Gandhamadhava temple, general view.

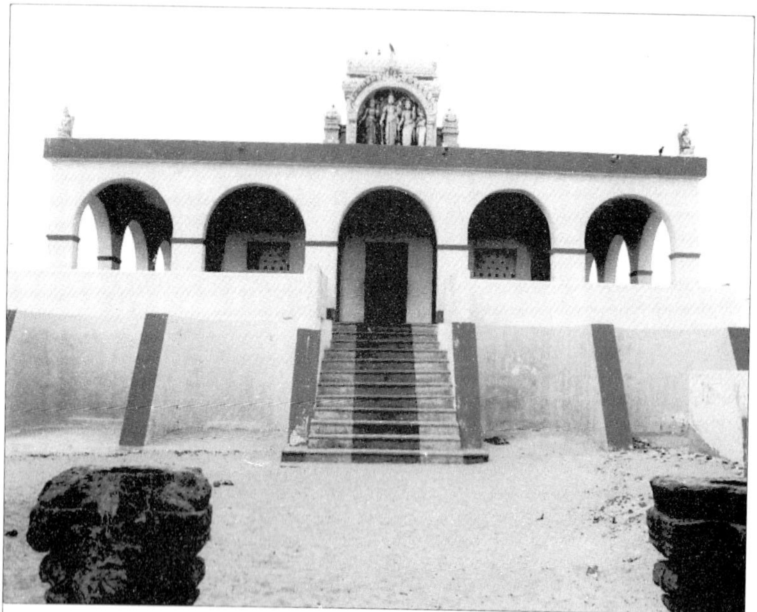

253. Ramesvaram, Kodandarama temple, general view.

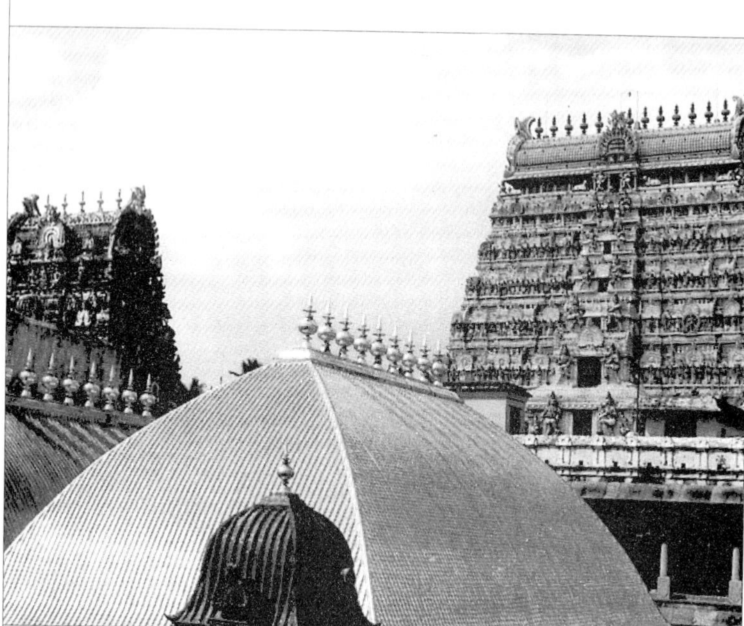

254. Chidambaram, Nataraja temple.

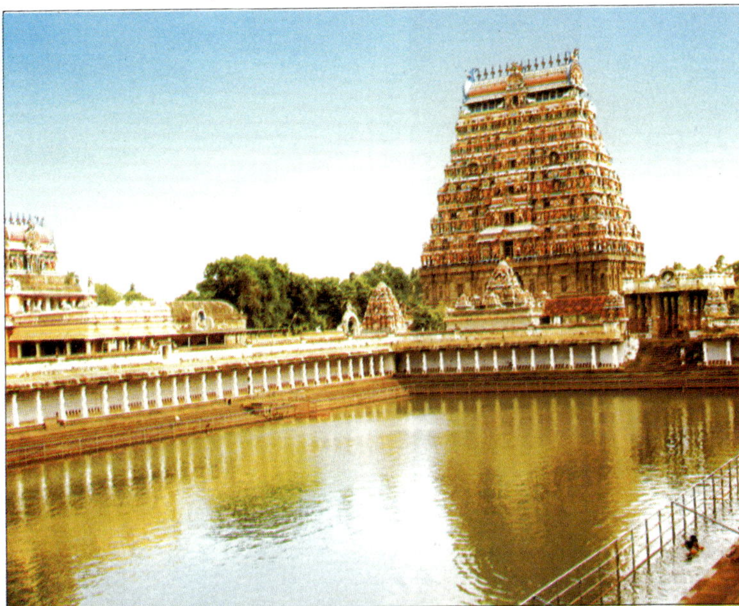

255. Chidambaram, Sivaganga tank with north tower.

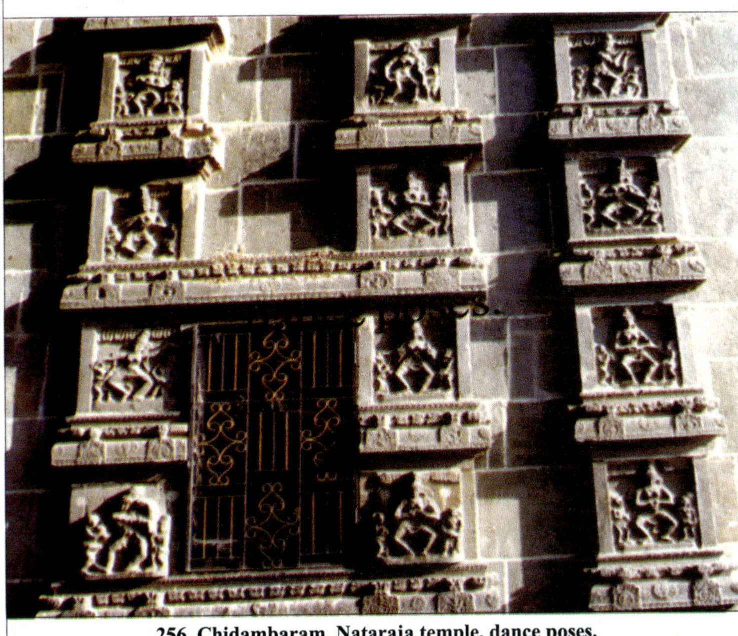

256. Chidambaram, Nataraja temple, dance poses.

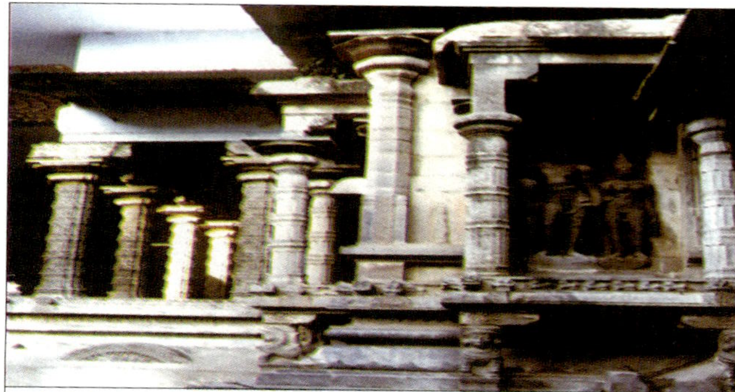

257. Chidambaram, Nataraja temple, *nritta-sabha,* partial view.

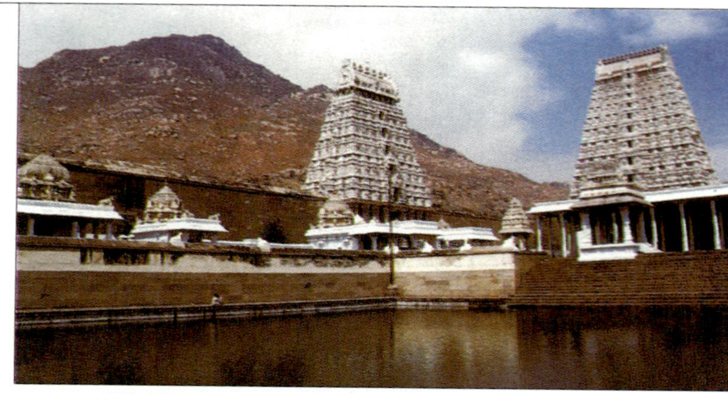

258. Tiruvannamalai, Siva temple, tank and *gopuras*.

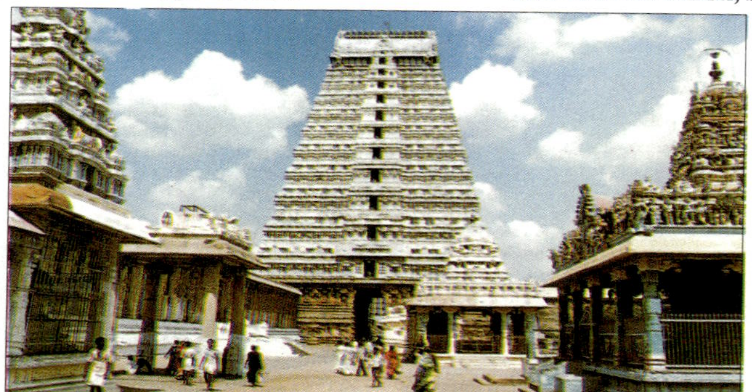

259. Tiruvannamalai, Siva Temple, small shrines and Gopura.

temple begins, as several beautifully carved halls *(mandapas)* have become shopping arcades. Families are stretched on stone floors between pillars, dozing away after an outing. Do they know that saints sang at this very spot, creating miracles? Do they know from within its massive precincts, had sprung art forms, music, dance and literature. Children scurry down to the green water of the pond of the golden lotus, where a thousand flowers of poetry blossomed in successive assemblies *(sangam),* making Tamil a supreme force, children to-day laugh and play oblivious of their heritage. Men in uniform who look like the guards of the temple exchange loud words, congregating in clusters along the corridors. Do they realise that mighty dynasties lavished most of their skill and resources on the art and architecture of their temple?

According to *sthalapurana*, Meenakshi was the daughter of a Pandyan king. Much to the shock of her parents she was born with three breasts. An angel foretold that she would loose third breast when she meets her would be husband. In due course she crowned the queen of Madurai. She ivaded many kingdoms. At last she marched on Mount Kailas, the abode of lord Siva. On seeing Siva, her third breast disappeared.Lord Siva asked her to return to Madurai. He also promised her to marry her eighth day. Accordingly, Lord Siva came with sages and gods and married Thadatatagai, otherwise Sri Meenakshi, which literally means the one with fish eyes. The worship of the mothergoddess, or *Shakti*, is personfied in the worship of Meenakshi as a loving, sustaining female energy.

The Meenakshi temple of Madurai (PL. 235) can be taken as typical of the Madurai style. It is actually a double temple dedicated to Sundaresvara and his consort Meenakshi. The outer high walls (259 x 221 m) are enclosing these two shrines and other structures with four large *gopuras* on the four sides. As we enter from the main entrance by the east (PL. 236) we are led through a beautiful pillared corridor into another entrance surmounted by a smaller *gopura*. Most of this second enclosure is covered by a flat roof. In the third and innermost enclosure is situated the sacred shrine which consists of *garbha-griha, antarala* and the *sabha-mandapa*. The *garbha-griha* is surmounted by a small *vimana* rising above the flat roof covering the other two compartments also.

All the corridors and halls situated within the three enclosures have long colonnades of pillars of bizarre designs. There are in all nearly 2000 pillars in the Madurai temple. The simple pillars have square mouldings while the huge and more intricate ones have rampant animals, figures of deities or portraits of royal persons for motifs. These figure sculptures so cut out as to form along with the main shaft a common support to the capital. The figures are of more than life size and highly elaborate in workmanship.

The sanctuary of Meenakshi is situated to the south of the main temple. This structure with its two concentric enclosures is roughly half the size of the main temple. In front of the temple of Meenakshi is the beautiful "Pond of Golden Lilies", a reservoir (50.3 x 36.6 m) surrounded by steps and a pillared portico on sides. Its picturesque appearance is enhanced by the background of the southern *gopura* which reflects on its waters (PL.237).

Large and small there are in all eleven *gopuras* to the Madurai temple looming over the city, the largest and the highly developed of them being the one on the southern gateway. By far this is the most massive and ornate *gopura* rising to a height of 45.7 m (PL.237). Its summit is a barrel roof with usual *chaitya* gable at the ends. The lofty base and the concave curves of the whole structure give to soaring quality greater even than its height suggests. The central rib of the tower is a pile of miniature pavilions rising one upon another and adding greatly to its massiveness and strength. The surface is covered all over with stucco figures of deities and semidivine characters freely form the inexhaustible Hindu mythology and present the appearance of a pulsating mass of masonary.

Another noteworthy and spacious structure in the temple complex is the hall of thousand pillars (PL.238) erected in the year 1560 A.D. by Arianayakam Mudaliar, minister of the founder of the Nayaka dynasty. This is situated in the north-east corner of the outer *prakara* and measuring 73.2 m x 76.2 m, which faces south, lies along side of the wide, pillared approach to the main temple. Its interior is symmetrical in the arrangement of the pillars and includes a central aisle leading up to a small shrine of Sabhapati at its northern end. Regarding the sculptures on the pillars Fergusson observes: "surpass those of any other hall of its class I am acquainted with". A number of sculptures bear the iconic forms of Siva alongwith the whole pantheon of other deities like dancing Ganesa (PL.239), Subrahmanya, Saraswati, Manmadha and Rathi. A museum of many antiquities, sculptures and interesting pieces of art is arranged here (PL.240).

The *pudu-mandapa* or Tirumala's Choultry situated out side the main entrance and infront of the main gateway was built between 1626-1633 A.D. by Tirumala Nayaka. This is a large open hall (106.7m x 32m), and is distinguished for its four rows of pillars, which are elaborately carved. The decorative carving on the central pillars consists of 10 life size statues of the Nayaka kings. The latest statue is that of its builder, Tirumala Nayaka. In other *mandapas* in the temple complex the *gaja-vyala* pillars (PL.241) are mostly favoured.

Utsavas or festivals take place in the Madurai temple all the year round every month. Chief among them is Chaitra festival or the *kalyana* (marriage) *utsava* of Meenakshi and Sundaresvar. It is celebrated in April- May. The floating festival takes place in January or February. In this festival idols of Meenakshi and her lord Sundaresvar are taken from the Meenakshi temple in a splendid procession to the Mariamman Theppakulam and placed on a soft decked with flowers and diyas after which the raft is floated in the tank.

The *svarga- vilasa* of the Tirumala Nayaka Mahal (PL.242) and the royal enclave were other achievements of Nayakas. It is about 1km south-east of Meenakshi temple. This palace was built in 1636 A.D. by Tirumala Nayaka and designed by an Italian architect. It consists of two parts, namely *svarga-vilasa* and *ranga-vilasa*. In the *svarga-vilasa* portion (PL.243) the darbar hall and *nataka-sala* are fairly preserved. It is a shiny example of Indo-saracenic architecture. The central dome of the palace is an attractive feature soaring to the height of 20 m, with its long canopied corridors and pillars rising to 10m, giving the hall a majestic appearance. There were turrets and heavy walls created to protect residents. The well-laid out gardens and ornamental fountains must have created a salubrious environment amid the bustle of the royal household and marked place.

The town of *Srirangam*, 7 km north of Tiruchirapalli (or Trichy), has a picturesque location. It is an island formed by the river Kaveri and its tributary Kollidam. According to a local puranic myth, Lord Ranganatha agreed to dwell on the island of Srirangam at the request of the river goddess Kaveri herself and the temple is associated with the great Vaishnava saint, Ramanuja. The additions made by Nayakas of Madurai to the Ranganatha temple of Srirangam contributed in no small measure to make it by far the largest of south Indian temples and world's biggest Hindu temple. We know of temples within towns, but only in Srirangam an entire town is located within the temple. This is the largest of Dravidian temples, spread over an enormous area of 150 acres, and is dedicated to Vishnu as Ranganatha reclining on *Adisesha*-the cosmic serpent. Unlike the Madurai temple, this has only one sanctuary, an ancient structure small in size and architecturally insignificant. As we see it today with its seven concentric enclosures, twenty one *gopuras* (PL.244), bazaars and residential colonies laid out within its walls, it looks more like a township than a temple. While the sanctuary dates back to about 11th century, the surrounding enclosures and the pavilions inside belong to 17th and 18th centuries.

The outer most *prakara* is a rectangle, measuring about 877.8 x 754.4 m. Of the 13 gateways which lie axially to the main shrine (north-south) at least six are notable for their size and workmanship. These ceremonial gateways with soaring pyramidal towers are hollow brick towers covered with brightly painted stucco sculptures. Barrel vaulted roofs at the tops of the towers are crowned by gilded pot finials (*kalasas*), visible from all over the town.The giant 13 tiered *Rajagopura* (PL.245) of the seventh enclosure is 72 m high; the highest temple *gopura* in the world has recently been renovated.

The three outer courts are not of any special architectural or even religious significance. They are just like the surrounding town and are lined with shops-cafes, vendors selling flowers, fruits and garlands, houses for the temple employees, stables for the temple animals etc.

The architectural portion of the temple begins with the fourth court, the outer wall which measures 376.4 x 258.8 m and has entrance *gopuras* on the north, south and east. The temple of Venugopala in the fourth enclosure is in Hoysala style datable to 13-14th century A.D. Slim, delicate maidens holding various musical instruments, while one carries a parrot, particularly the figure of Venugopala with his legs crossed and playing the flute come alive on the niches of its outer walls in high relief.

Architecturally, the finest part of the Srirangam temple is the "hall of thousand pillars" situated within the fourth enclosure near east *gopura*. It measures 152.4 x 48.8 m externally. It has 900 massive pillars. Opposite this can be seen the celebrated 'horse-court' or *Seshagirirayar-mandapa*, which contains rows of pillars carved as furiously rearing horses (PL.246) with mounted warriors attacking fierce animals and *yalis*. Each horse rears up aggressively to a height of nearly 2.7m were battling ferocious beasts and the strength and vigour of these animals is most emphatically conveyed. Beneath the raised hoofs of these animals were composite statuary of soldiers with drawn swords and extended shields. The next or third enclosure possesses *gopuras* on the north and the south. Beyond south *gopura*, the *garuda-mandapa* is seen with pillars of the central bay are decorated with portraits of the Nayaka donors in the posture of prayer. In this enclosure two ponds namely *Surya-pushkarani*, (sun-pond) and *Chandra-pushkarani*, (moon-pond) are situated.

The second enclosure is occupied prominently by pillared halls with a long processional passage on the west. It provided with entrances on north and south. The first or inner most enclosure faces the south and consists of the circular sanctuary set within a square compartment which is again surrounded by a larger rectangular chamber. The golden domical *vimana* (PL.247) crowned with a four golden vases (*kalasas*) projects above the flat roof outside.

The ecologically sensitive and beautiful landscape of Srirangam once inspired many poets, but now it is fast deteriorating. Many beautiful groves and gardens are giving way to dense building blocks. The quaint river banks are buzzing with building activity.

Srirangam is called *Bhooloka Vaikuntam*. It is believed that Vibhishana worships the lord here every day at midnight. A big festival takes place here on *Mukkoti Ekadasi* or *Vaikunta Ekadasi* in *Dhanurmasa* (December-January).

The Jambukesvara (Siva) temple at *Tiruvanikkaval* is also called Tiruvannayaka koil. It is at a distance of 3km from the great temple at Srirangam. It belongs to the same period and style, but much smaller in size when compared to other temples of Madurai style. It consists of four concentric enclosures, the two outer being open while the two inner are covered courts. Although not comparable in size to the Ranganatha temple it far surpasses it in the beauty of its architecture. The *Sundara pandya-gopuram* belongs to 13th century. The deities are known as Jambukesvara (Siva) and Akhilandesvari. In this *kshetra*, Siva is believed to have sat under the jambu tree and practised penance to have *darshan* of Vishnu in order to get rid of the sin *Brahma hatya* (killing a Brahmin). In the *garbha-griha* water springs up and oozes perenially all through the year.

On the crest of a famous rock, 83 m high (PL.248) of *Trichy (Thiruchirapalli)* is the fortified temple of Ganesa (PL.249) popularly known as Uchi Pillaiyar koil. The shrine commands a panoramic view of entire city and river Cauvery. Ganesa whom the Tamilians more endearingly call Pillaiyar or Vinayakar is a very popular deity and has a small temple in almost every place when there is a habitation in south India. The rock cut temples of Pallava affliation at the middle of the hillock exhibit rock-cut architectural traditons of Mahabalipuram.

Another well-known example of this style and of the same period is the *Ramesvaram* temple near Adam's bridge which separates Sri Lanka from India. From the time immemorial Ramesvaram has played an important role in stirring the Hindu consciousness. Pilgrimages to Kasi and Ramesvaram are sacred aspirations of spiritual life of Hindus. Ramesvaram and Sethu are situated on the island of Ramesvaram which lies in the south-east extremity of Ramanathapuram District. Continuous and high sand dunes present a lovely, natural sight along the seashore around Ramesvaram. The area of the island is 50 sq. km.

Ramesvaram, a Saiva-*kshetra* is one of the 12 *Jyothirlinga-kshetras* in India. The site is hallowed by legendary associations with Rama, the epic hero who defeated Ravana, the demon king of Lanka, who on his way back to Ayodhya, halted at Mount Gandhamadhana at Ramesvaram. Then he thought of performing *puja* to lord Siva to ward off the sin of having killed Ravana, a Brahmin, though he was a *rakshasa*. He bade Hanuman to bring Siva-*linga* from Kailasa; the god departed him on the mission, but could not come back with a sacred *linga* from Kailasa, witin the auspicious time. Thus, Rama had, with the idea of worshipping Siva in the auspicious time he had in mind, installed *linga* made out of sand by Sita and performed the *puja*.

The *linga* is called Ramalinga, Ramesvara and Ramanathar. This mythological account gives the name to the sacred spot, Ramesvaram. However, the *linga* that Hanuman had brought from Kailasa was installed north of Ramalinga and called Visvanathar, Kasi-*linga* and Hanuman-*linga* and ordained that the pilgrim should worship Hanuman-*linga* first before going to the shrine of Ramanatha. This custom still continues. The consort of Ramesvar is Parvatavardhani.

The temple at Ramesvaram (PL.250), like that at Madurai or Tanjore, was built on a settled plan, but with results which are very different. While the Tanjore temple which is hardly half the size of the Ramesvaram temple produces the éffect of an integrated architectural entity, the latter fails to convey that impression. Like the Meenakshi temple, the Ramesvaram temple also consists of two shrines which are enclosed by three concentric enclosures, the outer of these measures 268 x 205 x 6m and has four *gopuras* on cardinal directions. The *gopura* which crowns the eastern entrance is imposing, being 46 m high, with 11 storyes, built in the 17th century.

By far the grandest parts of the Ramesvaram temple are the pillared corridors around it, extending nearly 1,220 m in length totally, the breadth varying from 5.2 to 6.4 m. The height is about 9 m. Of its three corridors, the third is celebrated, one of the marvels of southern India (PL.251). It was erected during the late 18th century by Sethupathi, Muthurama Linga. The pillars, about 3.3 m high each, are enormous blocks of granite, richly decorated and well proportioned. Set close to one another, they run along the entire corridor. The perspective presented by these pillars running uninterruptedly to a length of about 210 m is a breath taking sight. In the words of James Fergusson "The glory of temple resides in the corridors.... Each pillar or pier is composed, twelve feet in height, standing on a platform five feet from the floor, and richer and more elaborate in design than those of Parvati porch in Chidambaram". The 5.2 m high *sudai nandi,* datable to 1568 A.D., in this temple is majestic.

The Devi (Parvata Vardhani) shrine is situated to the south of Ramalingesvara. Every Friday goddess is decorated with *navaratnas* (nine kinds of precious stones), and taken in a golden palanquin in procession round the *prakara*.

From the 15th century begins the record of dated constructions mainly associated with Sethupathis. In 1434 A.D. Udayan Sethupathi and a merchant built the western *gopura* and the outer *prakara*, in stone. About a century later, in 1540, Tirumala Sethupati erected parts of the second corridor. Figures of this benefactor and of his son, Raghunatha, appear in the temple.

There are 22 *thirthas* or places in the temple itself where the devotee are asked to bathe, for the expiation of their sins. It begins with the *agni-thirtha* or the sea in front of the temple and concludes with the *kodi-thirtha* within the temple. There are a few sites of interest around Ramesvaram that a tourist may like to visit. *Dhanushkodi* is 18 km from Ramesvaram. This is the southern most tips of the island and the point where the Bay of Bengal and the Indian Ocean meet. The bathing *ghat* is called *sethu* which is held very sacred and pilgrims are asked to bathe here and offer prayers and perform rituals for removing of their sins. Sri Rama is said to have bridged the gulf here in his invasion of Lanka.

There km west of Ramesvaram temple there is a temple known as the Gandhamadhana temple of later Pandya period in a sandy elevation (PL.252).The temple had undergone reconstruction. It is said that Hanuman made his wonderful leap to Lanka from this peak. *Sri Rama padam* placed on a *chakra* on stone enshrines here. *Kodanda Rama Temple* situated on a sandy hillock, 8 km from Ramesvaram (PL.253). Besides the stone images, there are images in bronze of Sita, Rama, Lakshmana and Hanuman. Image of Vibhishana, brother of Ravana is also there and the story is that here he sought the protection of Rama at this place and was crowned by him. *Sethukkarai,* 4 km from Tiruppullani is the famous Sethukkarai or Sethu Coast. Here we can see the relics of the great bridge believed to have been constructed by the *Vanarasena* (army of monkeys) for Sri Rama to across the sea over to Lanka to rescue Sita.

Equally venerated, and no less remarkable for its architectural merit, is the Nataraja temple (PL.254) at *Chidambaram* in Cuddalore District, whose growth extended over a period of nearly seven centuries, from the 10th to the 17th century. Though the temple consists of a number of structures built in various periods, it retains great symmetry of plan. The orientation, right-angles and parallels have been maintained throughout. It stands on an area of nearly 40 acres and has five *prakaras*. According to myth, Siva danced here to celebrate his victory over ritualist ascetics. This temple has played major roles in the lives of saints and poets. As in all major Saiva temples in Tamil Nadu, the sixty-three Nayanmars (Saiva saints) commemorated in the *Periya Puranam* have their images set out in a long row, against the north wall of the second *prakara*.

The earliest parts of the temple date back to the time of Imperial Cholas (10th to 13th centuries A.D.), who adopted Nataraja as their beloved family deity (*kulanayaka*), who often described themselves as "bees at the lotus feet of Nataraja". It was the Cholas who gilded the sanctum's roof, added enclosure walls, pavilions, *gopuras* and *Devi* shrine. Their work was continued by the Pandyas during 13th-14th centuries.

The *sthalapurana* (local legend), the *Chidambara-mahatmya,* tells that a legendary king, Hiranyavarman, from the north, built the temple out of gratitude for being cured of leprosy after a dip in the Sivaganga tank at the place. It has been plausibly suggested that this account was based on the historical Chola king Kulottunga (1070-1118). Hiranyavarman is said to have invited 3000 priests of the temple who had earlier gone to the north and employed them in the temple.

Chidambaram is unique; it is the only Siva temple in India where he is worshipped as a dancing Nataraja rather than a *lingam.* Lord Siva performed the *Tandava*. Siva Tandava is of 108 types. Of these, 12 form major types. Coming to the technical aspect of these dances, the *Agamas* say that each of the *Tandavas* explained and symbolised the *panchakrityas*, five divine acts of Lord Siva: creation, sustenance, dissolution, concealment and bestowal of grace rather than merely destruction. According to the *Agamas*, Siva is said to have danced Kali or *Urdhva tandava* at golden-*sabha*, Chidambaram. The lord raises his right leg over his head, making an abtuse angle of 180 degrees with left leg. Siva did this *Tandava* to Vanquish Kali in a dance contest. The right leg is lifted right up to the head, giving the dance the name urdhva. Kali could not do so and thus conceded Victory. This is also known as *Kali-Tandava*. Siva banished Kali to the northern boundary of the town and thus she agreed to cede her right on this holy spot.

According to legend Adisesha and Vyagrapada, an ardent devotee were witnessed Siva's cosmic dance of bliss. Adisesha after taking permission from his master, Vishnu, descended to earth as *Patanjali* (the one who has descended).Vyagrapada, did astute penance and obtained the claws of a tiger so that he could climb high up in to a tree and obtained the sacred *bilva* leaves and flowers with which he could shower the lord. Lord Vishnu also looked down in rapt admiration from the heaven.

Inside the *chit-sabha* (sanctum) which faces south, a bronze image of Nataraja is enshrined. Infront of this serving as a *mandapa* is the *kanaka-sabha*. A Vishnu shrine is situated on the east at right angles to the *chit-sabha*. In the second *prakara* in axial line with *chit-sabha* is the *nritta-sabha* (dance hall) which faces north and north to it is the *mulasthana* (where the deity is consecrated), facing east. To the east is the *deva-sabha* (hall of the gods). The Sivaganga tank, the Devi (Sivakamasundari) shrine, the hundred-pillared hall, the thousand-pillared hall, the Pandya Nayaka Subrahmanya shrine and a Ganesa temple are situated in the third enclosure. The Sivaganga tank is bounded by flights of steps and pillared arcades with the fine north *gopura* (PL.255) in its rear, which reflects in water forms an effective scene.

The four *gopuras* each stand to a height of 42 m, with bases of granite and the super structures of brick and mortar. Of the four, only the southern *gopura* is in exact alignment with Nataraja in the *chit-sabha.* The west and south *gopuras* were built during the Maravarman kulasekhara Pandya reign in 13th century A.D. The east *gopura* is also of 13th century. The north *gopura* was renovated by Srikrishnadeva Raya in the first half of the 16th century. A small stone image of Srikrishnadeva Raya in the round in a niche in the door way below this *gopura* is noteworthy. The decorative carving on the *gopuras* consists of divinities, forms of Siva such as Somaskanda, Kalyanasundara, Bhikshatana or Kankala etc. A granite wall of 9 m high enclosing the four main gate ways was renovated by Veerappa Nayaka in 17th century.

Since the temple is devoted to the Lord of Dance, there are sculptural representations of all 108 dance poses (PL.256) found in small panels on the inner walls on either side of the east and west *gopuras* with the names inscribed under them.

The oldest surviving structure in the inner two *prakaras* is the *nritta-sabha* (PL.257). It was built in the reign of Kulottunga III (1178-1216 A.D.). The *kapotabandha-adhishthana* has figural decoration in the *gala.* The socle and base had wheels and steeds (now covered up) as else where. The *sabha* contains a shrine of *urdhva-tandava* Siva. A small image of dancing Kali is on the floor beside the Urdhva-tandava *murti* (image). Dancing girls and musicians form friezes on the basement of the thousand-pillared hall and the *nritta-sabha. nritta-sabha* is a porch of 56 pillars, delicately carved with dancing figures.

The largest building of the temple is, "The hall of the thousand pillars" (the *raja -sabha*) for which the temple is famous was built in the 17th century. It measures 101 x 59 m. The huge *sabha* with massive pillars nearly 5 m high, and is roofed with a brick vault formed of radiating arches, in imitation of the wooden roofs of the other *sabhas.* This hall is used for the *abhisheka* (ablution ceremony) of Nataraja and Sivakamasundari as the culminating session of the two great festivals, the *mahotsavas* in Ani and Marghazi. In the two small pavilions, situated on the north-west corner, the images of Sivas forms-Bhikshatana Murti, Vrishabharuda Murti are preserved. The *nritta-sabha* strongly resembles the stone chariot pavilions *(ratha-mandapas)* from Tribhuvanam, Palaiyarai and elsewhere.

In the *chit-sabha* to the right side of Nataraja there is the proverbial secret of Chidambaram (*Chidambara-rahasya*), where several strings of golden *bilva* leaves hang in front of a curtain, behind which is empty space, but it is said to be *akasa-linga*, one of the *panchabhuta* (five) *lingas*. *Akasa* in other words is nothingness, or void, and thus, the *linga* is said to be there, but it not visible-actually nothing exists there but, people believe that there is actually the *akasa-linga*. This make-believe process is the essence of *Chidambara-rahasya*. Here it has been provided to worship the empty space itself as god.

The wooden walls of *chit-sabha* are composed of four planks in sections, each 35 cm wide, set between wooden pillars of the same width. 28 wooden pillars are setup to support the roof, where as the *kanaka-sabha by* 18 wooden pillars. The wooden doors between the pillars are copper plated. The two roofs of wood are both rectangular with curvilinear roofs recall the roof of the Draupadi-*ratha* at Mahabalipuram. (The same type of roof is found on all the *sabhas,* and also over the sanctums of other shrines). The *chit-sabha* has copper tiles plated in gold, the *kanaka-sabha,* despite its name, has copper tiles. The granite pillars of exterior of the *chit-sabha* look elegant. It is here in the *kanaka-sabha* that Siva and Vishnu are both to be seen side by side as though to proclaim that there is no difference between the two manifestations of the Lord.

Tirumanjana utsava in the month of June-July, and *Arudra Utsava* in the month of December-January are celebrated here.

Tiruvannamalai or Arunachalam, is one of the major sacred places of Tamil Nadu, with a great temple of Siva (PL.258), against a hill, many processions, and frequent festivals, especially that of *Karttigai,* the festival of fire. The Siva temple dedicated to *jyotir-lingam* today is the outcome of a millennium of successive additions, alterations, and extensions, of the original enclosure containing the main shrine, being enlarged in the process. What is now known as the first enclosure is infact the platform around the main shrine. The *gopuras* (PL.259) marking the four cardinal points, particularly the exterior ones, are very imposing. In the second enclosure are seen several deities, either free standing or in small shrines. Most of these shrines and images are not original. They have been replaced by modern ones.

The third enclosure can be dated to 12th and 13th centuries, from inscriptions and on the basis of stylistic features of some of its structures, such as some small shrines containing *lingas*, a pillared hall and the gateway known as the *kili-gopura* (parrot tower). On the east-west axis stands in the third enclosure, another *nandi*. The Devi shrine is situated on the north side, on Siva's left as usual. The shrine was thoroughly renovated in the 19th century by the Nattukkottai Chettiars.

The 4th and 5th enclosures and their buildings are datable to 14-16 centuries A.D. The Brahma Tirtha Tank, originally out side the temple precincts, is now in the fourth enclosure where two pillared halls were erected on the west side, as well as one on the east, the *puravi-mandapa.* The eastern *gopura* (Ballala-*gopura*) was built by the Hoysala king Ballala III and within its passage there is a niche housing a statue of king Ballala. The fifth enclosure consists of four gateways which are much higher than those of the inner enclosures; this distinctive composition, (increasing in height) is already evidenced in the 11th century at Tanjore with two gateways, became a regular feature for all temples with several enclosures. In the fifth courtyard are found the huge thousand pillared hall and, the Sivaganga tank surrounded by a colonnade.

Here Siva is honoured as Lingodbhava, issuing from a column of flame. Every year on the day of *Karttigai* (November-

December) or *Deepam* festival, a great fire is lit in his honour on the summit of the hill. Those who have vows will offer ghee and camphor in plenty to this *deepa*. It, therefore, burns for two or three days at a stretch. The Ramana Ashram here is well known.

The temples at Tiruvarur (Tanjore District) and Srivilliputtur (Tirunelveli District) are a few more examples of Later Dravidian style. The original shrine at Tiruvarur belongs to 9th century A.D. This temple-complex consists of Siva and Parvati temples surrounded by a cloistered court and three concentric walls enclose the entire complex of structures. The three storeyed gateway on the east, erected in 18th century, is the excellent part of this temple. Here note worthy is the pilasters, the sunken recesses, the rearing hippogryphs and the pillars enshrining sculptured images employed to maximum aesthetic effect. The temple at Srivilliputtur is renowned for its massive *gopura*, of about 60 m high, built in thirteen storeys, excluding its barrel-shaped roof.

There are many temples of the 19th century built in the Dravidian style, conforming to the same pattern but which come nowhere near their predecessors in size or architectural effect. The art of temple building is still known to many families in South India, bequeathed to them by generations of ancestors and their inherited talents are found in the innumerable towers and *gopuras* which have been, and are being renovated by them inasmuch as several new constructions. Religion is still a living force with the people and it is not unusual for wealthy persons to demonstrate their piety by patronising construction of new temples.

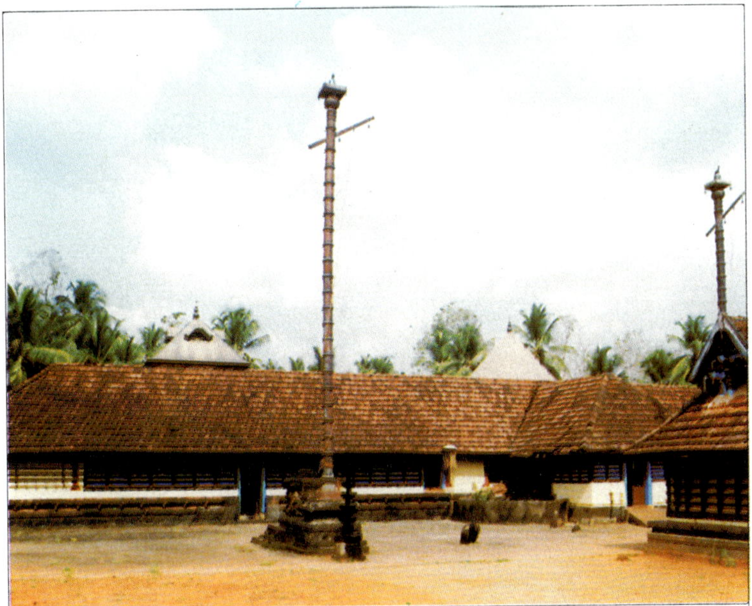

260. Manjeri, Ayyappan temple complex.

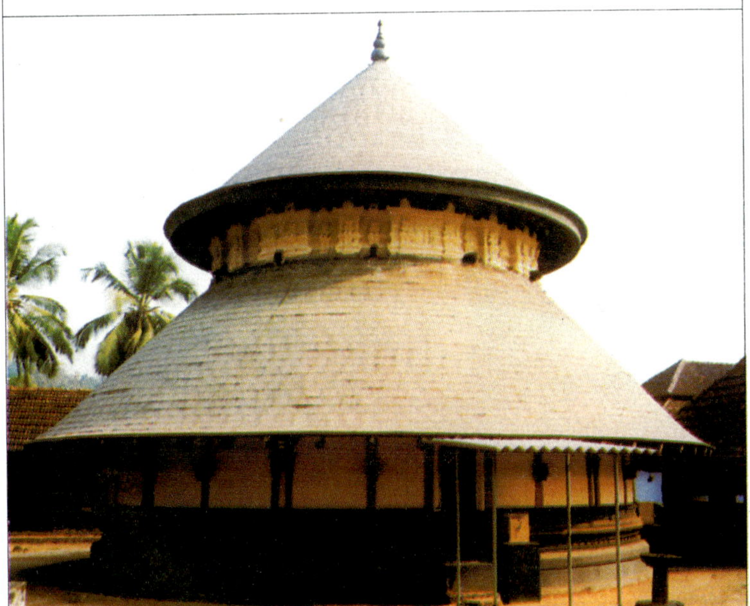

261. Manjeri, Subrahmanya shrine.

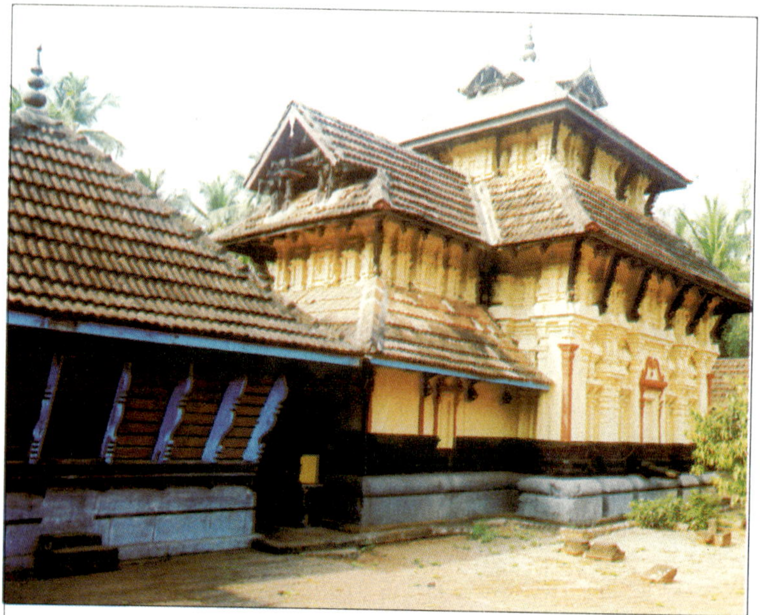

262. Manjeri, Velayudhan temple.

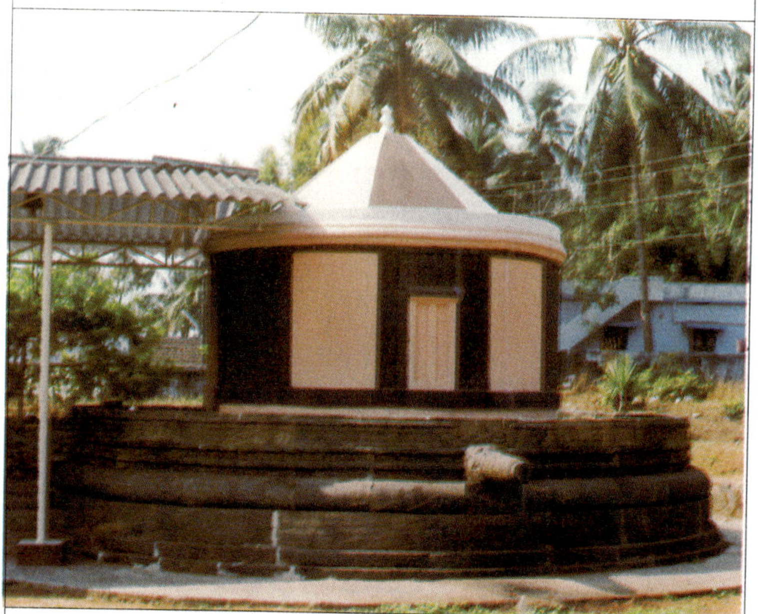

263. Palghat, Siva temple.

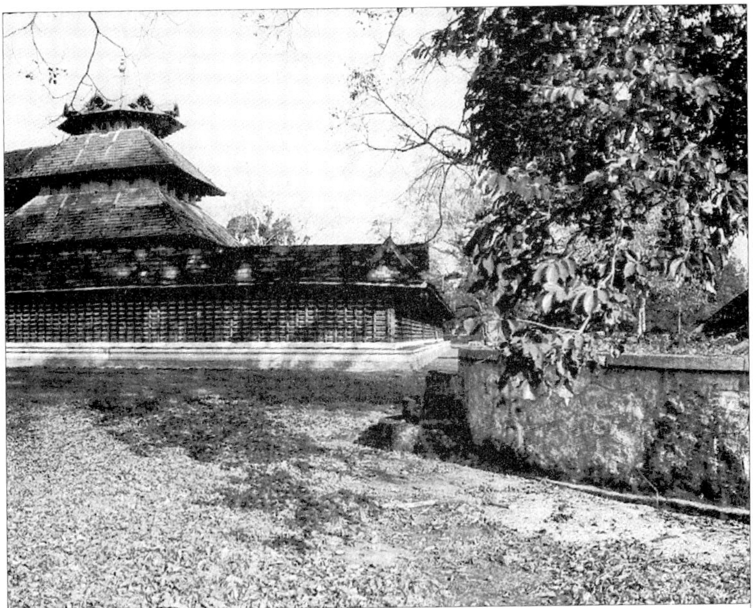

264. Peruvanam, Siva temple, Madattilappa shrine.

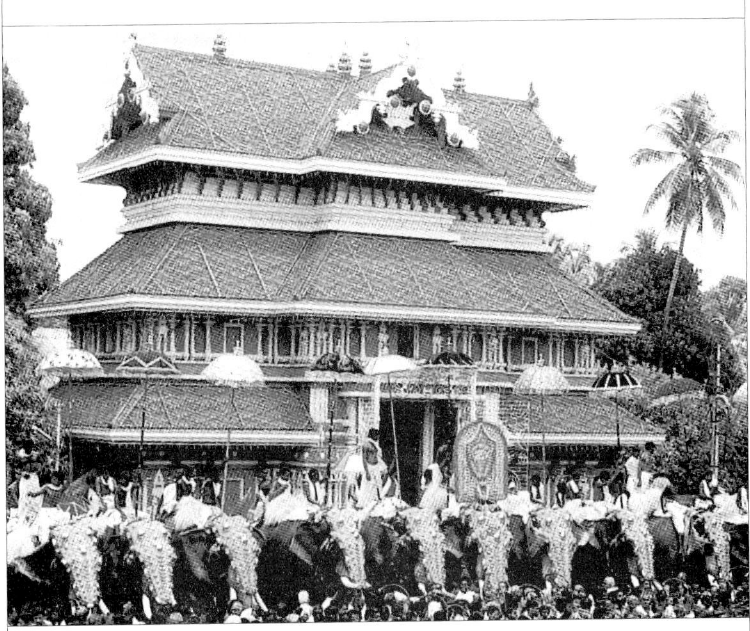

265. Thrissur, Vadakkunatha temple.

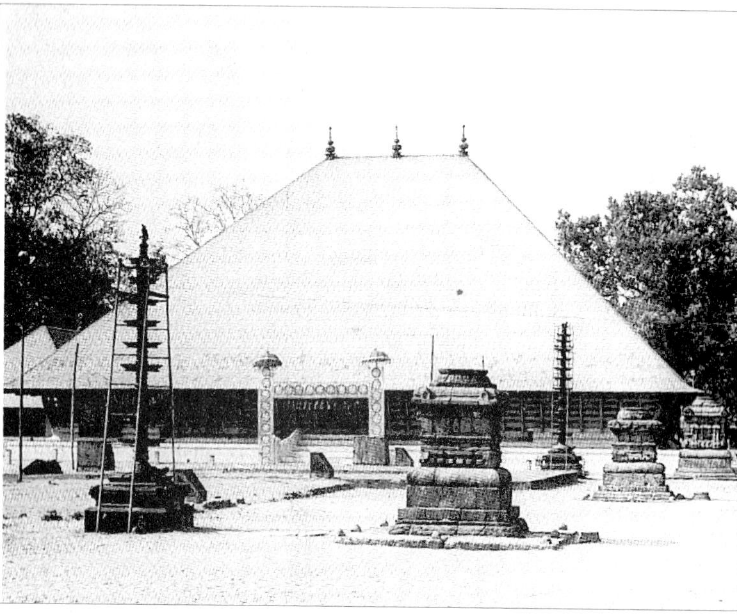

266. Thrissur, Vadakkunatha temple, Kuttambalam.

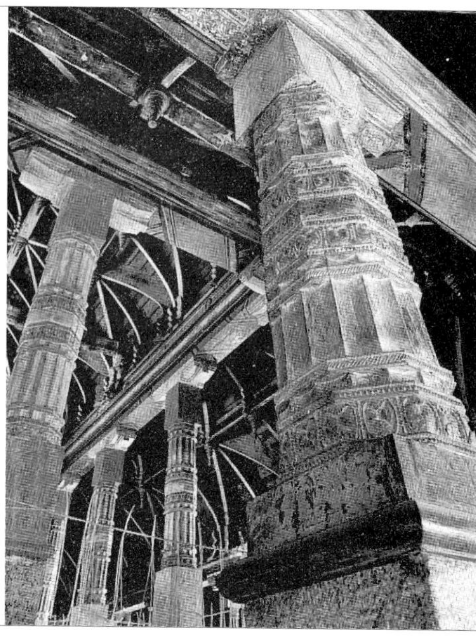

267. Thrissur, Vadakkunatha temple, carved ceiling.

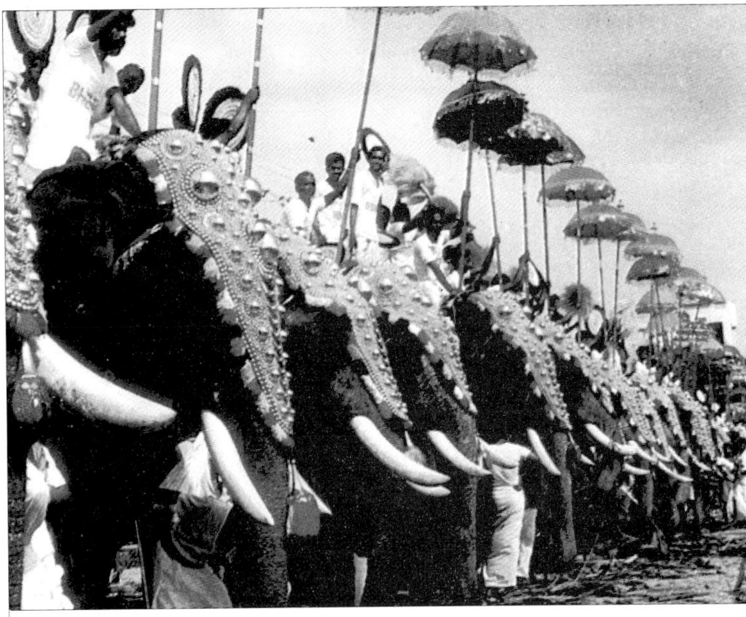

268. Thrissur, procession of elephants.

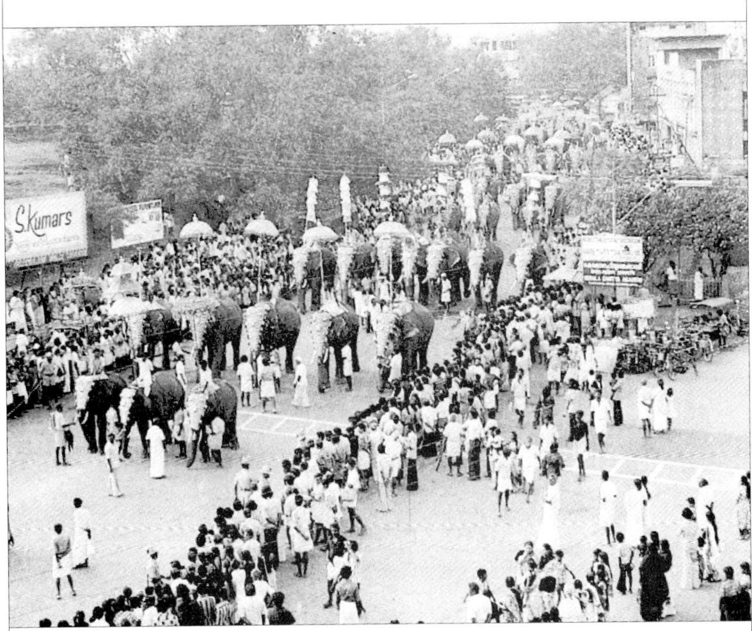

269. Thrissur *pooram*.

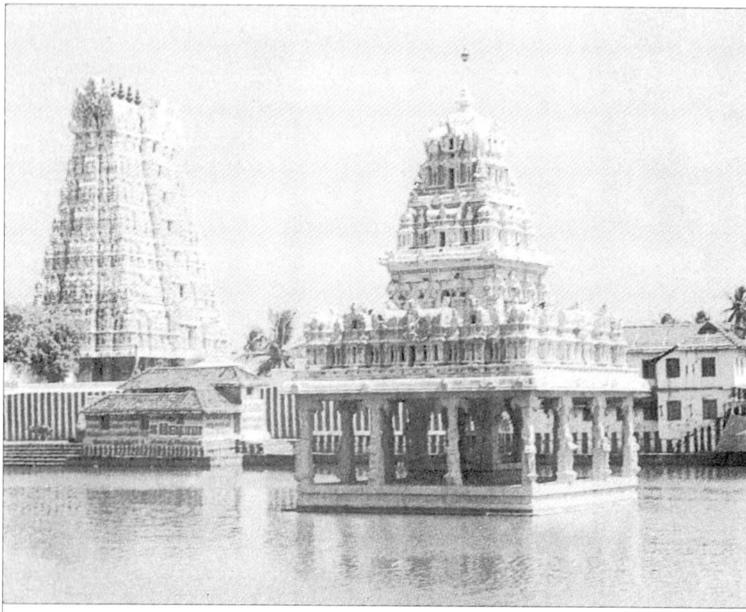

270. Suchindram temple, *gopura* and tank.

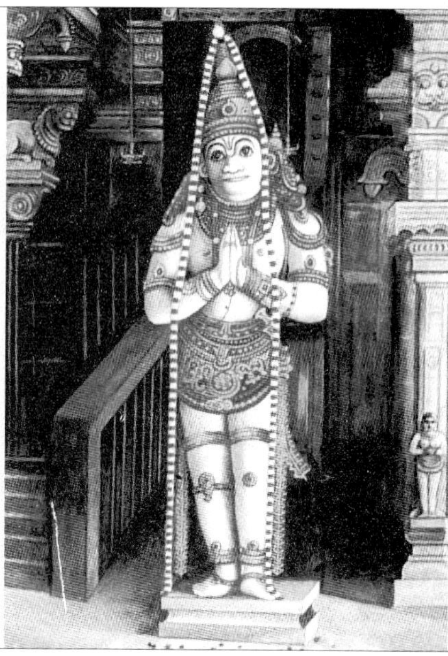

271. Suchindram temple, Hanuman.

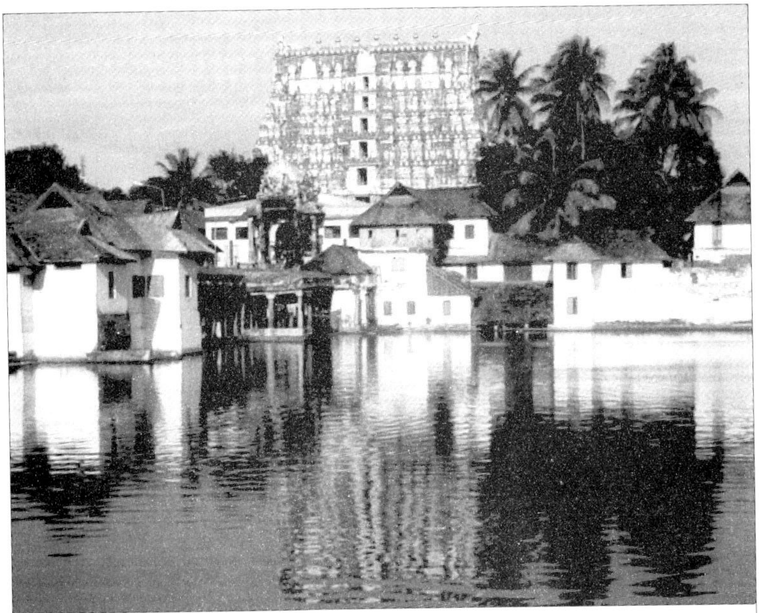

272. Thiruvananthapuram, Padmanabha temple, gopura and tank.

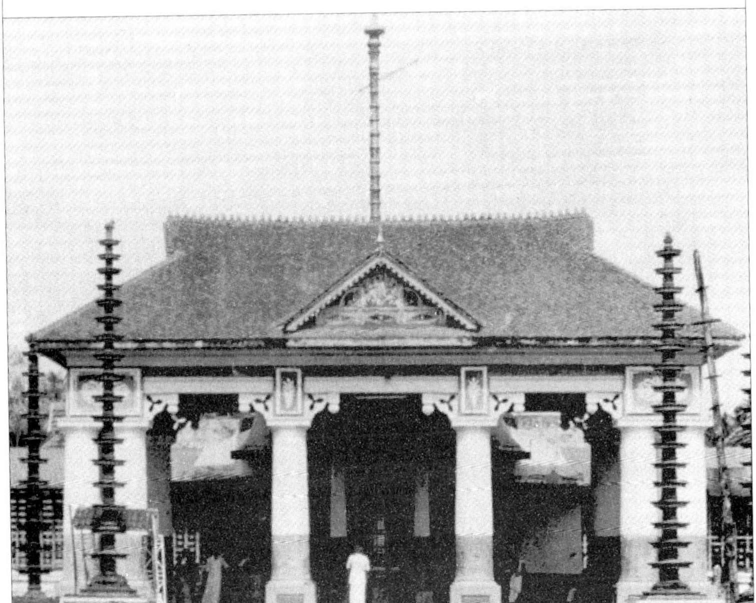

273. Vaikom, Peruntiru Koilappan temple.

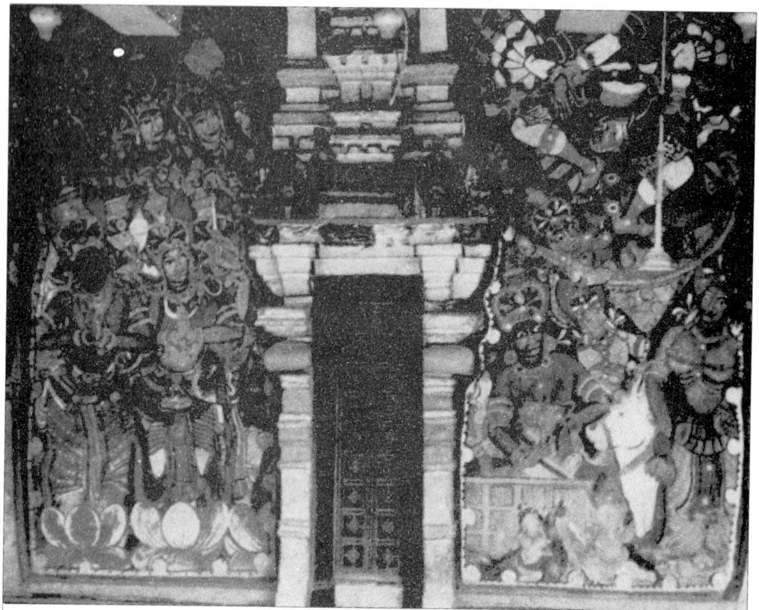

274. Vaikom, Peruntiru Koilappan temple, dancing Siva.

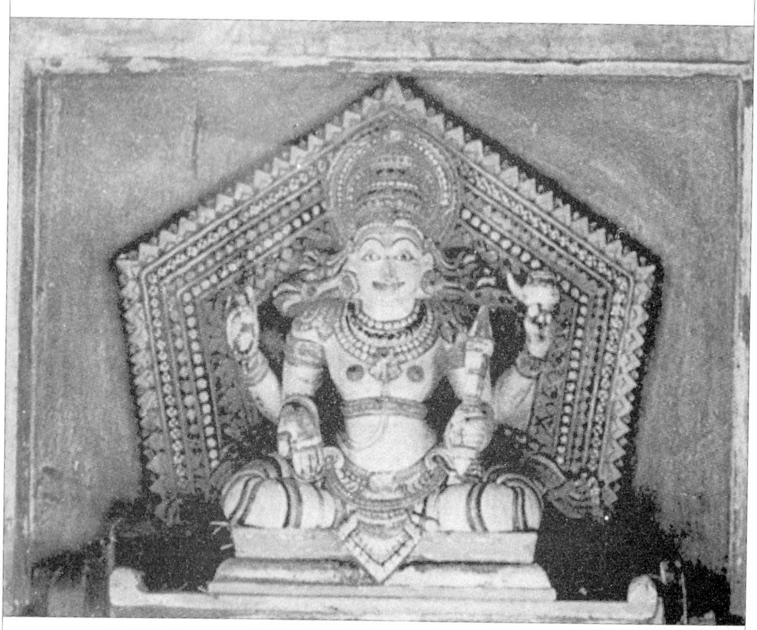

275. Villiapally, Ponmeri Siva temple, Surya riding the chariot.

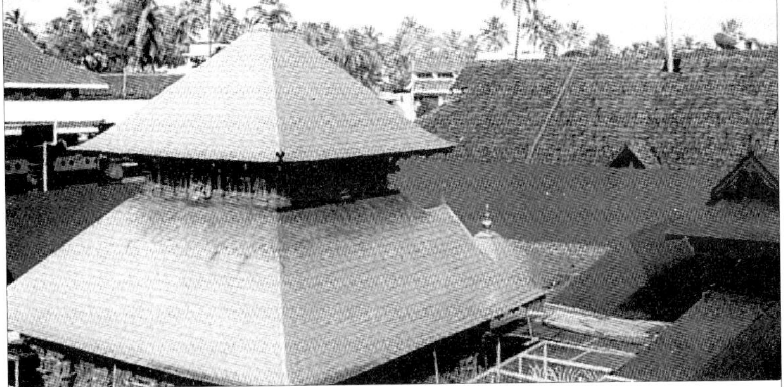

276. Guruvayur, Srikrishna temple.

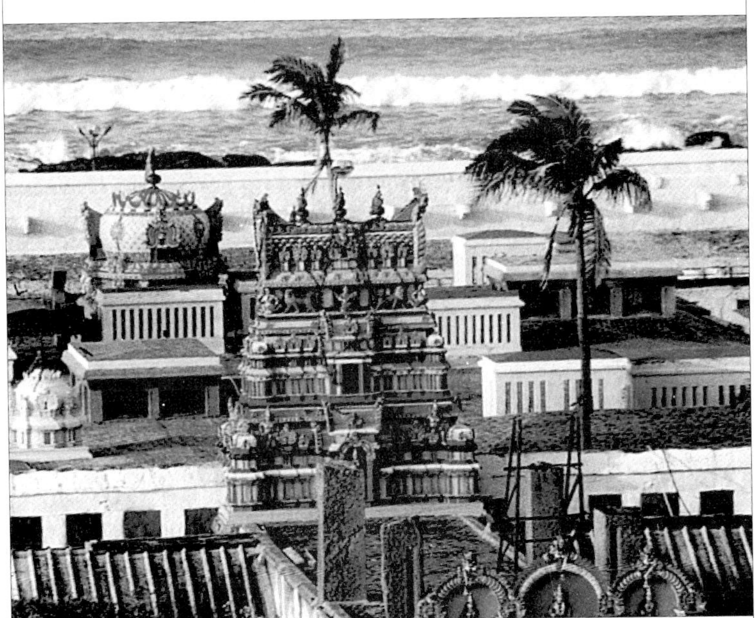

277. Kanyakumari, Kumari Amman temple, general view.

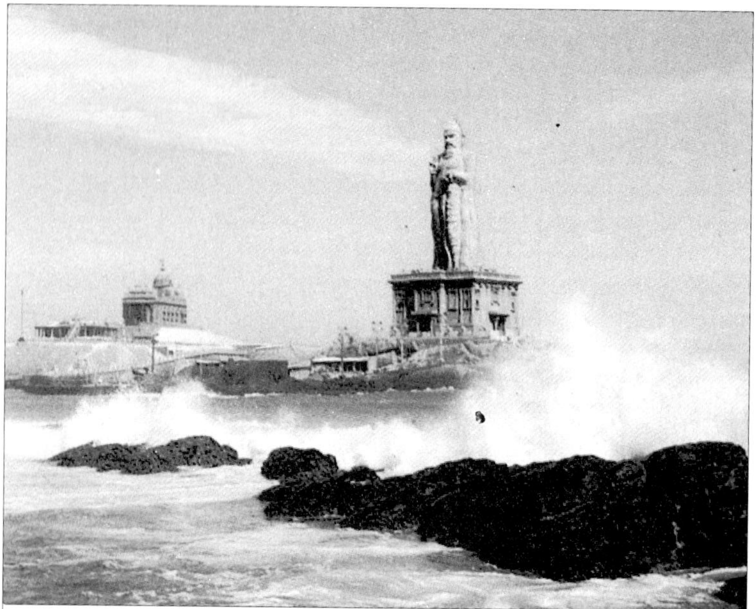

278. Kanyakumari, Vivekananda rock-memorial and Thiruvalluvar statue.

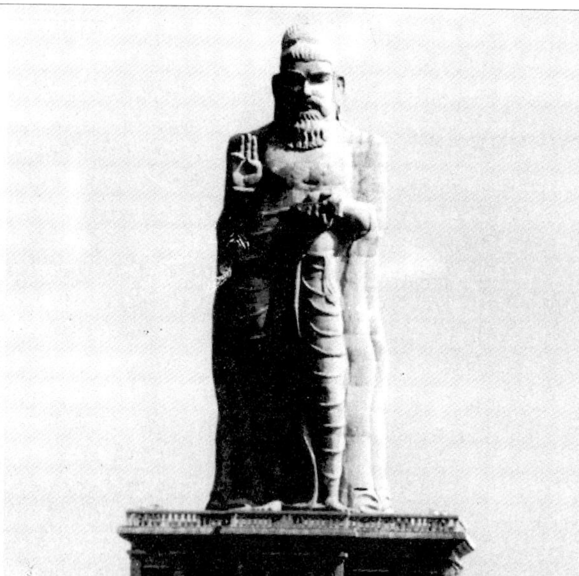

279. Kanyakumari, Thiruvalluvar statue.

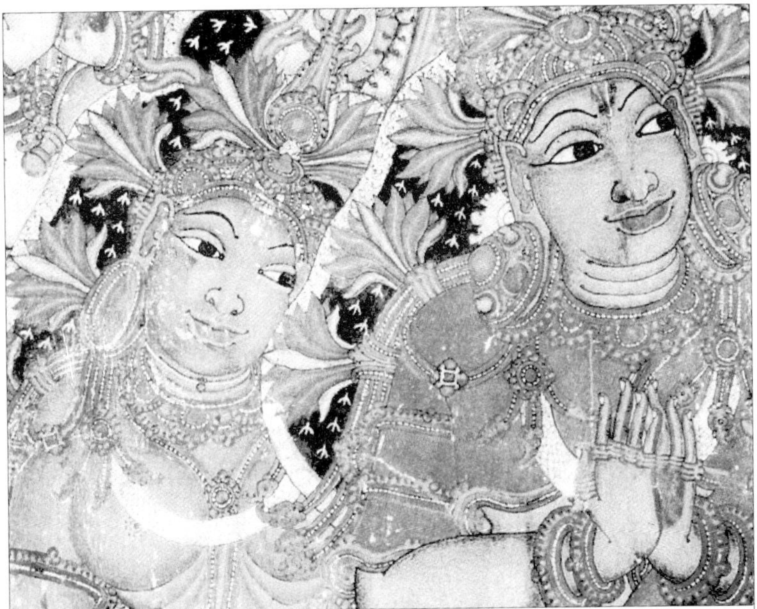

280. Cochin, Mattancheri palace, Rama and Sita.

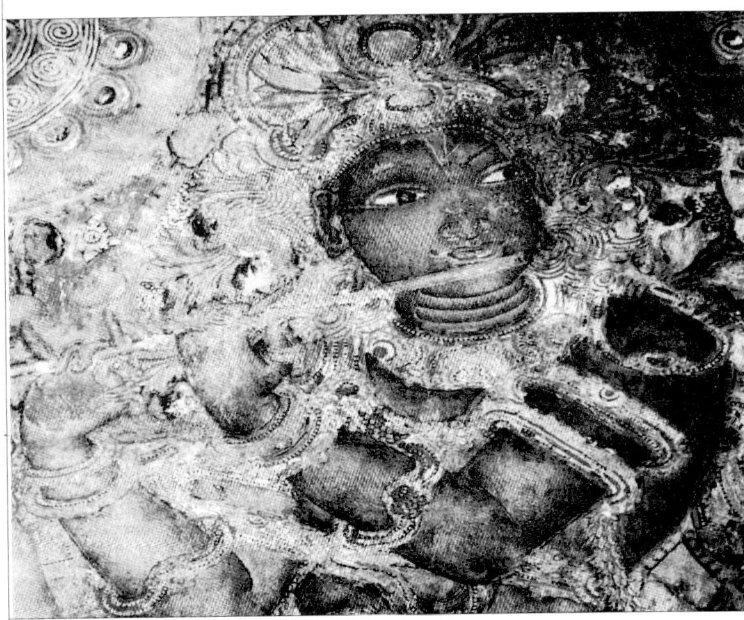

281. Cochin, Mattancheri palace, Venugopala.

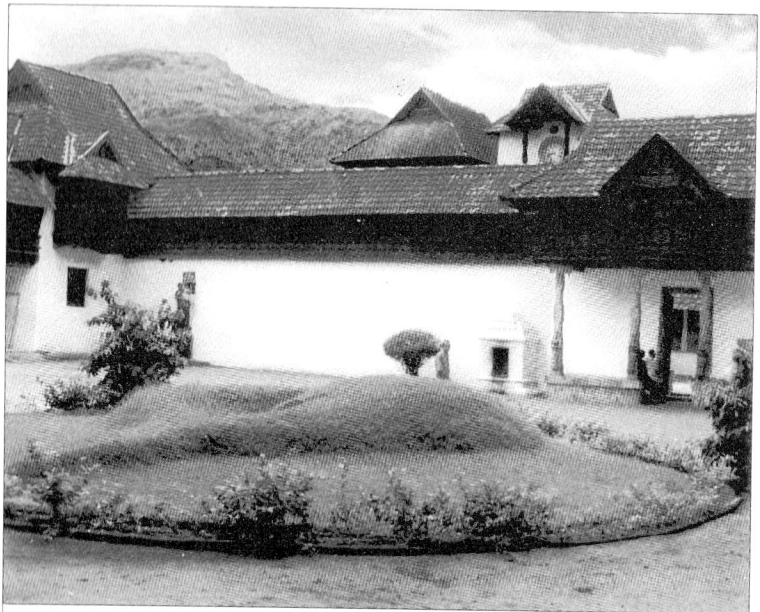

282. Padmanabhapuram palace.

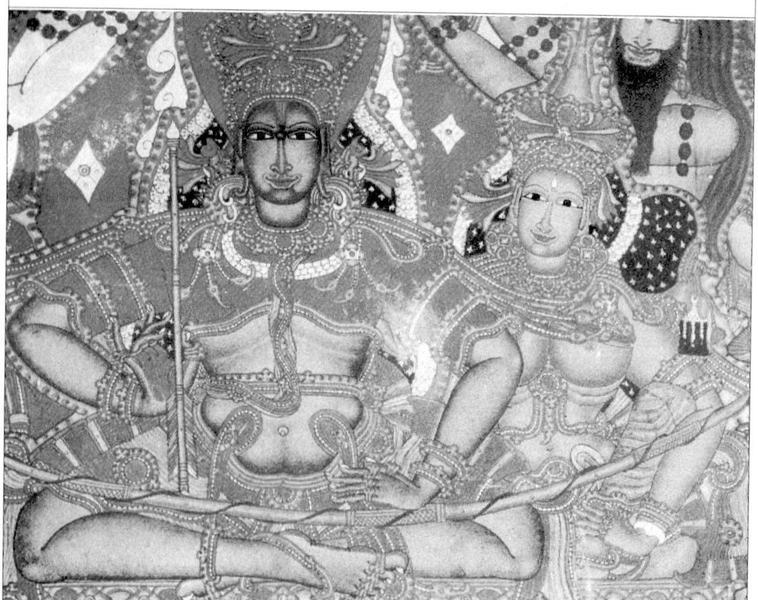

283. Padmanabhapuram palace, Rama and Sita.

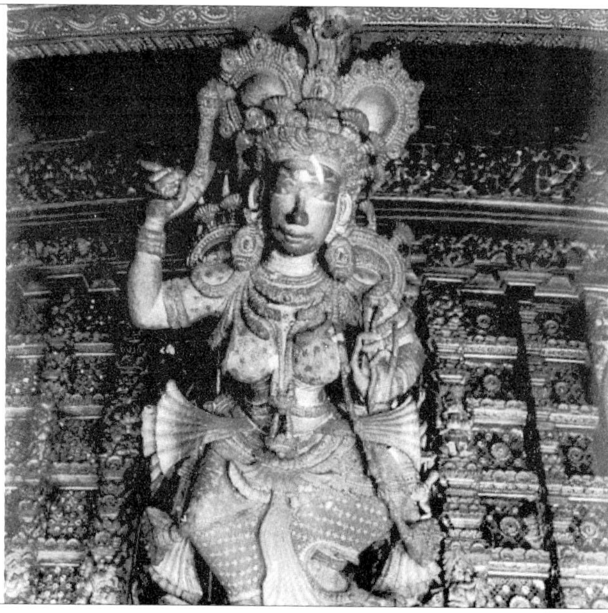

284. Female dancer, angled strut, Mahadeva temple, Ettumanur.

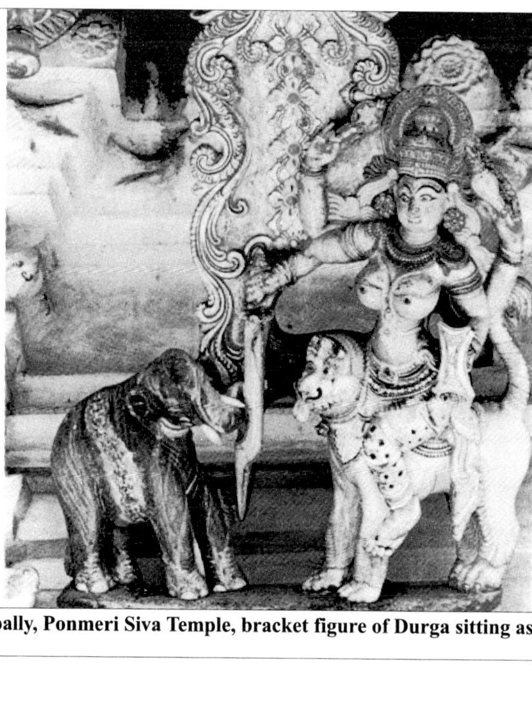

285. Villiapally, Ponmeri Siva Temple, bracket figure of Durga sitting astride a lion.

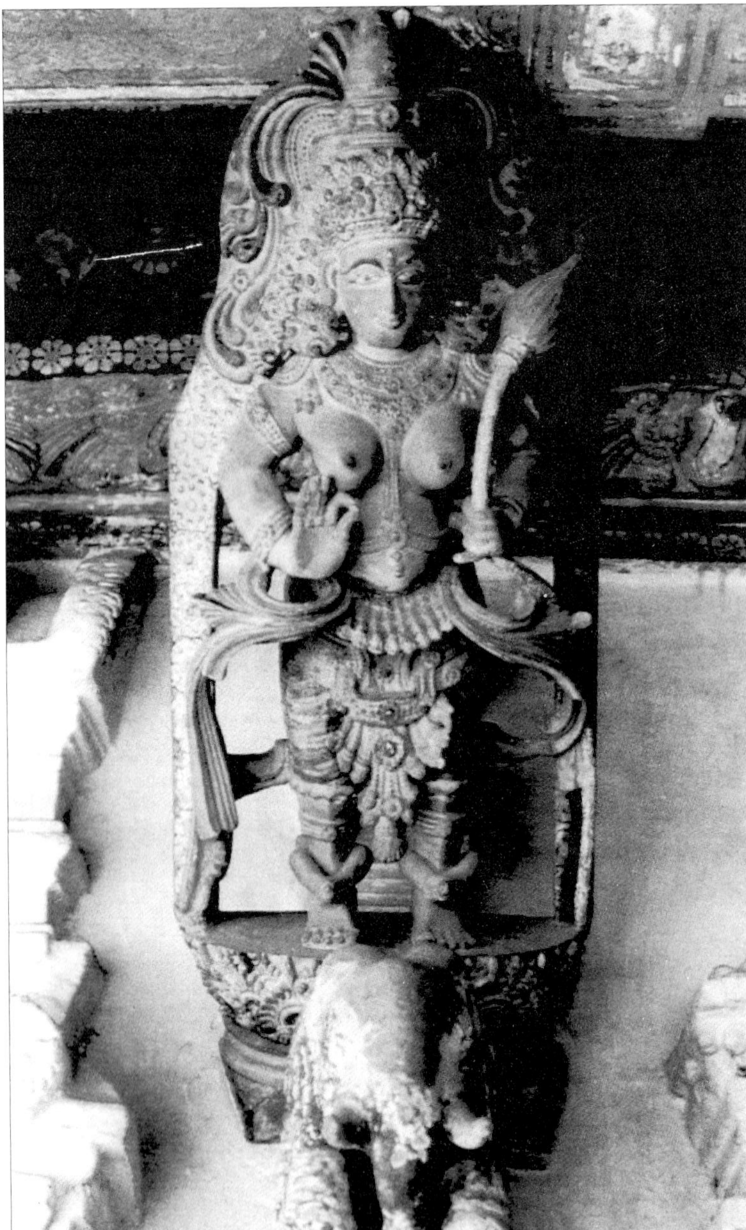

286. Parvati, angled Strut, Mahadeva temple, Peruvanam.

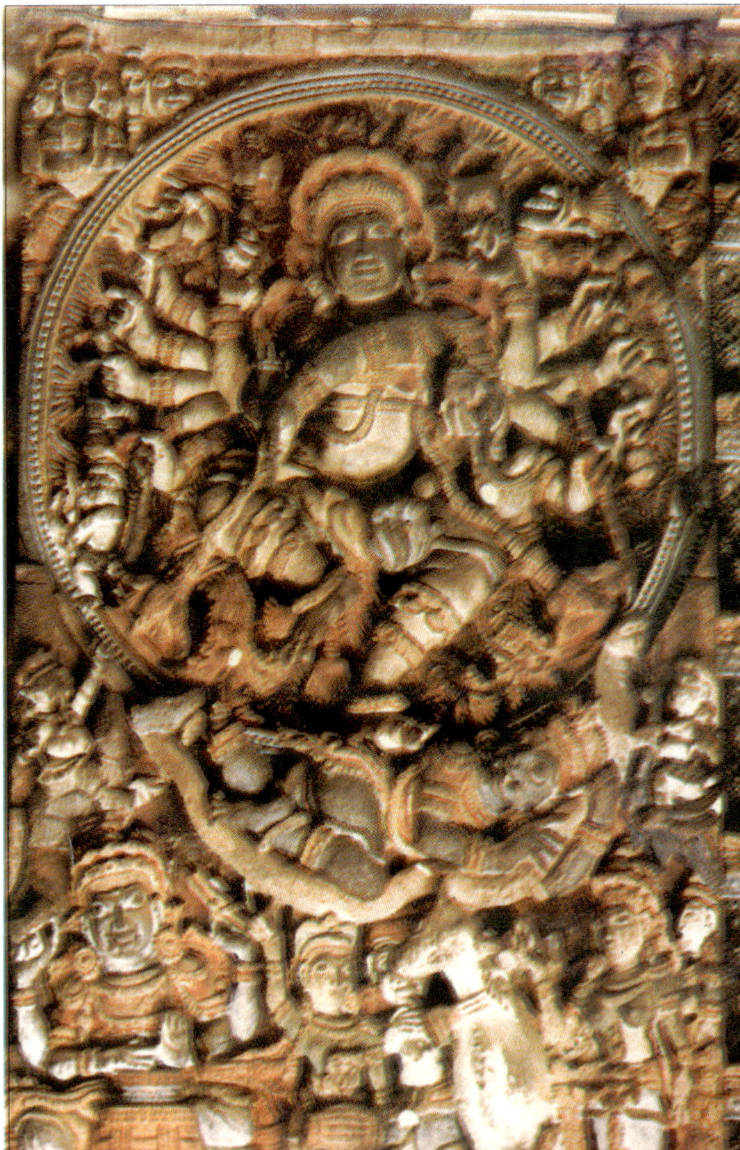

287. Nataraja Panel between window screens temple, Ettumanur.

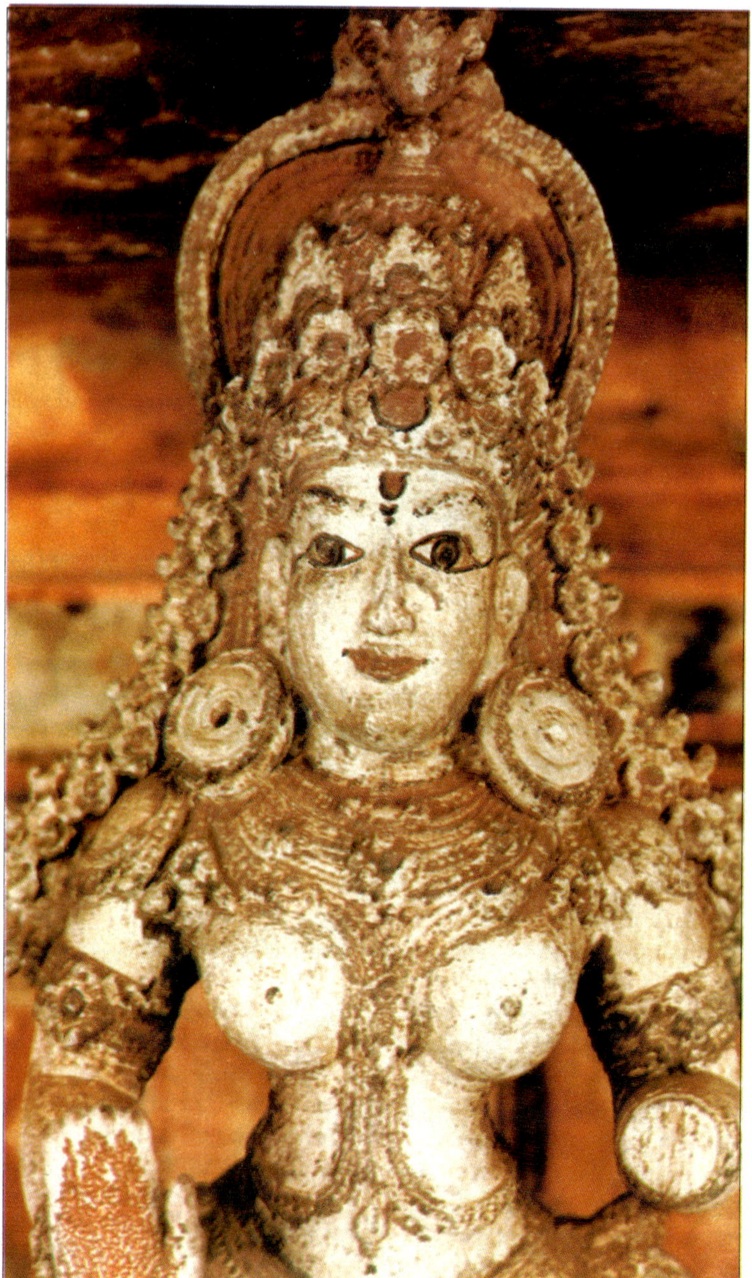

288. Female attendent, angled strut, Rama temple, Triprayar.

12

Kerala Style

Kerala's lush country side is regularly dotted with densely populated settlements that follow the principal roads and waterways. Green and serene, Kerala is replete with lagoons and lakes. Infact, the entire southern narrow strip of the Indian peninsula is green throughout. Its sensuous surroundings offer a taste of the exotic. Kerala has a touch of *sthalapurana* dating back to the legendary Parasurama who is associated with the famous Vaikom Siva temple. Parasurama, one of the ten incarnations of Lord Vishnu, threw his armaments in to the sea to atone for the sin of killing 1,000 Kshatriyas. The sea forgave him and the water soon receded giving birth to the fertile land of Kerala.

Every village in Kerala has atleast one Hindu temple that blend imperceptibly with the houses, surrounding coconut palms and bamboo groves. The temples are built of the same timber and tiles as the nearby houses and are rarely higher than the coconut palms around them. They are enclosed with compound walls and entered through modest gateways. The temples present a deeply sanctified environment where ancient traditions still continue. Paintings in Kerala show their existence right up to 1800 A.D. by which time it seems to be emptied of all content.

Most of the Kerala (now comprises Malabar and the erstwhile princely states of Cochin and Travancore) temples now existing are not very old, the oldest dating from medieval or post medieval times. The oldest ones, because of the perishable materials of construction, have been lost, only the stone *adhishthanas* and loose sculptures remain. These give us an idea of the continuity from at least the 10th century A.D. The gabled or multiple-roofed structures of Kerala, built of laterite stone, bricks, wood and tiles present a completely different appearance from their architectural counterparts elsewhere in South India.

The walls are usually laterite blocks which are abundant in the area, and can be cut and shaped easily when freshly quarried. Because of their rough and pitted surface, the walls are heavily plastered and the few decorations are picked out in stucco. The walls made of entirely wood in the districts of Kottayam and Alleppey form a good ground for mural paintings which take the place of relief sculptures. The Kerala temples are thus for their rich colour paintings executed on the lime plastered walls in fresco-technique.

Like the Draupadi-*ratha* at Mahabalipuram, the Kerala temples are simple in their form and have only the four essential parts-the *adhishthana* or base, the *bhitti* or wall, the *sikhara* or roof, and the *stupi* or finial.

The typical Kerala temple or *srikoil,* where the main image of the deity or *linga* is housed, can be circular or apsidal or square or rectangular and rarely even elliptical in plan, the structure being raised on a socle (a plain or moulded stone base). The main building lies on an east-west axis and is surrounded by a rectangular cloister. The roofs are by far the most dominant part of the Kerala temples, and their forms are adapted to suit the high rainfall of the region.The circular shrines, which are rare in other states of South India, constitute a dominant type and are found in southern parts of the state, especially in the Allppey and Quilon regions, which was once under the influence of Buddhism. On the contrary, temples with apsidal ground-plan is seen occasionally all along the west coast up to Thiruvananthapuram and also in central Kerala. The famous Siva temple at Vaikom shows elliptical ground plan. For enshrining Anantasayi Vishnu and also *Sapta-matrikas*, a rectangular plan is generally favoured as noticed in the temples at Thiruvananthapuram and Angadippuram.

The temple roofs are as a rule covered with thin tiles. Great attention is paid to the construction of these roofs, the length, thickness and the joints of the rafters being regulated by rules laid down by ancient treatises on architecture (*Vastu vidya)*.

These roofs can be single or double. The *srikvil* of Subrahmanya at Manjeri is dated to the 12th century A.D. This temple is an example of the double roof. The roofs-whether conical, pyramidal, or ridged are often multiple, two or three storyed, and on that account not only add to the height and majesty of the structures but provide greater opportunity for the image carver to display his skill on and around the struts that support the roofs. On the principal *srikvil* of the Peruvanam complex, for instance, at the upper level of the struts are found Vishnu seated on the serpent Sesha, triple-headed Siva and Siva and Parvati in the north, east and south.

An ancient Siva temple at Beypore, a small sea port at Kozhikode in Malabar, in its elevational features, it strongly recalls the Nepalese double roofed temple of the late medieval period.

Though the architecture of the Kerala's temples is simple, the brackets, struts and uprights on the exterior and the ceiling inside the building are often carved into beautiful imagery. We see in them the artistic ancestors of the wonderful wood and ivory carving for which the state is to this day renowned. Where the walls were the brick and mortar the surfaces were often covered by mural paintings "like a tapestry in which the buildings appear clothed". Even the wood carvings are some times coloured and made to merge with the paintings on the walls, reminiscent of the cave temples of Ajanta. That wall paintings constituted an important embellishment of ancient temples in South India is also borne out by many Dravidian examples as in the Kailasanatha temple at Kanchipuram, the Brihadisvara temple at Tanjore and the more recent paintings in the Meenakshi temple at Madurai.

However, the temple architecture of Kerala can be classified in to three major stages of development: Early phase (800-1000 A.D.), Middle phase (1001-1300 A.D.) and Late phase (1301-1800). As a style of architecture the early phase was patronized by the Cheras of Mahodayapuram, the Ays of south Kerala and the Mushikas of north Malabar. In this phase the temples follow either a square, circular or apsidal plans.The *namaskara-mandapa*, square on plan with its pyramidal roof is detached from the main temple. The quadrangular *nalambalam* or *chuttambalam* encloses the *srikovil* and the *namaskara-mandapa.*

At the entrance of *nalambalam,* the stone *bali-pitha* is invariably seen, a regular feature of the temples of Kerala and Tamil Nadu. Temples with square ground plan, an earlier tradition, is distributed throughout Kerala. The Siva temple at Tali (near Wadakancherry), the Krishna temple at Thirukulasekharapuram, the Kilatali temple at Thiruvanchikulam, all in Thrissur district, the Mahadeva temple at Kazhakuttam, Thiruvanantapuram district, the Siva temple in Ganapati-kshetram at Indyanur, Malappuram district, all these temples on stylistic as well as on epigraphical data,may be dated to the 9th or 10th century A.D. These shrines on plan, consists of a narrower *maha- mandapa*, an *ardha-mandapa*, a square *garbha-griha*, with a circumambulatory passage all round and a two-storeyed *vimana.*

The ruined Lakshminarayana shrine in the Ayyappan temple-complex at Panniyur, Palghat district, and the deserted shrine in the famous Bhagavati temple at Kodungallur, Thrissur district, are examples of *sandhara vimana.* In style these recall Kilatali Siva temple noted above. The *sandhara vimana* form, that was developed in the north India in Gupta period and its adaptation in the temples in Kerala is due to the influence of the Chalukyan or the Pallava traditions.

The laterite built ruined temple at Eramam, Cannanore district, is almost identical to the above temples in features. On plan; it is a *sandhara* temple with a square *garbha-griha* enclosed by square outer walls. A loose figure of Vishnu of 9th-10th century A.D. is noticed in the temple. An inscription of Mushika king dated 11th century is associated with the temple.

We have noted that the Kerala style (indegenous) of temple building co-existed with the Dravida style (south Indian) in southern parts of Kerala. It is perhaps on account of its geographical contiguity.

The Parthasarathi temple at Parthivapuram, Kanyakumari district, was erected by Ay ruler Karunandadakkan in 866 A.D. belongs to typical south Indian tradition or Dravida style. It is a highly renovated structure showing three storeyed *sandhara-vimana* on square plan. The temple inscriptions offer a good picture of the activity of the *salai* or Vedic school attached to this temple originally.

The circular temples constitute an important group in Kerala though they are rare in other parts of south India. They are almost contemporaneous with the square or rectangle temples.

The circular Narasimha temple at Ramantali, Cannanore district is a *sandhara* temple and recalls the Perumpaludur example. Its exterior circular wall encloses the circular *garbha-griha* externally while the interior is square. The exterior wall has functional doors on all the four sides and this type of the temple known as *sarvatobhadra.* The earliest inscription here is dated to 928 A.D. A stone image of Sasta is preserved in the precincts of the temple which is dated to the 9th century A.D.

The Ayyappan temple (PL. 260) in the Karikkad-Kshetram (4km from Manjeri bus stand) at *Manjeri,* Malappuram district, belongs to this phase although it is associated with an inscription of the 11th century. A *nirandhara* temple, on plan, features a rectangular *maha-mandapa* and a square *garbha-griha*. In its plan it recalls the Agastyesvara temple at Chilamakuru, Cuddapah district in Andhra Pradesh, datable to 8th century A.D. The circular Subrahmanya shrine (PL. 261) at the same place, is ascribed to middle phase. On its *adhishthana* a 12th century inscription is found. It has a double storeyed *vimana* of the *sarvatobhadra* type having four functional doors on cardinal direcitons. A row of 12 pillars adorn the circumambulatory path around the square *garbha-griha*. The Velayudhan temple in the same compound is also a worth visiting (PL. 262).

The temples in the middle phase in Kerala normally consist of *sandhara-vimana* in a developed form, a functional circumambulatory path, either single or double, around the *garbha-griha* with pillars. Another interesting feature of this phase is the Dravida *vimana* in miniature, which is square, circular or apsidal on plan with *griva* and *sikhara*. Middle phase, thus, stands as the synthesis of two styles, Dravida and Kerala, the former in its miniature form is housed in side a typical Kerala style of temple with sloping roofs. The circular temples of Kerala are interesting examples recalling the circular Buddhists examples of Sri Lanka.

The little Siva temple (PL. 263) at Tirunillai, in the out skirts of Palghat (4 km from Palghat railway station) belongs to 11th century A.D. and has undergone renovation and paintings. It has a granite *adhishthana* and circumambularoty path around the circular shrine, constructed with bricks, internally a square wall has an octogonal *griva* and *sikhara* built on corbelled arch.

The Niramankara temple at *Nemam*, near Thiruvananthapuram, has an inner shrine, built of brick with a Dravida *vimana,* enclosed by a circular outer wall. A row of 8 pillars aligned in a circle in the circumambulatory path around the *garbha-griha* are noticed and two more on either side of the inner shrine. This temple belongs to 14th century A.D. The figures of Vishnu (housed in a subsidiary shrine) and Brahmi are noteworthy. Though an early date is suggested by some scholars, these may not be earlier than 10th century A.D.

The Tiruvembilappan temple at *Venganellur*, Thrissur district, is associated with an inscription of the12th century A.D. The inner *vimana* is raised on a rectangular plan complete from its *adhishthana* to *stupi*. Encircling the *garbha-griha* two rows of pillars are met with, dividing *pradakshina-patha* in to two segments. The temple is a *sarvatobhadra* type as it exhibits four functional doors on the outer circular wall.

The Trikotesvara Mahadeva temple at *Punalur*, Quilon district, was raised in *Kollam* 421 (1245-46 A.D.). Built with granite, features a square *vimana* with octagonal *griva* and *sikhara*. In the ambulatory around, eight pillars are employed, two on each side of the sanctum.The renowned shrines like Vadakkunatha temple at Thrissur, the Irattaiyappan shrine in the Siva temple at Peruvanam, Thrissur district, had their beginning in the middle phase.These are datable to 11th-12th centuries A.D. Both shrines are circular, enclosing a square Dravida *vimana* as the *garbha-griha* and consisting three functional doors.In both the instances, the shrine's rear part is dedicated to Devi.

The Rama temple at Triprayar, Thrissur district, with a foundation inscription dated to 11th century A.D. has a circular *ekatala srikovil* with three functional doors.

The Vamana temple at Kizhavellur, Kottayam district, consists on plan an apsidal *garbha-griha* with a *gaja-prishthakara* roof ('elephant's back') above it. Laterite slabs were used for building the structure. The *pradakshina-patha* is punctuated by a row of fourteen pillars. On epigraphical grounds this temple may be dated to 1035 A.D.

The Kodavalam Vishnu temple at Pullur, Cannanore district, is the best example of the style of north Malabar. It is built of laterite blocks and set in a *sandhara* scheme with a single *pradakshina-patha* around the square *garbha-griha*.Unlike three or four doors, it has only two one in front and the other at the rear of the shrine. The other two in the form of *ghana-dvaras* or 'false doors' a feature common in the temple architecture of Kerala. An inscription of 12th century is associated with the temple.

The Siva temple at Thiruvanchikulam and Madattilappan shrine (PL.264) in the Siva temple at *Peruvanam* (near Thrissur) are identical structures to that of the Kodavalam Vishnu.The former, despite renovations in later times looks more ornate and retains many of its older features. The latter is a *tritala* type with octagonal *griva* and *sikhara*, a unique feature to the temples of Kerala. Stylistically these temples may be dated to the mid of the 11th century A.D.

The Siva temple at *Trivikramangalam*, 5 km east of Thiruvananthapuram, is dated to the 11th century A.D. The shrine and the *mandapa* opposite represent the visual Kerala type of architecture.The flights of steps that lead to the main shrine through the central entrance from either side is interesting. The side of the banister is decorated with a gaping *makara* head at the top and another at the bottom complete with floriated tail. The decoration is very finest than the similar example at Kadangur. A pair of granite *dvarapalas* at the shrine door is noteworthy.

In south Kerala, a few temples built in south Indian style and also in Dravida style are to be seen. The temple known as Kattilmadam at *Chalapuram*, Palghat district, is built in stone in pure Dravida style. A Square *nirandhara* shrine, on plan, features octagonal *griva* and *sikhara*, both made of single piece. The Parasurama temple-complex at Tiruvallam, near Thiruvananthapuram, in which Parasurama shrine with a stone body and brick work superstructure under gone renovation. The adjacent Brahma shrine is square, on plan, enclosed by an outer circular wall. An inscription of Venadu ruler Vira Keralavarman dated Kollam 399 (1224 A.D.) is noticed on the *adhishthana* of the Brahma shrine. It is interesting to note that in this complex circular Dravida *vimanas* and kerala style temples exhibit side by side.

The late phase of temple architecture in Kerala covers the period from 1301-1800 A.D. The significant examples of this phase had their origin in early phase. During the period, new adjuncts like *balikkal-mandapa, kuttambalam*, subsidiary shrines, *gopuras* on all four sides with multiple roofs covered with tiles, etc., were added to the existing big temples. These towers are neither tall nor imposing unlike those of later south Indian temples. Generally the central shrine is fronted by a square *namaskara-mandapa* with pyramidal roof. The other adjuncts like the open-air *pradakshina-patha*, cloistered *nalambalam*, the *vilakkumudam* affixed with a galaxy of lamps, paved outer *pradakshina-patha* and *prakara* or *prakaras* are aligned in orderly succession around the *sri-kovil* or main shrine.

Some temples in south Kerala exhibit another pillared structure known as *balikkal-mandapa*, in front of it there is *valiambalam*, the front part of the *nalambalam* provides entrance in to the temple. A *dipa-stamba* or *dhvaja-stamba* is situated facing the *balikkal-mandapa*, which enshrines the *bali-pitha*. From 14th century A.D. the larger complexes have *kuttambalam*, the venue for artistic performances and *teppakulam* (temple-tank).

One of the largest temples in Kerala, the Vadakkunatha (PL.265), is spread over nine acres on a small hillock in the centre of the *Thrissur* town. The temple is said to have been built by Parasurama. Legend also has it that Adi Sankaracharya was born after his parents, who were childless for many years, prayed at the temple. It is a multi shrined complex having three principal shrines dedicated to Vadakkunatha *alias* Ten-kailasanatha or Siva, Sankaranarayana and Rama. Several smaller shrines are spread around the outer courtyard. The Ayyappan or Sasta shrine, apsidal on plan, situated outside the *nalambalam* enclosure, there by indicating the gods dethronement from the higher position enjoyed earlier. Near *kuttambalam* a small shrine with Dravida *vimana*,dedicated to Krishna is located. The presiding deity Vadakkunatha is not visible, as it covered under a 4m high mount of ghee formed by the daily *abhisheka* (ablution) with ghee over the centuries. It is a wonder that the ghee, inspite of high temperature,doesn't melt. The Sankaranarayana shrine has beautiful 17th century murals depicting the story of Mahabharata.All the three central shrines have *namaskara-mandapas* with beautifully carved wooden pillars. The *kuttambalam* (PL.266) is a lovely wooden structure with a sloping roof and intricately carved ceiling (PL.267).

The four magnificent *gopuras* and the laterite *prakara* around the temple quadrangle are an imposing piece of craftsmanship and skill. Each *gopura* has beautifully carved out wooden pillars and wooden bracket figures.The four massive *gopuras* were renovated by Sakthan Thampuran in the late 18th century A.D. He was the very architect of Thrissur and became the ruler of the erstwhile State of Cochi. It was he who made the sprawling Thekkinkadu maidan, the major venue for Thrissur puram. He himself is said to have drawn up the 36-hour hectic schedule of the pooram festival.The festival during April-May is a time of incredible splendour. A procession of elephants (PL.268) in jewel-crusted trappings, fanned with whisks and carrying ceremonial umbrellas and refreshing scenes of public participation, takes the deity on a chariot round the main temple.

The Puram programme (PL.269) begins with the *ezhunnallippu* (procession carrying deity) of the *kanimangalam Shasta* in the morning and is followed by the *ezhunnallippu* of the six minor temples on the Pooram day.*The ezhunnallippu* programme is considered to be a ritual symbolizing the visit of the Devi from the Paramekkavu and the Thiruvambadi temples to the Vadakkunatha temple.

For the elephant lovers and devotees of Thrissur the annual *anayottu* (ceremonious feeding of elephants) ritual, held on the first day of the month of *karkkidakam* in the precints of the Vadakkunatha temple has become an exiciting component of thir festival calendar just like the pooram festival. The belief that offering *poojas* and delious feed to the elephants is a ritualistic way to propitiate Ganesa is what draws a large number of devotees to the event. The special feed included sugar cane leaves, coconut and jaggery and *pooja prasadam*.

During late phase subsidiary shrines, ranging from one to ten, were added to the temple complexes. The Vamanamurti Maha Vishnu temple at Trikkakara, Ernakulam district, circular on plan, possesses eight sub-shrines within the complex, where as the Siva temple at Kandiyur, Alleppey district, has ten sub-shrines.

Sixteenth-seventeeth centuries witnessed construction of lofty enclosures, sculpted corridors and the ornate *balikkal-mandapas* are rather cramped in some examples and practically concealed the main shrine. Notable examples where the main temple completely hidden behind the enclosures are Suchindram and Thiruvanantapuram. The nuclei of both the complexes belong to 9th or 10th century A.D.

Suchindram means the place where Indra worshipped god to make himself pure *(suchi)*. It is also called *Sivindram* thereby meaning that Indra worshipped Lord Siva here. The Sthanunathasvami temple at Suchindram, Kanyakumari district, Tamil Nadu, an adjacent area of Kerala, in Travancore region, is the most typical example of the Dravidin style.The temple is complete with its *gopura*, pillared pavilions and the tank (PL.270). The *navaratri-mandapa* belonging to 16th century A.D. is an exquisite lithic translation of the conventional wooden structure of Kerala. All the details of the original wooden model are carved on the ceiling and pillars.The ceiling is not flat but a coffered one "rose above the beams by a bracket construction which has the shape of a four sided collar ceiling". The *gopura* belongs to 17th century, which is imposing, well proportioned, and elegantly executed is the finest in Kerala.The pillars of the dance pavilion have the female figures, which are believed to be the temple dancers who donated the pavilion. The ceiling panels represent floral decorations. The *rishabha-mandapa* contains a huge *nandi* which with its thin white coat of plaster looks as if it was made out of rice flour. Close to the *citra-sabha* display a monolithic Hanuman, 5.1m high (PL.271) is noteworthy.The temple also has many other *mandapas*: Kulasekhara- *mandapa*, Vasanta-*mandapa*, Champakaraman-*mandapa*, Virapandyanmani - *mandapa,* Udayamartanda-*mandapa*, etc. The sculptures and reliefs here recall the late Vijayanagara and Nayaka idioms.

The temple here is venerated by both Saivites and Vaishnavites. It enshrines on a single *lingam* known as *Sthanumalaya*, (Siva as *Sthanu*, and Vishnu as *Mal* and Brahma as *Aya*) the triple aspects of the god.

Another well known example of the Dravidian style is the Padmanabhasvami or Ananta sayana temple at *Thiruvananthapuram*. This temple was completely renovated in the last two centuries. The open pillared *mandapa* round the complex with stone pillars, and the super structure of the eastern *gopura*, built of brick, are in Dravida style. While the subsidiary entrance to the north of the *gopura* has gable roof and *kilivasal-nasikas* in traditional Kerala pattern.Though the *gopura* (PL.272) built in Dravida style, is squattish and does not convey the commanding dignity of other well known temple *gopuras* of south India.The *gopura* at Madurai, for instance, soars skyward.

The central shrine, built of stone, is rectangular on plan to house the Anantasayi (reclining) form of Vishnu. The image of Lord reposing on serpent Ananta is viewed through three doors. The three doorways reveal the face, navel and feet of the reclining figure of Seshasayi Vishnu, a magnificent representation of Padmanabha. The original image was made of wood. The present image has been created using 1200 *Salagramas* and shaped using mixture of lime, granite, molasses and mustard. The Lord in *yoga nidra* pose is offering *bilva* leaves to lord Siva. The super structure is two storeyed with pent and gable-roof patterns for its storeys. The walls are painted but later restorations have ruined the charm of these frescoes though the contours show the faces of glory. There are subsidiary shrines dedicated to Krishna, Kshetrapala, Narasimha, Srasta, Garuda, etc.

The Adikesavaperumal temple at *Tiruvattar*, Kanyakumari district, is renowned for its covered passage which has 222 pillars exquisitely carved with *dipa-lakshmis* and other reliefs.Here, in this period the open outer *pradakshina-patha* has been converted in to a covered passage.The highly embellished *balikkal-mandapas* as instanced at Vaikom and Varakala occur this period.

The Perunthirukoilappan (Siva) temple (PL.273) at *Vaikom*, Kottayam district, is elliptical on plan, standing alone without any subsidiary buildings. The legendary Parasurama is associated with this famous temple. This temple is the best example for the typical Kerala temple architecture. It is topped with a cone shaped roof that is absolutely geometrical, covered with copper, and crowned by a dazzling gold *stupi*. The *sri-kovil* is datable to the 11th or 12th century A.D. Its wooden panel walls were added in the 15th or 16th centuries and that a second renovation took place in 18th century mainly to treat the murals. Siva oriented wall paintings have been retouched extensively and the colours are probably brighter than their original ones. The entrance *gopura* of the temple may be a late 18th or early 19th century construction with its European style pillars integrated into the typical Kerala temple court yard by the adumbration of tall brass lamps (PL.273). A wall painting inside the Vaikom temple painted in typical Kerala style with a violently dramatic Siva dancing while the devotees look on with wonder (PL.274) is noteworthy.

The Ponmeri Siva temple at *Villiapally*, Calicut district, has two roofs over the *sri-kovil* with a projecting double gable at the front. Wooden struts with figures 1m long support both roof projections, while larger supporting images in the round, stand beside the *sri-kovil* door. The *dvarapalas* 1.8 m tall, carved in granite, are flanked the doorway. The walls project and recede in shadowed, architectonic multiplication, in contrast to the active organic volumes of the figures. The ceiling and roof underside of the *namaskara-mandapa* is full of paintings with dazzling colours. On the middle of the ceiling is occupied the Surya riding the chariot (PL.275) is 12 inches high, adapted in an aurole which is not round but triangular. The symbolic toy horses, which are an unusual configuration of ten, are adjusted to the throne to make an image in wood, which may fix the imagination of the folk worshippers to the abstract Aryan god of the Gayatri hymn is note worthy.

Like Kerala, South Kanara (west coast of Karnatak state) also has some temples which show striking resemblence to the architecture of the Himalayan region. The Mudabidiri (32 km north east of Mangalore) Jain temples are datable from 12th to 16th centuries A.D. They are built of stone recalling the wood work. The Chandranatha temple is a splendid example of Mudabidiri group and is dated to the early 15th century A.D. It consists of three *mandapas*, all connected and combined with the *garbha-griha* in which the image of Jain *Tirthankara* is installed. The pillars in their decor and smoothness exhibit similar features noticed in the Belur and Halebid temples. The entire superstructure is a common multiple roof with open triangular gable-ends, identical in all aspects to those of Kerala.

The *sri-kovil* of the celebrated *Guruvayur* temple (PL.276), dedicated to Krishna (Guruvayur-Appan), is square and two storeyed with metal sheet gable roofs. The main shrine is covered with *nalambalam* and *prakara*. All murals in the temple have been obliterated by successive renovations. These were of 17th century. A 33 m high gold-plated flag post and a *dipa-stambha* with thirteen circular receptacles are noteworthy. During the annual temple festival in February-March, Krishnattam dance, the precursor of kathakali, is performed here. Non-Hindus are not allowed to enter the temple. The management of the temple recently decided to allow women wearing *chauridars* to enter the shrine. Women to wear only sarees seem to have been relaxed. The authorities should also stop insisting that men should remove their shirts and wear only *dhotis* when they enter the temple.

At the Southern most land tip of India, where the Arabian Sea, the Indian Ocean and the Bay of Bengal meet, lays *Kanyakumari* and Amman temple (PL.277), an important pilgrim centre. Kanyakumari is famous for its beach and the spectacular sunrises and sunsets especially on full moon days. The place has been named after the goddess Kanyakumari Amman who is the popular deity of the area, an incarnation of goddess Parvathi, to have performed penance on these rocks, in order to obtain the hand of Lord Siva.

Two rocks reach out of the ocean, south east of the Kumari Amman temple, on one of them, *Sri Padaparai*, the foot prints of the Virgin goddess are seen. On this rock, Svami Vivekananda is said to have sat in deep meditation; and here stands the Vivekananda Rock memorial, built in 1970 (PL.278).

On the other rock the Tamil Nadu government has installed a statue of Saint Thiruvalluvar (PL.279) who gave us quintessential words of wisdom known as *Thirukkural.* The total weight of the statue is 7000 tons and 39.9 m high including the pedastal. It took 22 years to complete the statue and finally inagurated on 1st January 2000. The stones for the sculpture brought from Sirudhamoor, Pattumalaikuppam and Ambhasamudram hills.

Among the early Dravida temples in Travancore region, which resembles a spacious hall rather than the cubical temple, is the Guhanatha Svami temple of Chola period (1000 A.D.) at Kanya kumari. The pilasters, the roll cornice with its *chaitya* window motifs and lion friezes above them clearly indicate the influence of the Dravidian style.

In north India the Vishnu temples at Pushkar (Rajasthan) and Mathura (Uttar Pradesh) with their typical *gopuras* and elaborate structure complex represent the Dravida architectural style. These were built in the later half of 19th century under the religious influence of south Indian Brahmins.

The sculptural art of the temples in Kerala is seen mainly either on banisters or on *pranalas,* the latter being generally associated with a dwarf figure, showing the impact of Chola architectural tradition.The banisters carry deities, dance scenes, etc.In south Kerala the former motifs are common while the rest have figures of lion. Further a dwarf-figure in the pose of drinking the *abhisheka* (lustral) water from the *pranala* is invariably seen all over Kerala.In some cases the *valiambalam* pillars have reliefs of *dipa-lakshmis* and other figures which exhibit the features of late Vijayanagara and Nayaka style.The art of Tamil country is best represented in the reliefs from Vaikom, Varakala, Suchindram.Thiruvananthapuram and others.

The sculptures in the Suchindram temple represent puranic stories of Krishna, Subrahmanya and other deities. These belong to 15th century A.D. A bas-relief of the *visvarupa* form of Krishna is depicted on one of the walls of the *gopura* datable to 16th century A.D.It is notable for its unique features combining the three forms of Vishnu Siva and Brahma with their weapons and attributes, a theme representing *gitopadesa* of Arjuna to Krishna.

PALACES:

The 16th century Portuguese built Mattancherry Royal Palace near *Kochi* or *Cochin,* is a veritable treasure house of marvellous paintings depicting scenes from the Hindu epics. The plan of the spacious double-storeyed panoramic edifice, murals in the large rooms and temples bear testimony to the Portuguese easthetic architecture and superb engineering skill.

The Mattancherry palace was erected by the Portuguese in 1557 A.D. and presented it to the ruler of Kochi. A century later, it was thoroughly renovated by the Dutch and hence the building was also known as the Dutch palace.

The palace exhibits Kerala's domestic architectural (*nalukettus*) style in its design and execution.Enclosed by a high wall with entrances on the east and west, the double-storeyed palace, is a large rectangular structure with a large court yard in the centre.In the centre of the court yard features a temple dedicated to the tutelary deity of the ruling family, Pazhayannur Bhagavati.In addition, to the south of the palace there are temples for Vishnu and Siva. To the west of the palace is the large masonary tank. The covered Porch is reached through a flight of steps from the South. From this Porch one can enter into the spacious coronation hall, noted for its carved ceiling. It has, however, no wall paintings, but has virtually converted into a museum, exhibiting the dresses, turbans and three palanquins, belonging to the royal Kochi family. To the west of the coronation hall is a bed-chamber (*palliyara*) with low wooden ceiling whose walls are fully covered with murals executed in traditional style. Every inch of space painted here with sombre colour. White colour has been used sparingly. There are forty to forty five scenes, mainly devoted to the story of Ramayana (PL.280) beginning from the Dasaratha's *putrakameshti-yaga* (sacrifice wishing the birth of a child) after which Rama is born, until the return of Rama, Lakshmana and Sita to Ayodhya. In the small room, the entire epic is played out in a panoramic drama of magnificent proportions.

In a room called *kovinithalam* or staircase room to the south of the coronation hall the murals represent the scene of coronation of Rama, Guruvayur Appan, and Mahalakshmi and so on. The room belongs to 18th century. To the north of the *kovinithalam* is another room with only one painting representing Vishnu as Vaikunthanatha of the Tripunittura temple.

In the ground floor there are two halls constructed during 19th century. These were the bed chambers for the ladies in which contain the murals. One of them depicts scenes from Kalidasa's *Kumara Sambhava* and the adjacent room contains five large sized murals depicting various *puranic* themes, like Siva dallying with Mohini, Krishna as Govardhanagiridhari etc. In modelling of the figures these paintings recall Vaikom and Ettumanur examples. A spacious hall on the north and one on the east exhibit some of the paraphernalia of the royal house of Kochi and some of their weapons and furniture.

The earliest paintings of the 16th century are on the theme of Venugopala (PL.281). These panels are interspersed with slightly later Ramayana paintings. All the life is presented in these glorious paintings. The rich colours reflect the lush natural beauty of Kerala, while the strong voluminous figures with their beautiful head dresses have a close relationship with the dance dramas of the land. The mural paintings of Kerala are among the finest made in India. The exquisite shading to depict the fullness and roundedness of form reminds us of the great paintings of Ajanta and Alchi, in Ladakh.

The ASI had reorganized the Mattancherry palace museum, providing lighting of international standards in the gallery that features life size portraits of the 19th century kings of Kochi made on canvas by local artists. A new gallery on Kerala history has panels on the story of Parusuraman and the archaeology and history of Kerala, Kochi's in particular.

Padmanabhapuram, the seat of the Travancore royal family from 1601 to 1790, is one of the best examples of the Kerala's *nalukettu* (four buildings) style wood architecture and probably the best preserved wooden palace (PL.282) in India.

The oldest parts of the palace date back to the mid 14th century and the well preserved 18th century murals that form a rich heritage in this part of the country are note worthy.

There are actually 14 palaces, spread over 6.5 acres. The complex, comprising individual structures of teak wood and granite and linked by a maze of corridors, colonnades, verandahs, and courts, is enclosed by massive stone walls 9m high. The earliest of the buildings here is the *Thai-kottaram* (Mother's palace). On plan; it is in *nalukettus* style with a well defined court yard in the centre. Of the several edfices with gabled tiled roofs, the most noteworthy are the entrance-hall, the council-chambers, the theatre, the *puja-mandapa* and the stone temple of Sarasvati fronted by a *navaratri- mandapa*.

Entry is through the *padippura* (main gate), an essential feature of any old Kerala house. Two equestrians carved in wood welcome the visitor into the *poomukham* or entrance-hall. The elaborately carved wooden ceiling and pillars of the entrance hall is eye catching. Especially fascinating are the flowers on the ceiling in number 90, each bearing a different design. A narrow wooden staircase leads to the *mantra-sala* or council-chamber on the first floor of the *poomukham*. Here, the king used to meet his ministers and other dignitaries. Traditional oil lamps provide light. The floor of this chamber has highly polished gleaming black floors, so bright as to image the surroundings in the surface. The secret method of laying this unique floor, utilising a special mixture of lime, burnt coconut husks, the white of eggs, coconut water, sand, laterite, and juices of herbs. This method of flooring has unfortunately fallen from use and is said to be lost.

The third court marks the beginning of the private chambers. The *upparikka- malika* (four-storeyed building) served as the king's quarters. The paintings in the third floor of these covering more than 40 scenes from the Hindu mythology are the master pieces of the Kerala mural tradition. The paintings depict Ananthasai Vishnu, Lakshminarayana, Ardhanarisvara, and Krishna with *gopis*, Nataraja, etc. The Sarasvati temple lies to the east of the *upparikka-malika*. Even today during *Navaratri*, Goddess Sarasvati is worshipped at the temple of the main palace in Thiruvananthapuram, conscreted and taken out in procession from Padmanabhapuram. On the west is the most beautiful part of the Palace the *navaratri-mandapa*, famous for its excellent woodcraft. The sculpted granite pillars lend an illusion of space. During the Navaratri festival, this hall would come alive with musicians and dancers who kept the audience enthralled for nine consecutive days.

Each room in the palace is unique. A guided tour through the maze of 108 rooms would leave one breathless at the sheer opulence of the furnishings, paintings, and exquisitely carved pillars and ceilings. The paintings made here are later than those at Mattancherry, the paintings are mainly on themes of Vishnu, Rama and Sita (PL.283). Unlike the Mattancheri paintings, the gods are presented in their iconic forms and not in narrative situations. The paintings again reveal the close relationship between the styles of art in diverse regions of India. The beautiful textiles as well as some of the forms recall the paintings of Alchi in Ladakh.

Although Padmanabhapuram (Kanyakumari district) now in Tamil Nadu, the palace is maintained by the Kerala State Archaeology Department as it had historical association with the dynasty of the rulers of Travancore. Raja Marthanda Varma, the ruler of Travancore, renamed the fort, the palace and the surrounding area as Padmanabhapuram in honour of Lord Padmanabha, the patron deity of the royal family of Travancore. It is one of the finest surviving examples of traditional Kerala architecture. There is a museum on the south-west corner of the palace where stone inscriptions, stone and wooden sculpture, weapons of the royal family are on display.

The temples of Kerala are very rich in wood sculptures. The wood carvers used teak, jackfruit and other woods to carve the sculptures and excelled, in providing their temples with a galaxy of gods and goddesses of lively, lovely and eye-treating wooden masterpieces.Most of the ceilings of the *namaskara-mandapas*, the *nava-grahas* (guardians of the eight regions, namely, Isana, Indra, Agni, Yama, Nirriti, Varuna, Vayu and Kubera, with Brahma in the coffer of the ceiling) are carved. The sculptures on the beams and rafters represent *puranas*.In *kuttambalams* also the epics and the *puranic* themes are frequently represented; the best examples come from Subrahmanya temple at Haripad (Alleppey district) and Subrahmanya temple at Kidangur (Kottayam district).The districts of Ernakulam, Allppey and Kottayam are renowned for wooden walls, magnificently sculptured with well defined panels and decorative motifs.

The wood carvings yielded images in the round as well as in reliefs. The latter category recall goldsmith's art demanding subtle execution with great skill, patience and devotion. The reliefs on timber walls include mythological scenes, decorative patterns and other narrations. The best examples of reliefs on walls come from temples at Ettumanur and Chengannur. The themes from Ramayana is represented with great deal of dramatic action and iconographic details. Mostly the individual scenes are preferred in rectangular panels as in the Kerala paintings.

Among the wooden sculptures in the round, the bracket figures, deities in the niches of *griva* and *dvarapalas* are good examples. The bracket figures represented at Peruvanam and Triprayar and other places, we encounter episodes from Ramayana, of which the Kiratarjuniya theme is a favourite one. Various deities, *gaja-vyala* figures in the brackets and perforated *jali*-windows are interesting examples recalling the Hoysala stone examples of Karnataka. The female bracket figures, the dancer from Ettumanur (PL.284), Durga sitting astride a lion (PL.285) from Villiapally, Parvati (PL.286) from Peruvanam, Nataraja panel (PL.287) from Ettumanur and female attendent (PL.288) from Triprayar are a few examples among the many interesting wooden sculptures.

The murals of Pandya origin in the cave-temple of Tirunandikkara, Kanyakumari district, can be regarded as the earliest in Kerala. The next early fragment is the Nataraja panel of the 16th century on the *gopura* of Siva temple at Ettumanur. The painting shows Siva as Nataraja who trampels the demon, Apasmara and the figure is enclosed within a circular rim as noticed at Aimanam and Edaseri Amsam in Kozhikode district. The gods and goddesses witnessing the spectacle from out side. In the Krishnapuram palace (near Thiruvananthapuram) are paintings of which the Gajendramoksha panel holds prime interest. On stylistic grounds this large panel may be dated to 16th century. On the walls of the Sankaranarayana temple in the Vadakkunnatha temple-complex at Thrissur, the battle of Kurukshetra was enacted, simultaneously, on the sides, Siva Nataraja, Dakshinamurti and Ganesa are represented.

The surviving panels in the Siva temple at Tripparangode may belong to later half of the 17th century A.D. The paintings shows configuration of Siva, in his incarnations as Ardhanarisvara Subrahmanya and Vishnu with two female figures, executed with great skill.

Some of the most important later wall-paintings are on the walls of Mattancheri palace, distributed mainly in three halls known as *palliyara* or royal bed-chamber, *kovinithalam* and the ladies chamber, are of the periods between 17th and 19th centuries A.D. Most of the panels in royal bed chamber, in horizontal planes, contain more than one scene depicting the story of Ramayana in sequence. Each figure is distinguished by a beaded border in bluish green especially on its upper part. In paintings white has been used sparingly but blue is absent. The walls of *kovinathalam* have paintings of divinities like Anantasayi Vishnu, Kudalmanikkasvami, Umamahesvara, Kiratamurti, Rama's coronation, etc. The use of lighter shades, introduction of dance-poses, elimination of beaded borders around different figures are discernable here.

The ladies' chamber in the ground floor has paintings in light colours while its adjacent room has walls painted unfinished in out line in red ochre over a white surface. The story of Kalidasa's *Kumara-sambhava* is a favourite theme here.There is a specially prepared plaster over which a layer of lime and the white colour is directly applied on the lime. The panels of Siva dallying with Mohini, Umamahesvara, Krishna with Gopikas, Krishna as Govardhanagiri-dhari are excellent specimens. Though mythological themes, these breathe an air of freedom, charged with an undercurrent of sensuousness.

Landscapes constituted a decorative element. Slimmer physiognomy and attenuated waist are evident. The nails, fingers and folds of cloth, etc.are precisely drawn with realistic colours.The modelling of the figures recall Vaikom and Ettumanur examples.

In Mattancheri murals two main trends are discernable. One is characterized by traditional line (royal bed chamber), the other mode has techniques adapted from the Western tradition (ladies chamber). Probably the brush work at the palace was carried out by two different schools of artists.

At Padmanabhapuram palace the paintings show the infiltration of western influence to some extent though it is clearly assimilated with the indegenius tradition. The Ganesa and Sasta panels press down on the eyes from the midst of nature forms.

On the whole, the mural paintings of Kerala, with their emphasis on dramatic scenes, elaborate costumes and memorable gestures of figures in intimate relation with each other, seems to be parallel to the living dance-forms of the Kathakali, Kudiyattam and other forms of the theatre of imagination.

The bronzes of Kerala mainly come from Suchindram temple and these date from 12th century onwards. Among these bronzes, Sabhapati or Nataraja, Siva and Parvati are notable examples of Chola tradition. Some of the best examples of Saiva and Vaishnava bronzes are also seen in the Thiruvananthapuram Museum which are datable to 13-14th centuries A.D. However, the earliest bronze image from Kerala datable to early 9th century A.D. is the standing four-armed image of Vishnu as Srinivasa (ht. 16 cm) exhibited in the same museum. Bronzes in typical Kerala idiom occur from 15th -16th centuriesA.D.An exquisite example of Vishnumaya, now in the Thrissur museum, reveals heavy modelling, elaborate ornamentation and stylized features. The *panchaloha* (made of five metals) *dvarapalas* of 17th century now in Thrissur museum were executed in hollow-cast process.

A group of metal images of 17th-18th centuries are preserved in the Siva temple at Thiruvanchikulam. These represent Nataraja, Umashita-Siva, Cheramal perumal Nayanar, etc. For the grace and elegance, heavy ornamentation and conspicuous *prabhavali* the figure of Nataraja is best example.

Glossary of Indian Architectural Terms

Adhisthana : basement of a temple, pillared hall or similar religious structure. It consists of mouldings, each moulding having a distinct name like *upana*, *jagati*, *kumuda*, *pattika* and so forth.

Antarala : passage or room between shrine and outer *mandapa*.

Ardha- mandapa : hall immediately infront of the principal shrine.

Asta-parivara : eight seperate shrines surrounding the main temple.

Bali-pitha : A stone platform on which ritual offerings are placed. In Kerala temples, there is one principal *bali-pitha* in front of the main temple entrance.

Balikkal-mandapa : the pillared hall raised above the principal *bali-pitha*.

Beki- bhairava : crouching human figure.

Bhadra-gavaksa : A square or rectangular porch with vertical posts and trellis and a bas-relief on the hind wall.

Bhutamala : A frieze of goblins shown below the roll cornice moulding.

Bhumi : storey.

Bhitti : wall.

Brahmakanta : A variety of pillar or pilaster quadrangular in form.

Citrakhanda : A pillar square in section and has a base.The shaft is made in to octagonal in the middle and occasionally a band connects the cube and lower parts of the shaft. The members of the capital are *lasuna* (pitcher), *tadi* (cushon shaped moulding with a convex profile),*kumbha* (vase shaped but inverted), *pali.* (inverted lotus) and *phalaka* (abacus).

Deva-kostha : niche enshrining a deity on the shrine wall.

Dvara : doorway.

Dvarapala : door-keeper at the entrance of a shrine or temple.

Dvi tala : two storeyed.

Dvi anga : having two proliferations, central and corner projections.

Eka tala vimana : one storeyed super structure of a temple.

Gaja -vyala : A motif depicting the combining features of an elephant and lion.

Gajakranta : a pillar having at its base an elephant standing on a lion.

Gajaprstha : the form of a superstructure in the shape of an elephant's back. It goes with the apsidal temples.

Gala : neck; a recessed moulding of a socle; a clerestory below the *sikhara*.

Garbha-griha : sanctum sanctorum.

Ghata-pallava : a pillar having at its base a *purnaghata* (vase and foliage).The capital is of *talapatra* consisting of square blocks, each decorated with palmette design.

Gopura : storeyed structure forming the main gateway of temple.

Ghanta-mala : bell and chain motif.

Griva : neck.The neck moulding below a *sikhara*.

Gudha-mandapa : closed hall, in front of *antarala*.

Hamsa-mala : a row of geese carved on the *valabhi* moulding below the cornice.

Hara : garland, necklace; connotes a row of miniature shrines called *kuta, sala* and *panjara* above the terrace.

Idal : Inverted Lotus like member under the abacus (*phalaka*) of a pillar with petals marked.

Jagati : platform or a terrace over which the shrine proper is built.
In the Dravida tradition, this term denotes the vertical moulding above the *upana* in the socle.

Jangha	:	wall; also denotes the shaft part in the pillar.
Kalasa	:	Pitcher used as the crowning member of a temple.
Kalyana-mandapa	:	Hall where the marriages of the deities are celebrated.
Kantha	:	a recessed moulding in the socle.
Kapota	:	over hanging cornice
Kati	:	wall
Khattaka	:	niche
Khura	:	hoof; the lowest moulding in the socle.
Kirttimukha	:	Lion's face
Kostha	:	niche.
Kumuda	:	the central moulding of the socle. It may be either *tripatta* three faceted or *vrtta* circular.
Kuta	:	a shrine on square plan with four sided roof with finial. Usually it is placed at the corner of each storey in the superstructure or in the *hara* over the terrace.
Kuttambalam	:	A Malayalam term for an edifice within a temple complex Where, dance, music and other recitals take place.
Lata	:	creeper.
Lalatabimba	:	it occupies the centre of the door lintel.
Maha-mandapa	:	a hall, closed or open, infront of the *ardha-mandapa* or *antarala*.

Manchabandha	:	*adhishthana* which does not have the *kumuda* but consists of other functional mouldings.
Mulaprasada	:	principal shrine
Madhyalata	:	central shoot or offset in the *sikhara.*
Makara-torana	:	decorative device above a niche with *Makaras* at ends with plumes hanging below
Mala	:	central projected part of the *Bhumija sikhara.*
Mandapa	:	hall
Mukha catusk	:	porch, open pillared pavilion, in front of the vestibule.
Mukha-mandapa	:	pillared hall, in front of the vestibule.
Nasika	:	chaitya dormer; a projected arched opening.
Nandi	:	bull, mount of Siva.
Nandi- mandapa	:	an independant pillared hall housing the *nandi* image, in front of the temple.
Natya-mandapa	:	dancing hall.
Namaskara-mandapa	:	also called *archana-mandapa* intended for congregation. It is detached from the temple and is square on plan with a Pyramidal roof.
Nava- ranga	:	Pillared hall.
Nirandhara	:	temple without an inner ambulatory.
Pada	:	pilastered wall.
Pada-bandha	:	If the *kumuda* is circular, the *adhisthana* is said to be of the *Pada-bandha* type.

Padma	:	moulding presenting the curves of the Lotus
Padma-pitha	:	lotus pedestal.
Panchayatana	:	when in an enclosure, four shrines, each in a corner surround the main shrine.
Pancha-sakha	:	five jambed as in a door way.
Panjara	:	miniature apsidal shrine (decorative motif).
Pattika	:	a projected moulding thick in size.
Phamsana	:	temples with pyramidal superstructure.
Pitha	:	base, socle.
Potika	:	corbel, bracket of a pillar.
Pradaksina-patha	:	circumambulatory path.
Prakara	:	enclosure wall.
Prasada	:	temple, palace.
Prastara	:	entablature over the wall or pillars.
Ranga-mandapa	:	an open hall used for theatrical purposes.
Ratha	:	chariot or monolithic temple car; a graded projection of the wall.
Rati-chitra	:	erotic figures.
Rucaka	:	square, a type of column.
Rekha	:	curvature.
Saduram	:	a square sectioned part of the pillar.
Sala-sikhara	:	wagon topped or barrel vaulted.
Salilantara	:	a recessesed portion in the wall.
Sandhara	:	temple with inner ambulatony.

Sikhara	:	cupola or the part above the *griva* or neck below the *kalasa*.
Simhapada	:	Lion base; mostly used in the pillars.
Sirsa	:	bracket.
Sri-kovil	:	the temple proper in Kerala tradition.
Stambha	:	pillar.
Sthapati	:	architect.
Stupi	:	finial of *vimana* or *gopura*.
Suka - nasa	:	'parrot's beak or nose'; architecturally, it denotes a projection over the *antarala* roof, adapting the design of the storey is decorated with a large horse-shoe shaped arch in front inset with a Siva-Nataraja or any deity related to the god enshrined.
Sundu	:	Elephant-truck; Fluted design of *Pranala*.
Tala	:	storey.
Torana	:	an arch; a gateway.
Tiruchuttumala	:	cloister around the enclosure wall.
Trikuta	:	three *vimanas* either arranged in a line or placed around a common hall.
Tripatta-kumuda	:	tri faceted *kumuda* moulding in the socle.
Trisakha	:	triple jambed.
Tritala	:	three - storeyed
Udgama	:	pediment.
Upana	:	the lowermost moulding of the socle.

Vatayana	:	window.
Vedika or Vedi	:	a railing like moulding in between *kapota* and *bhitti*.
Vedibandha	:	socle consisting of the mouldings *khura, jadyakumbha kalasa, antarapatra* and *kapotali*.
Venukosa	:	lateral offset of the superstructure.
Vimana	:	denotes the entire structure from the base to the finial,
Visnukanta	:	an octagonal pillar.
Vyalamala	:	a frieze of leonine form.
Yali	:	Leograph.

How to Reach there

ANDHRA PRADESH

Ahobilam: 26 km from Allagadda, 130 km from Kurnool, 320 km from Hyderabad, 520 km from Chennai and 275 km from Bangalore.Nandyal, 68 km away is the nearest railway station.It is well connected by road. Accomodation: A.P. TourismPunnami hotel, Ahobilam. ph:+91-08518-270104.

Alampur : 32 km from Kurnool, 180 km from Hyderabad, 600 km from Chennai and 350 km from Bangalore. It is well connected by road and rail. Accomodation: Best option is Kurnool with its wide range of hotels.

Amaravati: 35 km from Guntur, 45 km from Vijayawada (Via Undavalli), 350 km from Hyderabad. Convenient rail heads are Guntur and Vijayawada. Buses ply regularly between Guntur and Amaravati. Accommodation: Dharani tourist rest house, A.P. Tourism Punnami hotel (room (4) Rs. 275/-, dormitory per bed Rs. 50.), ph: 08645-55332, PWD guest house, Amaravati. 3 star hotels, budget hotels and lodges at Guntur and Vijayawada.

Bapatla: 53 km from Guntur in Guntur District. Accommodation: Basic acommodation at Bapatla.

*Bhairavakonda***:** 64 km from Kanigiri and 150 km from Ongole by road in Prakasam District. Accommodation: Basic accommodation (Lodges) at Kanigiri and Pamur.

Chejerla: 25 km from Narasaraopet and 70 km from Guntur by road in Guntur District.
Accommodation: Basic accommodation in Narasaraopet. Best option is Guntur with its wide range of Hotels.

Draksharamam: 25 km from Kakinada.
Accommodation: Lodges at Kakinada.

Gudimallam: 4 km from Papanayudupeta and 20 km from Tirupati in Chittor district.

Hanumakonda : 6 km from Warangal, 140 km from Hyderabad, 844 km from Chennai and 720 km from Bangalore. It is well connected by road and rail. Accommodation: A.P.Tourism Punnami hotel, Kazipet. Tourist information counter at Kazipet Railway Station.

Kanipakam : 75 km from Tirupati and 12 km from Chittoor
Accommodation: At Tirupati.

Lepakshi : 15 km from Hindupur 124 km from Anantapur in Anantapur District, 450 km from Hyderabad and 80 km from Bangalore. Buses ply frequently from Hindupur. A.P. Tourism accommodation : Punnami hotel, Lepakshi. Contact ph: +91- 08518-270104.

Mahanandi : 12 km from Nandyal, 95 km from Kurnool, 315 km from Hyderabad, 425 km from Chennai and 255 km from Bangalore. It is well connected by road.
Accommodation: APT Punnami Hotel, Mahanandi.

Markapur: Located 94 km from Ongole in Prakasam District.
Accommodation: Basic accommodation in Markapur.

Nagarjuna Konda: Via Nagarjuna Sagar 150 km from Hyderabad. The nearest railhead is Macherla; about 29 km from Nagarjuna Sagar. The museum can be reached by the launch service provided by the tourist department. Accommodation: A.P. Tourism Punnami Vihar, cell; 98480-07026, Punnami hotel (Vijayapuri South), Project house, Hotel Nagarjuna, Vijayavihar complex and cottages.

Palampet: 72 km from Warangal, 213 km frm Hyderabad, 914 km from Chennai and 790 km from Bangalore. It is connected by road from Warangal.
Accommodation: A.P. Tourism Punnami hotel, Warangal.

Simhachalam : 16 km from Vishakhapatnam, 665 km from Hyderabad, 750 km from Chennai and 950 km from Bangalore. It is well connected by road, rail and air. Accomodation: Star hotels and economy hotels at Vishakhapatnam.

Srikalahasti: 36 km from Tirupati, 640 km from Hyderabad, 230 km from Chennai and 300 km from Bangalore. It is well connected by road, rail and air. Accommodation: Devasthanam Accommodation, Trinetra guest house, Pudi, Ph: + 91 - 08578 - 262240 ext: 19 and private hotels, Srikalahasti.

Srisailam: 70 km from Nagarjunasagar, 220 km from Hyderabad. It can also be reached by an exciting 110 km boat ride from Nagarjunasagar. It is accessible by a ghat road on the hill from Dornala (49 km). Accommodation: Punnami hotel, ph: 08524-288311, (NonA/cRoom (3) Rs. 200), Ganga & Gowri sadan, Reddy Choulltry and other Choultries, Srisailam.

Tadipatri : 55 km from Anantapur, 350 km from Hyderabad, 600 km from Chennai and 340 km from Bangalore. It is well connected by road and rail.
Accommodation: Best option is Anantapur with its wide range of hotels.

Tirumala - Tirupati : 65 km from Chittoor, 592 km from Hyderabad, 180 km from Chennai and 250 km from Bangalore. It is well connected by road, rail and air. Accommodation: Tirupati has a number of star hotels and lodges to suit every budget. Guest houses/ Choultries are available both at Tirupati and Tirumala.

Tripurantakam: 40 km from Markapur and 93 km from Ongole in Prakasam Dist.
Accommodation: Low budget lodges at Markapur.

Undavalli: 5 km from Vijayawada. Accommodation: at Vijayawada.

Vijayawada: 267 km from Hyderabad, 450 km from Chennai and 700 km from Bangalore. It is well connected by road rail and air. Accommodation: Luxury, moderate, inexpensive Hotels; A.P. Tourism guest house, Krishnaveni Hotel.

Warangal: 157 km from Hyderabad. Warangal and the adjoining Kazipet fall on the Chennai - New Delhi grand trunk route. Hence train services are available to Warangal from all the major cities in India. Road: Warangal is easily accessible by road from Hyderabad and Vijayawada. Accommodation: Decent accommodation is available in Warangal with both Luxury and economy hotels. A.P. Tourism's 'Punnami' hotel with a bar and restaurant attached is ideally located at Hanumakonda, a distance of 2 km from Kazipet railway station and 14 km from Warangal railway station. Warangal Fort is 12 km from Warangal.

KARNATAKA

Badami: 150 km from Belgaum (closest airport), 100 km from Hubli and 71 km from Gadag.

Badami is a Station on the Hubli-Sholapur railway route. Pattadakal is 18 km, Aihole is 45 km and Mahakuta is 11 km from Badami.

Accommodation: Hotel Badami Court, Tel: 08357-265230; Mookambika deluxe Tel: 08357 – 265067; Hotel Anand Deluxe, beside bus stand, Ph: 08357-220074 (Rs. 300/-double bed room).

Belur: 39 km from Hassan, 155 km from Mysore and 234 km from Bangalore.

Accommodation: Hotel Hassan Ashok (ITDC), Hassan, Tel: 228730, 28731.

Traveller's Bungalow, Belur, Gayatri Lunch home, Near Bus Stand, Belur.

National Lunch home, Belur, Hotel Mayura Velapuri, Temple road, Belur.

Halebid: 16 km from Belur. Accommodation: Hotel Mayura Shantala.

Hampi: Hampi is 350 km from Banglore and 558 km from Chennai. Hospet (13 km) is the closest railway station; Bellary (74 km) the closest airport. There are regular buses between Hospet and Hampi. Hampi ruins are mainly situated between the villages of Kamalapuram in the south and Hampi in the north. Archaeological museum is situated at Kamalapuram. Accommodation: Karnataka State Tourism Development Corporation (KSTDC) has a hotel at Kamalapuram village which is the closest one can stay to Hampi. KSTDC also has a Hotel at Tungabhadra dam, 12 km from Hospet. However; there are some lodges and private economical guest houses (rooms) at Hampi itself.

Shravanbelgola: 52 km from Hassan and 95 km from Mysore and 150 km from Bangalore.

Accommodation: Hotel Hassan Ashok, Hassan, Hotel Raghu (double bed room Rs. 300/-) and Jain Choultries.

Somanathpur: 35 km from Mysore and140 km from Bangalore.

Accommodation: Basic accommodation at Somanathpur. Best option is Mysore with its wide range of hotels.

KERALA

Cochin or Kochi: 3 km from Ernakulam. Cochin is well connected by Air, Rail and Road. Accommodation: Sea Lord Hotel, Shanmugam Rd; Casino Hotel, Wllington Island; Woodlands, MG Rd, Ernakulam.

Guruvayur: 28 km from Thrissur. The nearest airport is Cochin (79 km). Accommodation Hotel Elite, East Nada; Panchajanyam Rest House, South Nada.

Ettumanur:12 km from Kottayam. Best option is Kottayam.Hotel Aishwarya (KTDC).

Manjeri: 5 km from Malappuram 25 km from Kozhikode. Nearest airport is Kozhikode. Accommodation: Basic Accommodation in Manjeri. Best option is Malappuram.

Padmanabhapuram: 53 km south of Thiruvananthapuram on way to Kanyakumari.
Accommodation: Best option is Thiruvananthapuram with its wide range of Hotels.

Suchindram: 18 km from Kanyakumari. Accommodation: Best option is Kanyakumari

Thiruvananthapuram: 920 km from Chennai, 851 km from Bangalore, 2065 km from New Delhi and 211 km from Ernakulam.It is well connected by air, rail and road.Accommodation: Mascot Hotel, Palayam; Hotel South Park, MG Road; Hotel Arya Nivas, Near Railway Station; Rajadhani Tourist Home, East Fort.

Thrissur: is well connected by air, rail and road.Cochin air port is 58 km away.Accommodation: There are several staying options in Thrissur town ranging from budget, mid-range to high-end. Hotel Luciya Palace, Marar Road; Central Hotel, Museum Road; Alukkas Tourist Home, Rly Station Road.

Triprayar: 40 km from Thrissur city. Accommodation: Best option is Thrissur.

Vaikom: 190 km from Thiruvananthapuram, 40 km from Kottayam.It is well connected by air, rail and road.The nearest airport is Cochin.Accommodation: Best option is Ernakulam with its wide range of Hotels.

TAMIL NADU

Chidambaram: 225 km from Chennai, 107 km from Thanjavur and 47 km from Cuddalore. It is well connected by air, rail and road. The nearest airport is Trichy (168 km). Accommodation: Hotel Tamil Nadu (TTDC), Railway feeder road, Ph. 04144-238739.

Darasuram: 34 km from Thanjavur and 5 km from Kumbakonam, almost at it out skirts.

Gangaikonda Cholapuram: 260 km from Chennai, 70 km from Perumbalur, and 70 km from Thanjavur and 36 km from Kumbakonam. A visitor from Chennai may take the train or bus to Kumbakonam from where buses ply to the place. Kumbakonam has private lodging facilities of a moderate kind.

Kancheepuram:71 km from Chennai and 64 km from Mahabalipuram. It is well connected by air, rail and road. The nearest airport is Chennai (71 kms).
Accommodation : Kancheepuram has moderate private lodging facilities (opp: bus stand). Hotel Tamil Nadu (TTDC); Abirami Lodge (Opp.Bus Stand) (Double bed room Rs.150/-)

Kanyakumari: 80 km from Tirunelveli and 245 km from Madurai. It is well connected by air, rail and road. Thiruvananthapuram (89 km) is the nearest airport. Kanyakumari is a major rail terminus; Nagarcoil, another important railway junction, 20 km away.
Accommodation: Cape Hotel, Hotel Tamil Nadu, and Kovalam Rd.

Kumbakonam: 38 km from Thanjavur. The nearest airport is Trichy (Tiruchirapalli) (95 km). A major junction, Kumbakonam is well connected by rail and road with all important towns and cities in Tamil Nadu.
Accommodation: Hotel Tamil Nadu (TTDC).

Madurai: 472 km from Chennai, 173 km from Ramesvaram and 245 km from Kanyakumari.It is well connected by air, rail and road to all major cities in South India.
Accommodation: Luxury, Moderate and inexpensive hotels. Hotel Tamil Nadu, Alagar Coil Rd; Hotel JK Residency, DMStreet. ph:0452-2340314 (Double bed room Rs. 350/-).

Mahabalipuram: 59 km from Chennai. Chennai is the nearest airport.
Accommodation: Luxury, Moderate and in expensive hotels.Surya camping site (resort) ph: 04114-242292.

Nagapattinam: 11 km from Keechalur.

Narttamalai: 16 km from Pudukkottai.

Padmanabhapuram:55 km from Thiruvananthapuram, connectcted directly by air and rail and road to most major cities.

Panamali: 21 km from Villupuram.

Ramesvaram: It is well connected by air, rail and road. The nearest airport is Madurai (173 km).
Accommodation: Alankar Tourist Home; Hotel Tamil Nadu and many Private lodges.Hotel tariff ranges from 150/-to 1000/-.

Srirangam: 7 km from Trichy (Tiruchirapalli) and 70 km from Madurai. It is well connected by air, rail and road.
Accommodation: Hotel Aristo; Hotel Gajapriya; New Sri Ranga Lodge (Opp.City union Bank), E.V.S. Street, Ranganagar.ph:0431-2432212 (Three bed room Rs. 300/-).

Thanjavur: 60 km from Tiruchirapalli,195 km from Madurai, 322 km from Chennai, and 106 km from Chidambaram. The nearest airport is Tiruchirapalli. It is well connected by rail and road. Accommodation: The accommodation ranging from economy to luxury is available at Thanjavur run both by Tamil Nadu Tourism Development Corporation and by Private Agencies.
Hotel Karthik (opp: old bus stand) – Ph.04362-278662, 278663. (Rs.350 +5% tax, double bed room)

Tirupparam Kunram: 10 km south west of Madurai.

Tiruttani: 86 km from Chennai.

Tiruvannamalai:190 km from Chennai; 107 km from Kumbakonam and 85 km from Vellore.The nearest airport is Chennai.It is well connected with all important towns and cities in Tamil Nadu.
Accommodation: There are lodges offering rooms at an affordable cost.

For further information and help in planning your tour, Contact:

(1) A. P. Travel & Tourism Development Corporation Limited,
Tank bund Road, Hyderabad-500 004.
Ph: +91-40-2233086, 2233087, 2233036.
E-mail:aptourd@ap.nic.in; website: www.aptourism.com

(2) Karnataka Tourism
49 Second Floor, Khanija Bhavan
Race Cource Road, Bangalore-560 001
Fax: 90 80 2352626 Email:discoverkarnataka@vsnl.net
Website: www.karnatakatourism.org

(3) Kerala Tourism Development Corporation
Thampanoor, Thiruvananthapuram-695 Ph: 0471-2330031, 438990.Fax:471- 434406.
Log on to www. Keralatourism.org

(4) Tamil nadu Tourism Development Corporation LTD.,
2, WallajahRoad, Near KalaivanarArangam Chennai-600 02 Ph: 91-44- 25383333, 25384444, Fax: 91-44 -25361385/ 25382772.
Website: www.tamilnadutourism.com
Email:dir-tour@tn.nic.in

Bibliography

Anitarau Badami, Apean in stone, *The Hindu*, Chennai, December 30, 1990, p.11.

Anjali Sircar, Superb Chola Bronzes, *The Hindu,* Chennai, Feb. 8, 1992.p.11.

Coomara Swamy, A.K., *History of Indian and Indonesian Art,* New York, 1927.

David Smith., Chidambaram, *Marg*, Vol. XLV No. 3 pp. 58-75.

Dennis Hudson., Kanchipuram, *Marg,* Vol XLV No. 3. pp. 18-39.

Devakunjari, D., *Hampi*, New Delhi, 1998.

Francoise L'Hernault., Tiruvannamalai, *Marg*, Vol. XLIV. No. 3 pp. 40-57.

Fergusson, J., *History of Indian and Eastern Architecture,* 2 Volumes, London, 1910.

George Michell., Carvings in Kerala Temples, *Marg,* Vol. XLIII. No. 3, pp. 17-40.

Grousset, R., *India (The Civilizations of the East series)* Tr.C.A. Phillips, London, 1932.

Hanumantha Rao, B.S.L., *Religion in Andhra*, Guntur, 1973.

____________________, *Srisailam, History and Culture* (Veturi Prabhakara Sastri Memorial Lecture), Srisailam, 1988.

Hanumantha Rao, D., Badami Chalukyan Architecture and its influence on Andhra monuments, *Archaeology of Andhra Pradesh, V.J.M, Centenary 1887-1987, Souvenir* pp.37-40.

Kameswara Rao, V., *The Lepakshi Temple,* Tirupati, 1982.

______________, *Select Vijayanagara Temples of Rayalaseema,* Hyderabad, 1976.

Krishna Dev, *Temples of North India,* NewDelhi, 1977 (Reprint).

Maya Jayapal; The stones of Hampi, *The Hindu*, Chennai, May 30, 1999. p. 11.

Meera Iyer; A landmark in ruins, *The Hindu*, Chennai, Nov 17, 1996. p.11.

Michael W.Meister., (Ed.) *Encyclopaedia of Indian Temple Architecture, South India, Lower and upper Dravida Desa,* (2 volumes), Delhi, 1983 and 1986.

Nigam, M.L., *Sculptural Art of Andhra,* Delhi, 1980.

Nilakanta Sastry, K.A., *A History of South India,* Madras, 1966.

Parabrahma Sastry, P; *The Kakatiyas*, Hyderabad, 1978.

Percy Brown, *Indian Architecture,* (2 Volumes) Bombay, 1959.

Raghavacharya, K.V., Srikalahasti, *The Hindu*, Chennai, February 20, 2001.p.5.

Rajendra Prasad, B., *Art of South India, Andhra Pradesh,* NewDelhi, 1980.

______________, *Temple Sculpture of Andhra Pradesh,* Hyderabad, 1978.

Rama Rao, M., *Temples of Tirumala, Tirupati and Tiruchanur,* Tirupati, 1982.

Ronald Bernier., Architectural Developments of Kerala Temples, *Marg,* Sept. 1979. pp.5-36.

Sarkar, H., *Monuments of Kerala*, New Delhi, 1992.

_______, & Nainar, S.P., *Amaravati*, New Delhi, 1980.

________, & Misra, B.N., *Nagarjunakonda*, New Delhi, 1987.

Siva Rama Murti, C., *The Art of India*, Bombay, 1977.

Srinivasan, K.R., *Temples of South India,* NewDelhi. 1979 (Reprint).

Subba Reddy, V.V., Two Stupa slabs from Dupadu, Prakasam District - Coastal Andhra Pradesh, *Quarterly Journal of the Mythic Society,* Vol. LXXXI Nos. 1-2. pp.33-37.

__________, Temples of Satyavolu, *Yuva Bharati,* Madras, May 1984. pp.37-40.

__________, The Art and Architecture of Amaravati *Stupa, Yuva Bharati,* Madras, August 1986. pp.21-24.

__________, Temples of Alampur, *Yuvabharati,* Madras, October 1984. pp.31-34.

__________, *Reddi Rajula Charitra (Telugu),* Guntur, 2004.

Theodore Baskaran, S., Poetry in Stone, *The Hindu*, Chennai, April 22, 2001, p.12.

Vidya Dehejia., *Looking Again At Indian Art,* 1978, NewDelhi.

Index

A

Acharya
  Nagarjuna, 28
  Ramanuja, Sri Vaishnava Sage, 142
Achyutaraya, 164
Adi Sankaracharya, 173, 209
Adishesha, 51
Aditya I, 111
Agamas and Tantras, 13
Agamic Knowledge, 12
Agastya Lake, 59
Ahobilam, Vaishna Pilgrim Centre, 170-172
Aihole Monuments, 62
  Montgudi Temple, 62
  Ravana Pahadi, 62
  Sun Temple, 62
Aihole, 60, 62
  School of Architecture, 65
Ajanta
  Paintings, 60, 103
  School, 101
Ajatasatru, 33
Akasa-Linga, 197
Alampur, 21
Alampur Museum, 68
Alwars (Alvars), 90, 120, 172
Amaravati, 22, 29, 32, 38
And Nagarjunakonda
  Sculptural Work, 45
Archaeological Museum, 32
  School of Art, 39
  Stupa, 32, 33
Anantasayi Vishnu, 50, 51
Andhra and Karnataka, 16
Andhradesa, 27, 28, 58, 73, 87, 88
Anuradhapuram, 108
Apsidal
  Chaityas, 34
  Shrines, 35
Archaeological
  Museum Alampur, 68
  Museums, 29
Architectural Scenes, 33
Architecture, 9
And Mural Paintings, (Vijayanagar Style), 164

Badami Chalukyans, 52-72
Of Buildings, 14
Of Our Ancestors in AP, (AOA), 10
Ahobilam, 10
Alampur, 10
Amravati, 10
Bhimeswaram, 10
Chezerla, 10
Draksharama, 10
Hanumankonda, 10
Kalahasti, 10
Lepakshi, 10
Mahanandi, 10
Pala Kollu, 10
Palampet, 10
Pancharamas, 10
Pillalamarri, 10
Satyavolu, 10
Simhachalam, 10
Srisailam, 10
Tadipatri, 10
Tirupati, 10
Tripurantkam, 10
Vijayawada, 10
Ardhnarisvara Image, 49
Arjun Ratha, 94
Art
And Arachitecture, 107
Of Bharava Konda Temples, 54
Of Nagarjunakond, 37
Arts and Architecture, 10
Asoka Emperor, 16, 27
Ayaka Platform, 42, 43
Ayyappan Temple Complex Panniyar, 204

B

Badami (Valapi), 59, 62
And Mahakuta, 58
Chalukya, 57
Complex of Temples, 60
Sculptures, 103
Bahustrutiyas, 36
Battle of
Tallikota, 154, 183
Asmaka, Teacher, 27
Belur
And Halebid, 141, 142, 214
Temples, 145, 146
Bhagiratha, 96
Bhairava Image, 51
Bhakti Cult, 48, 90
Bhandaramu Akkam, (Sani), 12
Bharhut, 32, 44
Bhuneshvari Devi, 173
Bhuta Mala, 52
Bodhi Tree, 43
Bouddha Sri Museum Guntur, 42
Brahma Shrine, 208
Brahmanical Shrines, 18
Brahmanis, 90
Brahmanism, 19
Brahmotsava at Tirupati, 15
Bronze Fort, 131
Bronzes of Kerala, 223
Buddha

Images, 38
Sujata Offering, 33
Buddhism, 16, 17, 27, 28, 30, 47, 90, 130, 203
And Jainism, 73
Buddhist
Architecture in India, 34
Art, 44
Aspdal Architectural Traditions, 16
Chaityas, 17, 23
Culture, 30
Establishment, 19
Establishment, Amaravati, 19
Establishment, Nagarjunakonda, 19
Inscriptions, 27
Monks, 40
Monuments, 27, 28
Sects, 35
Settlements, 27
Shrines, 40
Shrines in District Prakasam, 28
Chandavaram, 28
Dupadu, 28
Shrines in District Thanjavur (TN), 28
Nagapattinam, 28
Shrines in Guntur District, 28
Amaravati, 28
Bhattiprolu, 28
Goli, 28
Nagarjunakond, 28
Shrines in Krishna District, 28
Ghantasala, 28
Jaggayyapeta, 28
Sites in Andhra Pradesh, 32
Sites in India, 29
Stupa and Viharas, 47
Viharas, 47

C

Carved Figs of Narasimha—Siva, 61
Carvings, 37, 77
Cave
Architecture, 48
Shrines, 49
Temple of Ajanta, 204
Temples, 19, 58, 59
Mogalrajapuram, 19
Undavalli, 19
Centres of Trade and Commerce, 9
Ceylonese
Monastery of Thiruvadins Monks, 36
Monks, 36
Chaitya Griha, 16, 35, 36, 38, 41
Chalukyas, 103
Chalukya
Architecture, 65
Bhima, 75-78
Bhima Rule, 77
Rulers of Badami, 14, 58, 89, 91

Chalukyan
And Rashtrakuta Kingdoms, 20
Architecture, 21
Art, 68, 69
Art Centres, 90
Badami, 90
Pattadakal, 90
Kingdoms, 17
Style, 72
Chalukyas, 13, 58, 60, 62, 129, 131, 137
Of Badami, 65
Vaishnavas, 59
Chamunda, 79
Chandavaram, 44
Chandragupta Maurya, 126, 128
Chatturmukha-linga, 22
Chennai Museum, 158
Chidambaram Temple, 11
China, 28
Chola (s), 13, 28, 94, 108, 109, 182
Architecture Style, 82
Art, 110, 112, 114
Dynasty, 120
Iconography, 120
Ladies, 121
Paintings, 124, 125
Parantaka II, 113
Sculpture, 120
Ships, 93
Temple Architecture, 110
Temple Art, 107-128
Temple Complex, 113
Temples of Narattamalai, 103
Chulamanivarman Vihar, 28
Citra-Khonda Pillars, 53
Construction of Stupa with Svastika, 37
Cosmic Krishna, (Lord), 97

D

Daily Rituals, 11
Dakshinapatha, 27
Dance
And Music, 12
Of Siva at Chidambaram, 104
Dancing Nataraja, 197
Dasavatara, 156
Deccani Muslim Rulers, (DMR), 154
Ahmedanagar, 154
Bidar, 154
Bijapur, 154
Golkonda, 154
Gulbarga, 154
Devakulas/Devagharas, 16
Devi
Shrine, 85, 112, 158, 163, 192, 198
Temple, 138
Dhanushkoti, 193
Dharma
Chakra, 42, 44
Chakra in Ceiling, 104
Chakra Pravartana, 33
Sivacharya, 138
Dharmarajika Stupa at Taxila, 41

Dharmraja Ratha, 94, 95
Dhvaja-Stambha, 18, 19
Disposal of The Dead, 16
District
    Anantapur, 163, 164
    Guntur, 13, 42, 65
    Hasan, 141
    Kanyakumari, 205, 213, 214
    Karimnagar, and Nalgonda, 130
    Krishna and Guntur, 38
    Kurnool, 65, 167, 170
    Mahaboobnagar, 65
    Mysore—Dharwar, 142
    Of Kottayam and Alleppey, 202
    Prakasam, (AP), 11, 51, 137, 166
    Srikakulam, 14
    Warangal, 132
Domingo Paes, 159
Dravidian
    Architecture, 110, 131
    Temples, 188, 215
Durga Temples, 60, 61
Dynasties, 176
    Pallavas—Rayas, 176

E

Early Stone Age, 34
Eastern Chamtamula, 17, 18
Economy, 47
Educational Institutions, 12, 13
Ehuvalachem, 37
Ellora and Elephanta, 103
European Countries, 91
Excavations, 32, 34
Excavations at-, 16, 30
    Amaravati, 16, 30
    Bhattiproli, 16
    Chandavaram, 30, 42
    Dharanikota, 30
    Nagarjunakond, 40

F

Flying Gandharvas, 50

G

Gajapatis of Orissa, 151, 158
Gajendramoksha, 50
Gajendramoksha Panel, 222
Gandhamadhan Mountain, 191, 193
Gandhara School of Sculpture, 44
Ganesa Ratha, 93, 95
Ganga Dynasty, 84
Gaya (Bihar), 27
Ghatapallava Pillars, 67
Golakimatha, 13
Gold and Silver Ornaments, 11
Gomatesvara,
    And Mahavira, 59
    Jain Saint, 127
Gopuras, 14

H

Halebid, 142

Halebid Temples, 145
Hall of Thousand Pillars, 187
Hampi, 153-156, 161
Hanumankonda, 131, 132
Harappan Period, 39
Hari Hara I, 151, 153
Hari Hara II, 151
Hari Hara Raya II, 168
Hariti Knowledge, 19
Head Dress, 44
Hill Fort, 34
Hindu Temples, 17
Hinduism, 47, 151
  Art, 96
Hiuen Tsang, Chinese Traveler, 32
Hospet, 155
Hoysala (s), 13, 131
  And Kakatiya Temples, 146, 147
  Art, 141-149
  Empire in Karnataka, 135
  Kingdom, 11
  Of Mysore, 141
  Temples, 141, 143, 144, 146

I

Ikshvaku Dynasty, 18
Ikshvaku Rulers, 17, 35
Ikshvaku, 34, 40, 48
Image Worship, 16
Imperial Cholas, 107
Indian Archaeology, 40
Indragiri
  And Chandragiri, 126
  Hill, 127
Indrakeeladri Hill, 80
Indravarman, 48
Inscriptions,
  Aihole Inscriptions, 57
  Chejerla, 11
  Chezerla, 88
  Cholas, 175
  Draksharamam, 13
  Kalyan, 28
  Malkapuram, 13
  Mandagapattu, 88
  Mangelesa, 59
  Prataparudra, 11
  Tanjore, 108
  Velpura of M Kota Ganapati Deva, 12
  Vidhika, 33
  Yudhamalla, 80
Irrigation Programs, 155
Islamic Culture, 153

J

Jain
  And Hindus, 48
  Monks, 103
  Philosophy of Ahimsa, 104
  Sculptures and Ruins, 16
  Temples, 214
Jainism, 15, 16, 57, 59, 90, 109, 130
Jainism and Buddhism, 15
Janakachera, Temple Builder, 146

Jataka Stories, 37
    And Tales, 29, 31, 32
    Champeyya Tale, 37
    Dasaratha Tale, 37
    Dighitikosala Tale, 37
    Gata Tale, 37
    Mahahamsa, Tale, 37
Mandhatu Tale, 37
    Vessanlara Tale, 37
    Jatavarman Sundara,
        Pandyan King, 105
    Jyotirlinga (s), 167, 168
    Kshetra, 191

K

Kailasanatha Paintings, 101
Kakatiya
    Architecture, 131
    Art, 129, 131
Kakatiya Kings, 129
    Ganapati Deva, 129, 134-136
    Prataparudra Deva, 129, 132
    Rudra Deva, 129
    Rudramadevi, 129
Kakatiya
    Of Warangal, 129-139
    Structures, 137
    Style, 138
    Temples, 58, 130, 149
    Tripurantika, 137, 138
Kalabhras Invasion, 107
Kalamukhas, 137
Kalamukha Sect, 66, 113
Kalidasa Kumar Sambhavam, 217
Kalinga
    Age, 14
    Region, 84
    War, 27
Kalyan Mandapa, 21
Kalyani, 109
Kanchipuram (Kanchi), 87, 89, 99, 102, 103, 108, 181, 182
    Pallava Capital city, 99
Kandara II, 17
Kandarapura, 17
Kapotesvara Temple at
    Chejerla, 17
Karnataka
    Monuments of Chalukya,
        (KMC), 10
    Aihole, 10
    Badami, 10
    Pattadakal, 10
    Temples Architecture, 57
Karttikeya, 17, 18, 19
Kazipet, 131
Kerala
    Paintings, 221
    Style, 201-224
    Temples, 10, 202, 203
    Ayyuppan Temple at
    Manjeri, 10
    Mahadeva Temple, 10
    Padmanabha Svami
    Temple, 10
    Peruntirukoilappan
    Temple at Vaikom, 10
    Ponmui Siva Temple, 10

Vadakkunnatha Thrissur, 10
Khajuraho Temples, 115
King
- Ballala, 198
- Bukkaraya, 178
- Kakati Ganapati Deva, 138
- Narasimha Varman II, 99
- Prataparudra, 11
- Sailendra, 28
- Vinayaditya, 66

Krishna
- Deve Raya, 151, 152
- Temple Trivandrum, 204
- Valley, 44, 88

Kumbakonam, 111, 112, 120
Kurumbas, 154

L

Ladahkhan Temples, 60
Lajjagauri, 39
Lake Ramappa Cheruvu, 135
Lakshmi Narasimha, Monolithic Statue, 160
Lakshminarayan Shrine, 204
Lambadas, 154
Lepakshi, 164, 166
Lingaraja Temple Bhuvneshwara, 20
Lord
- Krishan, 141, 143, 144, 146, 158
- Rameswaram Temple, 12
- Sriranganatha (Kaveri Land), 11
- Venkatesvara, Lord of Seven Hills, 178

Lotus Mahal, 160

M

Mackenzie, Col., 32
Madhav-Varman, Vishnukundin King, 48, 80
Madurai Style, 183-199
Maha Sivaratri Festival, 170
Mahabalipuram, 54, 88, 91, 96, 97, 202
Mahabharata, 95
Maha-Chaityas, 35
Mahamaham
- Festival, 111
- Tank, 112

Mahamastakabhisheka, 127
Mahanadi, 21
- Pilgrimage Centre, 69

Maha-Parinirvana, 43
Mahasanghikas, 31
Mahastupa, 41
Mahayanism, 44
Mahendra Varman, 92
Mahendra Varman I, 88, 90
Mahendragiri Mountain, 73
Mahendravarman Rock Cut Architecture, 19
Mahisasaka Monastery, 36
Mahishasur, Demon King, 94
Mahishasurmardini, 62, 92, 93, 96, 143, 162
- Cave, 96

Malik Kafur and Khawaja Haji, General of Alaudin Khilji, 142

Mallikarjuna, 168
  Temple, 169
Mamallapuram, Port Town, 99, 103
  World Heritage Monument By UNESCO, 99
Mandalika Estate, 11
Manikyambi ka Peetha, 76
Marshall, John, 33
Mathas, 21, 152
Mathematics, 13
Mattencherry, 211, 220, 223
Mattencherry Royal Palace, Portuguese, 211, 220
Medieval Temples, 11
Megalithic
  Culture, 16
  Period, 16
  Tombs, 15, 16
Miracle of Sravesh, 33
Mogalrajapuram, 49, 50
Monastery, 34, 35
Monastery with Buddha Chaitya, 36
Mudabidiri Group, 214
Muhammad bin Tughlaq, 142
Mural Paintings, 203
Murals of Pandya Origin, 221
Muslim Invaders, 134

N

Nagai Temple, 13
Nagara
  And Dravida Style, 20
  Style, 71
Nagarjunakonda, 21, 38, 40, 41, 47
  Region, 17
  Sagar, 34-36
  Valley, 18
Nallamalai Range of Hills, 69
Nandi Shrine, 113
Nandivarman, 63
  Group, 102
Narasimha
  Deva I, 84
  Varman I, 88-90
  Varman-II, Pallava King, 28, 90
Nataraja Dwarfs, 59
Nataraja, Siva, 50
Navabrahma Group of Temples at Alampur, 65, 67
Nayaka
  Dynasty, 187
  Rulers, 145
Nayakas of Madurai, Military Generals, 183
North Indian Buddhist Sculpture, 44

O

Ornamented Chhatras, 43

P

Padarikarma Monastery at Nagapattinam, 28
Padmanabhapura Palace, 223

Paintings, 108
Paintings in Kerala, 201, 223
Pallava
 Architecture, 110
 Art, 98
 Dynasty, 102
 Kings, 19
 Simhavarman, 19
 Trilochna, 19
 Monuments, 92
 Rock Cut Caves, 124
 Sculptures, 97
 Structural Art, 100, 101
 Architecture, 101
Pillars with Lion, 101
 Temples, 51, 102
Pallavas, 13, 17, 55, 58, 84, 87-105, 107, 108, 110
 Architecture and Sculptures, 87
 of Kanchipuram, 48
 of Tamil Nadu, 51
 Shrines, 84
 Structural Temples, 87
Pampadevi, 155, 156
Panch Pandava Ratha, 93
Panchamala Kavya, 12
Pandharpur, 156
Pandya Kingdom, 11
Paramesvaravarman, I, 89
Parantaka I, 108
Parantaka II, 109
Parasurama
 Shrine, 208
 Temple Complex, 208
Parvati Shrines, 162
Patalganga, 167, 169
Peaks Seshadri—Venkatadri, 176
Pillard Corridor, 192
Planning
 Burials, 16
 Cities, 14
Polity and Administration, 129
Polonnaruva, 108
Pradakshina-patha, 44
Prakasa Mandapa, 21
Primitive Animism, 15
Prostitutes (Sanis), 12
Pulakisin, 21
Pulakisin, II, 57
Puram Program in Kerala, 210
Purna-Kumbhas, 31
Pushkarni Tank, 160

R

Rachamalla III, Ganga King, 127
Rajaraja, Chola King, 11, 28, 114, 118, 119, 123, 125
Rajaraja I, Chola King, 108, 124
Rajasimha, 89
Rajendra Chola, 114, 115, 118, 119
Rajendra Chola I, 109, 124
Rama Raya, 152, 154
Ramagrama Stupa, 43
Ramayana and Mahabharata, 146, 148, 165
Rameshvaram, 105, 191-193
Rani Rudrama Devi, 132, 133

Rashtrakutas, 75, 103
Rashtrakutas Princess, 76
Raya of Vijayanagar, 172
Reddis of Kundavidu, 172
Relief Sculptures of Vishnu, 93
Religio-Philosophical
  Development, 15
Religious Festivals, 14
Rituals, 13
River
  Bahuda, 85
  Godavari and Krishna, 28
  Gundakamma, 41
  Kauveri (Kaveri,
    Cauvery), 117, 188, 191
  Kollidan, 188
  Krishna, 17, 29, 34, 47,
    50, 74, 79, 80, 88, 167
  Malaprabha, 60, 62
  Manneru, 73
  Palar in Kaveri, 87
  Pennar, 161
  Tungbhadra, 153, 156
Rock Cut
  Monolithic Temples, 92
  Monuments, 89
  Technique of
  Architecture, 88
  Temples at
    Mogalrajapuram, 74
  Temples at Undavalli and
    Mogalrajapuram, 48
  Temples, 93
Rock Cut Cave
  Ajanta, 48
  Temples, 88, 92, 96
Roman Architecture, 40
Rome and Ceylon, 17

S

Sacrifices like Asmedha, 47
Sadasiva Raya, 154
Sailendra Kingdom, 93, 109
Saiva Sect at Amaravati, 23
Saivaite/Vaishnavite Thought,
  19, 20
Saivism, 90, 109, 130
Saivite Sects, 73
  Kalamukhas, 73
  Pasupatas, 73
Saivites, 151
Sakti Peethas, 76, 138
Salvation, 33
Sanchi, 32
Sangam
  Age, 107
  Dynasty, 151
  Literature, 176
Sangamesvar, 21
Satvahanas, 17, 27, 34, 47
  And Ikshvakus, 31
    Buddhism, 32
  Dynasty, 47
  In Karnataka, 44
Satyavolu, 21
Scenes of Folk Dancers, 136
Schools of Buddhism, 28
  Hinayana, 28
  Mahayana, 28
Sculptural Panels, 42
Sculptures, 33

of Alampur, 67
of Nagarjunakond, 37
of Vinadhari-
Dakshinamurti, 54
Shakti Sthalas, 80
Shrines, 135
Kalesvara, 135
Kamesvara, 135
Of Narasimha, 180
Of Sabhapati, 187
Sikhra, 20, 21
Simha Vishnu, 88
Simhala-dvipa, 93
Sipa-sastras, 20
Siva
And Karttikeya, 17
Purana, 169
Temple at Beypore, 203
Temples, 19, 158
Siva Concepts, 20
Ardhanarishvara, 20
Nataraja, 20
Somaskandamurli, 20
Sivaganga Tank, 198
Skandpurana, 66
Socio-Religious Reformation,
130
Somanathapur, 10
Belur, 10
Halebid, 10
Hampi, 10
South East Asia, 91
South Indian Buddhist, 16
Sravanbelgola, 10
Jain Monument, 126
Sri Krishnadeva Raya, 81, 155,
156, 160, 174, 177
Srirangam
Bhoolok Vaikuntam, 190
Town, 188
Srisaila Kshetra, 66
Srisailam, 14, 138, 167, 168,
170
Dam, 21
Temple, 11
Srivijaya Kingdom of Sumatra,
109
State Museum Hyderabad, 42
Sthala Purana, 83
Sthanapattu, Commercial
Head, 11
Stone
Carvings, 97
Ceiling, 16
Inscriptions, 9
Structural Temples, 97
Stupa
Architecture, 31
With Monastery with
Stupa Chaitya, 36
With Monastery, 36
Stupas at-, 13, 16, 32
Amaravati, 16
Bhattiproli, 16
Stupas in Andhra Pradesh,
(SAP), 28
Amaravati, 28, 30
Bhattiprolu, 28
Ghantasala, 28
Jaggayyapeta, 28
Nagarjunakond, 28
Sultans of Bijapur and
Golkonda, 183

Svastika, 16

T

Tadipatri Temple, 163
Tanjore Temples, 11, 115, 118, 124
Tantricism, 66
Tatacharya, Vaishnava Teacher, 152
Tax Free Grants of Village to Lands, 11
Telengana Region, 129, 138
Temple,
Adhikumbesvara, 111
Adikesava Perumal, 213
Ahobilam Narasimha, 171
Ahobilam, 172
Airavateswara, 119
Amaresvara, 73, 78
Architecture, 14, 15, 114
Architecture of Kerala-, 204, 209
As Great Landlord and Banker, 11
As Sapt-Santana, 10
Ashtabhuja-Narayana, 18
Ayyappan, 205
Bala-Brahma, 66, 67
Balasubrahmanyam, 111
Bejjanki, 129
Bhagawati, 204
Bhairavakena, 51
Bhaktavatsala, 105
Bhavanarayana Swamy, 82
Bhima-Lingesvara, 71
Bhimesvara and Panakesvara Swamy, 65
Bhimesvara, 76
Brahmanical, 40
Bramaramba, 169
Brihadesvara, 108, 109, 114, 115, 120
Chakrapam, 111
Chandra Sekhara, 73, 75
Chandranatha, 214
Chennakesava Belur, 144, 166
Chidambaram, 10, 109, 184, 194, 197
Chintala, Venkata, Ramana, 162
Darasuram, 10
Dasavarara at Deogarh, 50
Deogarh UP, 51
Dharmapuri, 129
Durga, 61
Ghanpur, 129
Golugesvara, 73, 74, 79
Hanumakonda, 129
Hariti, 40
Hatakesavaram, 170
Hazara Ram, 155, 157, 158
Hoysalesvara Halebid, 142, 146
In Western Ghats, 41
Jain, 57
Jalapsvara, 73, 74

Jambu Kesvara, 184, 190
Jogulamba Devi,
  Alampur, 69
Kailasanatha, 63, 89, 100,
  101, 104
Kakatiya Svayambhu
  Deva, 13
Kanchipura, 10
Kapoteswar, 23
Kedaresvara, 146
Kesava at Belur, 142-144,
  147
Kilatali Siva, 205
Kodamblur, 10
Kodandarama, 159
Kodavalam Vishnu, 207
Konarak, 120
Krishan, 155
Kumara Brahma, 66
Kumbokonam, 10
Lingaraja, 20
Lokesvara, 14, 63
Madurai, 10
Mahabalipuram, 10
Mahanandisvara, 69
Mallesvara, 73
Mallikarjuna Temple at
  Srisailam, 11, 64
Mandevya Narayana, 81
Manthana, 129
Matangesvara, 102
Meenakshi at Madurai,
  183, 184, 187, 188, 204
Moovar Koil, 113
Mukhalingam, 13
Mukhtesvara, 102
Nagesvara, 112, 122
Nagulapadu, 129
Narasimha Svamy, 170
Narasimha, 205
Niramankara, 206
Nodagisvara Svami, 18
Of Goddess Varanthika,
  141
Of Madurai, 184
Of Sarvadeva, 40
Of Siva at Tanjore, 108
Of Srirangam, 184
Of Tripura Sundari, 138
Padmanabhasvami, 212
Palampet, 129
Pampapatim, 155
Panakesvara, 69
Papanatha, 62
Papavinasa, 72
Parasuramesvara, 84
Parathasarathy, 205
Pushpabhadra Svami, 18
Rajarajavara, 108
Raja-Rajesvara, 73, 74
Rama, 207
Ramalingesvara, 161-163
Ramappa, 135
Ramesvaram, 10, 184,
  192, 193
Ranganatha, 188
Rock Cut Cave Temples,
  47-55
Saiva, 48
Sangaikondacholapuram,
  10
Sangameswara, 62, 64, 65

Sankari Devi, Sri Lanka, 69
Sarangapam, 111, 112
Siva, 208
Somesvara, 78, 111
Sri Kalalanestivara, 172
Sri Lakshmi Ganapati, 75
Sri Varaha Lakshmi Narasimha Svamy, 83
Sri Venkatesvara, 176
Srirangam, 10, 189
Srivilliputtur, 184
Svarga-Brahma, 66, 69
Svayambhudeva, 133, 136
Talagirisvara, 104
Tanjore, 10
Tinnevelly, 184
Tirumalai, 176
Tiruvalisvaram, 121
Tiruvallur, 184
Tiruvannamalai, 184
Trailokesvara, 63
Training in Fine Arts, Dances, Drama and Music, 9
Trikotesvara Mahadev, 207
Tripurantikesvara, 138
Undavalli Cave, 51
Uttara Kailasha, 114
Vadakkunatha, 211
Vaidyanatha, 114
Vaikom Siva, 201, 203
Vaikuntha Perumal, 89, 101
Vaishnava Siva, 47
Vamana, 207
Vamanamurti Maha Vishnu, 211
Varaha Narasimha, 84
Veerabhadra, 73, 158, 164
Veeranarayana, 146
Vijayala Cholesvara, 110
Virupakshi, 62-64
Virupakshi and Mallikarjuna, 63
Vishnu, 61
Visva Brahma, 67
Vitthala, 155, 156, 159
Yam and Siva, 59
Temples,
Centres of Learning and Imparting Knowledge, 9
Temples at-, 13
Badami, 13
Belur, 13
Hlebid, 13
Hampi, 13
Madurai, 13
Mahabalipuram, 13
Pattadakal, 13
Srirangam, 13
Tanjore, 13
Thousand Pillar Temple at Hanumakond, 133, 136
Tibet and China, 28
Tirthankaras, 59, 127, 128
Tirumala Nayak, 183
Tirumaladevi, Queen, 155
Tirumalai Nayak Mahal, 187
Tirupati—Srirangam, 152
Torana, 13, 136, 137
Trade with Romen World, 47
Traders/Merchants, 13
Trailokyanatha Somesvara I, 13

Trimukh Cave, 96
Trinity Miniatures, 49
Triratna, 31

U

Udayagiri Fort, 158
UNESCO, 99, 161
Upanishadic Concept of Religion, 15
Upanishads, 15
Urbanization of Structure, 16
Utsava Mandapa, 21
Uttama Chola, 109

V

Vaikom Siva Temple, 201, 203
Vaishnava Cave, 59
Vaishnavism, 109, 130, 152
Vaishnavite Temples, 14
Vajrayana, 29
Vakatakas, 48
Valley,
- Krishna, 44
- Nagarjunakonda, 34, 35

Varaha Cave, 96
Vatapi, 91
Vedas and Sastras, 13
Vedic
- Concept of Agni and Rudra, 22
- Learning, 89
- Religion, 47

Vedism, 15
Velikunda Ranges, 51
Vengi
- Chalukya (Eastern Chalukyas), 73, 75, 76, 78, 82
- Kingdom, 109
- Region, 81

Viharas, 41
Vijayalaya, 108
Vijayanagar, 13, 132
- Empire, 151-182
- Kingdom, 137
- Kings, 137, 183
- Monarchs, 151
- Paintings, 156
- Pillars, 174
- Traders, 28

Vijayapura, Capital of Ikshvakus, 47
Vijayawada, 48
Vijayawada Museum, 39
Vikram Chola, 84, 109, 121
Vikramaditya, 63
Village
- Committees, 14
- Dharnikota, Satavayana Capital, 29
- Harilayapura, 11
- Salakalavidu, 11

Virapurusha Datta, 10, 36, 37
Virasaivism, 138
Virupaksha, 151, 155, 156
Virupaksha-II, 157
Virupanna, 164, 165
Vishnu, 18
Vishnukundin, 19, 28, 31, 48
- Indravarman, 19

Kingdom, 88
Of Andhra Pradesh, 51
Vishnuvardhan, 142, 144
Shantla Devi, Wife, 146
Visvesvara-Sivacharya, 13
Dikshaguru of Kakatiya
King Ganapatideva, 13
Saivite Teacher, 13
Vrittis (Lands), 12

W

Warangal, 131, 132, 133
Wood Carvings, 203

Y

Yadavas of Devagiri, 141
Yaksha Fig., 32
Yasodhara Gautam, 38
Yogasala Mandapa, 21